Mahābhārata Now

Mahābhārata Now

Narration, Aesthetics, Ethics

EDITORS

ARINDAM CHAKRABARTI
SIBAJI BANDYOPADHYAY

Routledge
Taylor & Francis Group
LONDON NEW YORK NEW DELHI

First published 2014 in India
by Routledge
912 Tolstoy House, 15–17 Tolstoy Marg, Connaught Place, New Delhi 110 001

Simultaneously published in the UK
by Routledge
2 Park Square, Milton Park, Abingdon, Oxfordshire OX14 4RN

First issued in paperback 2015

Routledge is an imprint of the Taylor & Francis Group, an informa business

Typeset by
Glyph Graphics Private Limited
23, Khosla Complex
Vasundhara Enclave
Delhi 110 096

British Library Cataloguing-in-Publication Data
A catalogue record of this book is available from the British Library

ISBN 13 978-1-138-66011-3 (pbk)
ISBN 13: 978-0-415-71055-8 (hbk)

Contents

Foreword

When I see the first buds of purple wisteria hanging from the vines on the porch of the Rashtrapati Niwas, I can smell spring in the air. The publication of *Mahābhārata Now: Narration, Aesthetics, Ethics* has had that same effect on me. It is the first bud of a new species of cross-pollinated wisteria breaking out of its winter hibernation announcing the abundant flowering that is to come. Several years ago when I was thinking about the Indian Institute of Advanced Study (IIAS) and of its proper place in this vast and varied landscape of knowledge-making, both in India and in the world, and today, yesterday and the day after tomorrow, I was reflecting on its special character that allowed for both the delicate question and the grand pursuit. I reflected on the need to consolidate this distinct signature of the Institute. I dreamed of IIAS as a place where scholars could pursue the eternal questions of the human condition, think about honour, courage, truth, respect, dignity, loyalty, deference, authority, and rules, and do so while using both classical and contemporary frames of analysis. No frame, I felt, was too old fashioned and none was too pretentious. After days and months of considering possibilities, it became clear to me that a programme of 'contemporizing the epics' could be that signature activity I was searching for since it was capacious enough to accommodate many of the interesting questions that had preoccupied scholars in the humanities and social sciences. Contemporizing the epics allowed for a plural inhabiting.

The first step that we took towards achieving this goal was to organize an annual school on the *Mahābhārata*. In 2009–10, the first such school was held. This book is one of its outcomes. Two more schools have since been held. To see the material manifestation of that long held aspiration, a book of interpretations and arguments in print, is to see the working out of an idea with the help of a group of scholars led by Sibaji Bandyopadhyay, Arindam Chakrabarti and Sanjay Palshikar. To contemporize the epics, to make the community of scholars in the humanities and social sciences regard them as an invaluable resource from which they can draw questions, offer answers and contemplate puzzles, in their attempts to understand our contemporary predicaments, is indeed a large exercise of long gestation and even longer duration. The three schools, and this book, should thus be seen as the early steps in creating and expanding a new vocabulary for thinking about the human condition in contemporary times and thereby of staking out a distinct intellectual landscape. In bringing out the book of 12 chapters, with an insightful introduction, Sibaji and Arindam, as the first ones off the block, have done an Usain Bolt for us. Whether Bimal Matilal handed them the baton is perhaps an intriguing question to ask.

Why this deep desire to contemporize the epics? What is so symbolic about doing so at the IIAS? Do we not have enough good commentaries on the epics?

Is the long history of our engagement with the epic not a history of regular contemporization since it has been always used to speak to the present? Are the epics not already such an intrinsic part of our folklore, our stock of metaphors and illustrations, for them now to merit a special commitment by the IIAS? On these questions, I suppose, I need to offer both clarification and explanation. The first is that this exercise, which, I hope, will be a long-term commitment of the IIAS, is to contemporize the epics. Acknowledging the plural is important here for it allows interested and engaged publics to set conditions on what constitutes an epic, offer candidate texts for inclusion, make a fine distinction between an epic and a classic of literature, argue about whether *The Mahābhārata* and *The Rāmāyaṇa* alone deserve the hallowed label or whether the oral Telugu text *Palnativeerula Kathā*, or the Tamil text *Silappatikāram* or other such great works also qualify. By recognizing the existence of the plural, 'Epics', one has kept open the possibility of recognizing many claimants, to the status of an epic, from the different *bhāṣā*s of India and from the rich oral tradition of ballads. The first act of contemporizing is thus to democratize the field. By doing so one is inviting a discussion, from a diversity of viewpoints, on what requirements must be fulfilled for a work to be considered an epic.

This brings me to the second aspect of my ardour to contemporize. It has two sources. The first is embedded in the Indian civilizational space and draws its lineage from K. C. Bhattacharya's lecture, 'Swaraj in Ideas' (1954 [1931]). It stems from an anxiety that in this world of the politics of knowledge creation and dissemination, where power determines what is to be foregrounded and what backgrounded, our knowledge universe is deficient because the dominant curriculum of our universities gives little regard to deep scholarship in the Indian epics and valorizes instead either learning of instrumental skills or a Western academic canon. The humanities and social sciences discourse in India hence suffers from an ignorance of our epics. This amnesia is unfortunate because it deprives us of a rich body of moral conundrums, of descriptions about the intricate play of intentions, of the complexity of human relationships and, perhaps, even of their absurdity, of tragedy, deceit, steadfastness, and duty. It is also unfortunate because it leaves us disconnected from our cultural world — warts and all — that has had so many influences that have gone into its evolution and that is today available for both contemporization and secularization. This cultural world is also available for contestation. As a consequence when the work of contemporization and secularization is left undone we are rendered vulnerable to intellectual colonization by the West. This has happened in the past and continues to happen even today. Only now we do not recognize the process. Bhattacharya describes this colonization very graphically in his lecture:

> There is however a subtler domination exercised in the sphere of ideas by one culture on another, a domination all the more serious in the consequence, because it is not ordinarily felt, . . . slavery begins when one ceases to feel the evil and it deepens when

> the evil is accepted as a good. Cultural subjection is ordinarily of an unconscious character and it implies slavery from the very start . . . There is cultural subjection only when one's traditional cast of ideas and sentiments is superseded without comparison or competition by a new cast representing an alien culture which possesses one like a ghost (1954[1931]: 1).

One motivation to contemporize the epics (in the plural) is driven by the desire to both avoid such cultural subjection and to develop, within our own intellectual world, a temper of appreciation and criticism, humour and irony. When a society has developed and demonstrates many levels of appreciation, it is a marker of its intellectual autonomy. If it has also developed a capacity for irony, then we can read in that irony the self-confidence of that society.

The second source for my lament derives from the attitude, captured well in the television advertisement, of 'neighbour's envy, owner's pride'. They have done it, and done it well, and we have not. In the West, the epics have a (the) pride of place in their core university curricula, are required learning for anyone wanting the appellation of a 'learned' person, and, as a result, enjoy a high status in the corridors that matter. Their epics are the inspiration for art collections, theatre performances and museum collections. Naturally so. This is neighbour's envy. We too, therefore, must do what they have done not by copying their products but by imitating their practice. We, too, have to contemporize and secularize our epics by bringing them into seminar room presentations, India coffee house discussions, Jan Natya Manch performances and paintings by M. F. Hussain. Imagine regarding Hussain's works as an exercise of contemporizing the *Mahābhārata*, as an endeavour akin to what was done in the temples of Konarak and Ellora. His paintings are an occasion for celebration at many levels. This we have missed and have instead, succumbing to an obscurantist mindset, sent one of our greatest modern painters into exile. He was 90 years of age at the time. If, in contrast to what we have done, we are able see the epics as an intellectual and cultural resource that will allow us to do the various things mentioned earlier, and do so to meet the needs and desires of the contemporary world, neighbour's envy would be on the wane.

So, what would 'contemporizing' entail? There are at least three strategies that are available, some of which have been adopted by the essays in the book. The first would be to bring the contemporary tools of 'reading a text' to bear on the epic. In the case of the *Mahābhārata*, this could involve debates about authorship. Is it the work of one or several authors, written during a certain period, or is it a text that has been continuously modified? Should one see it as fixed or evolving? Is the oral tradition the source from where we will also draw our interpretations or will we rely mainly on written texts? Is it even appropriate, given the plethora of versions across India, to consider producing a critical version as V.S. Sukthankar has done for the Bhandarkar Oriental Research Institute, and which he details in his introduction to the first volume of the critical edition. Much of the contemporary scholarship on the epic has engaged with this exercise of 'reading the text'. This is a valuable strategy of contemporizing and has provided valuable details of the historical period when the epic was composed, the epic as *itihāsa*, of it 'entering our cultural DNA' (a description bequeathed to us by the late A.K. Ramanujan), of the diversity of regional versions and oral renderings, and of the perils of standardization. In this first strategy of 'reading a text', one could broadly see two pathways along which the contemporizing has taken place: the classical path whereby scholars such as V.S. Sukthankhar and Mukund Lath identify episodes which are then discussed and commented upon in detail with classical tools, and the modern path whereby scholars such as Uma Chakravarty and S.L. Bhyrappa use the tools of literary criticism and cultural studies to offer their views on aspects of the epic.

The second style of contemporizing would be to 'humanize and secularize the epic', an exercise akin do what Irawati Karve did in *Yuganta* (1968). Here she takes different characters or episodes and looks at them with contemporary eyes. For example, her discussion of Bhīṣma's arrogance at accepting the title of chief of the army at an age which, she calculated, would be in the eighties, even though he had never fought and won a war, brings out the issue of the play of ego and agency. The presentation of his persona, as one who aspires for power and glory, is a valuable intervention that secularizes the text. She does the same for several characters such as Draupadī, Karṇa, Kuntī, Kṛṣṇa, etc. She sees in Kuntī's life emotional responses ranging from magnanimity to meanness and, in doing so, presents a character in the epic that we can identify with. This second strategy of contemporizing the epic is to read it as an account of the human failings that mirror the virtues and vices of ordinary human beings as we encounter them in everyday situations. By reading the epic ethnograpically, and without the religious and metaphysical overtones that are usually given to it, Karve has humanized and secularized the text.

Another aspect of this second strategy is to not just look at the characters in the epic but to also look at institutions, for example, those related to war, treaties, truces, prohibition of battle after sundown or the complex infantry formations called (*vyūhas*). If we look at the rules by which the war was fought, the transgressions of these rules and the consequences that followed from such transgressions, we would find similarities with contemporary discussions in international law relating to the Geneva Convention on the rights of prisoners of war, about how the wounded in combat are to be treated, and how civilians in war zones are to be protected. One would find in the epic similarities with discussions concerning the International Criminal Court (ICC) on the doctrine of limitations, or on the defence that 'one was only following orders' not being regarded as an acceptable defence in cases when one is charged with crimes against humanity. M.A. Mehendale's *Reflections on the Mahabharata War* (1995) is an excellent study of the rules of war in the epic, and in reading it one finds interesting parallels with the Geneva Convention and the ICC. The discussions show both the rules that are to be observed, as agreed upon by both parties of combatants, and the penalties for the transgressions of these rules. For example, the use of the *brahmāstra* — which was supposed to be used only with an equal opponent — by Droṇācārya against common soldiers (and perhaps non-combatants), was a violation of the rule of war and perhaps resulted in the justified, but deceitful killing of Droṇa. While reading it, one is reminded of the contemporary use of napalm in Vietnam (remember the My lai massacre) and the use of depleted uranium artillery in Iraq. In both these cases, unfortunately, unlike in the epic the transgressors were rarely punished. It is noteworthy in this context that the collateral damage inflicted by Aśvatthāmā and Kṛpācārya on the Pāṇḍavas at the end of the war by slaughtering the latter's sleeping children was considered a criminal act in the epic. These discussions, in fact, lead to the very contemporary debates, in political and legal philosophy, on what are the conditions and limitations for a just war (Walzer 1992). A third possible line of contemporizing the epic, in this second strategy to secularize and humanize the epic, is to present it, as Peter Brooks has done so successfully in his film, as a universal story of the human condition of honour, revenge, uncertainty, and rectitude. Peter Brooks' film had an international cast of different races and different ethnicities. At the very minimum he has, by just doing this, made the story a universal story.

This aspect of exploring the human condition brings me to the third strategy of contemporizing the epic, the one that attracts me the most, which is to find in it 'moral puzzles that need to be analyzed' since they contain lessons for our individual and collective lives. The fun of complicating the self-righteous readings that are too easily given by many commentators, of searching for the 'right thing to do' in difficult situations, and of believing that such a search is valid in this post-modern world even if it does not result in an unequivocal answer, is what I think this third strategy offers and that I find very appealing. Jon Elster's *Ulysses and the Sirens: Studies in Rationality and Irrationality* (1979) that takes the story of Ulysses and the Sirens to develop a moral argument of pre-commitment, is an example of what can be done in this third strategy of contemporizing an epic. I believe the epics are such an intellectual resource available to us for mining since they contain a rich moral lode. They are also a moral minefield. The well-known episodes of Ekalavya's *guru dakṣiṇā*, Draupadi's disrobing, or Yudhiṣṭhira's little lie or Karṇa's loyalty to the Kauravas have been much discussed, so I will take three of the less discussed cases for our consideration of the epic as a rich and abundant resource for 'moral puzzles' that speak to our concerns today.[1]

The first story that can be explored is that of Gāndhārī and the blindfold. This is regarded by the dominant narrative as an act of great virtue. Accepting this storyline as a starting point — that Gāndhārī, as the loving and devoted wife,

[1] I am grateful to Sibesh Bhattacharya, Gangeya Mukherji, Surabhi Sheth and D. L. Sheth, for their comments on an earlier draft of this foreword and for complicating and embellishing my discussion of these three examples.

voluntarily blindfolded herself so that her husband Dhṛtarāṣṭra, who was blind, would not feel alone in his world of darkness — we can probe whether the best way to demonstrate her love for him was indeed to blindfold herself? Where does greater virtue lie? Where would she be more virtuous: in the solidarity of suffering which she showed by blindfolding herself or by optimizing the limited resources they shared of her eyesight by not blindfolding herself? Would she have served him better if, by not blindfolding herself, she could describe to him the world of colour, the wisteria and the promise of spring? Would she not have been more useful to him if she could describe to him the fleeting thoughts that could be read in the reluctant expressions on the faces of Yudhiṣṭhira and Arjuna? By depriving him of her trusted vision was she not being disloyal to him? Was she not diminishing the potential of her companionship since now she too had no visual way of cross-checking the stories that came to Dhṛtarāṣṭra, such as looking for the twitch in the face or the fidgety posture, of the story-teller. The trained and trusted eye, so much relied upon by spouses, who see things on behalf of their partners, that distant others do not see and that these others consider as trivia, which then are included in the subjects to be discussed in the privacy of the evening, was now unavailable to Dhṛtarāṣṭra. Her additional perspective would have been particularly valuable to him in his frequent moments of indecisiveness. In this second interpretation, the 'wife as helper' appears to be more true to her spousal duty than the 'wife as co-sufferer'.

There is another dimension, however, which is introduced to the Gāndhārī story which sees her act of blindfolding as a heroic act. By blindfolding herself she was able to achieve two things simultaneously. She was able to avenge herself on her husband for the deceit basis of her marriage to him (she was not told of his infirmity) just as Medea did to her husband Jason, in the Greek classic *The Medea* by Euripides, by killing their two children to punish him for his unfaithfulness to her. At the same time, in a paradoxical twist, Gāndhārī was able to achieve the iconic status of the devoted wife who voluntarily deprived herself of the pleasures of sight so that she could be one with her husband in his world of darkness. The 'wife as helper' would not have achieved this iconic status of the 'wife as co-sufferer' that Gāndhārī has enjoyed through the centuries, since it is a common story. By just looking at the act of blindfolding, we can, thereby, initiate a long discussion on what constitutes virtue, on the distinction between virtuous acts and virtuous consequences, on spousal duties that are to be distinguished from wifely duties, the former being gender-neutral and latter being gender-embedded, etc. This is an exercise of contemporizing the epics at its best.

The second story that can be explored in terms of moral issues, this time in the field of legal philosophy, is that of the minor Pāṇḍava, Sahadeva. According to the epic, he was gifted with the power of seeing the future but he would only reveal this future when he was asked. This capability placed a certain moral burden on him. How should he act in the face of a wrongdoing which he knew was going to occur, i.e., the killing of combatants at night, or the disrobing of Draupadī? Since he could see the future, was he morally bound to prevent the evil from occurring? What were the responsibilities of his moral persona and how do these travel in a social context, particularly in a heightened social context, i.e., that of war? Can one charge Sahadeva with being an accomplice to the crime, in the language of modern legal theory which would place upon him the obligation to intervene and prevent the crime from occurring? If one looks at the Geneva Convention, then he could be charged with war crimes, as Kurt Waldheim was, of not stopping the Nazi deportations from Greece when he was a 19-year-old camp guard. The defence that Sahadeva could offer that 'nobody asked me what would happen so I did not tell' would not be regarded as an acceptable defence just as 'I was only following orders' was not regarded as a proper defence post Nuremberg trials. By regarding Sahadeva in his persona as the Pāṇḍava who has the power to see the future, and exploring the moral basis of action that this power brings, I wish to initiate a moral–legal discussion on what being an accomplice entails. When is it justified to be merely an onlooker? When is one morally bound to intervene? The discussion can be further complicated by introducing the dimension of time. Does Sahadeva only have the power to see the near future or can he even see the distant future? What is the moral responsibility for the action that each vision brings? Does foreknowledge count as letting it happen, and if it does then are we guilty of not doing anything to prevent predictable global or local economic or ecological calamities? Will the former demand intervention, because he sees less, while the latter would recommend non-intervention, because he would see more and hence would see various principles of action in conflict among themselves thus giving him no clear basis for action? Contemporizing the epic would encourage us to look at some of these issues.

The third case relates to the place of the vow in the *Mahābhārata*. When one looks at the many vows made in the epic, Bhīṣma vowing to be celibate, Draupadī vowing to keep her hair loose till she could wash it in the blood of Duḥśāsana, or Arjuna vowing to kill Jayadratha before sunset to avenge his son Abhimanyu's killing, one finds that the vow seems to enjoy a moral pre-eminence as a basis for action. It is never overridden. There are no situations, subsequent to the taking of the vow, wherein the vow-maker can be justified in not fulfilling the vow because of some higher principle that comes into play. In the case of *dharma*, for example, there are contingencies in which *āpaddharma* can override what is normally one's *dharma*. But in the *Mahābhārata*, there seems to be no episode to relieve the oath-taker from fulfilling the vow? The case of Arjuna and his bow, the *Gāṇḍīva*, is illustrative of the power of the vow. Arjuna had vowed that he would kill anyone who insulted him or the *Gāṇḍīva*. When Yudhiṣṭhira insulted Arjuna and the *Gāṇḍīva* after his defeat at the hands of Karṇa, Arjuna was obliged to fulfil his vow. Kṛṣṇa, of course, could not allow this and advised Arjuna that abusing an elder brother was similar to killing him. Arjuna was thus permitted to abuse Yudhiṣṭhira which he did and thereby fulfilled his vow. So, how does one see a vow as a principle of action? What is its place in the order of moral precedence with respect to other moral grounds for action? Is one morally obligated to keep a bad promise or a promise, which upon subsequent reflection turns out to have been rash or un-benevolent just because it was a promise? Does it stand higher than *dharma*, in all its forms, as a basis for action, or lower? These are interesting questions that allow us to engage with the issue of the moral basis of action and of trumping principles which come into play in particular situations?

This brings me to the other issue raised earlier: Why the IIAS? If the three strategies of contemporizing the epics convey anything, it is that the epics are some of the richest intellectual resources available for us to draw from as we engage with the concerns of the present. They allow us to read and humanize them and analyze the different facets of the many moral puzzles that are found in them. Since the IIAS is mandated to explore the human condition and is tasked with asking the hard questions that society confronts, and attempt to work out the outlines of an answer, what better place than the IIAS to do so. The IIAS offers scholars the space, solitude, community, and opportunity, to explore these complex and fascinating set of issues, to suggest possible ways out of the problems we face. The epics offer us an abundance of questions that need to be probed if we are to enrich our intellectual lives as individuals and as a society. There are no two ways about it. Therefore, contemporize the Epics, at the IIAS, we must. And here is the first flower.

22 March 2013

Peter Ronald deSouza
Indian Institute of Advanced Study (IIAS)
Shimla

References

Bhattacharya, K. C. 1954[1931]. 'Swaraj in Ideas', Lecture delivered in October 1931 under Sir Asutosh Memorial Lectures Series, organized at Chandernagore by Charu Chandra Roy, in *Visvabharati Quarterly*, 20: 103–14.

Elster, Jon. 1979. *Ulysses and the Sirens: Studies in Rationality and Irrationality.*

Euripides. *The Medea.*

Karve, Irawati. 1968. *Yuganta.*

Mehendale, M. A. 1995. *Reflections on the Mahabharata War*. IIAS.

Walzer, Michael. 1992[1977]. *Just and Unjust Wars: A Moral Argument with Historical Illustrations*. 2nd edition. New York: Basic Books.

Acknowledgements

This volume of essays on the contemporary relevance of the *Mahābhārata* was supposed to be edited by three of us who drew up the book proposal together on a balmy afternoon in Sanjay Palshikar's spacious office at the Indian Institute of Advanced Study (IIAS), Shimla, in April 2010. In spite of his dropping out of the editorial team, the editors would like to register their indebtedness to Sanjay's careful and caring, skillful and mindful role in co-organizing the workshop on *Mahābhārata* from which this volume arose.

Peter de Souza is known for being a 'director with a difference', even for IIAS, 'an institution like no other in the world', devoted to research in the humanities that has had a glorious line of great minds starting from India's Platonic Philosopher-President Sarvepalli Radhakrishnan. The inspiration, administrative support and unflagging enthusiasm for the publication with which Professor de Souza has driven us through the arduous process of getting this unique collection of papers out can never be acknowledged adequately. As the editors know from the small measure of self-knowledge they can claim, the erudition and intellectual fecundity of Indian intellectuals vary inversely with their ability to honour deadlines. Our contributors have almost falsified this generalization. We remain grateful to all of them for staying within the limits of time and space which, sometimes, we ourselves have failed to respect.

We missed Shashank Thakur who took care of the logistics of the Summer School in 2010, during the process of the publication. We recall with fond gratitude the help we have received from Somnath Ghosh, Srinivasan Subramanian and Agniv Ghosh while preparing the final manuscript.

We remain grateful to Rakhi Sarkar of 'Cima Art Gallery' for permission to use Ganesh Pyne's masterpiece 'The White Hands' as a cover-image for our volume. Sadly, before seeing our published volume wrapped in the stunning colours and lines of his imagination, Pyne entered that penumbral place that his drawings so often draw us near to. As in the *Mahābhārata* story as on this tiny sorry planet in the cosmos, as meditated upon by the first chapter of this book, it is all a chancy game of dice. We have a trickster Śakuni of past-oblivious cult of speed and cyber-globalism to contend with, when publishing a volume of fearlessly critical essays on the Sanskrit Epic of All Times. There is no telling how it will all end.

Introduction

Arindam Chakrabarti
Sibaji Bandyopadhyay

The Concept of 'A *Mahābhārata*' and the Concept of 'Now'

There is one Leaning Tower of Pisa and a uniquely particular Qutub Minar. We have the concept of a tower, but we cannot have any concept of a Qutub Minar. Apparently, there is only one book, a collection of texts, a *saṃhitā*, originally called 'Jaya', known for the past 2,500 years as the *Mahābhārata*. How can we then talk about the general concept of a *Mahābhārata*? To form a general concept, we need multiple instances sharing a set of common properties. The answer to this question is straightforward. We can have the concept, for example, of a *Gītā*, because, in the *Mahābhārata* itself, there are many *Gītās*: *Parāśaragītā*, *Haṃsagītā*, *Vyādhagītā*, *Kāmagītā*, *Brāhmaṇagītā*, *Anugītā*, besides the *Bhagavadgītā*. Likewise, there are many *Mahābhāratas*; many versions in Sanskrit, many versions in regional vernaculars, but more deeply, each era, perhaps each civilization, writes and rewrites its own *Mahābhārata*. In the twentieth-century *Parva*, a novel by S. L. Bhairappa in Kannada, and *Andhaa-Yug*, a play by Dharamvir Bharti in Hindi, are examples of new *Mahābhāratas*, to say nothing of Peter Brook's French production of the stage and film version of the *Mahābhārata* with an international cast — comprising an African Bhīṣma and a Korean Droṇa, for instance — or the Bollywood movie *Rajneeti* in the twenty-first century. Some of these *Mahābhāratas* may remain unwritten, but handed down from generation to generation through spell-binding performances by Pandavani-singers like Teejan Bai, or keep transforming themselves (introducing, for example, additional semi-divine jester-characters) in Javanese Wayang Shadow puppet theatre (recognized by United Nations Economic, Social and Cultural Organization [UNESCO], as a 'Masterpiece of Oral and Intangible Heritage of Humanity'). 'Because, every age has its own unwritten (but avowed in consciousness) *Mahābhārata*, perhaps authored by their own great poets' (Das 2007: 54). This last remark was made by Jibanananda Das in an essay suggestively titled 'Perennial, Qua What?' ('Ki Hishebe Shaashwata'). Jibanananda Das (1899–1954) is still celebrated, on both sides of the Bangladesh border, as by far the greatest poet of undivided Bengal in the post-Tagore period. Although he wrote many novels and essays, his poetry defies all literary critical categorizations. It is at once deeply rural and deeply urban, intimately personal and local yet timelessly cosmopolitan. One of the reasons why we start this introduction with his essay on the *Mahābhārata* is that the paradox of the perennial as the contemporary, the uniquely classical as repeatably modern, is best exemplified and theorized in his words and thought. We cannot be completely comfortable with the translation 'perennial' of the word *shaashwata*. But in this memorable essay, Jibanananda observes that, if, in order to count as *shaashwata* a book has to perennially maintain its original textual integrity and remain just as alive in people's consciousness as it did at the time of its composition, then the *Mahābhārata* is *not* a *shaashwata* text. Yet, Jibanananda maintains, the *Mahābhārata* is a living text, now, in the twentieth century. To solve this paradox of not being ever-unchanging yet being alive now as ever before, it is important to first acknowledge that we have not absorbed *Mahābhārata*'s wisdom straight from either the Sanskrit text or its Bengali translations. Our relationship with the *Mahābhārata* is mediated by many later indigenous as well as foreign texts, in particular, those written in the last four to five hundred years. It is today's *Mahābhārata* — that is, the *Mahābhārata* informed by an ever-changing constellation of modern writing — which allows us to enter into the centuries-old *Mahābhārata* with our ears and eyes open. Emerging out of our contemporary experiences the *Uttar-Mahābhārata* equips us to compare and contrast the 'New' in relation to the grandness of the 'Old' *Mahābhārata*. Despite not being *shaashwata* by itself, *Mahābhārata*'s relevance, at least in India, is *shaashwata*. This means, it is mandatory for every (Indian) post-*Mahābhārata* text to have the *Mahābhārata* as one of its components. The *Mahābhārata* thus will remain a living text till the last day of human civilization. There is nothing in our literature that can measure up to *Mahābhārata*'s vastness of range. Gifted with an unsurpassable subtle suppleness the *Mahābhārata* always lends itself to later readings and appropriations. This quality of remaining usable without being *shaashwata* is also there in varying degrees in the works of Homer, Dante, Shakespeare, Rabindranath and such others. But what is unique to the original epic, if there ever was one, is that 'The *Mahābhārata* held together its own age – gave it road-directions; told stories spanning over a very wide space-time of the history of the world; showed an extra-ordinarily sensitive unique capacity to touch the heart by its style of telling tales, by elevating ordinary small things to divine proportions, and by reflecting clearly and luminously the most esoteric things in the mirror of the heart' (Das 2007: 52)

What is most ironic is that while we are all at pains to demonstrate that the *Mahābhārata* is *shaaswata* in some tenuous sense, the *Mahābhārata* itself announces unequivocally that all works, all that is living and nonliving, is *a-śāśvatam* ('un-perennial'); everything that is done ends in ruin, days end in nights, accumulations in decay, unions in divorce, and life in death (*Śāntiparvan* 27.29). These two claims — of eternity and perishability, of the classicalness and the contemporaniety, of the oldness and the newness of the *Mahābhārata* — could be reconciled if we reflect on the simple fact that all times are present times. The adverb 'now' is closely connected to the metaphysically maddening pronoun 'I'. In grammatically characterizing the first person singular pronoun. K. C. Bhattacharya (1983) remarks that 'I' is a general term, just as general as the word 'unique'. Now, this current moment, is also unique in the sense that every moment is a now. The universality and eternity of the *Mahābhārata* is best appreciated if we appreciate the omni-contemporaneity of 'a now'. In this collection of the newest essays on one of the oldest books, we have tried to capture the perpetual renewal, the electricity, and the dynamics of the 'current' human *itihāsa* called *Mahābhārata.*

The Background

In April 2010, the Indian Institute of Advanced Study (IIAS), Shimla hosted a two-week long Spring School on the *Mahābhārata* from 14 to 28 April 2010. Each of the 14 days had two sessions. Fifteen Resource Persons invited by the institute spoke on various aspects of the *Mahābhārata* in the morning-sessions. Twenty-five student-participants from different parts of India, carefully selected from a large pool of applicants, presented papers on a wide range of contemporary issues relating them to the *Mahābhārata* in the afternoon-sessions. The Spring School was jointly coordinated by Sanjay Palshikar and Sibaji Bandyopadhyay.

At the end of the Spring School the institute requested the resource persons to consider developing the lectures they had delivered into full-fledged essays. Since the responses were both positive and warm, the institute decided to bring out a book to be edited by Arindam Chakrabarti and Sibaji Bandyopadhyay. On the basis of the topics covered by the contributors, the editors have named the volume *Mahābhārata Now: Narration, Aesthetics, Ethics.*

Summary of the Chapters

The *Mahābhārata* is at once an archive and a living text; a museum and a laboratory; and a sourcebook, complete by itself, and an open text, perennially under construction. A storehouse of information, the *Mahābhārata* furnishes ample material to any professional interested in 'excavation'; and the professional may don the hat of, say, an anthropologist, a historian, a sociologist, a linguist, a literary critic, a historian of ideas, or a creative philosopher, to work out, even if provisionally, some or the other well-integrated meaning. On the other hand, in the course of entering the *Mahābhārata*, there is almost no one who does not undergo a sense of *déjà vu* — an inescapable feeling that the 'present' s/he inhabits is only a re-play of 'happenings' already recorded; an eerie sensation that most of the ethical dilemmas, the logical puzzles and the unavoidable impasses which baffle the modern man, as well as the mood of irresolution following every resolution that keeps plaguing him/her have already been punctiliously check-listed.

Thus, in the case of the *Mahābhārata*, two interpretative paths — one devoted to the uncovering of a shadowy past and the other engaged in negotiating the contemporary — keep intersecting. Scholars — who are engrossed in sifting through various confusing variants in order to bring coherence to a chaotic corpus, and absorbed in the pursuit of transforming a 'literary unthing' into a critically codified text that can shed light on India's past with sufficient cogence — collaborate, wittingly or unwittingly, with amateurs who, even while critically reflecting on 'current affairs', remain more or less convinced that the *Mahābhārata* is no less than 'a chronicle of events foretold'. This double play of 'freezing' and 'de-freezing' — the double move of construing a decisive 'body of words' that can be employed to prove or disprove any scientific hypothesis in relation to the past, and of reckoning the same as being a tool that can be employed to decipher the mysteries of the present — renders a magical quality to the *Mahābhārata*.

The urge to discover in the *Mahābhārata*, the repetition of *before*, *during* and *after* provides, in turn, a master-key to the analysis of the 'compulsion' known as the *compulsion to repeat* which holds the modern Indians in its grip — a 'compulsion' palpably evident in a number of their 'philosophical', 'aesthetic' and 'political' undertakings.

The 12 essays collected in this anthology are just as self-consciously 'scholarly' as they are charged by a sense of *nowness*. Whatever may be their domain of enquiry — 'narrative styles', 'problems of aesthetics' or 'ethical paradoxes' — all the essayists have underscored the theme 'Today' in their articles. This particular emphasis is what renders a 'unity of purpose' to the collection. It would be foolhardy to claim (or expect) that there would be 'evenness' in terms of either diction of thought or quality of language in the essays brought together in this volume. The *Mahābhārata* not only promotes the cause of *difference*, but also does so with a great fanfare. And therefore, every attempt to untie the text tied up in tight yet loose knots is bound to yield a result, which cannot but be positively unique. With due respect to 'singularities' of achievement, the editors have deliberately refrained from imposing conditions on the contributors mining the *Mahābhārata* from today's perspective which might have brought on 'uniformity' in style, length, scope, or for that matter, in ideological orientation. The volume is divided into three sections: Narration, Aesthetics and Ethics.

On Narration

One of the purposes of this section is to record briefly (*a*) the means by which the editors of the critical edition (published between 1933 and 1966) brought out by the Bhandarkar Oriental Research Institute, Pune, construed a (more or less) running narrative out of the available Sanskrit manuscripts of the *Mahābhārata* scripted in various Indian alphabets; and (*b*) the interpretative opportunities offered by the critical edition in conjunction with the previously printed versions of the Sanskrit *Mahābhārata* in tackling the knotty problem of narration.

The moot point is: even after the long editorial journey undertaken by the makers of the critical edition, the *Mahābhārata* remains as messy as ever. Despite its tremendous success in laying motorable roads into the 'jungle of tales' and lessening the baffling 'wild' noises which often misled earlier sojourners into the trap of an endless labyrinth, the critical edition fails to extract from the manuscript tradition the authentic *Mahābhārata* that can be certified as 'the autograph copy of the work of its mythical author, Maharṣi Vyāsa'. But the 'failure' itself is of great significance. It signals the fact that we have at last reached the last post in the affair of solving the enigma of inconsistencies. The Pune edition delineates that limiting horizon from which all attempts to 'clean' the book within the parameters of manuscript tradition look pathetically quixotic. This being so, it allows one to hazard strongly grounded yet novel hypotheses relating to the multifarious *techniques* of narration one comes across in the *Mahābhārata*.

In this section, keeping in mind the 'timeless nowness' of the *Mahābhārata*, experts probe the nature of the writing/telling of the text at three grades of depth. The first chapter titled 'Of Gambling: A Few Lessons from the *Mahābhārata*' by Sibaji Bandyopadhyay starts with the significance of the number four for Vedic–Purāṇic cultures and goes on to relating a brief history of dice games. True to the tradition of reading the *Mahābhārata* as an illustrative commentary on the Vedas, this opening chapter then delves deep into the mysterious Gambler-hymn of the *Ṛgveda*, comparing the radically different uses the gambling theme is put to by the Nala–Ṛtuparṇa story and the Yudhiṣṭhira–Śakuni story in our text. Interspersing an acute analysis of Kauṭilya's *Arthaśāstra*'s warnings against dice-game-addiction, with Hollywood comedian W. C. Fields' definition of horse-sense as what prevents the horse from betting on people, and allusion to the debate in post-Einsteinian physics, this carefully crafted chapter also works as a commentary on the cover image — the Ganesh Pyne masterpiece — that we have chosen for the volume.

The second chapter titled 'Methodology of the Critical Edition of the *Mahābhārata*' by Saroja Bhate emphasizes the history and politics of preparing a critical edition of the *Mahābhārata* which existed in different versions in different parts of the country at different times, and whose pre-modern Sanskrit commentators had also spoken self-consciously about alternative readings of crucial verses.

The third chapter titled 'Significance of the Early *Parvan*s: Modes of Narration, Birth Stories and Seeds of Conflict' by Sibesh Bhattacharya goes into the earlier parts of the text, problematizing their narrative strategies. It thematizes the trope of extraordinary stories of the births of the central characters.

Although philosophers, both in medieval Sanskrit and in modern English, have formulated a separate 'systemic' Philosophy of Vyāsa or Philosophy of the *Mahābhārata*, when we approach it with sharp ethical or metaphysical questions, in answer, the book, Bhīṣma or Kṛṣṇa tells us one or more stories and leaves it at that. Its job seems to be simply to describe in suggestive detail the actions of different people (sometimes, a self-disguising god, a disgruntled mongoose, trees, or birds, or even an insect crossing the road while a mighty chariot is racing through) in particular situations. Seeing this in the light of Ludwig Wittgenstein's advice to philosophers 'Do not explain, just describe', the fourth chapter titled 'Understanding Yudhiṣṭhira's Actions: Recasting *Karma-Yoga* in a Wittgensteinian Mould' by Enakshi Mitra tries something really radical. Criticizing the explicit belief–desire–activity–fruit model of human action, this chapter proposes to re-describe Yudhiṣṭhira's sometimes confused, sometimes akratic, sometimes virtuous, sometimes indecisive actions in the epic in a 'holistic' way, absorbing the alleged desire-causes as well as the alleged fruit-consequences into the action itself. This Wittgensteinian way of rethinking human actions, the author claims, helps us make a better sense of the doability of deeds without desire for action, transcending results or fruits.

On Aesthetics

Mahābhārata, first and foremost, is a poem, a consummate example of literary art and the art of story-telling. The chapters of this section dwell on the poetics of this ever-fresh work by offering: (*a*) a survey of the host of aesthetic categories deployed in pre-modern times by various schools to study the *Mahābhārata* as well as a sustained search for a paradigm that might transcend their intrinsic limits; and (*b*) an attempt to situate the relationship between Kuntī and Karṇa in terms of an aesthetic norm informed by the psychoanalytic approach to mother–son bonding.

The first chapter titled 'Aesthetics of the *Mahābhārata*: Traditional Interpretations' by Radhavallabh Tripathi revisits the ancient debate on the question of what is the dominant aesthetic milieu and relishable juice (*rasa*) of the *Mahābhārata*, in terms of the state-of-the-art Sanskrit aesthetics. Is it a theatre of cruelty, a drama of bravery and heroism, an invocation of horror or pity and compassion or disgust, or a sublime poem inspiring tranquility and detachment arising out of the fragility of goodness? The second chapter titled 'Karṇa in and out of the *Mahābhārata*' by Nrisinha Prasad Bhaduri zooms in on an inter-textual literary assessment of the singular character of Karṇa both in the *Mahābhārata* as well as in other Sanskrit poems all the way up to Rabindranath Tagore's modern interpretation of that complex character.

On Ethics

This section raises a host of issues which are of pressing importance to today's men and women. Broadly speaking, the essays deal with: (*a*) feminist/anti-casteist/pro-egalitarian critiques which focus upon some of the moral blinkers that block many of *Mahābhārata*'s insights from developing into full-scale concepts; (*b*) studies on modern blinkers which make it incomprehensible that what are often routinely written off as regressive elements in the *Mahābhārata* actually offer insights worth pursuing; and (*c*) systematic analyses of modern/post-modern explorations surrounding themes such as 'terror', 'conversation' and 'violence', with the express aim of tying them with relevant material from the *Mahābhārata*.

The six essays of the last and longest section bring contemporary ethical, social and political concerns to bear upon different moral issues in the *Mahābhārata*.

Some of the live problems of twentieth-century moral philosophy that these essays use the rich resources of the *Mahābhārata* to address are: the possibility of using care and humility as bases for an ethically responsive epistemology, sexuality and power-play involving royal consorts and royal maids, contextual and non-universalizable ethics of situations, the question of violence and retaliative cruelty, and the ethics of pubic fearless speaking of the truth against power. The care perspective has emerged in Western philosophy as a feminist alternative to Kantian and Consequentialist approaches to morality. The first chapter titled 'Care Ethics and Epistemic Justice: Some Insights from the *Mahābhārata*' by Vrinda Dalmiya seeks to find echoes of the care perspective in some concepts of the *Mahābhārata* concentrating on the idea of what the author calls 'relational humility' as a necessary condition for successful caring encounters. Whether feminist, Foucauldian or vernacular, the registers in which the *Mahābhārata* is re-read in these essays, make the text come alive as providing us the most post-post-modern vocabulary for a collective as well as existential examination of the self, society and humanity.

Of all the tales of moral travesty that the *Mahābhārata* weaves together to remind us of the occasional smallness of the greats, Uma Chakravarti picks the most shameful episode of Draupadī's public harassment which forms the pivot of the epic's plot. She reviews critically contemporary responses to Draupadī's legal–political question: 'Can a slave who has even lost his ownership of him-self have enough claim over his wife to be able to stake her in a gambling bid?' Interpreting such bodily gestures as hair-pulling and stripping as ancient — and current — signals of sexual domination, control and enslavement, and alluding to the now famous Mahashweta Devi's story which re-creates Draupadī as a mauled and dehumanized dalit woman Dopdi, Chakravarti raises, for our times, the new question: 'Can we pose Draupadī's question about the ownership of a slave's female slave (= wife) from the point of view of the *dāsī*-in-general? If women are booties in battles for power and honour, to be battered in public both in ancient as well as contemporary Delhi, men's valour, virility and patriarchal prestige seem to be eventually proven by military might and homicidal prowess.

Since the text never tires of telling the story of well-trained massacre-artists and bloody revenge such as breaking the chest and drinking the blood of the villain for the sake of keeping a promise of love, does the *Mahābhārata* regard killing of the enemy as not just permissible but obligatory while singing praises of 'non-cruelty' as the heart of righteousness? Was Arjuna supposed to kill his teacher or his own (unacknowledged) elder brother 'non-cruelly' with no desire for the fruit of the lethal act? That is a question which is as relevant today for all the war-mongering nations that are spending so much money, time and words on peace-talks (in Palestine, Korea or Kashmir).

Prabal Kumar Sen deals with the charge that the situational (*āvasthika*) ethics of the *Mahābhārata* is at best a form of moral relativism and, at worst internally incoherent. Citing and analyzing numerous contexts from within the text where irresolvable moral dilemmas thicken almost into a bifurcated conscience of either Yudhiṣṭhira or Bhīṣma or even of the divine adjudicator Kṛṣṇa himself, Sen draws fine distinctions between moral subjectivism, moral agnosticism, moral skepticism, moral syncretism, moral pluralism, and moral doubt. Does the question of an ethics, properly so-called, even arise where there is such a metaphysical pull towards determinism? Using the recent works of philosophers like Jonardon Ganeri, Sen's chapter warns us against extracting any monolithic 'ism' from this descriptive text which, for all its discourse on *dharma*, couches its normative content in a naturalistic idiom: human beings and human societies come in different shapes with different conceptions of a good life.

Rabindranath Tagore had characterized the early twentieth century as 'an earth drunk with violence'. The twenty-first century, beginning with the US' escalating carnage-competition with al-Qaida maintained its resemblance with the end of the *Mahābhārata*. Jibanananda Das, whom we invoked at the opening of this introduction, uses the epithet 'blind', both for the mouse-hunting night owl and the ruthless world-leaders without whose advice the twentieth-century world-peace-making would be impossible As he uses the spotlight of deconstruction — a la Derrida and Spivak — on the *Sauptikaparvan* ('Book of Sleep') which contains the bloodiest episode in the Kuru–Pāṇḍava war, Anirban Das brings out, in his essay, the lurid 'colors of violence' by bringing in the provocative trope of communal cannibalism: why do communities, violently coded group-identities, still need to mutilate, kill, cook, and eat the Other in order to construct a Self?

Given the relentless gruesome details of archery, weapon-wielding techniques, complex lethal formations of infantry and cavalry, and numerous methods of calculated carnage, when the *Mahābhārata* breaks into moral didactic praise of non-violence, it sounds just as hypocritical to the contemporary reader as a twenty-first-century Indian election-campaign speech. How could such a battle-fascinated saga be taken as a poetic–ethical–narrative recommendation of non-violence? That is the challenging question that Gangeya Mukherjee takes up in his literary–philosophical essay. With copious references to contemporary hermeneutic debates over the text's attitude towards 'war as sacrifice', Mukherjee slowly but surely arrives at the conclusion that in the face of unavoidable violence, the *Mahābhārata* explores the possibility of living truthfully but with self-censure, with compassion and dispassion. In spite of the *Gītā*'s notorious 'encouragement' of just war, to take Yudhiṣṭhira's voice as closest to the narrator's own, is to take this chronicle of combat as exemplifying a poetics of peace. This problematizes the concept of *mokṣa* in the middle of embroilment in *real-politik*, for the post-modern ethical man.

Though it teaches no single code of conduct to all of us, what the *Mahābhārata* does teach by example after example and by self-critical theorization is never to stop asking questions of oneself and never to stop conversing about how to live. Through its hundreds of *itihāsam purātanam* and especially the *Śāntiparvan* ('Book of Peace'), we are compelled to think about the very ethics of conversation without which all conversation about ethics turns into mere waste or war of words. Keeping Michel Foucault's concept of 'Fearless Speech' (*parrhesia*) in mind, Arindam Chakrabarti foregrounds the politics of linguistic performances which we witness in the dialogue about dialogues that takes place between Janaka and Sulabhā towards the end of the *Śāntiparvan*.

Dialogue as Sacrifice: Is Anyone Listening?

Together, these three sections afford us a three-dimensional depth-perception of the eternally recurrent saga of being-in-the-world which 'has been sung before, is being sung now, and will be sung again in the future' (*Ādiparvan* 1.24).

One uncontroversial ecological future of our planet, at this point, is that it will be a *waste land*, of the kind that is described at the end of the *Mahābhārata* war when the narrator announces in a thunderous voice: 'Happy times are over, terrible times have come, . . . the earth has lost its youth (*prithivī gatayauvanā*)' (*Ādiparvan* 119.6). In his Upaniṣad-inspired classic poem from *The Waste Land*, T. S. Eliot (1969: 73) asked, uncannily echoing the spirit, as it were, of the dirge in the *Mahābhārata*'s *Strīparvan* ('Book of Women'):

> What is that sound high in the air
> Murmur of maternal lamentation
> Who are those hooded hordes swarming
> Over endless plains, stumbling in cracked earth
> Ringed by the flat horizon only
> What is the city over the mountains
> Cracks and reforms and bursts in the violet air
> Falling towers
> Jerusalem Athens Alexandria
> Vienna London
> Unreal.

Tradition regards the epic *Mahābhārata* as a narrative commentary on the Vedas. In the voice of Eliot (ibid.: 74), the Vedas gave the earthlings of the twentieth century the ethics of gift, *dā* for *datta* as in the long *Dānadharmaparvan* (*Mahābhārata*, Book XIII):

> Ganga was sunken, and the limp leaves
> Waited for rain, while the black clouds
> Gathered far distant, over Himavant.
> The jungle crouched, humped in silence.
> Then spoke the thunder
> DA
> Datta: what have we given?
> My friend, blood shaking my heart

> The awful daring of a moment's surrender
> Which an age of prudence can never retract
> By this, and this only, we have existed
> Which is not to be found in our obituaries.

What, one may ask of this volume, does the perennial thunder that is the *Mahābhārata*, tell us *now*?

While it does tell us to give, not to be cruel, and to practise work without attachment to the fruits of action, the *Mahābhārata* does not teach us any single clear universal morality. *Dharma*, it says, is sensitive to time and place (Prabal Kumar Sen's essay in this volume is a nuanced elaboration of this situation-sensitivity of the *Mahābhārata* ethics). Morality must be always ready with a bifurcated judgment because in concrete life-contexts it faces deadly dilemmas. After all, Death and Dharma are one and the same divinity, the real father of our hero Yudhiṣṭhira, Yama — does not 'Yama' mean both self-restraint and a two-some? — who wields a noose of double bind. You are dead if you do, you are dead if you don't do what is right. In the end everyone is dead. Hard times make right actions wrong, and bad becomes the only good available. Truth often comes tainted with untruth and violence. Angry ascetics get duly snubbed by dutiful housewives and finally instructed by philosopher-butchers. In one story, for instance, friendship between a generous king Brahmadatta and a miraculous bird called 'the Worshipped One' (Pūjanī) turns bitter, when the little prince kills the bird's child by accident, and the bird blinds the prince in an act of motherly revenge. The king requests the bird to stay on as his friend for the fault was his son's. Pūjanī leaves the royal palace, afraid of unending revenge-cycles and unforgettable resentment. 'How can one who has known the taste of grief, of oneself as of others, feel like talking about moral matters?' says the bereaved bird-mother silencing all moral homilies mouthed by the 'forgiving king' who wants her to stay on. In another story, a cat and a mouse become friends in need, but never trust each other, and one is taught not to trust anyone too much. Yet, non-cruelty (*ānṛśaṃsya*) as *never inflicting on others what one cannot bear oneself* is repeatedly formulated as the essence of *dharma*. In yet another story, during a 12-year 'global warming', not a drop of rain falls, rivers dry up, cities and villages turn into deserts, all charities and services collapse. The holy sage Viśvāmitra roams the earth in desperate search of food. Finally, he breaks into the bedroom of an untouchable hunter and tries to steal a piece of stale dog-meat. The low-caste 'dog-eater' (*śvpaka*) tries, in a long ethical discourse in the Book XII or 'Book of Peace' (*Śāntiparvan*) of the *Mahābhārata*, to convince the high-caste sage that he should not be touching, stealing or eating this prohibited food, while the sage argues that when survival is at stake, eating any food is permissible. With profound irony and stark realism, the narrator of this story Bhīṣma — himself lying on a bed of arrows (of unanswered moral questions?) — demonstrates how starvation reverses the moral stances of the vegetarian upper caste and the carnivorous lower caste. The only morality left at such times would be 'saving life'. How do you decide which is the morally preferable option in such times of extreme crisis? The *Mahābhārata* offers a thumb-rule: 'Dharma *has been prescribed for the sake of flourishing of living beings. Whatever promotes sustaining and enhancement of life, for sure, is* dharma' (*Śāntiparvan* 110.10).

But this is not the only conception of *dharma*. In a similar crisis, a pigeon performs the supreme *dharma* of hospitality by throwing itself in a fire to become food for a hungry hunter who had just captured its partner pigeon. The hunter repents, and the pigeon is welcomed to heaven as a noble moral exemplar. Though extolling such heroic self-sacrifice, the text becomes more and more self-critical about any didactic moral discourse.

Our volume starts with reflections on the chancy metaphysics of the *Mahābhārata* where a dark and devious divinity — who is as much Kṛṣṇa as the poet Kṛṣṇa Dvaipāyana Vyāsa — gambles with our lives. It ends with an analysis of the dialogue between Janaka and Sulabhā, a young ascetic woman who suddenly arrives at the court of the philosopher-king, to test his wisdom. Bewitched by her beauty, the chauvinistic king nervously asks the nun, 'Why are you here? Why, in spite of having such a young and shapely body, have you renounced the world? Why do you want the impossible mingling between you and me?' (*Śāntiparvan* 308.54–59). In response, step by step, Sulabhā teaches the narcissistic king Janaka a series of moral and psycho-linguistic lessons about how not to speak in a civil assembly and what makes a dialogue a genuine piece of communication. Her fearless speech about proper and improper speech makes the reputed philosopher-king hang his head in silence. For our own talkative times, where the world-wide web of electronically transmitted words, through the bytes of computers and ego-centric jingle of 'I-phones', fills our days and nights, our cities and villages, with the aggressive drive to 'communicate', the *Mahābhārata* offers not only a dialogic ethic but also an articulate ethics of dialogue.

Vyāsa tells us that king Janmejaya told that Bhīṣma told Yudhiṣṭhira the tale of Sulabhā telling Janaka how to use words justly. But Vyāsa also ends the book by lamenting that he is crying in the wilderness raising both his hands but 'no one is listening' (*na ca kaścit śṛṇoti me*) (*Svargārohaṇaparvan* 5.49). In 12 chapters, we are about to renew and retell some of his stories and the history of humanity — but is anyone going to listen?

15 January 2012

References

Bandyopadhyay, Sibaji. 2008. *The Book of Night: A Moment from the Mahabharata*, trans. Ipsita Chanda. Kolkata: Seagull Books.

———. 2002. *Uttampurush Ekbachan: Ekti Bhaan*. Kolkata: Disha Sahitya.

Bhattacharya, K. C. (ed.). 1983. *Studies in Philosophy*. New Delhi: Motilal Banarsidass.

Das, Jibanananda. 2007[1955]. 'Ki Hisebe Shaashwata' ('Perennial, Qua What?'), in *Kabitaar Kathaa*, pp. 51–60.

Eliot, T. S. 1969. 'Waste Land', in *The Complete Poems and Plays of T. S. Eliot*. London: Faber and Faber.

Sukthankar, V. S. et al. (ed.). 1991. *The Mahābhārata for the First Time Critically Edited*, vol. 1: *Ādiparvan*. Pune: Bhandarkar Oriental Research Institute.

———. 1961. *The Mahābhārata for the First Time Critically Edited*, vol. 13: *Śāntiparvan*. Pune: Bhandarkar Oriental Research Institute.

———. 1959. *The Mahābhārata for the First Time Critically Edited*, vol. 19: *Svargārohaṇaparvan*. Pune: Bhandarkar Oriental Research Institute.

PART I
Narration

Of Gambling

A Few Lessons from the Mahābhārata

Sibaji Bandyopadhyay

I

> I, at any rate, am convinced that *He* does not throw dice.
>
> — Albert Einstein (1971: 130, emphasis original)
>
> (Popular variant: 'God does not play dice with the universe'.)

The number *four* is of immense significance in the textual imagination of India. Used for centuries to configure a variety of discursive *units*, the number has a special *force* accrued to it long ago. The piling of categorical measures onto number four has been so persistent and thick that one may even suspect the working of an organizing principle behind it. There is nothing to prevent one from speculating that the driving motive has been such as not only to compose a network of foursome bundles but also to arrange them in terms of a somewhat *convergent* series. It is as if, (despite many loose ends), there is a *design* implicit in the taxonomy scaled to degree four — a pattern that on its own proffers a slippery *limit* which, albeit indistinct and distant, casts a long shadow on the other four-pronged elements and functions as their ultimate referent.

As the fourth numerical embraces many a theoretical and practical aspects of existence; enumerates a plethora of *forms* of the 'social organization', 'calibrated life-style' and 'graded life-end'; and traverses the entire spectrum ranging from the 'ineffably abstract' to the 'grossly mundane', the impression that it has a ubiquitous quality about it is inescapable. Who can navigate the ocean of Indian texts without the guidance of lighthouses such as: the corpus of hallowed texts collectively called the Four Vedas; the amalgam of rank and prestige signified by the Four *varṇa*s; the stipulated stages of life or the Four *āśrama*s; the endowments of *dharma–artha–kāma–mokṣa* ('customary as well as customized propriety–material gain–pleasures of love and lust-deliverance'), holistically termed the Four *varga*s; *dharma*'s *catuṣpāda* or the Four Aspects of Right Conduct; Brahmā, the creator of the universe, who speaks in many voices with his Four faces; the cyclical movement of Ages construed by progressive degenerations and regenerations resulting in the Four *yuga*s — no, the Brahminical grammar is *not* thinkable without the *numerum quattuor*. But, of all the quadruplets which 'conceptual package' brings to that grammar a semblance of consistency?

Kālo 'smi, 'Time am I' — so said Kṛṣṇa when He revealed his True Identity to Arjuna just before the all-consuming War ensued on the battlefield of Kurukṣetra (*Gītā* XI. 32). The 'Superself' Kṛṣṇa taught the 'Superman' Arjuna (Sukthankar 1998: 121): Time was the prime mover of the universe (Radhakrishnan 2008: 279); being Time-incarnate, Kṛṣṇa was not only 'world-destroying' (*Gītā* XI. 32) but also came into being *yuge-yuge* (from age to age), to protect the good and ruin the wicked (*Gītā* IV. 8). The transcendental heightening of the temporal combined with *yuga* or the Age's four-fold division starting from the time of righteous prosperity to that of rapacious villainy, and thence on a reverse-journey of upward-climb from the state of utter degradation to that of absolute perfection gives the *clue* to spot the four-based unit we are interested in — it must be something that has the capacity to schematize vagaries of time in accordance with codes of some chancy game.

As in many other Indian texts, so also in Manu's *Book of Laws* we find mention of the Four Ages. In Chapter I, Verses 81–86, Manu exposits on them with a fair amount of details. Chronicling the tale of decay and destitution with increasing gloom, Manu names the successive four *yugas*: *kṛta*, *tretā*, *dvāpara* and *kali* (Bühler 2001: 22–24; Bandyopadhyay Sastri 2000: 37–39; Doniger and Smith 1991: 12).

A Set of 10 Dice: Proto-historic and Early Historic Mohenjodaro and Bhita Ivory
Courtesy: Indian Museum
Photograph: Somnath Ghosh

Now, it so happens that the words *kṛta*, *tretā*, *dvāpara* and *kali* correspond exactly with the words for (a) the number of dots on the sides of the four-sided Indian die (Monier 2005: 301, 462, 503, 261) and (b) the throws of dice (Doniger and Smith 1991: 11). The *akṣa* or die — usually made out of the fruits of the *vibhītaka* (*Terminalia Bellerica*) tree, each the size of a hazelnut — was four-dotted: the dot of four was called *kṛta*, those of three, two and one, *tretā*, *dvāpara* and *kali* respectively. The throw from a lot of die onto the game-board or *adhidevana/ iriṇa* yielded the four following results: if the total count were divisible by four the thrower obtained *kṛta* or 'winning'; if after dividing it by four the remainder were three he obtained *tretā* or 'trey', if two, *dvāpara* or 'deuce'; and, if one, what he earned was *kali* or 'losing' (Lüders 1906: 2–3).

The fantastic coincidence of names of Ages and throws of the dice is made even more scintillating by Manu just before he begins to set forth the characteristics of the four *yuga*s. He says in I. 80: 'The Epochs . . . are countless, and so are the emissions and re-absorptions (of the universe); as if he were playing, *parameṣṭhī*/ Supreme Lord/Brahmā does this again and again' (Bühler 2001: 22; Bandyopadhyay Sastri 2000: 36; Doniger and Smith 1991: 12).

So, contrary to Albert Einstein, Manu did think that God (or some Supra-power) plays with the universe and that too relentlessly. At any rate, (even if Viṣṇu, the god of preservation does not), there is ample evidence that Śiva, the god of destruction, plays dice with all creation (Doniger 2009: 321–22). But then, Einstein too had his moments of doubt.

At first perturbed by the news that an experimental result may disprove his theory of gravitation but later relieved to learn that the result was wrong, Einstein is reported to have quipped in May 1921: 'Subtle is the Lord, but malicious He is not' (Clarke 1971: 339). Reaffirming Einstein's long-held faith on God's straightforwardness — 'I, at any rate, am convinced that *He* does not throw dice' — this remark on the Almighty's intrinsic Goodness is permanently inscribed in stone above the fireplace in the Faculty Lounge of the Mathematics Department of Princeton University. However, Jamie Sayen's book *Einstein in America: the Scientist's Conscience in the Age of Hitler and Hiroshima* (1985) informs us that in the despairing days of the Third Reich and the subsequent nuclear disaster, Einstein had, perhaps temporarily, changed his stand. Indicating that in opposition to the timid expectations of believers of divine graciousness, God led — or rather misled — people to believe they understood things that they actually were far from understanding, Einstein had said then: 'I have second thoughts. Maybe God *is* malicious' (Sayen 1985: 51, emphasis original). Einstein's double-take on the *nature* of God and therefore of the cosmos becomes more pertinent to the connection between *yuga*s and the game of dice once we recall what happened on 16 July 1945. Watching with his naked eyes the first atomic explosion on the desert-field of New Mexico's Los Alamos — a spectacular and deafening burst that, by the way, provided the most convincing practical demonstration of the veracity of Einstein's theoretical formulation on the issue of extracting energy from matter — J. Robert Oppenheimer, reputed to be the 'Father of Atom Bomb', felt that the awesome scene was only a replay of sorts. Overtaken by the beguiling sensation of the 'Uncanny' — the experience of witnessing the coming into the open of a thing meant to remain secret and hidden (Freud 2003: 132) — Oppenheimer was reminded of Chapter XI of the *Gītā*. Of the two verses from the *Gītā*'s 'The Lord's Transfiguration' (*Viśvarūpadarśana Yoga*) Chapter that flashed in the mind of the nuclear scientist then, one was XI. 32: 'Time am I, world-destroying, grown mature, engaged here in subduing the world' (Junck 1985: 208).

Such happenstances can hardly be ignored. The metaphoric deployment of the dice by physicists sworn to the creed of 'determinacy' as well as by those bent upon transcending the tenets of 'total determination', coupled with the invocation of the *Gītā* at one of the most dangerous moments in modern times, does, on their own, pull us towards the *Mahābhārata*. It seems, the most celebrated dice-game recorded in world literature, the one in the *Mahābhārata* famous for the ethical dilemmas it dramatizes, has much to offer to the person who (like Albert Einstein) does his best to resist the idea that even while Nature is secretive 'she' is not bent on trickery, and also to the person who (like Niels Bohr or Werner Heisenberg) is willing to hazard the guess that there is an element of elusiveness in the workings of Nature which gives to the 'femme fatale' the appearance of being purposefully deceitful.

II

> God plays dice with the universe. But they're loaded. And [our] main objective . . . is to find out by what rules were they loaded.
>
> — Joseph Ford
> (Quoted in Gleick 1987: 129)

Accused Pleads Not-guilty

In retrospect it appears as if we have a foreshadowing of a Kafkaesque situation in *Ṛgveda* VII. 86 (Wilson 2000a: 310–11; Doniger O'Flaherty 1994: 213–14; Brereton 1992: 11–12; Bandyopadhyay 1976: 183–84). The hymn composed by Vasiṣṭha provides a tragicomic portrayal of a man harassed by one of the chieftains of authority for reasons unknown to him. Bandied from pillar to post, the distraught protagonist fails to cognize why god Varuṇa is hell-bent upon persecuting him. He keeps asking himself what was the transgression that has so upset his beloved Lord; he enquires upon the wise but all that the knowing men tell him is, 'Varuṇa has been provoked to anger against you'. Not being able to name the provocation, the hapless man stands indicted sans the slimmest chance of self-defence. So, in utter confusion, he supplicates to Varuṇa by tabulating the misdeeds for which he, in want of conscious intention, could in no way be *personally* responsible. Branded 'guilty' *before* having done anything wrong, the devastated soul pleads for the mighty god's mercy for crimes *not* committed by him. The humble supplicant lays out for his dreaded Master's consideration a list of mischief not blighted by pre-meditation. It contains: (*a*) sins of ancestors; (*b*) follies of younger generations; (*c*) reflex actions of individuated physical body; (*d*) objectionable dreams during sleep; and (*e*) the four things that lead one astray quite involuntarily, namely, liquor, pride, ignorance and dice.

A Dicey Author?

Ṛgveda X.34 is the fabulous hymn that explores the psychological trappings of the feeling of involuntariness that seizes a man whenever he engages in a dice-game (Wilson 2000b: 274–77; Doniger O'Flaherty 1994: 240–41; Bandyopadhyay 1976: 500–1).

As ancient archival records — records that constitute the Vedic-Brahmanical tradition — testify, the author of *Ṛgveda* X.34 was Kavaṣa Ailūṣa. And, what is extraordinary is that there is a 'biographical' detail regarding the *ṛṣi* (sage/seer) which may have had a direct bearing on the hymn. Damodar Dharmanand Kosambi, one of the front-ranking Marxist historians of India, drew attention to the fact that the poet of the 'touching' *Ṛgveda* X.34 was once ostracized by a band of self-righteous *ṛṣi*-priests (Kosambi 1998: 124–25, 105–6). Now, there are (at least) two tellings of Kavaṣa's humiliation.

Kauṣītaki Brāhmaṇa, a later Vedic text, narrates this story in XII.3: observing the presence of Kavaṣa on the banks of Sarasvatī, a group of sages who had assembled there to perform some sacrificial rite shout out, 'thou art the son of a slave-girl, we shall neither eat nor drink with thee'; Kavaṣa then turns to Sarasvatī and the river goddess responds favourably to his prayer by swelling forth; frightened by the sight, the pure-born *ṛṣis* promptly revoke the expulsion order and install Kavaṣa to the post of Master of Ceremony (Haug 1863b: 112).

The story is little more elaborate in *Aitareya Brāhmaṇa* II.19–20 (Haug 1863b: 112–13). The haughty *ṛṣis* not only cast Kavaṣa out of their company but also plan to push him off to a desert so that he dies of thirst without being able to contaminate the holy waters of Sarasvatī. But, as in the *Kauṣītaki*, so also in the *Aitareya*, the river goddess shows herself to be partial to Kavaṣa. The result: those who had excommunicated the so-abused fallen sage a minute earlier hurriedly readmit him to the fold of the revered Brahmins.

But there is one salient difference in the two tales. While sages in the *Kauṣītaki Brāhmaṇa* oust Kavaṣa for the sole reason of his being a son of dāsa woman (*dāsī*), sages in *Aitareya Brāhmaṇa* do so because Kavaṣa, besides being a *dāsyāḥ putraḥ*, was a *kitava* or gamester (Haug 1863a: 39). It may not, therefore, be too wrong-headed to assume that the existential charge that makes *Ṛgveda* X.34 one of the most lasting documents of human pathos owes a lot to the intense and intimate experiences of a bankrupt gambler (Bhaduri 1988: 43).

The Recurrent Lament

Written in the form of a monologue, *Ṛgveda* X.34 gives a harrowing account of a compulsive gambler. The hymn delineates the straits of a gambler who — after the dice, the 'hazelnut eardrops of the great *vibhītaka* tree', stop 'rolling on the furrowed board' and their paralyzing spell breaks — begins to realize the enormity of losses he has suffered. Many of the benighted man's self-castigations revolve around the injuries he has inflicted on his sweet-tempered spouse: 'Because of a losing throw of the dice I have driven away a devoted wife'; '[now] my wife pushes me away'; 'other men fondle [my] wife'; 'the deserted wife grieves'.

The unfortunate fellow is bereft of everyone's 'sympathy'; because of the *consequences* of his *unconscious* acts the wretched fellow is scorned by all and shunned by society: 'His father, mother, and brothers all say to him, "we do not know him. Tie him up and take him away"'.

Yet he remains incorrigible. He honestly owns up to his irremediable weakness: 'When the brown dice raise their voice as they are thrown down I run at once to the rendezvous with them, like a woman to her lover'. Quite in the spirit of the poet of VII.86, the lamenter of X.34 compares the bewitching dice with the intoxicating 'drink of Soma'.

Habituated to decry himself the moment he wakes from the big sleep of mindless wagering, the waster gushes forth in great poetry. One such specimen: 'Handless, the dice master him that has hands . . . and goad like hooks and prick like whips'.

In its deployment as a demarcated category, *anxiety* connotes a specific affective state — a state in which one invariably refers to some original reaction to helplessness by reproducing it in fresh danger-situations and each such reproduction functions as a *signal* for help (Freud 2001: 166–67). Seen from this angle, X.34's pathetic better is certainly an anxious-ridden person. The matter is made murkier by the fact that 'danger' here is represented by the gambol of capricious yet real things in 'meeting-halls', i.e., in the dens of (seasoned) gamblers — hence, what overtakes the man is not a fanciful but a *realistic anxiety* (Bandyopadhyay 2012: 403).

However, the *signal* for help the troubled soul (routinely) emits has a sinister edge to it. To save himself from the 'force of dice's terrible sorcery', X.34's (perpetual) loser closes his monologue with this rather malevolent prayer: 'Let someone else fall into the trap of the brown dice'.

The Ranking of Vices

Kauṭilya maps a cluster of vices springing from excessive desire in terms of the magnitude of damage caused by them in Book VIII, Section 3 of his treatise on political science, *Arthaśāstra* (Kangle 2006: 209–11, 2003: 393–96; Rangarajan 1992: 137–40). The vices — again, the Sign of Four crops up — are associated with 'hunting', 'gambling', 'women', and 'drink'. What gives to the craving for these 'objects' the quality of excessiveness is 'insatiability' — a happy expression for the uncontrollable impulsion to carry on could well be 'just one more' (Doniger 2009: 321).

Kauṭilya expresses his repugnance for 'gambling' by translating its moral hazards in the language of health hazards. He warns, the gambler — irregular in habits (but almost always sedentary) — is prone to contracting stomach, urinary and bowel disorders. Yet, remarkably, Kauṭilya disagrees with earlier commentators as far as the rank of 'gambling' in the hierarchy of vices is concerned: he considers it more harmful than 'hunting' and 'drinking' but less calamitous than 'lusting after women'. The reason the author of the *Arthaśāstra* advances in verse 53 of Section 3 in Book VIII, for plotting 'woman-addiction' in the lowest of the four-rung ladder of debasement and not 'gambling' is: a gambler can be reformed but a man given to womanizing is beyond cure. Nevertheless, in verses 44–45, Kauṭilya introduces a brilliant metaphor to illustrate how impossibly difficult it is to get out of the clutches of gambling. He says: 'The same wager won by one is, to the loser, a fish-hook which becomes a source of enmity; a gambler never knows how much wealth he has got, tries to enjoy wealth which he has not got and loses it before he can enjoy it'.

To provide legendary examples of being pierced by the ever-dangling fish-hook, Kauṭilya, in verse 43, refers to two characters from the *Mahābhārata*: Nala and Yudhiṣṭhira. Let us take a look at Nala first.

Gambler Turns a New Leaf

In the Book III of the *Mahābhārata*, viz., *Āraṇyakaparvan* ('The Book of the Forest') we meet with handsome Nala, the king of Niṣādhas. Accomplished in deeds, virtuous in conduct, learned in the Vedas, upright in dealing with his subjects (*Āraṇyakaparvan* 55.8–9),[1] Nala is an exemplar of the (Brahminical) paradigm of benevolent sovereignty. Befittingly, Damayantī, the luscious Princess of Vidarbha — skipping suitors such as the three world-guardian gods Indra, Yama and Varuṇa as well as the fire god Agni — chooses Nala as her husband. One celestial — albeit, the viler among them (*Āraṇyakaparvan* 55.5) — takes great umbrage at Damayantī's rejection of the divinities, particularly because he too desired to have Damayantī as his wife. That dejected celestial is none other than Kali. Hugely offended by the damsel's effrontery, Kali decides to wreck Nala in every possible way.

Accompanied as he was by Dvāpara, he turns to his comrade-in-arms for sympathy and support. And then conspiracy is set afoot. The lethal Kali plans to capture Nala's kingdom by means of the dice into which Dvāpara would ensconce himself (*Āraṇyakaparvan* 55.12–13).

[1] For all textual citations from the Nala episode in the *Āraṇyakaparvan*, see Sukthankar (1942).

Next, Kali does two things. Seizing upon a minor ritual fault committed by Nala he lodges himself in the body of the unsuspecting king (*Āraṇyakaparvan* 56.3). Thereafter, Kali inflames the passions of Nala's brother Puṣkara and ensures him that just one bout of dice-game would be enough to gain him the throne of Niṣadhas (*Āraṇyakaparvan* 56.4–5).

Goaded on by the demonic pricks of Kali, the possessed Nala goes all out on a gambling spree. His brain is then so fogged that he remains to the end oblivious of the fact that Puṣkara's dice is loaded with Dvāpara. Kauṭilya in his *Arthaśāstra* quotes one of his predecessors as having said that the gambler becomes enraged when somebody talks to him when he is in trouble and keeps playing even when his mother is dying (Kangle 2003: 395; Rangarajan 1992: 139). Nala too lives up to this description, for, heedless of entreaties of Damayantī, of his counsellors and well-wishers, driven by Kali and duped by Dvāpara, the poor man continues to play and lose. Nala has to perforce stop when his brother Puṣkara tells him that he has nothing left to save his consort. Tauntingly, says Puṣkara: 'Will you hold Damayantī as your stake now?' (*Āraṇyakaparvan* 58.3). But, Nala does not rise to the bait — he does not speak a syllable to his brother (*Āraṇyakaparvan* 58.4). Perhaps, it was this restraint unnatural for a gambler which portended — as Kauṭilya argues in the *Arthaśāstra* (VIII.3.53) — that Nala would not remain enslaved by the dice.

After a protracted period of tribulations, Nala enters into the service of king Ṛtuparṇa. One day, while driving the king's chariot the expert horseman Nala chances upon a *vibhītaka* tree in full fruit and Ṛtuparṇa says: 'Now you watch my great talent at counting! In this tree, the difference between the leaves and the nuts still on the tree and those fallen on the ground is a hundred and one. Both those branches have five crores of leaves — take off the two branches and their twigs and you get from them two thousand one hundred and ninety-five nuts' (*Āraṇyakaparvan* 70.6–10; Buitenen 1975: 353). Not ready to swallow the tall claim, Nala puts the king to test only to be further baffled: Ṛtuparṇa indeed hits the bull's eye (*Āraṇyakaparvan* 70.10–21). Dazed by the marvel Nala asks the king: 'I want to know the magic by which you knew their number' (*Āraṇyakaparvan* 70.22). Ṛtuparṇa then tells him: 'Know that I know the secret of the dice and am expert at counting' (*Āraṇyakaparvan* 70.23).

It is a tell-tale sign that Nala's discovery of Ṛtuparṇa's fabulous forte takes place at a site occupied by a *vibhītaka* tree. Had not *Ṛgveda* X.34 authored by sage Kavaṣa opened with the information that *vibhītaka* was the 'great tree' from whose 'hazelnut eardrops' were fashioned the Indian brown dice.

Humbled, Nala then requests Ṛtuparṇa to teach him the fine art of dice-play in exchange for his secret knowledge of horses (*Āraṇyakaparvan* 70.24–26). Agreeing to the barter, Ṛtuparṇa imparts to Nala the trick of grasping large measures with lightning speed — pronto, Kali loses his stranglehold on the deposed ruler of Niṣadhas (*Āraṇyakaparvan* 70.27–28).

Hollywood comedian W. C. Fields (1880–1946) — the renowned prankster who advertized his fondness for liquor with such scandalous abundance that physicians decorated the exhibitionist by naming a special characteristic associated with alcoholism 'W. C. Fields Syndrome' — has this wisecrack attributed to him: 'Horse sense is the thing a horse has which keeps it from betting on people'. Doubtless, given his expertise in horses, the same sentiment must have hit Nala at a crucial juncture of his life centuries before it became a laughing matter in America.

Freed of Kali's vicious grip — and, by extension, of Dvāpara's — Nala issues a challenge to his brother. He says to Puṣkara: 'Let the game of dice begin again. Let Damayantī and everything else, that I have, be my stake' (*Āraṇyakaparvan* 77.4–6). Believing himself to be as secured against odds as before, Puṣkara makes public his inmost lecherous craving. He declares boldly: there is no fun in betting unless you do it with your near and dear ones; I shall be *kṛta-kṛtya* or fulfilled when I lay my hands on Damayantī, who is, 'as ever, the darling of my heart' (*Āraṇyakaparvan* 77.14–15). But, of course, the tables are turned now: playing straight with unweighed dice the skilled Nala makes a mockery of the untutored braggart.

The interesting thing about the Nala yarn is that it is recounted to Yudhiṣṭhira, the eldest Pāṇḍava; and, in terms of sequencing, the *raconteur*'s interjections on Nala come *after* Yudhiṣṭhira, to his eternal shame, has surrendered himself to a wanton ludic impulse in the *Sabhāparvan* ('The Book of the Assembly Hall'), Book II of the *Mahābhārata*. If the purpose of telling Nala's story to Yudhiṣṭhira was to deliver a moral lesson to the latter, then surely the purpose was lost — it was like putting the horse before the cart, or, better still, locking the stable after the horse had bolted.

In contrast to the sobered-up Nala, Yudhiṣṭhira, while participating in the utterly unfair dice-duel in the *Sabhāparvan*, is so captivated by the allure of brown pieces that he loses himself completely in the 'chaos' caused by the rigorous 'rules' of a 'science of bias' — this spectacular event of a 'loaded' play makes the return to the *Mahābhārata* even more compelling.

III

> Chaos is lawless behaviour governed entirely by law . . . Dice are a bad metaphor for genuine chance, but a much better one for deterministic chaos.
>
> — Ian Stewart (2002: 12, 365)

A Saga of Bad Faith

In the Book I of the *Mahābhārata*, viz., *Ādiparvan*, Chapter 1 has a set of confessions spread over verses 95–159 made by the sightless Kuru king Dhṛtarāṣṭra after the Great War had concluded (Sukthankar 1997: 15–25). Of these, 55 verses (*Ādiparvan* 1.102–56) carry the heart-rending refrain, 'when I heard that . . . I lost hope of victory' (Buitenen 1983: 25). Two of the 55 instances in which, (on hindsight) the blind-as-bat Dhṛtarāṣṭra claimed to have undergone the crushing feeling of *losing* relate to the dice-game in the *Sabhāparvan*. In verse 105, the Kuru lord says: 'When I heard that Yudhiṣṭhira . . . was divested of his kingdom, yet still was followed by his inscrutable brothers . . . I lost hope of victory'; in verse 106, he speaks of Draupadī, the common wife of the five Pāṇḍavas, who, with tears in her throat and in a single garment because of her being in menstruation, was dragged into the assembly-hall where the dice-game had been taking place (Sukthankar 1997: 17; Buitenen 1983: 25).

Before starting off with his heart-rending lament: 'I lost hope of victory', Dhṛtarāṣṭra says in verse 97: 'I have no preference between my own sons and the sons of Pāṇḍu' (Sukthankar 1997: 15; Buitenen 1983: 24). But, just verse 105 is sufficient to show how thoroughly implicated he was in 'bad faith' — the news of Yudhiṣṭhira's loss was not what made the eyeless king feel he was doomed but the news that although pauperized due to the eldest Pāṇḍava's obduracy the five sons of Pāṇḍu were still united! However, the one good thing about this theme of 'bad faith' in the *Mahābhārata* is that it opens ways for forging other (insidious) connections.

Two Tribes of Deceivers

The Sanskrit word *cār* — related fundamentally to *motion* — has a special meaning attached to it. For example, Manu of his *Manusaṃhitā* (VII.184) advises the king desirous of battle to 'establish his spies properly' and the word for spy there is *cār* (Bühler 2001: 245; Tarkaratna 2000: 184; Doniger and Smith 1991: 147). *Cār* standing for 'spy', 'scout' or 'secret emissary' endows a far-sighted king with the attribute of being *cār-cakṣum* — he is that statesman who has the perspicuity to employ *cār*s in lieu of his *cakṣuḥ* (eyes).

The word *cār*, (not etymologically but phonetically), conjures on its own another Sanskrit word: *cor*. While on surface it simply means 'thief', Kauṭilya broadens its scope in the *Arthaśāstra* (IV.1.65): 'Merchants, artisans, craftsmen, nomadic mendicants, actors, jugglers and similar persons are all thieves [*cors*], in effect, if not in name' (Kangle 2007: 131; Kangle 2003: 259; Rangarajan 1992: 242). The phonetic assonance between the Sanskrit *cār* and *cor* is made even louder for our benefit by the Sanskrit-derived word *cār*, which, for instance in Bengali, means the number *four*.

Obviously, contrived as they were, the throws of a handful of (presumably) *cār*-dotted die in the *Sabhāparvan* could not have taken place without the active participation of some *cor* and *cār*. The question, then, is: who were they?

Crooks' Cooking

Śakuni, the Kuru king Dhṛtarāṣṭra's brother-in-law, asks his sister Gāndhārī's husband to inquire into the reason why Duryodhana, the eldest scion of the Kauravas and the king's favourite, has all of a sudden become exceedingly dejected and prone to brooding (*Sabhāparvan* 45. 4–5).[2] The fond father finds out what is driving Duryodhana crazy is the Pāṇḍava's magnificence-cum-munificence — he is on the brink of mental collapse because he can no longer stomach his cousins' ever-increasing fame and material prodigality. Coached by his maternal uncle Śakuni, the sore and sour Duryodhana proposes that Dhṛtarāṣṭra should take the initiative to organize a duel of wits between the two branches of the Kuru clan via a game of dice in which Śakuni, the Grandmaster of Dicing, would act as Duryodhana's proxy (*Sabhāparvan*.45.39–40). Shaken though by his son's distress, Dhṛtarāṣṭra tells him that he would decide on the matter only after consulting his wise counsellor Vidura. But Duryodhana knows very well: Vidura, the son of a palace-maid of *śūdra* origin and his father's half-brother, would on no account approve of the scheme trumped up by Śakuni; so, lest the *dāsyāḥ putraḥ*, the moralizing paternal half-uncle of his, queers up the pitch, Duryodhana threatens to commit suicide if Dhṛtarāṣṭra acts upon Vidura's advice and spoils the sure-fire plan of despoiling the Pāṇḍavas (*Sabhāparvan* 45.41–44). Panicked by the threat, the loving father bows to his son's wishes and orders carpenters to build 'a big hall of a thousand pillars and a hundred doors' fit for a royal competition (*Sabhāparvan* 45.46).

The moment Vidura hears that the 'Gate of Kali' was upon them, he hastens to intervene. As feared by Duryodhana, the pious mentor implores the Kuru king to put a stop to the proceedings at once (*Sabhāparvan* 45.50–52). After a little dillydallying, Dhṛtarāṣṭra appeals to his son to fall in line with the sagacious Vidura (*Sabhāparvan* 46.5–6). Duryodhana retaliates by delivering a long and vivid description of the Pāṇḍava's riches only to end it by saying: 'Father! Don't let the enemy's luck please you!' (*Sabhāparvan* 50.25). Softened by his son's plea and fortified by Śakuni's assurance — 'Be sure, the dice are my bows and arrows, the heart of the dice my string, the dicing rug my chariot. I shall take the fortune Duryodhana is grieving after from Yudhiṣṭhira. I shall throw the dice and defeat the fool!' (*Sabhāparvan* 51.1–3) — Dhṛtarāṣṭra deputes Vidura to invite Yudhiṣṭhira to a (friendly) match (*Sabhāparvan* 51.26).

Śakuni had observed earlier that while he was the world's greatest expert at dice, Yudhiṣṭhira, in spite of his passion for the sport, was a very poor player (*Sabhāparvan* 45.36–38). And, certainly, Vidura was fully aware of this terrible asymmetry. So, even when he dutifully passes on Dhṛtarāṣṭra's message of invitation to Yudhiṣṭhira, the astute counsellor adds the caveat that along with Śakuni, the 'overplaying and dexterous knower of dice', Duryodhana has a battery of rank *kitava* or gamesters in his camp (*Sabhāparvan* 52.13, 9). Yudhiṣṭhira is no fool either. He quite appreciates the danger awaiting him: 'Most dangerous gamblers have been collected, who are sure to play with wizard tricks' (*Sabhāparvan* 52.14). Yet, he does not display an iota of hesitation in accepting the challenge.

[2] For all citations from the *Sabhāparvan*, see Edgerton (1995).

Yudhiṣṭhira again picks up the theme of wizardry as he prepares to begin with the game. He beseeches Śakuni to desist from adopting crooked means (*Sabhāparvan* 53.3). Śakuni brushes off Yudhiṣṭhira's remonstrance apropos 'trickery' by dignifying it as the tactics required of every worthwhile contestant. He says: 'A scholar surpasses a non-scholar only through *his* trick or *nikṛti* — but people don't call that a trick' (*Sabhāparvan* 53.11). The analogy may have been false, but, Yudhiṣṭhira, instead of pursuing the argument, asks the opponent to commence the game.

Then Duryodhana inaugurates the betting sport by, first, staking his gems and treasures, and, second, by officially appointing Śakuni his proxy; Yudhiṣṭhira registers his protest against the substitution but lets it pass. Trailed by a company of royal dignitaries, Dhṛtarāṣṭra and other Kuru elders enter the pearl-studded majestic Assembly Hall (*Sabhāparvan* 53.15–18).

In total, Yudhiṣṭhira places 20 stakes. Defeated each time, he loses every particle of his immense wealth, all his men and maidservants, turns his four brothers and himself into slaves sworn to serve the winner to their perdition, and ultimately, with nothing else left to wager, holds the Pāṇḍava wife Draupadī as stake and losing her, gets stripped of private property in the final-most sense of the term.

The game of 20 throws is punctuated by 20 exclamations of Vaiśampāyana, the principal narrator of the *Mahābhārata*. Of these four simply state the fact that Śakuni had won the throw (*Sabhāparvan* 53.25; 54.3,11; 58.43). But, the remaining 16 are phrased as: 'Śakuni decided, tricked, and cried "won"' (e.g., *Sabhāparvan* 54.7; 58.6). Doubtless, Śakuni was far superior to ordinary *kuhakas* (jugglers), who, as Kauṭilya opines in the *Arthaśāstra* were anyway '*cor*s, in effect, if not in name', for it was his skill in giving to transparent thievery the appearance of practised marksmanship, in his ability to re-present the 'foul' as 'fair' without any fuss, was what made his 'jugglery' so regaling to Duryodhana and his cronies.

After the tenth shot, Vidura tries to break up the game of treachery (*Sabhāparvan* 55.1–57; 56.1–10). He says, Śakuni's expertise in the dirty business of 'sleight-of-hand' is known to everybody (*Sabhāparvan* 56.9). Duryodhana immediately condemns Vidura as a traitor (as Pāṇḍava's 'secret emissary' or *cār* who has now shamelessly revealed his viper-self so long kept hooded by pretensions of virtue) and advises his father to not to 'lodge a hater from the enemy's party' in his house (*Sabhāparvan* 57.1–12). Berated thus — and, presumably, affected by the studied silence of the Kuru elders and the sight of Yudhiṣṭhira wholly engrossed in testing his luck — Vidura gives up (*Sabhāparvan* 57.20). Vidura's predicament furnishes, as it were, a made-to-order tapestry of ironies: (*a*) Duryodhana, the champion of Śakuni the cheat-*cor*, accuses him of being a *cār*-in-disguise; (*b*) sharing with *Kauṣītaki* and *Aitareya Brāhmaṇas*' *ṛṣi* Kavaṣa the misfortune of being the son of a slave girl but differing significantly from the *Aitareya*'s Kavaṣa who was (like Śakuni) a *kitava* or trickster, he sings a song of lament after being cast away by

Duryodhana which both echoes and pens a commentary on *ṛṣi* Kavaṣa's hymn in *Ṛgveda* X.34 (*Sabhāparvan* 57.13–21).

Surely, Yudhiṣṭhira was driven to bet on Draupadī by the prospect of excitement the tempting thought 'just one more' brings with it. In the first round of contest with his brother, Nala had not surrendered to his younger sibling Puṣkara's enticement to go for a blind bargain by pledging his wife Damayantī, but Yudhiṣṭhira, like gamblers who react with chronic keenness just as the brown dice raise their voice, went ahead when Śakuni said: '[T]here is your precious queen, and one throw is yet unknown. Stake [her]' (*Sabhāparvan* 58.31).

This scene, however, is not simply confined to the depiction of Yudhiṣṭhira's despicable lapse — it offers much more. Hearing the first Pāṇḍava agreeing to Śakuni's call, most of the assembled persons express horror: excepting one, the elders break out in sweat and their pained mutterings spell of 'Woe! Woe!'; the hall itself starts shaking; other kings begin whispering among themselves; Vidura buries his face in his hands and looks as if he has fainted; streams of tears rush down the cheeks of almost all the *kṣatriya*s (warriors) present (*Sabhāparvan* 58.38–40, 42). The only elder who acts differently is the same person, who in his post-War string of laments would say: '[W]hen I heard that . . . I lost hope of victory' in the context of Draupadī's public humiliation following Yudhiṣṭhira's defeat in the ultimate throw (Sukthankar 1997: 17). For, when Śakuni rolls the dice for the last time, the blind Dhṛtarāṣṭra, far too exhilarated to maintain composure, keeps asking, 'Has he won, has he won?' (*Sabhāparvan* 58.41).

Dhṛtarāṣṭra's anxious cry, 'Has he won, has he won?', rhymes perfectly with the sixth *ṛk* of Kavaṣa's *Ṛgveda* X.34 hymn in which we hear: 'Asking himself "will I win?", and trembling with hope, the gambler goes to the meeting-hall'. It may not be too risky to gamble with the idea that besides Yudhiṣṭhira, Śakuni and the retinue of court-swindlers, there was another in the assembly hall psychically oriented to reckless gambling. And, he was Dhṛtarāṣṭra. Using his brother-in-law via Duryodhana as his *cār*, the eyeless Kuru lord was the *cār-cakṣum* trickster or *kitava* directing the sham-show from behind. This equation has the merit of linking in a single chain (*a*) gambling, (*b*) discourses on deterministic chaos as well as on absolute determinism, and (*c*) chaotic or otherwise unfolding of Time — for, mired in bad faith as he was, Dhṛtarāṣṭra pontificates much too much on the subject of Destiny.

At the very onset of the match, Śakuni, boasting of his prowess, admonishes Yudhiṣṭhira by saying: 'The handling of dice can defeat our foe; that is why you say that it's Time that does it' (*Sabhāparvan* 53.5). Śakuni's cunning tying of Dice, the good metaphor for deterministic chaos, with Time, symbolizing in this case implacable determinism, provides adequate raw-material for instituting further investigations.

IV

> The distinction between the order of Vishnu and the disorder of Shiva . . . [lies in the way] in which divinity makes itself manifest: benevolence and wrath; harmony and discord. In the same way, mathematicians are beginning to view order and chaos as two distinct manifestations of an underlying determinism.
>
> — Ian Stewart (2002: 17)

In between issuing his first command to Vidura to call over Yudhiṣṭhira for dicing with his cousin ('Go at once on your chariot . . . and bring Yudhiṣṭhira. My decision shall not be circumvented. [*Sabhāparvan* 45.56–57]) and its swift retraction ('Enough of the dicing' [*Sabhāparvan* 46.7]), Dhṛtarāṣṭra says: 'I tell you, Vidura! I deem it supreme destiny (*param daivam*) that makes this befall' (*Sabhāparvan* 45.57). The sightless Kuru lord may have been unaware of the ludicrousness of courting personal authority for promulgating a royal announcement and then immediately imputing it to forces beyond human control, but his judicious counsellor is not. Saddened (as well as amused) by the king's quick switch from the first person singular signifying free agency to its forthright dissolution, Vidura mockingly comments on Dhṛtarāṣṭra's invocation of *daivam* or destiny in a hushed mutter: 'It is not!' (*Sabhāparvan* 45.58).

And then, when he finally makes up his mind to put a final seal to his eldest son's plot of defrauding Yudhiṣṭhira and orders Vidura to go over to the Pāṇḍava quarters and communicate his intention of hosting a (pleasant, amiable) game of dice, Dhṛtarāṣṭra says with a great deal of pomposity to his half-brother: 'No quarrel [that may stem from the dicing game] bothers me, Steward. For otherwise fate would run counter to dicing. This world submits to the Placer's design; and thus does the world run, not by itself' (*Sabhāparvan* 51.25). Dhṛtarāṣṭra here cleverly combines two themes: he lets it be known that he subscribes to the view that the universe is governed according to laws set by the (unfathomable) *Dhātā* or Placer and, in the ultimate reckoning, human effort is void of meaning; next, appending an extra gloss to Duryodhana's contention, '[since] the ancients bequeathed us the rules of the game there is no evil in it' (*Sabhāparvan* 51.12), he insists that dicing enjoys the sanction of ineluctable Providence. Reeking though of hypocrisy, this double-speak of Dhṛtarāṣṭra has the merit of enunciating simultaneously at one stroke the principle of pure determinism via the persona of the *Dhātā* and the principle of qualified determinism via the chaotic fallout of Fate-decreed dice-games.

From Natural Sciences to Psychology

Kitava Kavaṣa's *Ṛgveda* X.34's ninth *ṛk* describes graphically the seductive dance of dice, the enthralling hip-hop, witnessing which may denude one of all sense of volition: 'Down they roll, and up they spring. Handless, the dice master him that has hands'. The hand — the part of human anatomy that bespeaks of man's *tool-making* capacity and therefore of his ability to alter natural course of things and restructure the environment he inhabits — is what gets arrested by the hypnotizing dance. To maximize the theatrical potential of this dreamscape, let us take a cue from Sigmund Freud. Defending the act of 'over-interpretation', (the mode of 'reading' derided by votaries of consciousness-centric rationalistic explanation), Freud writes in *The Interpretation of Dreams* (1900): '[J]ust as all neurotic symptoms, and, for that matter, dreams, are capable of being "over-interpreted" and indeed need to be, if they are to be fully understood, so [are] all genuinely creative writings' (1998: 299).

Exercising the liberty of over-interpreting we might go so far as to say: *Ṛgveda* X.34's spellbound subject's loss of self-possessing subjectivity is nothing short of symptomatic of the weakening of the anthropocentric *hamartia* or 'error of judgment' that impels man to fall prey to the *māyā* or Nescience of imagining that he is the Master of universe. This, in its turn, leads automatically to the observation: activating a process of 'transference' the traumatic emptying of oneself culminates in ascribing to the 'handless' tool the (supernatural) power of manhandling the tool-maker. And, paradoxically enough, the surrendering to the charms of the 'instrument', to the indecipherable mechanizations of the 'machine', also becomes a source of (perverse) rapture for the captivated.

Speaking generally, the sour–sweet excitations of subjects caught up in any performance that induces the sensation of being full-with-hollowness — articulated for instance, during 'drinking', 'lusting' or 'gambling' — are products of a particular *style* of 'hunting'. Reversing Kauṭilya's 'Order of Vices' we may classify the other three as different tropes of the dangerous-of-all vices, meaning, that venal happening at which all of a sudden the subject and the object change positions, and the *hunted* assumes the role of the *hunter* and the *hunter* that of the *hunted*. While each may be clubbed under the heading of 'hunting-without-hunting', what separates 'gambling', 'drinking' and 'lusting' is the *quality* of expectations of pleasure-pain associated with them.

The recklessness of 'losing one's head' to which all gamblers are inclined can perhaps be better rationalized if we pursue the metaphor of dicing prized so highly by physicists with little more stringency. Now that classical determinism has become *bi-focal* and has branched out in two directions, one towards 'order' and the other towards 'chaos', it may be profitable to re-think the profile of the gambler by expediently *psychologizing* the implications of the *loci* of the two different paths.

The property that distinguishes the grammars of 'order' and 'chaos' is, while the former is *prospective* in character, the latter is *retrospective*. Both tend to tame (intrinsically ungovernable) chance, but they do so by following (apparently) opposing codes. The grammarian of 'order' deals with events whose outcomes have the potential of predictability. The grammarian of 'chaos', on the other hand, deals with events whose outcomes can be ascertained only after they have actually occurred. Although both obey iron-clad, inviolable laws, the two types of events differ in nature so radically that their manner of *determination* too differs radically: while an 'order'-oriented event lends itself to *a-priori* reckoning, a 'chaos'-oriented event has to await *a-posteriori* explication. Since a very small deviation from equilibrium produces chaos out of order, if we consider the events that are sensitive to small changes, meaning, those that are exceedingly susceptible to feedbacks, we are likely to encounter chaotic happenings which defy being described in advance with any kind of *exactitude* (Gribbin 2004: 30, 56).

The two forms of 'chaos', notorious for driving people involved in forecasting them crazy, relate to 'weather' and 'stock market'. A specialist had once ruefully complained: '[W]e can predict the weather accurately provided it doesn't do anything unexpected' (Stewart 2002: 119). The same cynicism can be traced in utterances of even the most cocksure venturer busy taking stock of stock-market fluctuations. It, therefore, is not extraordinary that a bit of an idiotic, ridiculously clownish Indian character in H. R. F. Keating's 1986 detective fiction *Under a Monsoon Cloud* — one in the series which has its hero, the Bombay police inspector named Ganesh Ghote — threads together (*a*) the steps of swift-foot horses (in unison with which throb the pulses of bookies and betters thronging the side of racing tracks), (*b*) the fickleness of women (who are nonetheless lusted after by men), and (*c*) weather-forecast (without which no outing can be planned with sufficient rigour), to create and recite with regular periodicity this memorable aphorism: 'The galloping of a horse, the mind of a woman, whether the monsoon will be good or bad, even the gods cannot be predicting' (Keating 1986: 12–13).

In Want of Spell

Dhṛtarāṣṭra justifies his acquiescence to his obstinate son's (childish) clamouring in the name of *Dhātā* or Placer, and so does Yudhiṣṭhira when he accepts the Kuru king's invitation to participate in a dice-game with Duryodhana. Although aware that Duryodhana's team is packed with gamesters proficient in 'wizard tricks', Yudhiṣṭhira says to Vidura, Dhṛtarāṣṭra's steward-messenger: 'But this world obeys the Placer's (*Dhātā*'s) design — I do not refuse now to play with those gamblers' (*Sabhāparvan* 52.14). Making blatant his eagerness to jump into the fray and give into the masochistic delight of being caught up in the chaos of non-anticipatable results — the masochism surfaces precisely because he has the fore-knowledge that by blocking free play of chance his opponent wields the whip, as do sadists in orchestrating power-shows — Yudhiṣṭhira declares to the world: 'Fate takes away our reason as glare blinds the eye; man bound as with nooses obeys the Placer's sway' (*Sabhāparvan* 52.18).

It appears as if Dhṛtarāṣṭra and his nephew Yudhiṣṭhira are victims of a corrosive disease for which the modern jargon is 'Obsessive Compulsive Disorder'. The fascinating aspect of the disorder is that it may make one hyperactive to the extent of being self-destructive. It, therefore, is noteworthy — despite undergoing the sense of 'losing' or *Kali* at several crucial turning points of which we learn in the *Ādiparvan* (102–56: '[W]hen I heard that . . . I lost hope of victory') — Dhṛtarāṣṭra not only does nothing to prevent the devastation but also lends a helping hand to actualize it. Yudhiṣṭhira too colludes with his uncle when he wittingly makes a fool of himself by staking Draupadī — public disgracing of a *Kṣatriya* woman in front of a group of *Kṣatriya* men being the epitome of *Kṣatriya* disgrace, the festering enmity between the Kuru cousins becomes even starker.

After the sordid display of Duryodhana's villainy, Dhṛtarāṣṭra takes two conciliatory steps in quick succession. First, as a gesture of goodwill Dhṛtarāṣṭra waives Duryodhana's authority over all the gains made by him and prays that by not taking to heart Duryodhana's offensiveness the *dharma*-abiding Yudhiṣṭhira will keep the brotherly bonds with his brethren intact (*Sabhāparvan* 65.2, 10, 15). Second, moved by Duryodhana's plight and anguished appeal, Dhṛtarāṣṭra brushes off the Kuru elders' and his wife Gāndhārī's protests to issue forth a fresh notification on the continuation of dice-play even before the Pāṇḍavas reach their land (*Sabhāparvan* 66.1–37). Reverting to type, the blind king, often addressed as 'Bull of the Bharatas', promulgates the order: 'Bring [the Pāṇḍavas] back at once, even if they are far on their way; [they] must come back and play the game again' (*Sabhāparvan* 66.24), and seeks justification for his reversal of decision on the ground that if his line were fated to end then surely he was powerless to avert the calamity (*Sabhāparvan* 66.36). Yudhiṣṭhira too reverts to type: just as he hears of his venerable uncle's bidding he readily complies by saying: '[I]t is at the disposing of the Placer that creatures find good or ill; although I know, dicing at the old man's behest will bring ruin I cannot disobey his words' (*Sabhāparvan* 67.3–4).

In the second round of combat only one stake is stipulated. The stake is: the losing party will have to roam the forests clad in deerskin for 12 years and spend the 13th year disguised among people; if the losers are discovered while they are supposed to be in disguise they would be further penalized, and the penalty would entail a renewal of the 12-year banishment to the woods (*Sabhāparvan* 66.18–19).

And, not unexpectedly, Śakuni again defeats Yudhiṣṭhira. Decidedly, it required great effort on Yudhiṣṭhira's part to keep himself undiscovered for 12 long months. For, when, upon the commencement of the 13th year, the five brothers and Draupadī take shelter in King Virāṭa's court the eldest Pāṇḍava chooses to dress up as a gambler! At the beginning of Book IV of the *Mahābhārata*, viz., *Virāṭaparvan* ('The Book of Virāṭa'), in verses 19–22 of Chapter 1, he tells of his plan to his co-exiled companions: '[W]hen I come to King Virāṭa I shall be the Royal Dicing Master of the king; I shall pose as a Brahmin by the name of Kanka, one who knows the dice and is an ardent gambler' (Vira 1936: 6–7; Buitenen 1978: 28). Unable to contain his fascination for the dice — 'those made of beryl and gold and ivory, the phosphorescent nuts, and the black and red dice' — Yudhiṣṭhira invents his alter-ego in the shape of Kanka whom he (doubtless, lovingly) presents to the world at large as 'Yudhiṣṭhira's bosom friend'. To maintain the masquerade with so thin a mask indeed was marvel of a performance which, while it hid the gambler-agent's true identity, also permitted him to openly pander to his 'Obsessive Compulsive Disorder'!

Of Obsession

'Obsessive Compulsive Disorder' of any form is bound to lead towards an ego-construct premised on some or the other specific mix of the active and the passive. The ego overtaken by extreme addiction has to perforce *amplify* the urge for surging forward on its own steam as well as the propensity to display its diminution in the face of adverse circumstances — a dual condition which no ego can wholly annul or circumvent.

The word *cathexis* — derived from the Greek *kathexis*, meaning, 'holding' — is usually used to describe investment of libidinal energy in a person (e.g., 'father'), an object (e.g., 'leather jacket'), or an idea (e.g., the *Brahman*). And, there are two kinds of 'holding': freely flowing cathexis that presses on towards discharge, or *mobile cathexis*, and its opposite *quiescent/bound cathexis* (Freud 1991: 302–3).

In contrast to the non-addict, meaning, the lucky person adept in withdrawing his libidinal investment from one object of adoration and re-investing in another, the incurable addict, by remaining forever glued to some single target, has his libido almost completely entrenched in 'bound cathexis' — 'held' by some charmed object, the fetishist 'holds' on to it with such erotic intensity that it nearly engulfs his entire being. It, therefore, is extremely telling that of all his callousness the perpetual gambler's negligence towards his loyal wife is most heavily underlined in Kavaṣa Ailūṣa's hymn in *Ṛgveda* X.34, or that dazzled by the phosphorescent nuts' glow *Mahābhārata*'s Yudhiṣṭhira ends up pledging his dear consort. Both texts delineate with admirable clarity men's withering of erotic impulse for women when they get inextricably attached to dicing. The question, then, is: since it is axiomatic that nothing can supply better fodder to the fuelling of 'death-instincts' or *Thanatos* than monomaniacal *love*, what happens to those who are single-minded in their devotion to gambling?

Unquestionably, Yudhiṣṭhira was a man of many parts. He was not as besotted as Dhṛtarāṣṭra that he could match his uncle's frank nonchalance regarding annihilation-of-all. It was not Yudhiṣṭhira but Dhṛtarāṣṭra who had washed his hands off as for the eventual outcome of gambling was concerned by declaring, 'Surely, if our line must end, I shall not be able to avert it' (*Sabhāparvan* 66.36). Nonetheless, let us take the theoretical leap of calling the syndrome of 'Obsessive Compulsive Disorder' focalized on gambling, *Yudhiṣṭhira-complex*. For, after all, it was Yudhiṣṭhira who in the *Āraṇyakaparvan* of the *Mahābhārata* — the same book in which he heard Nala's story — had touched upon the theme of mysteriousness of death-instincts. He had answered Dharma-in-disguise's question: 'What is the strangest of things', by saying — and, it must be put in parentheses that this oft-quoted exchange can only be located in the *Mahābhārata* manuscripts copied in the Devanāgarī character — 'Even while witnessing daily the passing away of living beings, humans long for immortality: that is the strangest of things' (After *Āraṇyakaparvan* 297.61 – [59]–[64] [Appendix I, Section 32]).

Anyone fixated with the *Yudhiṣṭhira-complex* is psychologically programmed to court 'determinism'. Smitten beyond release by a special trope of 'hunting-without-hunting', the insatiate gambler is at the same moment *predisposed* to capitulate without bothering about its upshot *and* seek solace for his capitulation by passing on the responsibility to 'Destiny'. The attribute differentiating the gambler from every other species of 'creature of habits' is his *double* subscription to 'lawless behaviour governed entirely by law' and 'lawful behaviour governed entirely by law' — the former eluding precise foretelling and the latter, amenable to (even if, only rhetorically) prophetic divining. The thrill of combining the *precipitous* afforded by the retrospective with the *sagacity* buttressed by the prospective is what drives the gambler on. The Science of Gambling can well be defined as the art of simultaneous adherence to 'deterministic chaos' and 'deterministic order', of simultaneous obeisance to wrath-discord manifesting in Śiva and benevolence-harmony manifesting in Viṣṇu.

It is indeed striking that in spite of being mesmerized by the rapidity with which luck turns during play many a man hooked to it has instinctively sensed the structural closure imposed by 'deterministic chaos' in gambling, e.g., the one whose passion for gaming is punctiliously recorded by Fyodor Dostoevsky (1821–81) in his 1867 novel *The Gambler*.

The Dostoevskian hero of the novel — Dostoevskian, precisely because he transparently mirrors Sigmund Freud's 1928 character-sketch of the novelist as being composed of pathological addiction to gambling, severe neurosis, a 'strong destructive instinct directed mainly against his own person' which triggers the masochistic impulse of construing 'gambling as a method of self-punishment' (Freud 2001: 196, 177, 178, 191) — does feel strongly that there is something 'morally mean and foul' about gambling (Dostoevsky 2004, Chapter 2: 1).

But then — in a manner similar to *Ṛgveda* X.34's lamenter, who, like a woman-in-love, runs to the rendezvous with brown dice the minute they call out — Dostoevsky's hero falls into convulsions just as the sound of chinking of money reaches his ears even two rooms away from the gambling room; and when, caught up in a rush of good fortune, he keeps pushing on, he compares his heightened state successively with that of a man in fever, disoriented by madness and entranced by dream. However, the same internally lacerated person proves to be remarkably insightful when he makes the quasi-mathematical observation: 'I deduced one conclusion which seemed to be reliable — namely, that in the flow of fortuitous chances there is, if not a system, at all events a sort of order. This of course is a very strange thing' (ibid., Chapter 17: 2, Chapter 14: 3–4, Chapter 4: 1).

The artistry involved in the Science of Gambling is brilliantly illustrated by the Kafkaesque bewilderment of *Ṛgveda* VII.86's protagonist — the fate of incurring god Varuṇa's displeasure for partaking in innocent pleasures such as dicing puzzles him to no end. The superb eloquence of *Ṛgveda* X.34's self-flagellating protagonist makes the artistry even more poignant when he shrieks with evident knowledge: 'Handless, the dice master him that has hands'.

The artful science may be further developed if we give a psychological twist to one of the key concepts of Chaos theory. The idea in its rudiments is: if a system residing in steady state, e.g., a pile of sand sitting quietly on a table in equilibrium, keeps receiving newer inputs, it may at some stage arrive to the 'edge of chaos'; unless a 'delicate balance' between input and output, e.g., between the amount of sand added to the pile-at-rest and the amount of sand falling off the corners of the table, is established, the tiniest increment may cause the overstepping of 'critical value' and bring about an avalanche. The technical term for the precarious state of 'edge of chaos', the grit required for remaining stationed on the safe side of 'boarder-line', is *self-organized criticality* (Gribbin 2004: 158–59).

Admittedly, more taken by the nomenclature than any exact isomorphic relationship between 'gambling' and 'steady state', we postulate: in contrast to persons with the temperament of (reformed) Nala, those struck by the *Yudhiṣṭhira-complex* are likely to lose 'self-organized criticality' at some stage and move beyond the brink of precipice. So, it is immaterial how violently gamblers (e.g., Dhṛtarāṣṭra) adduce to hidden motives of insurmountable Destiny once the gaming gets done; the vulnerability structural to psychic organization of people prone to *Yudhiṣṭhira-complex* is sufficient to turn them into perpetrators of colossal catastrophes, into unwittingly witting Terminators.

Play and Non-play

The Dutch historian Johan Huizinga (1872–1945) — one of the founders of modern culture theory and a trained Orientalist whose doctoral thesis was on the clown-figure in Sanskrit drama — proposed in his overwhelmingly influential treatise *Homo Ludens: A Study of the Play-Element in Culture* (1938): as species-specific characterization of the human–animal the terminology *Homo Sapiens* or 'Man the Wise' was (profoundly) dubious, the appellation *Homo Faber* or 'Man the Maker' was not satisfactorily exclusive, but the sobriquet *Homo Ludens* or 'Man the Player'/'Playing Man' was quite apposite (1960, Foreword). Huizinga advanced the rather daring thesis that rather than being just one of many cultural manifestations *play* was constitutive of culture itself (ibid.: 19). He argued it was not at all astonishing that 'ritual' and 'play' were substantively similar in constitution: in essence, every ritual was legitimately reducible to an irreducible play-concept; hence, there was no formal discrepancy between 'consecrated spots' delimited for performance of sacred rites and 'play-grounds' such as 'the arena, the card-table, the magic circle, the temple, the stage, the screen, the tennis court, or the court of justice' (ibid.: 26, 10). '*Identification* or mystic repetition or *representation*' that, for example, one found in Vedic sacrificial rites which aimed to represent 'a certain desired cosmic event' so as to 'compel the gods to effect that event in reality', could well be called 'playing it' (ibid.: 15). Intimately linked to 'playing' was 'knowing', for one *knew* only through *play* (ibid.: 105). Problems demanding solutions augur 'competitions' crafted in terms of oracles, wagers, lawsuits, vows, or riddles, and nowhere was the 'function of ritual riddle-solving' contests most clearly articulated than in the Ṛgvedic lore 'pregnant with the wisdom of the Upanishads' (ibid.: 105, 26). Despite their tendency to throw up inconsistent explanations and 'innumerable contradictory interpretations of ritual riddles', the 'cosmogonic speculations' of Vedic *Brahmaṇa* literature too were marked by 'fundamental play-character' (ibid.: 108).

In the context of Huizinga's emphasis on human beings' unquenchable appetite for play and their inexhaustible capacity for *rule-making* and *rule-breaking* — a 'spoil-sport' rudely flouts rules to 'shatter the play-world itself' and thus deprives other players the 'fun' of experiencing 'seizure' which grant them temporary release from everyday banalities, but the 'cheat', like Śakuni, pretends to play and therefore 'acknowledges the magic circle' even while secretly disregarding the enshrined laws of the game (ibid.: 11, 17) — gambling's curious properties begin to look ominous.

Thus far we have deduced: for the player bugged by *Yudhiṣṭhira-complex*, 'gambling' is a 'play' teleologically tilted to culminate in his own as well as everyone else's detriment to the point of extermination. This allows a generalization, terrifying in its highly probabilistic applicability: *Homo Ludens* in his gambler-avatar has the potential to confound man's *Homo Sapiens* self with such completeness as to wreck his *Homo Faber* career with no hope of recovery or retrieval.

V

Every Thought emits a Dice Throw

— Stéphane Mallarmé (2006: 181)

Gaming is a principle inherent in human nature. It belongs to us all.

— Edmund Burke (1780: 26)

The Double Bind

The marvellous riddle-solving play that we witness in the *Āraṇyakaparvan* of the *Mahābhārata* contains an exchange on the subject of Time. Dharma-in-disguise asks *Yudhiṣṭhira* — again, it must be put in parenthesis that this piece of dialogue can only be located in the *Mahābhārata* manuscripts copied in the Devanāgarī script — 'What is the *vārtikā* or news' and *Yudhiṣṭhira* answers: 'In this cauldron of the world . . . Time is cooking all creatures. This is the news' (After *Āraṇyakaparvan* 297.61–[70]–[71] [Appendix I, Section 32]). There is no denying that the most striking of all contemporary News is: today's cauldron of world is far more heated than it was during *Yudhiṣṭhira*'s days and the all-devouring Time is so impatient now that it might polish off everybody at one single stroke. At some critical historical conjuncture, *Homo Sapiens*' inquiry into laws of nature, along absolute deterministic lines, got so enmeshed with *Homo Ludens*' natural willingness to derive nerve-wrecking sensations from incalculable risks along chaos-bound deterministic lines that the chance of human species' total ruination is now realistically genuine. One of today's implications of the axiom 'to know is to play and to play is to know' is: the *knowledge–play* nexus compounded by the doings of nuclear physicists and gamblers of various shades, including merchant-speculators who dribble-dabble with capital in stock-markets, has immortalized the 'Hiroshima moment' to such an extent that no matter what intricate plans of surveillance the liberal states devise to better the 'independence of their parliaments', gas chambers in concentration camps like the one in Hitler's Auschwitz loom larger and larger in the distant yet ever-approaching horizon. Nevertheless, there is this comforting thought that while 'every thought emits a dice throw' no 'dice throw at any time' 'will abolish Chance'. But, such is the twisted logic of Time that it appears it is this statement from the *Mahābhārata* which best epitomizes the present, the Age rightfully deserving the epithet 'Age of Final *Kali* or Losing', 'Time am I, world-destroying, grown mature, engaged here in subduing the world' (*Gītā* XI.32).

War of the End of the World

The scenario of an ending that proffers no beginning — a scenario quite alien to pre-modern theoreticians of 'Movement of *Yugas*' such as Manu, the lawmaker — complicates the issue of taking an ethical stand against the machinations of those engaged in 'subduing the world'. When, poised at the 'edge of chaos', the impulsion for 'just one more' may go so far as to actualize the hitherto available accounts of doom/apocalypse/*pralaya* in various pre-modern myths, any critique fashioned in the language of Ethics sounds morally vacuous. But, if not a saving grace but still a consolation, there is another dimension of *play* which might engender a tempering ethical effect not tainted by crass moralism.

In *Homo Ludens: A Study of the Play-Element in Culture*, Johan Huizinga argues: 'the profound affinity between play and order' places 'play' squarely within the domain of Aesthetics; 'play has a tendency to be beautiful' precisely because along with all aesthetic practices it too is 'animated' by the 'impulse to create orderly form'; it, therefore, is not accidental that words used to 'denote the elements of play'— for example, *tension*, *poise*, *balance*, *contrast*, *variation*, *solution*, and *resolution* — 'belong for most part to aesthetics'; on the whole, Art is inseparable from play; combining the human-animal's characteristics of the *Homo Sapiens* and *Homo Faber* in admirable proportions, *Homo Ludens* finds one of its best expressions in playful art (Huizinga 1960: 10, 158–72).

The *Mahābhārata* happens to be one of those texts which have had the fortune of being continually revisited and ceaselessly worked upon by people of varying temperaments, ideological assumptions and backgrounds. It is a narrative that 'relentlessly muddy the water of traditional morality, [and] is a canvas mostly dark, with sudden gleams of moral heroism, splashes of brilliant colours of all possible passions and crisscrossing lines of philosophical riddles', but is 'above all, a poem of life' (Chakrabarti 2011: 9). Being so, this Tale of War and Peace with no 'closure' in sight in the shape of any 'proper ending' remains 'open' to endless reiterations and renewals. The *Mahābhārata*'s magnificent quality of the *iterable* — and Jacques Derrida pointed out in his 1971 lecture 'Signature Event Context' that since the word *iter* probably comes from *itara*, 'other' in Sanskrit', *iterability* is inextricably allied to *alterity* (1988: 7) — makes it an extremely handy tool to fabricate alternative sketch-texts each adept in raising ethical problems in the guise of Art, meaning, creating something which *withholds* morally suffused frontal attacks and is yet critically alive. The cultivated *disinterestedness* of *art-play* allows for *quietness* — and that may speak volumes even at the perilous hour human beings find themselves now.

Satyajit Ray (1921–92), one colossal in the arena of world-cinema, had perhaps misjudged when he said: '[O]nly in the distant past was there violence on a heroic scale' (Seton 2003: 254). Dismissing contemporary violence as being merely mean and petty, Ray contemplated on making a two-part film of epical dimensions on the *Mahābhārata* in the early 1960s to prove, among other things, that he possessed the finesse to depict grand violence with great adroitness, but given the capital-intensive nature of celluloid cinema and his elaborate plan to have an international cast including the Japanese actor Toshiro Mifune of Akira Kurosawa's *Rashomon* and *Seven Samurai* fame, no moneybag came forward to fund the film and Ray was forced to drop the project (ibid: 254, 256). But then, the *Mahābhārata* never ceased to charm Ray. At a later date, while confessing that he was truly incapable of 'tacking the War at all', he toyed with the idea of concentrating on a part which could capture the text's essence — and the part that he thought did so brilliantly and also offered great 'cinematic possibilities' was the dice-game episode! Ray rationalized his decision by saying: 'It shows all the characters, and all their aspects' (Robinson 1990: 284). Sadly however, this film too remained unmade.

Surely, there have been many such aborted plans to build on the *Mahābhārata*. Leaving aside the missed opportunities and also skipping literary or cinematic adaptations, let us concentrate on a seized opportunity fleshed out in the medium of painting. We choose the canvas for two reasons: one, it has been filled up only recently; and two, the picture there deals with the dice-game of the *Mahābhārata*'s *Sabhāparvan*.

From December 2010 to January 2011 a Kolkata-based art-gallery put up an exhibition titled 'Ganesh Pyne: His Mahabharata'. Consisting of a series of paintings by the internationally reputed artist Ganesh Pyne (born, 1937) it was a collection of his personal interpretations of the *Mahābhārata* in lines and colours.

Pyne focused on isolated, discrete moments and yet, despite the dispersal, the set of pictures was thematically internally cohesive. The overriding sentiment in them was *Terror*. Sometimes comically, at others brooding gloomily, Pyne attempted to capture the Spirit of Terror in its many hues through his *re-telling* of the *Mahābhārata*. Certainly, the creative outburst was instinctively attuned to the sense of the uncanny that attends any impending catastrophe.

In one of the paintings we encounter Śakuni and Yudhiṣṭhira: they are seen dicing, but the setting differs dramatically from the one described in the *Sabhāparvan*: it appears as if the two are all alone in some dark cave-like enclosure; a lamp, whose flame has the distinct tactile feel of the phallic, lights up the game-board or *adhidevana*; Śakuni's eyes are so glazed that it seems he is sightless; Yudhiṣṭhira, as though to penetrate the impenetrable glassy eyes of the rank cheat so 'forearmed' as to play the game 'blindfolded', keeps staring at Śakuni; and the two hands of Śakuni, caught in the frieze of throwing a single die onto the board, are starch-white. The painting is named: *The White Hands*.

In his literary contribution to the catalogue of the *Mahābhārata* paintings — the piece is titled 'Moving Images' — Ganesh Pyne himself gives an allegorical reading of the dice-scene. He adds the clause 'heart-burning' to the flame-erect glowing lamp and likens it to the 'fate of Yudhiṣṭhira'. He further explains that in order to underline that everyone, including Yudhiṣṭhira, were aware of Śakuni's 'treacherous' intent, he has chosen to paint Śakuni's hands white. He employs just two words to suggest the menacing implication of the tool-making animal's, *Homo Faber*'s malfunctioning hand-tool; they are: 'Untainted whiteness' (Pyne 2011: 13).

This, then, is the riddle: what if white-treachery continues to be (mis)recognized as untainted and the number of people tainted by *Yudhiṣṭhira-complex* keeps exponentially rising will be the fate of those who are yet to come?

References

Bandyopadhyay Sastri, Manubendu (ed.). 2000. *Manusaṃhitā*, Chapters 1–3. Kolkata: Sanskrit Pustak Bhandar.

Bandyopadhyay, Hiranmoy (ed.). 1976. *Ṛgveda-Saṃhitā*, 2 vols. Kolkata: Haraf Prakashani.

Bandyopadhyay, Sibaji. 2012. 'Defining *Terror*: A "Freudian" Exercise', in Sibaji Bandyopadhyay, *Sibaji Bandyopadhyay Reader*, pp. 359–472. New Delhi: Worldview Publications.

Bhaduri, Nrisinha Prasad. 1988. 'Juakhelar Utsa Sandhane', *Desh* (Kolkata), 26 March, pp. 18–22.

Brereton, Joel. (trans.). 1992. '*Ṛgveda* 7. 86', in Ainslie T. Embree (ed.), *Sources of Indian Tradition*, vol. 2. New Delhi: Penguin Books.
Bühler, G. (trans.). 2001[1886]. *The Laws of Manu*, in *The Sacred Books of East*, vol. 25, ed. F. Max Müller. New Delhi: Motilal Banarsidass.
Buitenen, von J. A. B. (trans.). 1983. *The Mahābhārata*, vol. 1: *The Book of the Beginning*. Chicago: The University of Chicago Press.
———. 1978. *The Mahābhārata*, vol. 4: *The Book of Virāṭa*. Chicago: The University of Chicago Press.
———. 1975. *The Mahābhārata*, vol. 3: *The Book of the Forest*. Chicago: The University of Chicago Press.
Burke, Edmund. 1780. 'A Plan for the Better Security of the Independence of Parliament', speech delivered in the House of Commons on 11 February 1780. London: Printed for J. Dodsley.
Chakrabarti, Arindam. 2011. 'A Tale of Two Trees, Twisted Tresses, and an Unstoppable Horse', in *Ganesh Pyne: His Mahabharata*, pp. 3–6. Kolkata: Centre of International Modern Art (CIMA).
Clarke, Ronald W. 1971. *Einstein: The Life and Times*. New York: The World Publishing Co.
Derrida, Jacques. 1988[1971]. 'Signature Event Context', in Jacques Derrida, *Limited Inc.*, trans. Samuel Weber and Jeffrey Mehlman. Evanston: Northwestern University Press.
Doniger O'Flaherty, Wendy (trans.). 1994. *The Rig Veda*. New Delhi: Penguin Books.
Doniger, Wendy and Brian K. Smith (trans.). 1991. *The Laws of Manu*. New Delhi: Penguin Books.
Doniger, Wendy. 2009. *The Hindus: An Alternative History*. New Delhi: Penguin/Viking.
Dostoevsky, Fyodor. 2004[1867]. *The Gambler*, trans. C. J. Hogarth. Page by Page Books.
Edgerton, Franklin (ed.). 1995[1944]. *The Mahābhārata for the First Time Critically Edited*, vol. 2: *Sabhāparvan*. Pune: Bhandarkar Oriental Research Institute.
Einstein, Albert. 1971. 'Letter to Max Born (December 4, 1926)', in *The Born-Einstein Letters*, trans. Irene Born. New York: Walker and Company.
Freud, Sigmund. 2003[1919]. 'The Uncanny', in *The Uncanny*, trans. David McLintock. London: Penguin Books.
———. 2001[1928]. 'Dostoevsky and Parricide', trans. V. Woolf and Koteliansky, in James Strachey (ed.), *The Standard Edition of the Complete Psychological Works of Sigmund Freud*, vol. 21, pp. 175–96. London: Vintage.
———. 2001[1926]. *Inhibitions, Symptoms and Anxiety*, trans. Alix Strachey in James Strachey (ed.), *The Standard Edition of the Complete Psychological Works of Sigmund Freud*, vol. 20. London: Vintage.
———. 1998[1900]. *The Interpretation of Dreams*, trans. James Strachey. New York: Avon Books.
———. 1991[1920]. *Beyond the Pleasure Principle*, in *The Penguin Freud Library*, trans. James Strachey, vol. 2. London: Penguin Books.
Gleick, James. 1987. *Chaos: Making a New Science*. New York: Viking Penguin.
Gribbin, John. 2004. *Deep Simplicity: Chaos, Complexity and the Emergence of Life*. London: Penguin.

Haug, Martin (ed.). 1863a. *Aitareya Brāhmaṇam of the Rig Veda*, vol. 1. London: Trübner and Co.

———. 1863b. *Aitareya Brāhmaṇam of the Rig Veda*, vol. 2. London: Trübner and Co.

Huizinga, Johan. 1960[1938]. *Homo Ludens: A Study of the Play-element in Culture*. Boston: The Beacon Press.

Junck, Robert. 1985[1956]. *Brighter than Thousand Suns: A Personal History of the Atomic Scientists*, trans. James Cleuch. Harmonsworth: Penguin Books.

Kangle, R. P. (ed.). 2006[1960]. *The Kauṭilīya Arthaśāstra*, part 1. New Delhi: Motilal Banarsidass.

———. 2003[1963]. *The Kauṭilīya Arthaśāstra*, part 2. New Delhi: Motilal Banarsidass.

Keating, H. R. F. 1986. *Under a Monsoon Cloud: An Inspector Ghote Mystery*. London: Penguin Books.

Kosambi, Damodar Dharmanand. 1998[1956]. *An Introduction to the Study of Indian History*. Bombay: Popular Prakashan.

Lüders, Heinrich. 1906. 'Das Würfelspiel im alten Indien', summarized in English by Giles Schaufelberger as 'Dice Game in Old India', http://mahabharata-resources.org/ola/dice.game.pdf (accessed 2 March 2013).

Mallarmé, Stéphane. 2006[1897]. 'A Dice Throw At Any Time Never Will Abolish Chance', in E. H. Blackmore and A. M. Blackmore (trans.), *Collected Poems and Other Verse of Stéphane Mallarmé*, p. 181. Oxford: Oxford University Press.

Monier, Monier-Williams. 2005[1899]. *A Sanskrit-English Dictionary*. New Delhi: Sharada Publishing House.

Pyne, Ganesh. 2011. 'Moving Images', in *Ganesh Pyne: His Mahabharata*, pp. 7–8. Kolkata: Centre of International Modern Art (CIMA).

Radhakrishnan, S. (trans.). 2008. *The Bhagavadgītā*. New Delhi: Harper Collins.

Rangarajan, L. N. (trans.). 1992. *Kautilya: The Arthashastra*. New Delhi: Penguin Books.

Robinson, Andrew. 1990. *Satyajit Ray: The Inner Eye*. Calcutta: Rupa & Co. in association with Andre Deutsch, London.

Sayen, Jamie. 1985. *Einstein in America: the Scientist's Conscience in the Age of Hitler and Hiroshima*. New York: Crown Publishers.

Seton, Marie. 2003. *Satyajit Ray: Portrait of a Director*. New Delhi: Penguin Books.

Stewart, Ian. 2002. *Does God Play Dice? The New Mathematics of Chaos*. Malden: Blackwell Publishing.

Sukthankar, V. S. 1998. *On the Meaning of the Mahābhārata*. New Delhi: Motilal Banarsidass and Bombay: The Asiatic Society of Bombay.

——— (ed.). 1997[1933]. *The Mahābhārata for the First Time Critically Edited*: vol. 1, part 1: *Ādiparvan*. Pune: Bhandarkar Oriental Research Institute.

——— (ed.). 1942. *The Mahābhārata for the First Time Critically Edited*, vols 3 and 4: *Āraṇyakaparvan*. Pune: Bhandarkar Oriental Research Institute.

Tarkaratna, Panchanan (ed.). 2000. *Manusaṃhitā*, Chapters 4–12. Kolkata: Sanskrit Pustak Bhandar.

Vira, Raghu (ed.). 1936. *The Mahābhārata for the First Time Critically Edited*, vol. 5: *Virāṭaparvan*. Pune: Bhandarkar Oriental Research Institute.

Wilson, H. H. (trans.). 2000a [1850–88]. *Ṛgveda-Saṃhitā*, vol. 3. Varanasi: Indica Books.

——— 2000b. *Ṛgveda-Saṃhitā*, vol. 4. Varanasi: Indica Books.

Methodology of the Critical Edition of the *Mahābhārata*

Saroja Bhate

The *Mahābhārata* (hereafter Mbh.) occupies a place of pre-eminence in the cultural history of India. It is, in fact, one of the paramount manifestations of all aspects of Indian culture. Late Dr V. S. Sukthankar, the first editor of the critical edition (hereafter crit. ed.) of the Mbh., describes it as 'the most inspiring monument of the world and an inexhaustible mine for the investigation of religion, mythology, legend, philosophy, law, custom and political and social institution of ancient India' (1933: iii). It has a venerable place in Indian mind and addresses itself as *pañcamo vedaḥ* or 'the fifth Veda' (*Ādiparvan* 57.74; *Śāntiparvan* 327.18). As a supposedly historical event — if at all — the Mbh. is held to have happened more than 3,000 years ago. As a supposed document of history, it has been in existence in some form since the beginning of Common Era (CE) (Fitzgerald 2009: 154–55, n. 10). The Greek Sophist Dion Chrisostom (40–105 CE) who is reported to have visited India stated: 'Indians possess an Iliad of 100000 verses'. There is also a reference to an inscription of fifth century CE, wherein the Mbh. is mentioned as *śatasāhasree saṃhitā* (a text of 1,00,000 verses). It is, therefore, clear that already in the first millennium CE, the epic had assumed a gigantic form and has been, indeed, handed down in this form through the centuries. Sukthankar describes it 'in bulk about four times as great as the Greek Epics, Iliad and Odyssey put together and one and a half times as our *Rāmāyaṇa*' (Gode 1944: v). In order to understand why and how the Mbh. assumed this monumental form, it is necessary to undertake a journey deep down in the past. Historians, archaeologists, anthropologists and linguists have been engaged in exploring the ancient cultures hidden in the Mbh. B. B. Lal, a well-known Archaeologist, has, for instance, published an extensive report of excavations at Hastināpura and other sites associated with the Mbh. carried out during 1950 and 1952. After 'a systematic exploration of over thirty sites mentioned either in the *Mahābhārata* itself or alleged to have been associated with the story according to local tradition' (Lal 1954–55: 7), he discovered that 'almost all the sites yielded painted Gray Ware from their low levels' (ibid.). After comparing the archaeological data with the text of the Mbh. and other ancient works he states the following:

(*a*) that a large number of sites associated with the *Mahābhārata* story contain the same ceramic industry, viz. the Painted Grey Ware.

(*b*) that the date of the *Mahābhārata* battle falls within period II at Hastināpura (ibid: 151).

He concludes 'that the sites of Hastināpura, Mathurā, Kurukṣetra, Barnāwā (Vāran āvata), etc. are identifiable with those of the same name mentioned in the *Mahābhārata*' (ibid.). However, he also points out at the end that this circumstantial evidence needs to be further substantiated by positive ethnographic and epigraphic evidence (ibid.).

Dr Lal appears to be inclined to accept the historicity of the epic war and its probable date as *c.* 950 BCE in agreement with the view of the well-known Purāṇa scholar F. E. Pargiter (ibid.: 149). There are, however, various views regarding the date of the Great War. In the absence of other substantial corroborative evidence, another group of scholars has always questioned the historicity of the event. There is, however, reason to believe that the seed of the epic narrative lay in the saga of the Great War sung by bards (*Sūtas*); thus, it must have been a historical event. According to the generally accepted scholarly opinion, *Jaya* was the name of the original epic as it appears in the beginning verse of the Epic. This was further developed into *Bhārata*, a poem of 24,000 verses (*Ādiparvan* 1.61). *Bhārata* assumed the form of *Mahābhārata* after series of narratives and a large bulk of didactic passages were added to it. The process of its growth from its birth continued for several centuries until the epic was finally established as *śatasāhasree saṃhitā*, 'a sacred text with a hundred thousand verses', sometime around third or fourth century CE. It must be noted that it was handed down by word of mouth through the centuries. Nevertheless, it must have been committed to writing 'at different epochs under different circumstances' (Sukthankar 1933: lxxix). Although it is difficult to state exactly when the practice of committing the text of the Mbh. to writing began, there is some evidence to show that a manuscript (ms.) of the Mbh. became a sacred text all over South-East Asia in the latter half of the first millennium CE. There is a reference, for instance, in one sixth-century CE inscription, not in India, but in Kampuchea, that a Brahmin named Somaśarman offered a complete copy of *Bhārata* to Lord Tribhuvaneśvara and arranged for its recitation (Chandra 2009: 25). According to another inscription belonging to mid-seventh century CE, a person who tries to destroy the ms. of the Mbh. donated to a temple would incur a curse (ibid.). Recitation of the text of Mbh. in holy places such as temples became, and still continues to be, a part of Hindu rituals in some parts of India. This rise of the Mbh. from the level of a popular narrative to the status of a sacred text of Hindus must have given a fillip to the enterprise of writing down this massive compendium of religion and ethics.

Variegation or diversity is the striking feature of Indian culture and it is reflected in the Mbh. tradition in all possible ways. For example, when it was being orally transmitted, the bards almost recomposed it by adding their own compositions and drawing relevant content from their respective cultural backgrounds. Secondly, since the content was more important, no careful attention was paid to the stylistic and structural aspects of the text, though care was taken to preserve the core. This diversity, at the level of both form and content, was bound to find its reflection in the written tradition as well. Script was yet another dimension added to the variegation. We have, thus, in India, the text of the Mbh. available in eight different scripts. The next step in the development of Mbh. tradition is turning it into a melting pot on account of the interweaving and interlacing of different kinds of texts. While on the one hand the ms. were being copied, on the other hand, the oral tradition continued to be transmitted. Often the copyist did not copy only from one ms., they had, at a time, several copies representing different regions and times, and added verses and passages not found in their exemplar from other copies. To add to the medley, both oral and written traditions drew upon each other. This process of transfusion must have continued for centuries. Pointing at this interesting phenomenon pervading the whole history of the transmission of Mbh., Sukthankar, who was the first to get lost into the 'bewildering profusion' of the textual tradition, remarks that the Mbh. is a work 'which must have been growing not only upwards and downwards but also laterally like a *Nyagrodha* (Banyan) tree, growing on all sides' (Sukthankar 1933: lxxvii). After having waded through the forest of versions of the Mbh. produced at different places and at different points of time, he arrived at a conclusion that 'even in its early phases the Mbh. textual tradition must have been not uniform but polygenous' (ibid.: lxxix). The strange vagaries of the ms. tradition which every editor of the crit. ed. had to encounter can be justified only if we assume extensive mutual borrowings, indiscriminate crossing and re-crossing of the two parallel traditions.

So, what is the Mbh. we have arrived at, at the end of this journey into the past centuries of its origin and growth? We find ourselves in a grove of fig trees where it is difficult to locate the original, the 'father' tree which has procreated with its own root-like branches. In other words, we are in the midst of several Mbhs and are unable to reach the 'Ur-Mbh.'. To quote Sukthankar, '[w]ith the epic text as preserved in the extant Mahābhārata ms., we stand, I am fully persuaded, at the wrong end of a long chain of successive synthesis of divergent texts, carried out providentially in a haphazard fashion, through centuries of diaskeuastic activities' (ibid.: lxxxii).

This is the background against which an urgent need for a standard crit. ed. was strongly felt. It was voiced, for the first time, in the West, naturally because in India the text was approached with devotion and faith and it hardly mattered whether one textual tradition agreed or disagreed with another. In 1897 at the 11th session of the International Congress of Orientalists held at Paris, M. Winternitz, a German Indologist, expressed an urgent need for a crit. ed. of the Mbh. In the next session the Sanskrit Epic Text Society was founded to consider the proposal. In one of the subsequent sessions a committee was formed and that committee recommended that the work be undertaken by the International Association of Academics. In 1904 the suggestion was accepted and a resolution to that effect was passed. The academies of Berlin and Vienna sanctioned some funds. Prof. H. Lüders, a German Indologist from Goettingen, prepared a specimen of the crit. ed. of the first 67 stanzas of the *Ādiparvan* based exclusively on 29 ms. available in European libraries. 'The tender seedling planted with infinite care did not, however, thrive in the uncongenial European soil' (ibid.: II). The First World War broke and the work came to a halt. It was a happy coincidence that the Bhandarkar Oriental Research Institute was founded on 6 July 1917 and 'enthusiastically undertook the work, making a fresh start, fortunately without realizing fully the enormousness of the project or the complicacies of the problem' (ibid.). In 1919 the project was officially launched and in 1923 a specimen crit. ed. of *Virāṭaparvan* was prepared by Dr N. B. Utgikar. Sukthankar took charge as General Editor in August 1925 and continued for the next 17 years. Thereafter, Dr S. K. Belvalkar and, following him, Dr P. L. Vaidya carried the task forward as General Editors. Ten editors edited individual *parvans* and finally, on 22 September 1966, publication of the complete set of 19 volumes of the crit. ed. of Mbh. was announced by the institute. Thus, it took scholars more than 50 years to present to the reader a single uniform text of the Mbh. as gleaned from all extant manuscripts. From the inception of the idea of a crit. ed. in 1897 to its complete execution in 1966 is the period of 69 years of the coming into being of the standard text of the great epic.

Now, let us try to understand its methodology of the preparation of the crit. ed.

The text of the Mbh. has come down to us in two recensions, Northern and Southern. Northern recension is available in five scripts, while Southern is available in three scripts. There are, thus, in all, eight versions of the Mbh. Mode of narration is different in these two versions: 'Southern recension impresses us by its *precision, schematization and thoroughly practical outlook*, . . . [whereas] Northern recension is distinctly vague, unsystematic and *more like a story rather naively narrated*' (ibid. xxxvi, emphasis added). Due to this difference in the mode of narration as well as due to indiscriminate mutual borrowings, the total number of verses in each version is different. Some of the longest and shortest versions differ in their extent by about 13,000 stanzas (i.e., 26,000 lines). And yet there is a distinct family resemblance which proves beyond doubt that both the Northern and Southern recensions spring from a common source. It was therefore decided to reconstruct the original through comparative analysis. With each recension embracing a plurality of versions and each version being divided into a multiplicity of subgroups the reconstruction was a challenging task. The job was similar to that of a musician who was asked to compose a melody out of a heterogeneous mixture of jarring, cacophonous notes. It was realized by Sukthankar that the classical canons of textual criticism applied to ancient Latin and Greek manuscripts could not be satisfactorily applied to the Mbh. manuscripts with their luxuriant growth and indiscriminate fusion of versions. The method of tracing an archetype and setting up a *stemma codicum* could not be applied to the fluid text of Mbh. with conflated manuscripts. The editors, therefore, decided that their objective would be 'to reconstruct *the oldest form of the text which it is possible to reach on the basis of the manuscript material available*' (ibid., emphasis added).

A peep into the workshop of the editors reveals ms. of all sorts, both complete (very few, about 10), incomplete (about a 1,000) and written in eight different scripts in good or bad handwriting, and in good or bad state of preservation. From this massive bulk those ms. which, in turn, were copies of older ms. were separated and discarded. The ms. for each *parvan* were then sorted. Specialists in different scripts as well as Sanskrit language were engaged at different places like Shantiniketan and Tanjore to collate the ms. Collation sheets were prepared and individual stanzas from every reading found in different ms. were noted on the sheets for every individual verse. Thus, the entire corpus of Mbh. textual tradition in the form of individual verses and their variants became available on collation sheets to the editors. The next stage was to single out the stanzas common to all versions and to separate stanzas and passages not found in all versions. At this stage rules were set up for deciding the text of the crit. ed. The first principle was to accept as original the text that was uniformly documented in all versions. This principle is stated in the formula:

If N=S, then original.

It means, the text that was found in both 'N', i.e., Northern and 'S', i.e., Southern recensions is to be understood as original. Sukthankar calls it the principle of '*originality of agreement between what may be proved to be (more or less) independent versions*' (ibid.: lxxxvi–vii, emphasis added). After a careful inspection of all the versions, the early editors were able to ascertain that both the recensions were independent copies of an orally transmitted text of Mbh. fixed in written form at a certain point of time. This was felt mainly due to the fact that while the Northern and the Southern recensions disagreed on the presence or absence of a passage, one of the Northern versions shows frequent agreement in petty verbal details with the Southern version. The editors felt that this agreement between the two recensions on small, isolated readings must be due to common inheritance.

After the original was thus gleaned from all the available data, the stanzas that were not uniformly found in all the versions were dealt with by using other principles. Dr M. A. Mehendale has discussed these principles in detail, giving illustrations from the text (2009: 7–9). For example, when the editors found many readings equally acceptable, their choice naturally was the reading that was documented by the largest number of versions and supported by intrinsic probabilities. In a more complex situation when two or more groups of each recension showed agreement and thus evinced equal intrinsic merit, the foremost editor decided, as a rule, to adopt the readings of the Kashmir version which was, according to him, the least contaminated because of its difficult script as well as the difficulty of access to it. Similarly, in case of equal intrinsic merit, he adopted as a stop-gap, the reading of the Northern version as it is regarded as closer to the original. For example, the following readings:

> N: *maharṣeḥ pūjitasyeha sarvaloke mahātmanaḥ|*
> S: *maharṣeḥ sarvalokeṣu pūjitasya mahātmanaḥ|*

convey the same meaning: [O]f the great sage, the great soul, who is worshipped in the whole world'. The editor preferred the N. The doubtful readings were marked with wavy lines below the word.

Another principle that was followed by all the editors was: keeping emendation to the minimal. The editors have always been averse to rejecting or correcting readings. '*Interpretation has in general been given preference over* emendation' (Sukthankar 1933: xcii). For example, in the whole *Ādiparvan*, there are only 35 emendations. Emendations are shown in the crit. ed. by a star sign.

A comparison of both recensions showed that many passages were added in the course of time. Sometimes they are incorporated in the text and sometimes scribes added them either in margins or on separate folios. Such passages are either included in the critical apparatus given on every page below the text, or in the appendix depending upon their extent. It is interesting to note that some passages in the appendix are about an episode already well-known as a part of the Mbh. narrative. For example, it is well known that at the time of the *svayaṃvara* of Draupadī, Karṇa who wanted to try his luck by lifting the bow and aiming the target, was insulted by Draupadī who said, 'I will not marry the son of a charioteer'. This statement of Draupadī is missing in Southern and almost in all Northern versions. It appears, in fact, in only six Devanāgarī ms. and the version known to Nīlakaṇṭha, one of the well-known commentators of Mbh. It is, therefore, absent in the crit. ed. Similarly, the famous prayer by Draupadī to Kṛṣṇa at the time of dragging of her garment (*vastraharaṇa*) at the royal assembly and Kṛṣṇa's subsequent appearance providing an infinite chain of garments to her is relegated to appendix since it is absent in some versions, and even in those in which it is present it shows interpolation of this type. After the inclusion of all such interpolations in the appendix, the total number of verses of the text of Mbh. is reduced to about 75,000 from the massive 100,000.

This is a brief account of the methodology of preparation of the crit. ed. of Mbh. It has yielded a critically constituted text which certainly does not claim to bear the autograph of any one of the three traditional authors, Vyāsa, Vaiśampāyana or Ugraśravas. It does, however, claim to be the core and essence of all the extant ms. Since the available ms. cannot be placed further down beyond the fifteenth century, the text cannot be traced to antiquity; it probably belongs to the medieval period.

What has this crit. ed. for which 1,259 ms. were collected and examined and about 800 manuscripts were collated, achieved for a common reader? The Mbh. exists for general students, not as a Sanskrit text alone. *Mahābhārata* is, in fact, the name of a wider tradition which 'has existed in ancient and "medieval" India in several forms (oral, written, dramatic, dance, puppet performances) in many languages and in numerous versions and it is entirely uncharted as such a super-textual tradition' (Fiztgerald 2009: 153). Apart from establishing that 'a single Sanskrit version of the *Mahābhārata*, fixed in writing, was at the base of the entire manuscript tradition of the Sanskrit Mahābhārata' (ibid.: 152), the crit. ed. has also proved to be a highly fixed and stable form of the Mbh., probably 'the one through which one gains the most knowledge about the Mbh. tradition' (ibid.: 155).

The crit ed. has, however, its own limitations. For instance, it still contains passages or verses which are mutually contradictory. One example will suffice to illustrate this. In the *Ādiparvan* there is a description of Mādrī, Pāṇḍu's second wife, committing *satī* (self-immolation) after Pāṇḍu's death (*Ādiparvan* 116.31). It is described that Mādrī mounted the funeral pyre and consigned herself to the flames. In the following chapters (*Ādiparvan* 117.30, 118.18–30) however, there is a description of the dead bodies of Pāṇḍu and Mādrī being carried to Hastināpura from the forest and Bhīṣma performing their funeral rites. This and a few other contradictions of similar nature have been retained by the editors since they appear in all the eight versions. A careful study involving deeper textual criticism is thus needed to solve the problem of contradictions.

Though the publication of the crit. ed. was hailed by Mbh. scholars all over the world — since a uniform, authentic text based on all extant ms. was made available for the first time — a few scholars were opposed to this methodology. Bruce M. Sullivan records, for instance, the criticism levelled by Madeleine Biardeau, a French Indologist who was against the very idea of a crit. ed. of the Mbh. Sullivan writes, '[S]he believed that there never was a single written text of the Mbh, "the Archetype", from which all the manuscripts have evolved but instead that the various manuscripts are simply written versions of the story' (1999: 19). In other words, 'Biardeau sees the Mbh. not as one text in variant versions but as many variant versions which together constitute an epic tradition and it is precisely the variants which are of the greatest interest to her' (ibid.: 20).

In spite of all appreciation as well as criticism received by the crit. ed. since its publication, it cannot be gainsaid that it has a unique unparalleled place in the whole history of the Mbh. textual tradition. It forms, in fact, the foundation of the whole Mbh. tradition.

References

Chandra, Lokesh. 2009. 'The Mahābhārata in Asian Literature and Arts', in Kalyan Kumar Chakravarty (ed.), *Text and Variations of the Mahābhārata: Contextual, Regional and Performative Traditions,* 25–36. Samīkṣā Series II, National Mission for Manuscripts, Indira Gandhi National Centre for Arts. New Delhi: Munshiram Manoharlal.

Fitzgerald, James L. 2009. 'India's Fifth Veda: The *Mahābhārata*'s Presentation of Itself', in Arvind Sharma (ed.), *Essays on the Mahābhārata*, 150–70. New Delhi: Motilal Banarsidass.

Gode, P. K. 1944. 'Preface', in V. S. Sukthankar, *Critical Studies in the Mahābhārata*, pp. v–xi. Bombay: V. S. Sukthankar Memorial Edition Committee and Karnatak Publishing House.

Lal, B. B. 1954–55. 'Excavation and Hastināpura and other Explorations in the Upper Gangā and Satlaj Basins 1950-52', *Ancient India: Bulletin of the Archaeological Survey of India*, 10 and 11: 5–151.

Mehendale, M. A. 2009. 'The Critical Edition of the Mahābhārata: Its Constitution, Achievement and Limitations', in Kalyan Kumar Chakravarty (ed.), *Text and Variations of the Mahābhārata: Contextual, Regional and Performative Traditions*, pp. 3–24. Samīkṣā Series II, National Mission for Manuscripts, Indira Gandhi National Centre for Arts. New Delhi: Munshiram Manoharlal.

Sukthankar, V. S. (ed.). 1933. *The Mahābhārata for the First Time Critically Edited*: vol. 1, part 1: *Ādiparvan*. Pune: Bhandarkar Oriental Research Institute.

Sullivan, Bruce M. 1999. *Seer of the Fifth Veda: Kṛṣṇa Dvaipāyana Vyāsa in the Mahābhārata*, New Delhi: Motilal Banarsidass.

Significance of the Early *Parvans*

Modes of Narration, Birth Stories and Seeds of Conflict

Sibesh Bhattacharya

I must naturally begin by clarifying what I mean by early *parvans*. The expression 'early *parvans*' obviously implies an attempt to divide the *parvans* of the *Mahābhārata* into some kind of sequential order like early, middle, late, etc., or some other variants. The expression also implies grouping. While choosing the term I have not considered all the 18 *parvans*. First, it was not necessary to do so for the purpose of this essay, and secondly, such an exercise lies way beyond my competence. By early *parvans*, I simply mean the first two *parvans*, viz., *Ādiparvan* and *Sabhāparvan*. I think it ought to be admitted right at the beginning that both the choice of the expression and the *parvans* included therein may not be found to have much to it more than my personal preference. There is no *āpta* (credible) tradition to back either. The expression 'early *parvans*' can include with some justification, besides *Ādiparvan* and *Sabhāparvan*, the next three *parvans* up to *Udyogaparvan*. And, in a threefold division (say, early, middle and late) of the *Mahābhārata* in view of the total number of *parvans*, the clustering of the first five *parvans* together would look more equitable and proportionate. Let me then try to explain why I thought of including only the first two *parvans* to constitute what I call 'early *parvans*'.

These two *parvans* together, I think, hold a defining position and significance in the text. From the point of view of the development of the main story, that is, the internecine rivalry between the two branches of the same lineage culminating in an all-consuming war, the *Ādiparvan* and *Sabhāparvan* take us, as it were, to a point of no return, a point from where the events had to inevitably move towards the tragic climax, the terrible war. It is in these two *parvans* that we witness not only the process of preparing the ground, cultivating the soil and sowing the seeds, but also the fructification, the initial nurturing and the growth of the seeds sown. These two *parvans* together seem to have already charted emphatically the course that the rest of the story was to run. From this angle, they thus may be considered as forming a unit.

Apart from the development of the central narrative, these *parvans*, particularly, the *Ādiparvan* has some other significant and interesting features. Some of these features highlight certain important characteristics of the text, particularly the modes of narration. From the points of view of the modes of narration and the narrative devices employed, the importance of *Ādiparvan* can hardly be over-emphasized. Dealing, as the *Ādiparvan* naturally does, with the 'origin accounts', it contains a number of birth stories. Some of these birth stories, at least to me, seem to make a symbolical statement that the major protagonists of the central narrative were no run-of-the-mill characters, but were 'extraordinary' human beings and appropriately, therefore, had extraordinary births. Thus, the following sections will mainly deal with the following three themes as they appear in the early *parvans*: (*a*) modes of narration and narrative devices, (*b*) birth stories, and (*c*) development of the main story.

I may also mention in passing a couple of things more. First, for the present essay, I have relied almost exclusively on the internal evidence from within the text of the *Mahābhārata* (Critical Edition) and have used external material very sparsely and that too only as supporting evidence and for asides. Second, I have taken the text as it stands now. The issue of whether the text grew out of an original nucleus gathering grafts from various writers at different points of time, and similar other issues have not been considered. Third, the discussion on the composer or the narrators of the *Mahābhārata* figures in this essay only in the context of the modes of narration and has nothing to do with any effort to determine the historical truth about the authorship of the *Mahābhārata*.

Modes of Narration and Narration Devices

Let us first briefly take note of the narrators of the *Mahābhārata*. That the *Mahābhārata* was said to have been an orally narrated text is well known. Although it taxes our modern mind and belief rather heavily, the text consistently asserts that this gigantic composition was orally narrated.[1] These narrations/recitations, took place on two different occasions as recorded in the text itself (*Ādiparvan* 1–19, 1.57-58, 4.1–2, 53.31–36, 54.16–24). On the occasion of the snake sacrifice (*sarpasatra*) king Janamejaya requested Kṛṣṇadvaipāyana Vyāsa to narrate the story of the great battle that his ancestors had fought. 'Sir, you had seen', said the king, 'with your own eyes both the Kurus and the Pāṇḍavas. I want to listen to their life stories (*carita*) narrated by you (*kathyamānam tvayā*). Even though they could smoothly achieve all their undertakings (*akliṣṭakarmanam*), how this difference grew between them and how this all-destroying (*bhūtāntakaraṇam*) war arose, tell me the history (*vṛtta*) of all these' (*Ādiparvan* 54.18–19). Vyāsa then asked one of his students, Vaiśampāyana, who had accompanied him to the sacrifice to narrate the story (*Ādiparvan* 54.21–24). The exact words of Vyāsa to Vaiśampāyana are

[1] Stupendous memory feats of early Indians have been amply attested. Entire Vedic corpus was committed to memory. Elaborate techniques were developed to help memorization and correct recitation. Predilection to use oral devices was not due to unfamiliarity with writing, since writing had been known and used in India at the very least since the Harappan period.

interesting and worth quoting: 'You have heard from me (*yān mattvaḥ śrutavān asi*) how the cleavage developed in the past between the Kurus and the Pāṇḍavas. Narrate (*ācakṣva*) all these to him' (*Ādiparvan* 54.22). Vaiśampāyana then narrated the whole of the *Mahābhārata* at the snake sacrifice.

This was the first recitation of the great epic. We may note here another minor point. Some verses in the text raise doubt whether Vaiśampāyana was the sole reciter/narrator during the snake sacrifice. There are some indications that Kṛṣṇadvaipāyana himself, at times, assumed the role of narrator. Some verses state that after the daily rituals were over, on some days the *Brāhmaṇas* would relate the stories from the Vedas (*vedaśrayaḥ kathāḥ*); on others, Vyāsa would narrate the *Mahābhārata ākhyānam* at the sacrificial hall (*Ādiparvan* 53.31–34). However, commentators like Nīlakaṇṭha, Haridāsa Siddhāntavāgīśa and others say that in these places 'Vyāsa' should be taken to mean Vaiśampāyana deputizing for Kṛṣṇadvaipāyana as the narrator, and not Vyāsa literally (Bhaṭṭācārya 1383 [Bengali era]: 631). Vaiśampāyana, of course, can be justly regarded as the mouthpiece of Kṛṣṇadvaipāyana. Anyway, there should not be any difficulty in accepting that the snake sacrifice of Janamejaya was the occasion when the first public recitation of the text took place.

During the recitation at the snake sacrifice, Sauti Ugraśravas, son of Sūta Lomaharṣaṇa, was present. He apparently listened to the whole narration with great interest and rapt attention. It appears that the story of the *Mahābhārata* made a very deep impression on him. After the snake sacrifice was over, Ugraśravas made it a point to visit the region of Samantapañcaka where the Kauravas and the Pāṇḍavas had fought their deadly war (*Ādiparvan* 1.11–12). His interest in the story, thus, seems to have gone beyond the professional calling of a Sūta. After wandering about for a while, Sauti reached the hermitage of rector Śaunaka in a forest called Naimiṣāraṇya where the latter was engaged in the performance of a 12-year long *sattra* (sacrificial session). Requested by the assembled sages there, Sauti Ugraśravas repeated the narration of the *Mahābhārata* at Śaunaka's hermitage (*Ādiparvan* 1.8–19). It is this narration by Sauti Ugraśravas in Naimiṣāraṇya that constitutes the text of the *Mahābhārata*. The *Mahābhārata* opens with the description of his arrival at Śaunaka's hermitage and his acceding to the request of the sages to narrate (*pravakṣyāmi*) the wonderful creation (*adbhutakarmaṇaḥ*) of Vyāsa (*Ādiparvan* 1.1–23). Sauti Ugraśravas, thus, is the 'primary' narrator of the text of the *Mahābhārata*. It is in the course of his narration during Śaunaka's *satra* that the account of the earlier narration during the snake sacrifice figures.[2] This affords us a glimpse of the interesting, and complex, narrative structure that the text employs. The text begins by challenging the simple chronological order. It opens with a later event — an event not really related to the main story — the

[2] Ritual ceremonies, particularly the longer ones, provided occasions for the recounting of old heroic lore (Bhattacharya 2010).

arrival of Sauti to the *satra* of Śaunaka. And then it leisurely — some may even find it tediously slow and meandering — weaves the matrix of the main story. Later in this chapter, we will come back to this flashback technique in the text.

Let us briefly take a note of the composition and the composer of the work as mentioned in the text itself. That the *Mahābhārata* was composed by Kṛṣṇadvaipāyana Vyāsa has been stated several times in the text. Both the recitations by Vaiśampāyana and Ugraśravas refer to it (*Ādiparvan* 1.9, 15, 23; 53.31–34; 54.22). Vyāsa is said to have composed the *Mahābhārata* after organizing the Vedas into four divisions and after the passing away of Dhṛtarāṣṭra (*Ādiparvan* 1.52; 1.55–56). Presumably, he began composing it after the *svargārohaṇa* (ascent to heaven) of Yudhiṣṭhira. There was thus some time gap between the composition and the recitation of the text at the snake sacrifice, the reign of Parikṣita separating them. His own son (Śukadeva) was the first to be taught the *Mahābhārata* by Vyāsa. And then he taught it to some other competent disciples as well (*Ādiparvan* 1.63; 57.73–75). Besides Vaiśampāyana and prior to him, the *Mahābhārata* thus was learnt by some other pupils of the poet. It is not totally unlikely that there were recitations of the text prior to the one by Vaiśampāyana at the snake sacrifice. That a superb narrative (*ākhyānavariṣṭha*) had been composed by Vyāsa consisting of wonderful cantos and verses (*vicitrapadapravaṇaḥ*) seems to have been well known by the time Ugraśravas presented his narration at Naimiṣāraṇya (*Ādiparvan* 1.16). Because, that is what the assembled sages wanted to listen to. And then, there is a famous statement of Sauti right at the beginning of his narration: *ācakhyuḥ kavayaḥ kecitsaṃpratyācakṣate pare/ākhyāsyanti tathaivānye itihāsamimaṃ bhuvi* ('this has been narrated in past by some poets and is being presented now by others as this *itihāsa* will be presented still by others in future the same way') (*Ādiparvan* 1.24; 56.22). Ugraśravas proceeds with his narration and takes it up to the point of the snake sacrifice. The locale is Naimiṣāraṇya and the audience are Śaunaka and his band of disciples. As the narrative reaches the point at which the occasion of snake sacrifice is mentioned, Vaiśampāyana takes over as the narrator; the venue is Janamejaya's sacrificial hall and the audience are the assembled priests, sages and the king. And, we may surmise the presence of a large gathering of dignitaries and others as well, as was expected in a royal sacrifice.

It needs to be emphasized that with the commencement of Vaiśampāyana's narration Sauti's narration does not cease; it continues. Vaiśampāyana's narration is a part of the narration by Ugraśravas. When Vaiśampāyana completed narrating the story of the *Mahābhārata*, Sauti again takes up the threads of narration in the concluding verses of the work (*Svargārohaṇaparvan* 5.26–54). He begins by saying: 'Hearing this (account) from the best of the Brahmins during the sacrifice, that king Janmejaya was filled with wonder' (*Svargārohaṇaparvan* 5.26). Thus, it is a case of 'narration within narration'. Although Vaiśampāyana was made the narrator of the bulk of the *Mahābhārata*, from the point of view of the mode of narration, the Sauti Ugraśravas is the prime narrator and the primary location of narration is the hermitage of Śaunaka.

Normally, the flashback technique opens with the narration of a later event and then goes on to that of the main story located in an earlier time period. But once the main story is taken up for narration, the normal chronological scheme, i.e, from the earlier to the later, is usually maintained. But the mode of narration employed in the *Mahābhārata* is more complex. The narration moves back and forth in time and does not strictly follow a linear order.[3] And then, as is well known, the narration, leaving the main story, often meanders into disparate byways and then leisurely comes back to take up the threads of the main story. Further, the main story of the epic has been told in abridged form as well as in detail.[4] It has been told in abridged form more than once and in different modes of narration. These abridged narrations adopting different devices are found in the *Ādiparvan*. The first chapter itself contains two abstracts of the main story juxtaposed with each other. They supplement each other and from that angle the later one appears like a continuation of the earlier. At the same time, the two also offer a study in contrast.

The first one begins by invoking the imagery of two giant trees with roots and trunks and branches and foliages, the trees with contradictory characteristics: Duryodhana, the tree of wrath (*manyumayo mahādrumaḥ*) and Yudhiṣṭhira, the tree of virtue (*dharmamayo mahādrumaḥ*) (*Ādiparvan* 1.65–66). And then in 30 verses of straightforward narrative, it presents a crisp and synoptic sketch of events, beginning with the reign of Paṇḍu, leading to the terrible war (*vigrahe tumule*) wherein *kṣatriyas* slaughtered each other (*ahan kṣatram parasparam*) (*Ādiparvan* 1.65–94). It is more or less an impersonal outlining of the story. However, the clash is attributed here to the opposing values espoused by the two sides, imparting the train of events a kind of inevitability. In contrast, immediately following this synopsis, there is another one of the main events given in the form of 'lamentations' (*vilāpa*) by Dhṛtarāṣṭra (*Ādiparvan* 1.95–159). At the end of the war, in a monologue addressed to Sañjaya, Dhṛtarāṣṭra recalls the main events leading to the extermination of his line as he reflects over his role in bringing about the tragic outcome.[5] These intensely personal outpourings of his heart by the blind king, partly self-accusing and hugely self-pitying, are not only interesting for allowing a peep into the character of Dhṛtarāṣṭra but also from the point of view of the mode of narration.

---

[3] Early Indian concept of time generally was non-linear and cyclical; *kālasya kuṭila gati* was a well-known saying about the nature of the movement of time (see Balslav 1999).

[4] 'This work imparting great lessons has been presented both in detailed and abridged forms by the sage (Vyāsa) as the learned persons of this world desire both short and detailed enumeration' (*Ādiparvan* 1.49).

[5] The character of Sañjaya is suddenly introduced here without any preliminaries and without much clue as to his identity and role. The significance of his role becomes clear much later in the work.

That this *vilāpa* appears almost at the very beginning of the *Ādiparvan* is remarkable; its appropriate place, if chronological order of narration was followed, should have been in the *Strīparvan*. This is another instance of the employment of flashback device. But *vilāpa* has more significance than just this. Boldly defying the linearity of time, a much later occasion (end of the war) is seized upon to provide a brief, pointed preview of the tragic story about to unfold. Interestingly, this preview is clothed in the form of a post-facto viewpoint. There are other points of differences as well. While the first abstract highlights the main episodes in the story leading to the war, the second one underlines its tragic dimension. The first one presents an onlooker's perspective, the second that of an actor and a losing one at that. The second one highlights, as was natural from the perspective of a loser, the achievements of the Pāṇḍavas and the consequent despondency growing in the mind of Dhṛtarāṣṭra. A sense of gathering gloom and impending catastrophe pervades it. This mood becomes more pronounced when Dhṛtarāṣṭra starts reminiscing the phases of the war. It is interesting that in the first abstract, the war is disposed off in a single verse referring to the wasteful carnage it led to (*Ādiparvan* 1.94). But that is done in a rather dry and impersonal manner. Dhṛtarāṣṭra's *vilāpa* in the second abstract, on the other hand, gives far more details of the war and brings to higher relief the senselessness of the bloodbath.

In the Chapter 2 of the *Ādiparvan*, still a third abstract isgiven in the form of *parvasangraha* wherein a summary of each *parvan* is enumerated in sequential order. These synopses of the work serve several ends. These three summary presentations in succession, the second following immediately after the first and the third at the heels of the second, are obviously designed to hammer the outlines of the story into the minds of the listeners/readers at the very outset. This follows the same method as in the classical Indian musical recitals wherein the main *rāga* (musical mode) without embellishments is introduced right at the beginning. These synopses were absolutely necessary in a work of such vast proportions, abundant diversions and a highly complex architecture. Without this aid, the reader/listener ran the risk of either losing his way or interest or both. It was all the more necessary in an age when a work like the *Mahābhārata* was presented in the form of oral narrations before a listening audience.

This brings us to the last point that we would like to touch upon before closing this section: the oral nature of the text. The *Mahābhārata* maintains all through the form of an orally narrated work; in style and presentation it keeps up from end to end the look of a story being told to an assembled audience. Its style and format, however, are not that of a story being dished up to an audience from a platform or a stage. And, it is seldom declamatory. Both in form and style, the text is conversational in character. There is a narrator, and there is also an interlocutor. In the primary narration that took place in Naimiṣāraṇya, the narrator, as we have noted before, is Ugraśravas; the sages in the hermitage are the first interlocutors and then Śaunaka takes over that role. In the narration at the snake sacrifice, Vaiśampāyana is the narrator and Janamejaya is the interlocutor. The interlocutor helps in carrying the story forward by asking questions and making requests; his interventions also help in preventing monotony. We would like to stress that the mode of narration, except for the discursive parts like, say, that of the *Bhagavadgītā*, is not really dialogical in character; the mode of narration is conversational story telling mode. It is in the dialogical *saṃvāda* sections that the role of the interlocutor becomes that of a participant debater/discussant. In the early *parvans*, such debates/discussions occur very rarely. Even the discussions regarding the propriety of five men marrying a single woman (*Ādiparvan* 187.22*ff.*; 188–90), or the legitimacy of Yudhiṣṭhira's action of staking his queen in the dice game after losing his own freedom (*Sabhāparvan*, Chapter 60) do not fall within the category of *saṃvāda* debates.

The early *parvans* thus provide us a fair view of the basic character of the mode and devices of narration employed in the *Mahābhārata*.

Birth Stories

Let this section begin with considering the birth of Kṛṣṇadvaipāyana, known more widely by his nickname Vyāsa (*Ādiparvan* 57.73). Vyāsa's figure stands in an extraordinary relationship with the text and the story of the *Mahābhārata*. He is the author of the work and an important character in the story at the same time. He stands in the same relationship to the contending parties of the royal house of Kurus as Bhīṣma does. Biologically speaking, his relation with the Kauravas and Pāṇḍavas is closer than that of Bhīṣma; he is the progenitor of Dhṛtarāṣṭra and Pāṇḍu. He is the distressed witness of tumultuous events, the building of the cleavage between Kauravas and Pāṇḍavas leading to those very events, the passing of an era, from *dvapāra* to *kali*, and the dwindling of *dharma*. The work ends with his anguished cry: 'There are thousands of areas of pleasure (*harṣasthāna sahasrāṇi*) and hundreds of areas of fear (*bhayasthāna śatāni ca*), day in and day out they come and infect the fools, but not the wise men. With upraised hands I cry (hoarse) but nobody listens. *Dharma* begets both *artha* as well as *kāma*, so why not serve it' (*Svargārohaṇaparvan* 5.48–49). And yet, the *Mahābhārata* is not an autobiography or an account of reminiscences. It is a far wider work, a work of truly universal quality and dimension (*Ādiparvan* 56.33; *Svargārohaṇaparvan* 5.38).[6]

This great sage was born of an unwed mother, a fisherman's daughter called Satyavatī. His conception and birth took place in an unusual manner and in odd places. While an exceptional and lone passenger, the great sage Parāśara, was being ferried across the river by Satyavatī in her boat — Satyavatī in her maiden days used to ferry passengers across the river to help supplement her father's earnings — the

---

[6] The famous self-evaluation of the *Mahābhārata*: 'Whatever is found here, may be found elsewhere, but whatever is not found here does not exist anywhere'.

sage was so strongly smitten by her beauty that he cajoled and persuaded the girl to submit herself to him. And then through his mystic powers, the sage created a cover of mist and cohabited with the girl right there in the boat itself (*Ādiparvan* 57.54–69). Vyāsa was born out of this union. The unwed mother 'immediately' conceived as well as delivered (*sadyo garbhaṃ suṣāva sā*) the child on an island (*dvīpa*) (*Ādiparvan* 57.69).[7] The boy thus also came to be known as Dvaipāyana (placed in island) (*Ādiparvan* 57.71). The boy is also said to have grown up very quickly. All these, to say the least, are out of ordinary, even fantastic.

In comparison, the birth story of Bhīṣma does not have such fantastic elements. His mother was a regularly wedded wife of a powerful ruler; he was conceived and delivered in a normal fashion. Yet, it will not be correct to say that Bhīṣma's birth was totally free from unusual elements. If not the actual birth, the circumstances amidst which it took place were extraordinary. His mother Gangā was not an ordinary mortal; she was a river goddess. The condition laid down by her before agreeing to marry Śaṃtanu and her acts under the cover of that condition were truly extraordinary. The story is well known. She laid down a condition that no action of her would ever be questioned by her husband. She gave birth to seven sons one after another and, on each occasion, would drown the newly born baby in the Ganges. On the birth of the eighth son when the poor husband protested, she at once deserted the husband and disappeared taking the newly born infant with her. Gangā after bringing up the infant to boyhood returned him to Śaṃtanu (*Ādiparvan*, Chapters 92, 93). Similarly, the birth stories of the brothers Dhṛtarāṣṭra and Paṇḍu are also well known. They were conceived by their respective mothers, Ambikā and Ambālikā, through unwelcome levirate union with Vyāsa, Satyavatī's son born out of the wedlock. Pressed by their mother-in-law Satyavatī, the two sisters agreed to levirate for continuing the line of Kurus (*Ādiparvan* 99.44–49). While the elder one at the time of the union closed her eyes out of fright at the sight of the ugly Vyāsa, the younger one became pale in fear. The children born of these unions thus carried congenital physical defects: the son of Ambikā was born blind and the son of Ambālikā pale (anemic?) (*Ādiparvan* 100.1–18). The trail of extraordinary births continued in the next generation too.

Because of a curse, Pāṇḍu could not take the risk of uniting with his wives and fathering children (*Ādiparvan* 109.25–30). But if Pāṇḍu was cursed by a short tempered sage, we meet so many of these ill-tempered *Brahmaṇa*s in the *Mahābhārata*: his elder queen Kuntī, as a maiden, had received an extraordinary boon from one such *Brāhmaṇa* (*Ādiparvan* 104.1–7), whereby she could invite any god she wished, in order to have a son by him (*Ādiparvan* 113.31–35; 114.2). Persuaded by her husband[8] she had three sons by three gods, Dharma, Vāyu and

[7] This kind of immediate conception and delivery is also found in the case of the birth of Ghaṭotkaca, the son of Bhīma by Hiḍimbā.

[8] It needed a rather long persuasion before Kuntī agreed (*Ādiparvan*, Chapters 111, 112, 113).

Indra (*Ādiparvan*: 113.36-43; 114.1–27). When Pāṇḍu asked for a fourth, Kuntī refused saying it was not virtuous to have a son in this manner more than three times. 'It has been said by the sages that even in distress one should not give birth to a fourth (in this manner). (Third) onwards (in unions like this) a woman becomes progressively a *cārinī* and then a *bandhakī*.[9] You are learned and well versed in *dharma*, even then for the sake of (more) sons you are transgressing it; you must be saying this in a fit of forgetfulness', she said to Pāṇḍu (*Ādiparvan* 114.64–66). Yet, Kuntī did have earlier a fourth son in the same manner, the eldest of her offsprings, Karṇa whom she had conceived in her maiden days and cast away after the delivery (*Ādiparvan*: 104.8–13). Pāṇḍu then persuaded Kuntī to teach Mādrī the art of begetting sons by gods. This way Mādrī gave birth to the twins Nakula and Sahadeva (*Ādiparvan* 115.1–17).

Gāndhārī's hundred sons had even stranger births. Gāndhārī had conceived a year before Kuntī invited Dharma to father her eldest son (*Ādiparvan* 114.1). But her conception had been taking too long a time to mature. To add to her anxiety Kuntī had already delivered her first born while Gāndhārī was still nursing her conception (*Ādiparvan* 107.7–10). A contender to the throne with heavy legal backing, inheritance belonged to the eldest, had already arrived. The news of Yudhiṣṭhira's birth made Gāndhārī very sad (*duḥkhena parameṇa*) (*Ādiparvan* 107.15). Out of her anxiety, without letting Dhṛtarāṣṭra know it, Gāndhārī with excessive effort (*yatnena mahatā*) prematurely tried to hasten the delivery, but to her great mortification she found that she had only delivered a great lump of flesh hard like an iron ball (*Ādiparvan* 107.9–12). Dvaipāyana, who had given Gāndhārī the boon of hundred sons, having learnt of the mishap (through Yogic power of course) arrived there and divided this lump of flesh into hundred parts and put them in hundred pots. From these were born Gāndhārī's hundred sons (*Ādiparvan*, Chapter 107). Among them, Duryodhana was born first and then followed the other brothers. Duryodhana was born the same day as Bhīmasena was born to Kuntī (*Ādiparvan* 114.14). They grew up with intense dislike for each other.

Droṇa, the teacher of Kauravas and Pāṇḍavas, was 'pot-born' too, but he was pot-born in a more fundamental way than Gāndhārī's children. Droṇa was born untouched by mother's womb. In fact, he did not have any mother in any form whatsoever. Sage Bhāradvāja had gone to the river Gangā[10] for offering *havis* when he saw none other than the nymph (*apsaras*) Ghṛtācī draped in wet clothes with water dripping from them (*dadarśāpsarasaṃ sākṣādghṛtācīmāplutāmṛṣiḥ*). When a gush of wind drew away her clothes (*tasyā vāyuḥ samuddhūto vasanaṃ*

[9] *Cārinī* and *bandhakī* are variants of prostitutes.

[10] The account of Droṇa's birth is recorded twice in the *Ādiparvan*. The first and a slightly briefer version appears in *Ādiparvan* 121.1–5 and a marginally longer version in *Ādiparvan* 154.1–5.

vyapakarṣata), the sage was overcome by the sight; it led to ejaculation (*tato 'sya retaścaskanda*) (*Ādiparvan* 121.3–4; cf. 154.3–4). He put (*ādadhe*) the semen in the water pot (*droṇa*) he was carrying (*Ādiparvan* 121.4; cf. 154.4). Thus, Droṇa was born from his water pot (*tasminsamabhavaddroṇaḥ kalaśe tasya*) (*Ādiparvan* 121.5; cf. 154.5). Droṇa, therefore, had only a father, Bhāradvāja, for parent, and no mother. However, Droṇa was not the only one to have a 'motherless' birth; Droṇa's brother-in-law Kṛpa and Droṇa's wife Kṛpī, too, were not born of mother's womb. Their birth account was, to a large extent, similar to that of Droṇa. Their father Śaradvat, son of sage Gautama, had more aptitude for the craft of bowmanship than for Vedic studies (*Ādiparvan* 120.3). He used to practise the use of all arms with the same dedication as other Brahmacārins practised Vedic studies. Such dedication caused great anxiety in Indra who sent a heavenly nymph to upset his concentration and practice. Seeing the scantily clad beauty, Śaradvat too lost his control and ejaculated. The semen fell on a reed and split in two halves. Śaradvat, in the meantime, had left the place and gone after the nymph. From this split semen were born twins, a boy and a girl. King Śaṃtanu who had come there on a hunting expedition, took these infants into his care and brought them up. Because Śaṃtanu had taken pity (*kṛpā*) on the twins, they came to be called Kṛpa and Kṛpī (*Ādiparvan* 120.1–18).[11]

Even in the accounts of these two 'motherless' births, women did play an indirect role of initial motivators. There are other birth accounts in the *Mahābhārata* where women played no role at all. These births have been described as *ayonija* or non-uterine (*Ādiparvan* 153.8). Three such births are referred to: those of Kṛṣṇā, better known as Draupadī, Dhṛṣṭadyumna and Śikhaṇḍin (*Ādiparvan* 153.8). Dhṛṣṭadyumna and Śikhaṇḍin were born in a kind of made-to-order fashion, to perform a job that had been chosen for them even before they were born. Śikhaṇḍin's birth story is not recounted in the early *parvans*; the birth is just alluded to in a single verse (*Ādiparvan* 153.8). We will, therefore, take up the birth story of Dhṛṣṭadyumna and Draupadī.[12]

The birth of these twins was the direct outcome of Droṇa–Drupada hostility. The running antagonism between these two childhood friends forms one of the most interesting subplots in the *Mahābhārata*. This story will be taken up in some more detail in the next section. Here, we will touch upon only that part of the story which is relevant to the birth accounts of twins, Dhṛṣṭadyumna and Draupadī. Smarting from the injury — Droṇa had forcibly snatched half of Drupada's kingdom (*Ādiparvan* 154.23–24) — and insult by Droṇa, Drupada was consumed by the desire to avenge them. But considering Droṇa's resources and personal endowments as a redoubtable warrior, he despaired of ever achieving

[11] The account of the twins' birth is more detailed than that of Droṇa's.

[12] As they too were born simultaneously, we may call them twins like Kṛpa and Kṛpī.

his goal. Analyzing his own situation in comparison to Droṇa's, he ascribed his weakness to the want of a 'great' son (*nāsti śreṣṭhaṃ mamāpatyam*) (*Ādiparvan* 155.1–4).[13] Condemning his existing sons and companions (*jātān putrānsa nirvedāddhigbandhūn*), he scouted for and finally found a suitable priest ready to perform a ritual for the generation of a son, truly valiant, endowed with great prowess and high spirit (*sa ca putro mahāvīryo mahātejā mahābalaḥ*) who would be capable of slaying the son of Bhāradvāja (*bhāradvājasya hantāraṃ*) (*Ādiparvan* 155.1–34). At the end of the oblation (*havana*), the priest told the queen 'a twin for you has appeared' and invited her to eat the *havis* (offering). The queen asked the priest to wait for a while so that she could go and wash her mouth and have a bath (*Ādiparvan* 155.34–37). But the proud priest refused to wait and put the *havis* into the ritual fire. From the fire sprang a boy with flaming fire like complexion and equipped with arms and weapons (*Ādiparvan* 155.37–39). And then heaven spoke up: 'The prince to remove the distress of the king and for slaying Droṇa has been born' (*Ādiparvan* 155.40). From the same sacrificial altar also arose the princess Kṛṣṇā. As she arose from the fire, again the heaven spoke: 'The best of the women has been born who will cause the destruction of *Kṣatriyas*' (*sarvayoṣidvarā kṛṣṇā kṣayaṃ kṣatraṃ ninīṣati*) (*Ādiparvan* 155.41–45).

Thus, the course and purpose of the life of Dhṛṣṭadyumna, and to a slightly lesser extent, those of Draupadī as well, were charted even before they were born. The same was true of Śikhaṇḍin too. Śikhaṇḍin was born as Drupada's daughter who later became his son. Śikhaṇḍin became a man by the charms of a Yakṣa (a semi-divine being) (*Ādiparvan* 57.104; cf. 61.87).

Development of Story: The Seeds of Discord

The development of the story can be viewed at two different levels. One can look at it purely from the angle of inner dynamics of events in a sequence of cause–effect relationship: Event A automatically leading to Event B, and so on. However, there is another level of looking at it. It can be viewed in the light of *dharma* and its violations and the consequences flowing from them. The second plane calls for bit more elaboration.

The *Mahābhārata* has *dharma* for its leitmotif. The work opens with a reference to *dharma*. While requesting Ugraśravas to narrate the composition of Vyāsa, the assembled sages in Śaunaka's hermitage referred to it as a text embodying *dharma* that destroys the fear of committing sin (*dharmyāṃ pāpabhayāpahām*) (*Ādiparvan* 1.19). And it closes with Vyāsa's lament that despite its obvious advantages, people in their folly do not pay any heed to *dharma*. *Dharma* is one of the most frequently used expressions and concepts not only in the *Mahābhārata*. It had, and still has, a pervasive presence over the entire body of Indian culture.

[13] For Drupada's obsession and ruminations, see *Ādiparvan*, Chapter 155.

Although its general meaning is pretty clear, it has innumerable nuances. Thus, in spite of its wide use and familiarity, the concept of *dharma* has also something of an elusive aspect in it. The concept in all its subtleties and nuances is difficult to capture.[14] In a broad and general way, however, *dharma* may be taken to be the eternal principle that upholds and governs the universe; it is the ultimate fount of justice, the fundamental ground of discriminating between right and wrong.

Delineating on the import of the term *dharma*, Sukthankar approvingly puts forward the view of Bhīṣma on the matter as a good working guide:

> In reply to a question by Yudhiṣṭhira, Pitāmaha Bhīṣma, after explaining the difficulties in the way of defining it, gave some rules by which Dharma may partly be known, which I have found to be the simplest and at the same time the most profound exposition of the subject, if understood rightly. Dharma, says Bhīṣma, was ordained for the advancement and growth of all creatures; therefore that which leads to advancement and growth is Dharma. Dharma was ordained for restricting creatures from injuring one another; therefore that which prevents injury to creatures is Dharma. Dharma is so called because it upholds all creatures; therefore that is Dharma which is capable of upholding all creatures' (Sukthankar 1998: 81).

It may be noted that all along the emphasis is on the growth of 'all'. It is the larger good that is the normal criterion.

While considering the development of the storyline, we may keep in mind the famous maxim of Manu about the efficacy of *dharma* in terms of both its positive and negative impact. 'And, (when) *dharma* is slain, (it) slays; *dharma* protects (when) it is protected' (*Manusmṛti* VIII.15). Let us now turn to the storyline.

The reign of Śaṃtanu may serve a convenient starting point. Although certain general and conventional terms of praise for the character and qualities of Śaṃtanu appear in the text (*Ādiparvan* 92.19, 24), the most noteworthy events in his reign were his two momentous marriages. And both the marriages were the result of his crushing infatuation. In extenuation of his first marriage with Gangā, it may be said that he was something of a pawn in a divine design and that he was psyched up for the marriage by his father. But the fact remains that so overpowering was his infatuation that he accepted, almost knowingly, the insufferably difficult terms that Gangā imposed for the marriage. Her condition was: 'Whatever I would do (*yat tu kuryāmahaṃ*), either good or evil (*śubhaṃ vā yadi vāśubham*), you will neither restrain me nor speak ill of them (*na tadvārayitavyāsmi na vaktavyā tathāpriyam*)' (*Ādiparvan* 92.34). She, in fact, had laid open her hand, but Śaṃtanu

---

14 Even a *Mahābhārata* scholar of the stature of Sukthankar writes, 'I am not going to make the attempt to give you another perfect definition of Dharma, a task which . . . has taxed better brains than mine' (1998: 81). The difficulty of grasping the concept in its totality has been discussed at length by Sukthankar. However, he has also said that such an exercise is perhaps not altogether indispensable (ibid.: 80*ff.*).

blinded by his passion could not see. And from that point the events could only move toward the direction they did. We have already noted them in the earlier section.

Śaṃtanu's second marriage proved even more critical. It is a bit surprising that after the tragic consequences of his first marriage, Śaṃtanu, who is said to have been unparalleled among *Kṣatriyas* in the observance of *dharma* (*Ādiparvan* 94.5), should fall a prey to another spell of overpowering passion for a maiden. This happened when his eighth child himself was a young man of marriageable age. Śaṃtanu had already anointed Devavrata as crown prince (*Ādiparvan* 94.38).[15] Unable to either fight off his infatuation, he felt a sharp burning sensation running through his body (*śarirajena tīvrena dahyamāno 'pi*), or to give what Satyavati's father had demanded (*nakāmayata taṃ dātum varaṃ*), he began pining (*śokopahatacetanaḥ*) like an adolescent (*Ādiparvan* 94.52–53). Noticing this, Devavrata asked his father why he remained so miserable as if in a trance and did not even greet him (*kimarthamihabhikṣṇaṃ pariśocasi duḥkhitaḥ dhyāyanniva ca kiṃ rājannābhibhāṣ asi kiṃcana*) (*Ādiparvan* 94.55). Śaṃtanu's explanation that what was weighing heavy on his mind was the risk the great house of Bharata (*kule mahati bhārata*) ran because there was just a single son (*apatyaṃ nastvamevaikaḥ*) in the family was so pitifully thin, that it would deceive nobody, least of all the super-intelligent Devavrata (*devavrato mahābuddhiḥ*) (*Ādiparvan* 94.56–64). He promptly went to an old minister and found out the real reason for king's distress. The rest of the story is too well known to need recounting. By his great vows of renouncing the right to throne and of remaining a celibate, Devavrata became Bhīṣma of immortal fame. But the price that the dynasty had to pay! The dynasty lost one of its best possible rulers ever. For, Bhīṣma was an extraordinarily versatile and gifted man: an unconquerable warrior and an authority on politics and statecraft, he was equally at home in spiritualism and metaphysics. And, he was wise and virtuous.

This marriage of Śaṃtanu led to a chain of events that did not serve the best interests of the family. Two sons born of this union lost their father before they came to manhood. This was natural: Śaṃtanu was quite advanced in age when he married Satyavatī. These minors were crowned one after the other, but both died prematurely. While the elder died before marriage, the younger died without leaving any issue. We have referred to, in the earlier section, how Dhṛtarāṣṭra and Pāṇḍu were born to the two wives of Śaṃtanu's younger son Vicitravīrya through the custom of levirate and how the throne, bypassing the elder, went to the younger. Thus, the seed of discord got firmly planted. Śaṃtanu can hardly be absolved of the responsibility of 'fathering' the discord. It is noteworthy that an ancestor of Śaṃtanu, king Yayāti, had passed on his old age to his son taking on the latter's youth because he had not had enough of sensual gratification. Father making

[15] Śaṃtanu's encounter with Satyavatī took place at least four years after Devavrata's anointment as crown prince (*Ādiparvan* 94.40–78; 94.52–53).

unnatural demands on son's affection was thus not new in the family.[16] After Śaṃtanu's death, Bhīṣma had to assume the role of a guardian of the minor princes and this led him to abduct three daughters of the king of Kāśī for marriage to Vicitravīrya. Abduction was a sanctioned practice for marriage among *Kṣatriyas*, but the bride had to be willing. Before the marriage was to be solemnized, the eldest of the three sisters disclosed that she had already chosen king Śālva as her husband. 'You know what *dharma* is; therefore, please act according to *dharma* (*dharmajña tatastvaṃ dharmamācara*)', she told Bhīṣma (*Ādiparvan* 96.49). Bhīṣma, of course, let her off and allowed her to go to Śālva. But the damage had already been done; spurned by Śālva, the princess swore revenge on Bhīṣma. She became Śikhaṇḍin in her next birth and became the instrument of Bhīṣma's demise. The story of Śikhaṇḍin, we have seen earlier, belongs to a later *parvan*. And, here Bhīṣma was at fault, even if in a very minor way, he violated *dharma* while abducting the girls; consents of the girls were not obtained.

Some points about Droṇa–Drupada relationship have been discussed in the earlier section. We will add a few more details here. Droṇa and Drupada spent their early days as students at the hermitage of Agniveśya studying and playing together as was natural for young lads. Their fathers, sage Bharadvāja and king Pṛṣata, too, were friends (*bharadvājasakhā cāsītpṛṣato nāma pārthivaḥ*) (*Ādiparvan* 121.8; cf. 154.6). Droṇa, in spite of his personal attainments — he had mastered Vedas and Vedāngas (*Ādiparvan* 121.5; cf. 154.5) — apparently lived in poverty. Meanwhile, he had married and had a wife and son to look after. Having heard that the great warrior Paraśurāma had decided to give all his wealth to *Brāhmaṇas*, he went to him. But Droṇa was a little late; Paraśurāma had already given away all his wealth. He had just his weapons left with him. Paraśurāma offered to give Droṇa all his weapons and teach him their use. Droṇa gratefully accepted the offer (*Ādiparvan* 121.6–23; 154.8–13).

Paraśurāma's inability to render any material help prompted Droṇa to go and meet his old and dear friend Drupada (*priyam sakhayam jagāma drupadam prati*) (*Adiparvan* 121.23) who had succeeded his father as the ruler of Paṇcāla, and hail the latter as his friend. Drupada not only refused to honour the old friendship, but insulted and humiliated him in the harshest possible terms. He rebuked Droṇa for being churlish (*akṛteyaṃ tava prajñā*) and trying to establish friendship through force (*prasabhaṃ sakhā te 'hamiti*) and reminded that friendship can take place only between equals (*samaṃ*), that the poor cannot be a friend of the rich (*na daridro vasumato*); the ignorant, of the learned (*navidvān viduṣaḥ*); the eunuch, of the brave (*śūrasya na sakhā klībaḥ*); and the one who is not a king, of a king (*nārājñā saṃgataṃ rājñaḥ*), etc. (*Ādiparvan* 122.1–9; 154.14–15). Droṇa remembered every word of it and bided his time. Overcome with anger

[16] For this part of Yayāti story, see *Ādiparvan*, Chapters 78 and 79.

(*manyunābhipariplutaḥ*), he thought for a moment and drew up his plan in mind and silently left for Hastināpura (*Ādiparvan* 122.10–11).

Soon, Droṇa returned Drupada the blow for blow, the hurt for hurt. As *gurudakṣiṇā*, he got Drupada vanquished in war by his disciples. With his pride humbled (*bhagnadarpaṃ*), wealth lost (*hṛtadhanaṃ*) and captured (*vaśamāgatam*), Drupada stood before Droṇa. Recalling Drupada's old hostility (*vairaṃ manasā dhyātvā*), Droṇa said these memorable words to Drupada: 'I have by force devastated your kingdom, occupied your capital and your life is at the disposal of your enemy. Now, tell me what do you expect from a friend? But, O king, do not fear for life (*mā bhaiḥ prāṇabhayādrājan*), we are forgiving *Brāhmaṇa*s (*kṣamino brāhmaṇā vayam*), in the hermitage you have played with me in childhood (*āśrame krīḍitaṃ yattu tvayā bālye mayā saha*) and that has swelled my love and affection for you (*tena saṃvardhitaḥ snehastvayā me*). I am again asking for your friendship. I am granting you a boon (*varaṃ dadāmi te*). Receive half of the kingdom. Since one who is not a king cannot become the friend of a king (*arājā kila no rājñāṃ sakhā bhavitumarhati*), I am taking care to give you a kingdom (*ataḥ prayatitaṃ rājye*). Now, O Pāñcāla, you may consider me a friend, if you want to (*sakhāyaṃ māṃ vijānīhi pāñcāla yādi manyase*)' (*Ādiparvan* 128.6–12; 154.21–24). Drupada had no option but to agree, but since then it became his single-minded pursuit to avenge the insult. This, as we have seen earlier, led to the birth of Dhṛṣṭadyumna.

The story of Droṇa–Drupada antagonism is a cyclical repetition of arrogance, humiliation and reprisals and exemplifies the shattering consequences flowing from them. This sub-story got entangled with the main story of Pāṇḍava–Kaurava relationship and became more complicated after the marriage of Draupadī. It also perhaps foreshadowed the pattern of the grand alliances that were to emerge before the Kurukṣetra war. Drupada became the natural ally of the Pāṇḍavas. Did this push Droṇa to the other side?

Karṇa is an ill-starred and fascinating figure.[17] He had to carry the burden of, as it were, a curse all through his life and finally departed under its weight. He was born an unwanted child and cast away as newborn baby into the river of life, metaphorically as well as physically, helpless and totally vulnerable. Born of a union of illustrious parents, a royal upbringing was his legitimate due, but by an irony of fate, the illegitimacy of his birth (as the child of an unwed mother) leading to his upbringing by Sūta foster parents pursued and haunted his whole life. And in

[17] Sukthankar, however, does not think that Karṇa is a genuinely noble character and attributes the tragedy of his life, to a large extent, to one great failing in his character: his limitless pride. According to Sukthankar, what passes for his heedless generosity was his overweening pride of which he himself was the prime victim. After all, as Sukthankar argues, he was willingly party to and participant in all the diabolical deeds of Duryodhana (1998: 49*ff.*).

tune with his birth, he made his final exit unarmed, defenseless and hopelessly vulnerable. His death, however, is recounted in a later *parvan*. But already in the early *parvans*, the course of his life and fate are firmly chalked out. Some of the most crucial episodes in his life history figure there.

The Chapter 104 of the *Ādiparvan* describing his birth story[18] encapsulates practically the entire journey of Karṇa's life. It describes how he was born to an innocent, childlike and playfully curious mother in the first flush of her approaching womanhood; how the child mother was overcome by a sense of fear and shame after his birth, how she took the fateful decision of casting him off into the river; how Rādhā and her Sūta (charioteer) husband found the baby and brought him up as their child; how he became a redoubtable warrior, etc. But even more interestingly, it also tells us how he was born naturally endowed with invincibility, with *sahajāta kavaca kuṇḍala* (inborn armour and earrings), and how he gave that precious gift away to Indra who came seeking for it disguised as a *Brāhmaṇa* tearing it off his body. This episode powerfully hints at how Karṇa would meet his doom weaponless and without defense at the hands of Indra's son and protégé Arjuna in the final battle of his life.

There was some elemental aspect in the relationship of Karṇa with the Pāṇḍavas, especially Arjuna. Rabindranath Tagore in his famous poem 'Karṇa Kuntī Saṃvād' called it an invisible mysterious pull that drew Karṇa and Arjuna together into bitter mutual hostility and violence. Our text does not overtly refer to it, but there is enough to suggest the existence of some such thing. Otherwise what could be the reason for Karṇa to suddenly appear at the show of martial skills and challenge Arjuna (*Ādiparvan* 125.26*ff*.; Chapters 126,127). It could not have been just the abandoned child's natural urge to take on what he might have perceived as the unkind society responsible for the injustice done to him. If it was just that, why should he have singled out Arjuna for his hostility and hatred? Duryodhana was as much a symbol of power and privilege conferred by the same society as Arjuna, but Karṇa did not betray any feeling of hostility against him; in fact, he got instinctively drawn towards him (*Ādiparvan* 126.13–15). Some higher force was at work and was guiding the Karṇa–Arjuna affair inscrutably, leading it to its deadly finale. Their inborn mutual antagonism found its first open expression during the show of arms. From where the bitter animosity arose nobody, including the two adversaries, could be sure at this stage, except perhaps Kuntī.[19] She, watching the show from the ladies' enclosure recognized her firstborn and

[18] There are just 21 verses in the Critical Edition.

[19] When Karṇa made his dramatic entry in the show of arms and began challenging Arjuna, the poet pointedly stressed the fact that 'one brother not knowing the other brother' (*bhrātā bhrātaramajñātaṃ*), i.e., Karṇa not knowing that Arjuna was his brother, scorned and rebuked him (*Ādiparvan* 126.8–9).

realized the inexorable way the events were shaping. She swooned (*kuntibhojasutā moham vijñātārthā jagāma ha*).[20] With tortured soul she found that her youthful act of cruelty[21] now caught up with her; she was condemned to suffer secretly her loss, fear and guilt for a long time. These accounts, again, belong to later *parvans*. The show of arms cemented the bond between Karṇa and Duryodhana forever. And thenceforth, Karṇa was a prominent member of Duryodhana's inner circle, enthusiastically participating in all its schemes and transgressions including those in the game of dice.

The chief interest of the *Sabhāparvan* from the point of view of the development of the story lies in the game of dice. It is not necessary to dwell upon the significance of the game of dice; it is well known. With the various schemes of Duryodhana to destroy the Pāṇḍavas having failed, the *Ādiparvan* ended in apparent peace with the division of the kingdom. In contrast, by the end of the *Sabhāparvan*, the chance of peace was lost forever. The ultimate humiliation and injury hurled on the Pāṇḍavas — the attempted violation of their common wife — ensured that events could move only towards the final war of annihilation.

Significance

What do all these issues imply? Are all these merely parts of an interesting and edifying story? Or do they bear a deeper significance? These questions are natural and legitimate. But, answering these is not easy. First, they merge into a much larger question, the question of the meaning of the *Mahābhārata* as a whole, and go far beyond the scope of the early *parvans*. In his masterly exposition, Sukthankar has shown that the question of the meaning of the *Mahābhārata* is a multilayered question and has to be viewed at different levels. Second, the attempt to answer these questions will entail a rather radical departure from the methodology we have followed so far. Until now we have confined ourselves to the consideration of the overt, to the manifestly stated and expressed in the early *parvans* of the text. These questions demand going much beyond *avidhā*, the level of expressly denoted, and delving more and more into *vyañjana*, the level of suggestion and resonance. While *avidhā* is by and large objective in nature, *vyañjana* cannot help being subjective.

Although these questions really relate to the whole of the *Mahābhārata*, we will try to confine ourselves generally to the material in the early *parvans* alone.

[20] *Ādiparvan* 126.27–30 gives a graphic description of the mental and physical distress of Kuntī when she found that by a cruel twist of fate two of her sons were ready to shoot each other (*tāvudyatamahācāpau*).

[21] It is interesting that when Karṇa entered the arena of weapons show, the poet introduces him by describing him as born of the maiden womb (*kanyāgarbhaḥ pṛthuyaśaḥ pṛthāyāḥ pṛthulocanaḥ*) (*Ādiparvan* 126.3).

What does the narrative structure of the text signify? We venture to suggest that the narrative devices are not just clever and novel tools to stir and hold the interest of the listeners/readers. There is a purpose beyond that. The structure and the devices have been consciously chosen to serve a consciously chosen end. Their purpose is to convey the message that the story, basically, is one of universal import. At the apparent level, it is a story of a specific time–space locus. It is obviously time- and space-specific; it does not have the 'once upon a time' air or form. It concerns the history of a particular dynasty and thus liberally shares the characteristics of *vaṃśa* literature. Yet, it does not lie trapped and frozen in its defined locus. The form and the narrative devices signify the breaking of boundaries of the time–space context of the narrative. Thus, for the primary narration of the story the venue chosen is the hermitage in Naimiṣāraṇya removed in time and space from the actions of the story. There is more to it than just physical distance. The hermitage in Naimiṣāraṇya represents an ambience completely different from that of the Kuru–Pāṇḍava family saga. It is interesting that this story of violent family relations has for its audience the *Brahmacārins* living a life of peaceful pursuits away from family ties. Further, this predominantly *Kṣatriya* account is narrated to an assembly of *Brāhmaṇa ṛṣi*s. However, at the core *Mahābhārata* remains a *vaṃśānukīrtana* (glories of a dynasty); the major part of which is narrated to king Janamejaya in answer to his specific request for learning about the deeds of his ancestors. These two narrations symbolize the relation between the particular and the universal, and the movement from the one to the other. And the passage of the movement — from the universal to the particular — is interesting too. It begins with the universal (*Naimiṣāraṇya*) and then moves to the particular (snake sacrifice) and then back to the universal.

It is also pertinent to note that the snake sacrifice, the occasion for the second narration (second in order of appearance and not chronology) does not appear as an intrusive element but is neatly woven into the body of the main narrative. And the account of snake sacrifice, along with its background, is also an account of the Kuru dynasty from the time of Parikṣit to that of Janamejaya. In other words, the last part of the history of the house of Kurus is the one that is narrated first and then, following the 'flashback' technique, the rest of the narrative is taken up. We have already noted some other instances of the employment of this device in the second section.

Similarly, Dhṛtarāṣṭra's *vilāpa*, as we have seen earlier, strongly illustrates the calculated resistance to the one-way linearity of temporal movement. Dhṛtarāṣṭra's *vilāpa* skillfully mixes all the three temporal divisions — past, present and future — and deliberately alters their conventionally accepted interrelationships. We have already noted that if the chronological order were followed, the *vilāpa* should have been placed at the end of the war. The end of the war is the 'present' of the *vilāpa*, but in calculated defiance of chronology the *vilāpa* is placed right at the beginning of the narrative. Not just its positioning, but the form of its content too challenges the accepted idea of the passage of time. For the reader/listener, the lamentations of Dhṛtarāṣṭra serve as a preview of the story, but the preview comes in the form of post-facto perspective. And that is not all. The form of this post-facto overview is one of prognosis. Conscious efforts to symbolize the dissolving of time–space boundaries and the linearity of time are important elements of the modes of narrations in the *Mahābhārata*. The underlying intention is clear: the dead set linearity of time has been defied to convey that the story, although located in a particular timeframe, is not a prisoner of that timeframe; its significance overflows the boundaries of that particular timeframe.

Can the birth stories in the *Ādiparvan* be regarded as extraordinary in the same sense, say, as those of Lord Kṛṣṇa, Gautama Buddha, Mahavīra Svāmī, etc.? The circumstances and the manner of their occurrence make the *Ādiparvan* births interesting and remarkable. Their varied characters add to the interest in them and they touch many chords of emotions in us. Some are fabulous, some tragic, some even look comical. One can hardly miss the element of irony with which the *Mahābhārata* records numerous instances of renowned holy men and members of royalty falling easy victims to the pull of lust, leading to the birth of some outstanding people. But it must also be noted that the text does not play this element of irony up to the point of ridicule or censoriousness. It, on the other hand, weaves the narrative very slowly, almost imperceptibly, so as to show how these transgressions bore unfortunate consequences in the long run.

However, in spite of their interesting features, the *Ādiparvan* birth accounts do not rise to the level of the birth accounts of Kṛṣṇa, Buddha or Mahavira. There are no suggestions of anything similar to immaculate conception;[22] there are no dreams about divine beings entering the wombs of expectant mothers; no flowers blooming on the footprints of the newborn child as he starts walking right away; and no serpent spreading its hood to protect the newborn child from the incessant rains as he is being carried away from the prison where he is born. No mystique of supernatural piety surrounds the birth stories of *Ādiparvan*; instead they exude an earthy rawness. We may add that this is how the author of the *Mahābhārata* wanted to project the birth stories of its heroes. It is interesting that none of these heroes, not even Yudhiṣṭhira, could achieve the status of an *avatāra* (incarnation of a divinity). Kṛṣṇa is the only *Mahābhārata* character to find a place in Indian pantheon. And, the *Mahābhārata* story does not revolve so much around Kṛṣṇa as it does around the Pāṇḍavas and Kauravas.

By all measures, the *Mahābhārata* is a grand narrative. However, this grand narrative has some core ideas. Sukthankar has highlighted several key passages epitomizing the centrality of *dharma* in the *Mahābhārata*. In this context, we would like to underline two statements : (*a*) Gāndhārī's statement, *yato dharmastato jayaḥ* ('victory is where *dharma* is', *Strīparvan* 13.9), and (*b*) Sañjaya's statement

[22] Even the conceptions of Kuntī and Mādrī had more physicality than mystic divine elements.

at the end of the *Bhagavadgītā*, *yatra yogeśvaraḥ kṛṣṇo yatra pārtho dhanurdharaḥ/ tatra śrīrvijayo bhūtirdhruva nītirmatirmama* ('where there is Kṛṣṇa, the lord of the *yoga* and where stands Pārtha holding his bow, there reside the goddess of fortune, the victory, the prosperity, the unwavering law; this is my considered opinion', *Strīparvan* 18.78). These statements, from theistic point of view, have the same kind of ring as the *mahāvākya*s of the Upaniṣads.

Grand narratives in today's intellectual milieu, however, enjoy low esteem. They have become a synonym of grandstanding and are considered banal. But in the hands of really grand narrators, grand narratives even now continue to fascinate and command respect. Tolkien's *The Lord of the Rings* may be cited as an example. The *Mahābhārata* across the barriers of time continues to attract and baffle with undiminished vigour and promises to do so in future too.

References

Bhattacharya, Sibesh. 2010. *Understanding Itihāsa*. Shimla: Indian Institute of Advanced Study (IIAS).

Bhaṭṭācārya, Haridāsa Siddhāntavāgīśa (ed.). 1383 Vangābda (Bengali Era). 'Ādiparvva', in *Mahābhāratam*, vol. 2. Kolkata: Visvavani Prakasani.

Niyogi Balslav, Anindita. 1999. *A Study of Time in Indian Philosophy*. New Delhi: Munshiram Manoharlal.

Sukthankar, V. S. 1998. *On the Meaning of the Mahābhārata*. New Delhi: Motilal Banarsidass.

Understanding Yudhiṣṭhira's Actions

Recasting Karma-Yoga *in a Wittgensteinian Mould*

Enakshi Mitra

Although the *Mahābhārata* is a fusion of fictional and non-fictional narratives, most of which are controversially categorized by us as 'mythology', it can be treated more generally as a universal history of the human condition. At the heart of the text, proclaimed by the tradition as its cream, lies the moral psychology of action (*karma*) as expounded in the *Bhagavadgītā*. In the modern period ever since the time of Bankimchandra Chattopadhyay and Swami Vivekananda, the message of the *Gītā* is understood as a recipe for staying firm in wisdom in the midst of changes and unstoppable actions which is our life; and embracing work that is inescapable — such as the work of a butcher or a soldier in the battlefield — as liberating rather than binding. This new philosophy of work and style of agency would now be called karma-yoga and viewed as the carnal of the teachings of *Gītā*. The objective of this essay is, first, to critique what I call the *Mahābhārata*'s foundationalist/essentialist account of human action from a Wittgensteinian anti-foundationalist point of view, and then to try to reinterpret the actions of the epic's alleged hero — the righteous but confused Yudhiṣṭhira — in a non-traditional non-foundationalist way. One wittingly contentious claim I would like to make is that seeing our actions in this new way illuminates the notion of desireless-action or *karma-yoga,* making it available to unliberated moral strugglers, such as the virtuous but vulnerable Yudhiṣṭhira. Such a quotidian understanding of what it is to act for the sake of action and not for the sake of fruit of the action matches the overall scheme of the *Mahābhārata* which aims at offering a self-questioning complex set of ethical directions for socially involved worldly people and not for moral saints or world-renouncing prophets.

I shall be using the key term 'foundationalism' in a rather qualified and extended sense. Classical foundationalism amounts to a definition of epistemological enterprise, dividing all our beliefs into two groups: those that are self-supporting form the base, while the rest constitute the superstructure built on the base (Dancy 1985: 53). What is interesting and relevant for our present purpose is to expose the basic folly of all forms of foundationalism as professing a non-circular mechanism that externalizes the foundation from the founded and yet invests the former with an occult power to entail the latter.

Later Wittgenstein worked against this myth in both the spheres of language and actions, verbal and non-verbal practices. For him, language cannot be set on a foundation more primordial than language itself. No pre-linguistic private mental realm need to be postulated to explain the way language works. None of the usually proposed foundations — universals, objective thoughts, physical ostension, mental images, verbal rules, nervous excitements, brain-patterns, or even forms of life — can be claimed to have a pre-linguistic or 'basic' character. Each proposed foundation would open itself to further interpretation and thus lead to an infinite chain of interpretations until we are obliged to merge it with the founded in an unbroken continuum. Extending this insight to actions, he points out that desire, belief, volition, or intention for action cannot have a 'pre-actional' identity[1] but meshes up with the action. Similarly, there is nothing outside the action that could be called the fruit or consequence of the action.

While the *Gītā* instructs us to give up desire for fruit, both the narrative background and the *Gītā*'s proto-*Sāṃkhya* metaphysics and psychology of action lends support to a foundationalist view of *karma* or action. The *karma-yoga* of *Gītā* is undoubtedly cast in the prevalent doctrine of the own-nature or character of an agent as a mental reservoir (as a coherent system of beliefs, desires, intentions, and *saṃskāras*) being external to and yet entailing or causing all the subsequent actions that the agent is going to perform. It weaves a rigid cycle of *saṃskāras* determining actions, which in turn generate further *saṃskāras* and further actions, bringing an inviolable set of consequences along with them. The central characters of the *Mahābhārata* are destined to be and categorized as 'virtuous and 'vicious' right from their birth and thus expected to act in predictable modes. Yet, the body of the text abounds in an almost continuous slippage and blurring of boundaries — gods shading into men, men shading into gods, subhuman creatures guiding humans on moral matters, mono-andry shading into polyandry, virtue shading into vice and vice versa. In this routinely topsy-turvy world, characters essentially pre-destined from their birth to act in a certain way seem to have no place, because people act in unexpected ways all the time. Exceptions and uncertainties are more frequent than rule-abiding conduct. Notwithstanding its essentialist precept, this epic presents the most provocative playground of dissolving, in a Wittgensteinian fashion, all proposed foundations into a plethora of particular practices, describable but not explicable in terms even of the *Sāṃkhya* triple-*guṇa* theory of human nature.

This essay is divided in two parts. The first part takes off from the *karma-yoga* of *Gītā* and seeks to push the ontology of action in a non-foundationalist direction. Borrowing insights from later Wittgenstein, it seeks to construe *niṣkāma karma* as merging the putative splits between (*a*) the beliefs and volition (supposedly mental antecedents *of* actions); (*b*) the brute action consisting in the physical movement; and (*c*) consequences generated by the action (*phala*) into a continuum. The second part revisits these insights in the concrete live actions of Yudhiṣṭhira, the hero of the *Mahābhārata*.

---

[1] We take the liberty to use this ungrammatical expression throughout the essay.

Negotiating *Karma-Yoga* through a Non-foundationalist Direction

Let us set aside all internal differences amongst the Indian schools of philosophy on the nature the terms *karma*/'action' and *karmaphala*/ 'consequences' (a la *Bhagavadgītā*). To put the idea of *niṣkāma karma* in simplest possible terms: for the performer of such actions, the results generated from the deed ceases to be the end for the simple reason that it is not desired, and there can be no end conceivable apart from desire. (*Gītā* II.47).

Now one cannot act, whether in the *sakāma* or *niṣkāma* fashion, without conceiving a specific result of that action. An action as contrasted to a mere bodily event is one that is performed with an intention to achieve a particular result. What seems like an action of planting a sapling (with the result of getting its flowers or fruits in view) may be alternatively described as: (*a*) the exercise of creating a configuration of the earth, sapling and one's own body; (*b*) testing the density of the soil (where the sapling could have been replaced with any other object); and (*c*) creating a light-and-shade effect on the soil; and so on. Each of these actions is an intentional action yielding a particular result, without which the said action would be reduced to involuntary movements of the body forced to bend over with the sapling getting stuck accidentally into the earth. *Karma-yoga* or harnessing oneself to actions pertains only to voluntary actions within which the *sakāma*/*niṣkāma* dichotomy falls.

As all voluntary actions seem to be preceded by a desire for an end, in what sense does the *Gītā* enjoin one to abandon the end of an action? The answer, as already indicated, is this: starting with the minimal conception of *phala*, one has to flesh it out in and through an incomplete and continuous flow of actions. It is in this sense that a *niṣkāma karmī* does not project the end as outside the action, but absorbs it into the body of the action itself. It is in this sense that the action can be seen not as a means to an end but as an end in itself. And only when the end is externalized from the action that it becomes the object of desire. Each of the different actions described, if claimed to be performed in the *niṣkāma* style, have to be seen as inculcating or absorbing the end into itself.

The full import of absorbing fruit/consequence into the action itself — writing a doctoral dissertation as including getting the doctoral degree rather than as stopping with the submission of the dissertation — needs to be understood in the general background of Wittgenstein's treatment of speech-acts. When I use rude words and offend someone, is the person getting offended a *phala* (consequence) which I can pare apart from my speech-act of offending? We, as desire-motivated actors (*sakāma karmī*), externalize the end from the action, i.e., split up the seamless whole of action into the following fragments: belief–desire–*saṃskāra*–rule of action/action/end or *phala*. And once cut up into fragments, they have to be stitched up through various foundationalist mechanisms:

(*a*) It may be thought that that the strength of informed beliefs, desires, or volition is sufficient to bring about a unique action with a uniquely desired *phala*.

(*b*) Given the fact that most of the Indian schools of philosophy have an established theory of *saṃskāra*, i.e., cognition or action leading to a disposition to be revived into similar actions, a *sakāma karmī* can put his trust on this mechanism. A person taking lesson in driving, swimming, reading, writing, etc., rests assured in the supposition that his learning activities will stay latent in his mind in the form of a disposition to yield the desired *phala* on suitable occasions.

(*c*) Aristotle attempted to show actions not as offshoots in a causal chain leading from cognition, desire and volition, but as logically deducible as consequences from premises relating desires and beliefs in the following form of a practical syllogism:[2]

Any action of mine, which results in S, is desirable.
This action of mine results in S.
Therefore, this action of mine is desirable.

Aristotle equated the conclusion itself with the action.

The device to ensure a particular *phala* from a particular action may take the following form:

All actions executed through steps a, b, c, d, etc., yield the desired *phala* p.
This action is executed through steps a, b, c, and d.
Therefore, this action yields the desired *phala* p.

Wittgenstein's critique of all these foundationalist mechanisms (as already indicated) is chiefly directed against a purely pre-actional or 'mental' foundation, or a pre-applicational identity of rules, independent of and yet generating a unique action along with a unique consequence. The critique can be worked out in details through the following phases.

Against Believing, Hoping, Willing, etc., as Mental Foundations of Actions

Wittgenstein points out that studying phenomena like seeing, hearing, thinking, believing, willing, etc., invites a question of criterion, viz., what external behaviours

[2] Davidson discusses Aristotle's notion of practical syllogism in *Essays on Actions and Events* (2001). The issue is also taken up by Evnine in *Donald Davidson* (1991).

one must exhibit in order to be in that state. He argues resourcefully to drive home this insight:

(*a*) Hopes or expectations cannot be given an episodic, self-contained, private phenomenological quality of the present. Their content spills over to imbibe the social contextual precedents and public consequents of the situation (Wittgenstein 1984: Section 584). Suppose, the entire morning I am hoping that N. N. will come and bring me some money. If a minute is cut off from this context, 'will it not be hope?' The question can be answered sensibly only if we realize that whether we cut off a chunk of one minute or five hours from the stretch, hoping cannot preserve a purely mental status if the words do not belong to the language-game, if the 'feeling' of hope is displaced from the entire institution of money-lending in which it is situated.

(*b*) The diverse cases of hoping, expecting, or intending do not share a common self-identical character in the shape of a special mental undertone that can be retrieved through introspection. To dissipate such myths, Wittgenstein takes to his characteristic style of actual survey of cases where these terms are used (ibid.: Section 588): (*i*) I am revoking my decision to leave tomorrow; (*ii*) your arguments do not convince me, I stick to my previous decision; (*iii*) asked how long are you going to stay, I say 'Tomorrow my holiday ends'; and (*iv*) at the end of a quarrel, I say 'OK, I decide to leave tomorrow'. There is no characteristic typical experience of 'tending towards something' underlying all these diverse phenomena. Intention to say something does not consist in opening one's mouth, drawing one's breath and letting it out again. For, such things can happen in a completely different situation to feed a completely different concept (ibid.: Section 591). On the whole, the dimension of 'depth' in the cases of genuine intentions, as contrasted to faked ones, actually comes out through a flattening out of the depth in a painstaking description of the humdrum uses (ibid.: Section 594).

(*c*) Wittgenstein argues against the prevalent theory according to which willing is the primordial, indescribable and intractable foundation of action, but is itself not an action. As far as the popular slogan goes: 'it cannot be brought about', 'it comes when it comes' (ibid.: Section 611).

For Wittgenstein, a thing is ascribed a property not as a positive insular essence but in its relational contexts and contrasts with other practices, similar or dissimilar. To describe the will in the aforementioned way is to contrast it with the raising of my arms, which surely cannot be described in similar idioms. At the same time, the will *is* something that happens to me; I do not passively wait for it in the sense that I wait for the violent thudding in my heart to stop (ibid.). There is a sense in which I can bring about my will to swim by simply jumping into water (as I can bring about my stomach-ache by overeating) (ibid.: Section 612, 613).

For Wittgenstein, the way to solve the enigma of will as an uncaused phenomenon and yet bringing about voluntary actions has to be solved by revamping our usual notion of a causal mechanism. We think that the only way a causal mechanism can fail is on account of a discontinuity in the links of the chain. The will is unavailable as a link in the causal chain and that constitutes its primordial and pre-actional character. Wittgenstein points out that there is another way in which a causal mechanism fails, say, when the cogwheels turn soft, they run into each other, or they either mesh up with the objects to be meshed. It is not because of an irreducibly mental character of the will that it becomes unavailable as a link in the causal chain, but because it meshes up with other units of the whole.

Wish and will are not the sort of instruments to bring about the action, not in the sense of pliers and hammer that are instruments physically separable from the nail going down (Wittgenstein 1984, Section 614). Wittgenstein states quite explicitly that if a will is to be distinguished from a wish it cannot stop short of an action (ibid., Section 615). (And as we have seen — wishing, hoping, expecting, making an effort, spread out in motley of uses and behaviours). The action of raising one's arm is not a conjunction of two units: the will to raise the arm and the arm going up (ibid., Section 621).

Wittgenstein further points out that if one splits the willing subject from the acting subject, it is not only the former that is reduced to something without mass or inertia, or the pure mover that is never moved, but doing itself too, like an 'extensionless point' of a needle, would seem not to have 'any volume of experience' (ibid., Sections 610, 620). It would seem to be the real agent, pure action, and all the 'phenomenal happenings' would only be external consequences of this action (ibid., Section 620). 'I do' would be having a (putatively) definite sense severed from all experiences (ibid.). In other words, once we insulate the will in a mental reservoir, we also insulate the action into a putative boundary divorced from its consequences. On the contrary, most of the so-called consequences *of* the action are to be absorbed into the action.

A desire-actuated doer (*sakāma karmī)* may appreciate that his actions are not caused (but are at best inclined by) hopes, expectations and volitions. In other words, highly-strung desires, hopes or volitions may stop short of the action and therein lies the freedom of the agent. But what a *sakāma karmī* does not realize is that hopes, expectations and willing are not purely mental antecedents but are themselves laid out in motley of actions that may stop short of further actions.

The Nature of Karma, Saṃskāras *and* Phalas

In this section the nature of *karma*, *saṃskāra*, and *karma-phala*s are explored, following a broadly *Gītā*-line. This is followed by a Wittgensteinian critique of the foundational mechanism underlying these theories.

Karma can be fully characterized as the coherent and harmonious workings of a living and cognitively aware organism, whereby the life-breath (*prāṇa*), sensory and motor organs, mind, ego, and *buddhi* concur in the growth, reproduction and sustenance of human body. *Gītā* III.5 also states this quite explicitly: 'No one can remain even for a moment without doing work; everyone is made to act helplessly by the impulses born of nature'. Life-preserving activities of the *prāṇa* (like digestion, respiration) are also subsumed under *karmas*, for they, insofar as they can be stopped by the *yogis*, have a volitional element.

Any cognition or volition leaves its subtle impression (*saṃskāra*) on the *citta* (subconscious mind-stuff where all the *saṃskāras* are embedded) and is enlivened on suitable occasions (*Yogasūtra* II.12, 13; IV.8, 9). The activities of the *jñānendriyas* (sense organs) and the *karmendriyas* (motor organs) are like scooping up a handful of sand from a pot, which again settles down in the form of a sediment or lump. Metaphorically speaking, *saṃskāra* is that sediment, which though is an activity, is different from the full-fledged action that it generates or is generated by. *Saṃskāra* is the passivated, unmanifested or inertialized state of cognition or volition, residing in the *citta*. The word *triguṇaiḥ* (*Gītā* III.5) clearly suggests that all our actions are governed by an interplay of *sattva*, *rajas* and *tamas*,[3] or rather by an interplay of revelation and its *saṃskārika* sedimentation.

All the past *karmas* generate their *phalas* or consequences through the mediation of the *saṃskāra*. The obvious fact that all our efforts and engagements become smooth through repetition is another way of saying that it produces a habit or disposition. Once this disposition or *saṃskāra* is revoked in memory, it leads to further actions of our sense and motor organs, which in turn lead to experience of pleasure and pain.

Types of *Phalas*: Our *karmas* have three kinds of *phalas*, or rather the *saṃskāras* manifest themselves in three different ways: *jāti* (preservation of the body), *āyus* (life-span), and *bhogaphala* (pleasure and pain) (*Yogasūtra* II.13, 14). The activities of digestion, respiration and blood-circulation, belonging to *prāṇa*, sustain the body and produces *jāti* (next birth); the duration of these activities constitutes the life-span or *āyus*; insofar as these activities go on in a smooth and unhindered fashion, they produce pleasure, otherwise pain (*bhogaphala*). The *saṃskāras* figure as the reservoir of the eternal flow of actions throughout all the births and rebirths; all multiple aspects and anomalies of a character are inscribed in the *saṃskāras* (*Yogasūtra* II.12). *Gītā* III.33 speaks of *prakṣti* as the mental equipment with which one is born, as a result of the past acts that must run its course.

Types of *Saṃskāras*: *Saṃskāras* are of two types: (*a*) *smṛtiphala* or *vāsanā* and (*b*) *trivipāka* (*jāti*, *āyus* and *bhogaphala*). *Vāsanā* simply reproduces itself in memory; it does not effect any new construction. *Trivipāka* is geared to the instrumental

---

[3] The *sattva*, *rajas* and *tamas* are the three essential characteristics to which the physical universe is reducible. The *sattva* represents whatever is fine and light, the *rajas* stands for whatever is active, and the *tamas* represents whatever is heavy and opaque.

powers (*karmaśakti*) and once it matures into volition (*ceṣṭā*) it brings about certain changes in the nature of the instruments (*karaṇas*) themselves.

Vāsanā is compared with an intricate network consisting of many nodes, or with a book with all its pages closed in a single lump. A particular action is like opening a single page or tugging at a particular node. With respect to the agent A, his cognition or transaction with another agent B will open up all suitable and similar *saṃskāras* from that network, which were residing in the mind of A and an appropriate *phala* will be produced thereby.

It is this conjoined force of *saṃskāras* and *karmaśakti* (the natural powers of *karaṇas*) that constitutes *karmāśaya* or *trivipāka*. Unlike *vāsanā*, *trivipāka* fructifies not in the present but in the next birth. The cognition of *jāti*, *āyus* and *bhoga* leads to *vāsanā* while that of the internal functions of mind, sense organs and motor organs leads to *karmāśaya*. *Karmaśakti* — the raw, elemental, unstructured energy involved in all actions — falls into particular moulds or *vāsanās*, viz., *jāti vāsanā*, *āyuvāsanā* and *bhogavāsanā*. The primary energy once channellized or shaped into moulds is the *karmāśaya*. In fine, *vāsanā* provides the path allowing the *karmāśaya* to navigate through it. The *karmaśakti* of a person channellized into the mould of *caura vāsanās* (kleptomaniac tendencies) will produce certain typical memories. The channellized *karmaśakti* will further lead to certain characteristic experiences, descriptions and *caura* actions with suitable *phalas*.

Types of *Karmas*: The factor of freedom or volition on the part of the embodied agents puts *karmas* under two categories: *puruṣakāra* and *bhogabhūta karmas*. The former is what the agent does with his free will, and it is to these actions that the word *karma* can properly be attributed. In the latter case, the agent's will is completely overpowered by the functioning of the *karaṇas*, e.g., digestion, circulation, falling on the ground, doing something under gunpoint, habitual and impulsive actions, etc. The latter kind of actions are compulsively performed under the influence of past *saṃskāras* and external forces, while the former resist the flow of *saṃskāras* in some way or other. *Karmas*, once performed, accumulate a store of *saṃskāras*, which must lay out its scheduled *phalas* without the possibility of an exception or circumvention. However, the agent has full power to transform the existing trend of *saṃskāras* into a new trend through conscious training and cultivation. One has the option to introspect, comprehend the harmful effects of, say, *krodha saṃskāras* or *caura saṃskāras*, and mutate the trend by consciously desisting from new acts of *krodha* and *caura*. According to *Yogasūtra* (III.9, 10), 'an action is destroyed by an opposite action; similarly, a *saṃskāra* is destroyed by opposite *saṃskāras*, e.g., *krodha saṃskāra* is destroyed by *akrodha saṃskāra*.

The precepts of *Gītā* III.33–43 summarily concur with this. Though the bent of human nature (*prakṛti*) is predominantly evil, the evil disposition operates not automatically but invariably by appealing to our lower or sensuous self. While our impulsive reactions are not voluntary, our negotiations with impulses are voluntary and leave room for moral judgment. One has the freedom to realize that '[i]n respect of every object of sense there is love or hatred [and that] [o]ne should not come under the sway of either for they are one's foes' (*Gītā* III.37). One has the freedom to respond to the injunction: '*Kāma* and *krodha* — craving and wrath, born of the mode of passion — are the most sinful. Do thou subjugate them first so that you may bring down the ruinous foe' (*Gītā* III.37). On the whole, one has the freedom to understand his own *prakṣti* to decide which kind of work is best suited to him, which impulses to give vent to and which impulses to temper or control.

However, *Gītā*'s injunction of moral duties in accordance with one's *vaṛa* or caste actually falls back on a four-fold categorization of human nature (*svadharma*) (XVIII.41–44), which accommodates little interpenetration. Supposing that each category is a set pattern of *saṃskāras*, the question that arises is: to what extent would *Gītā* permit one to mutate them from one mould into another?

Draupadī in the *Mahābhārata* clarifies the nature of *puruṣakāra* as that which does not fall back either on providence or on sudden and sporadic coincidences (*Āraṇyakaparvan* 33.10, 11). While an agent does achieve some virtues by worshipping the gods, man, by performing *puruṣakāra* with his own efforts, achieves publicly observable results (*Āraṇyakaparvan* 33.16).

The fruits of *karma* categorized under three heads (*jāti*, *āyus* and *bhogaphala*) are direct and natural (*svābhāvika*). Strictly speaking, *phala* is the *vipāka*, the manifestation of natural powers of the internal organs and *karma*. This rules out the irregular (*naimittika*) consequences of external contingencies. For instance a person's intellectual endeavour will lead to cerebral excellence, as well as to appropriate changes in *jāti*, *āyus* and *bhogaphala*. But consequences like getting a high position or a high salary or social reputation are, again, not direct fruitions of *karma*. As Draupadī also points out, what a person achieves by the sheer force of his efforts is the *svābhāvika phala* (*Āraṇyakaparvan* 33.17). Drinking contaminated water works on our biological system and causes cholera. But contracting cholera is not causally determined by our *saṃskāras* of ignorance. The action of planting and watering a plant leads naturally to *bhogaphala* in our mind and not to the fruition of the plant. The latter is a natural manifestation of the inherent powers of the plant and not that of our act of watering. None of these external consequences are directly linked with our *saṃskāras*: it is the way we are affected by these external conditions (social reputation, cholera, fruition of the plant) that is the natural manifestation of our *saṃskāras* which are, properly speaking, the *phalas* of our actions.

Looked at this way, all internal, natural and supernatural consequences are directly or indirectly the fruits of our own actions. For, being thrown in this anomalous world of constant dangers and contingencies is ironically a regular and inviolable consequence of our own actions. One should thus shift his focus from *naimittika phalas* or external contingencies and focus on the internal ones. Attaining liberation from this trap of inviolable contingencies through strong *puruṣakāra* of spiritual exercises is also the fruit of our own actions.

We need to appreciate that while the external consequences of actions can be evaded or given away this does not apply to the internal fruits of our *karma saṃskāras* by any means. The doctrine of *niṣkāma karma* enjoins us not to nullify the natural fruits of our *karma*, for it is an impossible feat. What it enjoins us to do is, first, to renounce the indirect fruits noted earlier, and, second, to renounce the natural fruits as well, i.e., perform the action for the sake of action alone and not greed of the natural fruits, such as a better *jāti* in the next life, more *āyus* and a greater proportion of pleasure.

Thus, to the long inventory of translations of *karma*, *adhikāra* and *mā* of *Gītā* II.47, as well as the various modes of their semantic interplay recorded by Sibaji Bandyopadhyay, we can venture to add yet another (Bandyopadhyay 2010). We suggest that all these three expressions, as well as the term *phala*, have a double meaning at the same time. The particle *mā* means factual negation (*na*) of (unstated) *adhikāra*, where *adhikāra* means a *causal relation* between *karma* and *phala* (*naimittika* fruits). At the same time, *mā* means moral prohibition of (unstated) *adhikāra* in the sense of craving with respect to *phala*, i.e., *svābhāvika* fruits.

Further, principles of division classify actions as: (*a*) *dharma* or *śukla*, (*b*) *dharmādharma* or *śukla–kṛṣṇa*, (*c*) *adharma* or *kṛṣṇa*, and (*d*) *aśukla–akṛṣṇa*. Purely *dharma karma*s or *śukla karma*s, including ceremonies, are those that abstain from sinful activities like torturing, or killing plants or animals. All *dharma karma*s which are of a nature opposed to *avidyā*[4] fall into four major categories: (*a*) cultivation of peace, stability and equanimity of mind, i.e., destroying its *rajas* qualities and attaining *sāttvika* ones; (*b*) reflecting on God as the abode of all excellence that the agent comes presently to attain for himself; (*c*) charitable actions and giving up of attachment to material possessions; and (*d*) serving others and thus outgrowing one's ego. The *Mīmāṃsaka*s hold that the fruits of *yajña*s (sacrifices), whether perceptible or imperceptible (*dṛṣṭa* or *adṛṣṭa*) are generated by *karma* itself, without falling back on the external regulation of God. It is the collective will of the agents of sacrifice (whether uttered in the phonetic form of *mantra*s [hymns] or not) that have the mesmeric power of generating fruits through the process of offerings in the sacrificial fire of the *yajña*. However, all such *dharma karma*s can be performed with a view to attaining pleasure or happiness and, perhaps, cannot be *niṣkāma* in the proper sense of the term.

Thus, all actions — whether *bhogabhūta* or *puruṣakāra*; whether *sāttvika*, *rājasika* or *tāmasika*; whether *dharma*, *adharma* or *dharmādharma* — are evidently conceived and defined in the foundational framework (ibid.: 48–60), where the pre-actional *saṃskāra*s are ontically delinked from actions, just to form a rigourous closure over them and their *phala*s. When Yudhiṣṭhira stated that the fruits of virtue and vice, the root and destruction of actions, have a mysterious illusive energy which is kept in secrecy (*Āraṇyakaparvan* 32.33, 34), he probably referred

[4] *Avidyā* may be generally characterized as ignorance of the distinction between soul and physical matter.

to the intractable workings of the *saṃskāras*. Whether the *karmas* are grafted in a *satkāryavāda* or *ārambhavāda* scheme,[5] whether the agent is working *under* the sway of *saṃskāras* or *away* from them with the objective of reforming one's character-traits, *saṃskāras* *have* to be interspersed between the agent and the action.

Wittgenstein against Sāṃskārika *Foundations of* Sakāma Karma

Wittgenstein's reflections on unconscious wishes and motives, disposition, memory, and action (the last already discussed at length in Section 1.1), if given a systematic exposition, will bring out the inherent folly of the theory of *saṃskāras*.

First, memory and the subsequent actions, along with their *phalas*, cannot be explained as revival of *saṃskāras* (*vāsanā* and *karmāśaya*). Insofar as the similarity among a cluster of *vāsanās* as well as that between the cluster and the present experience is not consciously registered, the talk of such a group floating up to the conscious surface on a suitable occasion does not make sense.

Second, it may be granted for the sake of an argument that an objective (but unperceived) similarity is sufficient for the *saṃskāra* to be revoked in the shape of an image, and it is having this image that constitutes memory. However, whether the quality of 'pastness' can be said to be inscribed into the image (in the manner as redness may be) for the subject to represent is a matter of extreme contention.

An alternative metaphorical description in terms of the subject 'hauling up an image from the deep abyss of the past' does not explain memory. For the subject to have a notion of the past shows that he already has memory, and this phenomenon cannot figure as a non-circular explanation of memory. Man learns the concept of past by remembering (Wittgenstein 1984: 231), just as man learns the meanings of words and sentences in and through an incomplete flow of uses, not through grasping rules, ostension or brain-patterns, for such activities themselves are interpretative exercises.

Memory-images do not come with a special characteristic distinguishable from those of other mental images (ibid., Section 166). It is not conceivable that someone remembers for the first time in his life and says: 'Yes, now I know what remembering is, what it feels like'. We can, on the other hand, speak of learning what the phenomenological quality of a particular experience of 'tingling' is, when we get an electric shock for the first time in life (ibid., 231). Here, Wittgenstein clearly suggests that remembering is a game that we need to learn to play in the course of our lives. As he further explains (ibid., Section 604), our recognition of an object or a task (e.g., writing, driving, doing a sum) as that we have seen or learnt before, consists not in two images or two groups of images — one past

[5] *Satkāryavāda* is a doctrine that holds the effect as already latent in its material cause, while *ārambhavāda* considers the effect to be a new beginning that cannot be traced in its material cause.

and the other present — but in fusing them into one. In other words, this aspectual transition of one into the other is not an identification of a 'pastness' in the so-called memory-images reappearing in the present; it consists in a difference in 'fine shades of behaviour', which have 'important consequences' (Wittgenstein 1984: 204). It is my affirmation/denials in response to certain queries, my reaction of being surprised/not surprised at the present encounter with the object, my style in maneuvering with the object by drawing a picture, giving a model or a description — all these bits and pieces of behaviour that will shape up the difference between recognition and non-recognition; it does not hark back on the unconscious traces or objective essence of pastness (Further elaborations on the theme can be found in Wittgenstein 1984: 197, 198, 206, 207).

Let us now take note of the main thrust of Wittgenstein's critique of the Freudian theory of the unconscious before it can be fruitfully applied against the theory of unconscious *saṃskāras* (Wittgenstein 1967; Cioffi 1991). Generally, the Freudians look upon certain dream-experiences as calling forth a causal explanation in terms of unconscious wishes and motives. On Freud's conception of the unconscious when Dora speaks of Frau K's 'adorable white body' it is a homoerotic infatuation lying deep down in the unconscious, waiting to be discovered by Freud. Wittgenstein gives another example: while walking along the river with his friend, Taylor, Taylor extends his arm and pushes Wittgenstein into the river (Wittgenstein 1967; Cioffi 1991: 177). For Freud, even if Taylor describes the action 'as shooting out his arm to point to the church spire', it leaves open the possibility of the action being 'unconsciously intentional', that is, being caused by an unconscious rivalry with his friend that Taylor feels. For Wittgenstein, in all these cases, the Freudians failed to realize that such descriptions are simply clarifications and analyses; they call for further elucidations that are internal to the experience or action, making them what they are, and hence cannot be externalized in the shape of causal hypotheses (Wittgenstein 1980a: 68; Cioffi 1991: 169–73). Often, such descriptions are the less manifest features of the narrative, yet which gives it the substantial content, and of which the subject is capable of coming to a more explicit cognition (Wittgenstein 1967: 45–50; Cioffi 1991: 171). Such terms as 'less manifest' and 'more explicit' do not point to a realm of unconscious, but to certain features that belonged to a neglected phase before being absorbed into the ever-expanding body of meaning. The way Taylor described his action calls for not an unconscious rivalry but further inputs like a mild irritation slowly working up towards his companion coupled with callousness in his movements.[6] It is these neglected aspects of the narration that are added on; they always lay on the surface and not in the depths of the unconscious.

[6] Wittgenstein gave a different treatment of this example, one that Cioffi thinks does not go in his favour (see Wittgenstein 1967, Section 18, 19; Cioffi 1991: 177). We, however, have taken the liberty to use it in favour of the general direction of his critique.

Let us extend the crux of this critique to the theory of unconscious *sāṃskārika* foundations. A person's experience and description of particular objects, as well as his habitual actions of stealing them, cannot be traced back to his unconscious *caura saṃskāras* (kleptomaniac traces) which is absent in the case of so-called 'normal' descriptions and actions. The difference between a kleptomaniac and a non-kleptomaniac lies in the differences in subtle shades of descriptions and behaviour that they will exhibit when asked to present a picture, a model or a story of the object, or other relevant transactions. These marginal details will now invade the core, get absorbed in the ever-expanding and ever-indeterminate flow of meaning and not remain as unconscious and external causes of meaning and action. In other words, the so-called *sāṃskārika* foundations never foreclose actions and their *phalas*, but spread out in an incomplete and indefinite flow of verbal and non-verbal engagements. The hidden depths of the unconscious have to be dissipated into the immensely rich and open flow on the surface.

The stories of success and failures that come along with the *saṃskāra* -theory are misleadingly obvious. Repeated efforts of our *karaṇas* are said to turn our accumulated *saṃskāras* into power, making our efforts successful. Repeated efforts of writing generate *saṃskāras*, which, in their turn, invest our hands with the power of writing. It is by employing one's powers with superior knowledge and skill, and steadfast resolution that one's efforts become successful. Such power-theories, however powerful they may seem, are quite vulnerable to Wittgenstein's attack. He will say that superior knowledge and skill do not have an irreducibly mental content that precedes and yet entails the success of our actions. They themselves are actions, which penetrate into further actions and do not precede them. Imperceptible dispositions or powers are philosopher's myths.

The account of an agent's changing his *saṃskāras* for better or worse is open to similar treatments. Is the power to change one's *caura saṃskāras* to *a-caura saṃskāras*, or *krodha saṃskāras* to *a-krodha saṃskāras* inherent in further *saṃskāras*? Can the tool of a beginning-less cycle of *saṃskāras*, actions and *phalas* rule out the demand for an origin in time and the traditional charge of an infinite regress? Alternatively, the agent's comprehensions about the nature of his *saṃskāras* and their harmful effects are placed on a higher level so that such reflections on *saṃskāras* are themselves not subjected to *saṃskārika* determinations. (As already pointed out, *Gītā*'s precepts in III.33–43 makes room for freedom in one's negotiations with one's *saṃskāras*.) But does it amount to saying that the agent, say, the kleptomaniac, in his transactions with his *saṃskāras*, just acts as he acts, i.e., he engages in a series of *a-caura* activities foundation-lessly, in the Wittgensteinian style? No, because as per the constraints of the *saṃskāra* theory, these activities are again supposed to produce an opposite *saṃskāra* (a non-stealing or non-angry *saṃskāra*) in a reverse direction, which will again lead to the relevant memories, actions and their *phalas*. Thus, the entire second-level story also gets bogged down with false splits of a foundational mechanism.

Philosophers mistakenly think of knowledge as a state or process having a definite origin and duration. Then he tends to postulate dispositions as unconscious states of mind giving rise to conscious states of knowledge. But Wittgenstein points out that one can at best speak of dispositions in the sense of an apparatus in the brain manifesting in knowledge. The construction of this apparatus and the mechanism through which it works invoke two distinct concepts or criteria. Hence, the talk of brain apparatus manifesting in knowledge cannot be recast into the talk of an unconscious disposition giving rise to conscious state of knowledge. For Wittgenstein, this pair of terms, 'conscious' and 'unconscious', just covers up grammatical differences; it does not point to any ontical realm of the unconscious (Wittgenstein 1984, Section 149), just as the grammatical levels of nominative, comparative and superlative, e.g. sweet, sweeter and sweetest, do not point to optimal sweetness. We may add that the attempt of analytic philosophers (Carnap, Ryle for instance) to reduce disposition to a series of counter-factuals is welcome insofar as it dispenses with any realm of the unconscious.

A *sakāma karmī* may appreciate that his actions are not necessitated (but are at best inclined by) strongest *saṃskāra*s, the strongest dispositions (supposedly) created by repeated learning, or highly impassioned desires or intentions. In other words, a student, fully equipped with all mathematical competence and practical motivations, may desist from working out a problem in a test; a person, strongly bent upon stealing an object in opportune circumstances, may, at the last moment, desist from stealing. Intense desires, hopes and dispositions may stop short of the action and therein lies the freedom of the agent. But, what a *sakāma karmī* does not realize is that hopes, expectations, *saṃskāra*s, and intentions are not external or causal foundations of, but themselves penetrate into, a rich expanse of actions. This expanse, however, may not extend to certain other actions which these hopes, desires and *saṃskāras* — the supposedly mental causes — were expected to generate. The freedom of *sakāma karmī* does not lie in operating a non-necessitating causal mechanism, where some purely mental foundations incline but do not compel certain actions and their desired *phala*s. His freedom rather consists in one cluster of his actions not determining, rather not necessarily extending to, another cluster.

Niṣkāma Karma: *The Game of Non-foundationalism*

The ideal desireless actor, in our construal, does not operate in a causal or logical machine, where pre-formulated rules are supposed to generate a particular action with a unique result. He knows that rules, beliefs, conventions, or plans of action cannot compel him to act in a unique manner, but 'it makes it possible for [him] to hold by it and make it compel [him]' (Wittgenstein 1956, Part V, Section 45). He sets out with rules and plans of action as a formal or architectural requirement 'for the sake not of their content, but of their form' (Wittgenstein 1984, Section 217), not ossifying them into a closure, but fleshing them out through in an ever-incomplete flow of uses.

Let us note how our construal of *niṣkāma karma* runs along with its traditional conception in the *Gītā* before they are forced to part their ways. It is in the *sakāma karma* that the lust for *phala* tears the seamless whole and invents false devices to stitch them up. It is interesting to note in this connection that not only the ideas of personal benefits but even actions planning to achieve utilitarian ends through a causal or rationalistic mechanism turn out to be *sakāma*.

The terms *yogastha* and *samatvam* in *Gītā* II.48 connote inner composure and equanimity of mind — this is nothing but unruffled continuum of will, action and consequences. The false cleavages and lumps, false dichotomies of success and failure (*siddhi* and *asiddhi*) do not create yawning gaps in the whole, fragmenting it with anger, ambition, and pride on the one hand, and pain, doubt and despondency on the other.

Arjuna's apparent *vairāgya* (detachment) does not spring from true enlightenment but from narrow love for his kith and kin (*Gītā* I.31; II.6); it is actually faint-heartedness (*hṛdaya-daurbalyam*), it is *rāga* and not *virāga*. It is on empirical and not ultimate grounds that he adopts an attitude of inaction (*Gītā* II.3). It is the passions — the fear of losing and love for the kin — that splits up the continuum of action. Just as the desire for the 'fruits/rewards' splits up the action, so too does the fear of unpleasant consequences. For a *niṣkāma karmī*, the undesired *phala*s do not jut out but are absorbed in the actions. Arjuna is actuated not by genuine detachment, but by sadness, doubt and despondency (*viṣāda*) (*Gītā* II.1, 7). Depression and doubt come from the splitting up of the foundation of action from the action itself. The doubt about whether the rule or plan of action will lead to the desired result and not incur the fearful ones, the resignation and frustration arising out of the dilemma, and the undesirability of each consequence arising from each fork splinter the seamless whole of the action into fragments.

Yudhiṣṭhira, in a conversation with Draupadī, clearly suggests that it is the misconception of *phala*s as external to the action that crops up in the form of a sceptical attitude towards *dharma karma*s not generating their expected *phala*s, and *adharma karma*s bringing success in life (*Āraṇyakaparvan* 32.4, 5). Once a person conjures up the *phala*s as external concrete objects, he is not satiated by even by a massive quantity, while one who absorbs the *phala* into the action itself is contented with a little (*Āraṇyakaparvan* 32.19, 32, 36).

The *Gītā* heartens us to put in our best effort, assuring us that nothing that we do for self-development will go wasted. 'No such effort is lost nor is there any obstacle in the way of its coming to fruition' (*Gītā* II.40). The doer of good never comes to grief. (*Gītā* VI.40). Grief, pain, frustration, or fear of failure are lumps created by splitting the action into a foundationalist machine. Interestingly, this concept of *niṣkāma karma* seems to collapse into that of *sarvadhanī naraḥ*, which Yudhiṣṭhira defines as 'the man to whom the agreeable and the disagreeable, happiness and misery, the past and the future, are all alike' (*Āraṇyakaparvan* 297.64).

Karma-yoga is not renunciation *of* action but renunciation *in* action. The object of *Gītā* is to discover a golden mean between *pravṛtti* and *nivṛtti*,[7] and preserve the excellence of both. Both *pravṛtti* and *nivṛtti* forge a false split between desire and action. The fear that desire may cause bondage, coupled with the desire for renunciation of desire, is finally expected to lead to *mokṣa* (liberation). Ironically, such a way of renouncing actions insofar as it forges a false split between renunciation and *mokṣa* will fall under the category of *sakāma* actions.

The way we have conceived the *sakāma/niṣkāma* dichotomy as a contrast between the foundationalist and non-foundationalist games will lead to reading the role of doubt and despondency in *sakāma karma* in a different fashion. Scepticism often presupposes certain ontological myths as conceptually valid and then seeks to display our epistemological and logical tools as inadequate to match up to them. Postulating unconscious *saṃskāras*, volitions and rules of actions as pre-actional foundations, one then exercises doubts whether the foundation will be strong enough to imply the desired results. Scepticism may amount to an indulgence in formulating deviant hypotheses, externally rupturing the observed regularities in nature. This may lead to frustration or despondency, as also to renunciation *of* action and not renunciation *in* action, the former being nothing but a *sakāma karma*.

Of the fourfold categorization of *karmas* into *śukla*, *śukla–kṛṣṇa*, *kṛṣṇa* and *aśukla–akṛṣṇa*, the last one deserves special consideration. While all the other three kinds of actions keep the *karaṇas* in constant vibration, those of the fourth category are geared to a state when the *citta* will no longer undergo any modification in the form of any object (*citta nirodha*). The very sense of 'I' dissipates gradually, and without the sense of the subject there cannot be any cognition of objects. Without any cognition of objects, there is no scope of their sedimenting in the form of *saṃskāras* awaiting fructification into further *karmas*. In other words, as the conception of the object ceases to jut out of the *karma*, it also ceases to ossify into a desire for the end, thereby shaping up the *sakāma karmas*. With all *saṃskāras* exhausted, even the foundations of life-preserving activities (like digestion, respiration, etc.) are withdrawn. Thus, ironically, actions, in order to be *niṣkāma* in the strict sense of the term, need to nullify all representations, and ultimately all actions: *jñānāgni sarvakarmāṇi bhasmasāt kurute tathā* (*Gītā* IV.37). Positively speaking, the negative ideal of *kaivalya* (abstraction of the self) can be understood in the positive connotations of *ātmaśuddhi* and *brahmabhūyām* (*Gita* V.11; III.30).

Let us take *aśukla–akṛṣṇa karmas* that lead to the cessation of all actions and a dissipation of the subject as *niṣkāma karmas* in the true sense of the term. There is no way in which one can gloss over the foundationalist mechanism in which it operates: the entire system of the *saṃskāras* manifesting in *karmas* and *karma*

[7] *Pravṛtti* and *nivṛtti* are the two ideals of life. The former recommends living in the society and abiding by its obligations. The second stands for the negative ideal of renunciation.

phalas, and the device through which it changes into the intended direction have to be presupposed if the actions are ultimately to peter out in *samādhi* ('complete concentration') or *mokṣa*. Given this notion of *niṣkāma karma* in its richest and optimal content, can we distil it of its ontological baggage of *sāṃskārika* mechanism and the pure subject that *mokṣa* essentially invokes?

For Wittgenstein, it is through a series of progressive contrasts that the talk of pure subject or dissipation of subject/object dichotomy gets its sense. To 'turn my attention to my own consciousness' is to engage in a particular mode of behaviour: 'staring fixedly in front of me — but not at any particular point or object', glances are vacant, like someone admiring the illumination of the sky or drinking in the light (Wittgenstein 1984, Section 412). It is such clusters of uses that constitutes consciousness, one can go on contriving consciousness of consciousness of consciousness . . . by enacting clusters of clusters of clusters . . . in a series of gradual progression until he stops out of fatigue or boredom or any other philosophically unimportant reason. We can clarify this point with the help of another instance. The talk of 'absolute motion' gets its sense through an exercise of, say, constructing in computer graphics different sets of planets in ascending order of levels, where planets of each of the higher levels kept track of the actual motion, rest, velocity of the planets in the immediately lower rung. We do not capture the sense of 'absolute motion' by putting a supreme planet at the end of space so to speak, beyond mass, gravitation or any mode of relativization. (This line of argument is developed from Wittgenstein's comment in 1984, p. 53, footnote.) To use another example, '[A] proof that 777 occurs in the expansion of p, without showing where' works through evoking an image of a 'dark zone of indeterminate length very far on in p', where we can no longer rely on our devices for calculating'. Then, further out, we imagine another zone where we can again see something 'in a *different* way' (Wittgenstein 1956, Part IV, Section 27). The proof of absolute subject also thrives on a process of posing subjects of subjects . . . , as a tantalizingly long zone with a blurred edge where we magically cross over the indeterminate region and bump our head against the absolute subject — the terminus of *karma*. Here suddenly our discourse takes a different turn — from an innocuous play of grammatical contrasts to an ontological commitment. We think that after all we must be weaving a piece of cloth (the pure subject so to speak) 'because [we] are sitting at a loom — even if it is empty — and going through the motions of weaving' (Wittgenstein 1984, Section 414).

On our construal in the Wittgensteinian fashion, a *niṣkāma karmī* would not be one who ceases to represent or to act, but one who ceases to ossify objects and actions into a closure. He deploys all foundations of cognition or action (so-called real essences, ostensions, verbal rules, intentions, volitions, etc.) as architectonic or formal requirements. Wittgenstein elaborates this with special reference to rules: a rule does not compel me to act like this but 'it makes it possible for me to hold by it and make it compel me' (Wittgenstein 1956, Part V, Section 45). And it is an interesting fact, rather an interesting form of living that people set up rules for pleasure and then hold by them (ibid.). Our *niṣkāma karmī* perhaps realizes that '[o]ur requirement is an architectural one; . . . a kind of ornamental coping that supports nothing' (Wittgenstein 1984, Section 217). It is like constructing an ornamental gateway at the entrance of a building, or writing a caption at the beginning of a film, or designing a decorative cover of a book, where we find pleasure in using a picture, the picture of the entrance-structure or the beginning caption, somehow suggesting or even encapsulating the entire content of the building or the film. To a *niṣkāma karmī*, a rule seems like a 'short bit of hand rail' by means of which one can let himself be guarded further than the rail reaches' (Wittgenstein 1956, Part V, Section 45). 'But', Wittgenstein adds, 'there *is* nothing there; but there isn't *nothing* there' (ibid.). For a *niṣkāma karmī*, the need for a handrail, the architectonic need for an entrance-structure and the '*deep* need' for setting ad hoc ethical conventions and obeying them (Wittgenstein 1956, Part I, Section 74) are themselves not conventions. They are nothing short of our forms of living.

A *niṣkāma karmī* knows how to play the contrastive games with 'I' in an ongoing series of grammatical contrasts without lapsing into an ontological commitment. For him, the talk of 'absolute values' of ethics acquires its significance not from an ontological goodness, but rather in the same way as does the talk of 'absolute motion'.[8] For him, explanation or justification of language and action ends not in the cessation of action, but in the action itself — in simply what we do — in the forms of life (Wittgenstein 1984, Section: 217). The meaning of this phrase, however, gets enriched in further and further actions, in further forms of living — without sinking into a dubious domain of silence.

A Non-Foundational Reading of Yudhiṣṭhira's Actions

All these negotiations against the pre-actional foundations of actions get re-instated in the fictional narrative of the epic — a narrative unimaginably rich and multi-layered — where each character lives out his life through unpredictable vicissitudes in real time. Wittgenstein's attack on foundations can be best carried out through his 'look and see' (ibid., Section 66) or 'use'-survey method (ibid., Sections 30, 43, 120, 138, etc.) applied to the life of Yudhiṣṭhira, the hero of the epic. Yudhiṣṭhira was pre-ordained to be the foremost in all virtues — as truthful, powerful, ruler of the earth (*Ādiparvan* 114.7). We might say that according to the official doctrine of *karma*, these traits are the *saṃskāra*s that constitute his character and are supposed to unfold in pre-determined manner. Yet, we find an appreciable number of

[8] The somewhat scattered and unclear reflections on 'absolute values' by Wittgenstein (1965) need to be synthesized with the more complete and well-designed arguments in Wittgenstein (1984), particularly with respect to issues like measurement of absolute quantity and mathematical necessity.

his actions running contrary to these character-traits and his explicit professions. Without going into a theoretical engagement with the criteria of 'good' or 'bad', we shall first focus on those actions which are intuitively or common-sensically 'bad' or 'ignoble', rather 'uncharacteristic' of a character that is virtue incarnate. On the whole, we try to show that while his noble actions do not follow from his noble character — a supposedly perfect harmony of just beliefs, intentions and dominantly noble *saṃskāras* — his 'ignoble' or questionable actions also cannot be explained or justified on the basis of ignorance, false beliefs, situational codes of ethics, or non-dominant *saṃskāras*, all of which are supposed to fall in the margin without disrupting the dominant 'virtuous' core. We shall be primarily deploying his actions of the 'ignoble' category — a considerable number of its instances — without attempting to create an inventory of all of them scattered over the colossal text.

To start with the *Ādiparvan*, many of Yudhiṣṭhira's actions were connivances, and they challenge the customary divide between errors of commission and those of omission. When with Arjuna's persuasion, Droṇa trapped Ekalavya into cutting off his right thumb (*Ādiparvan* 123.26–38), when Kṛpācārya openly denied Karṇa the chance of a fair competition with Kuru princes because of his supposedly humble lineage (*Ādiparvan* 126.32), when Bhīma abused Karṇa with banally obscene metaphors (*Ādiparvan* 127.7), or later when Karṇa was again refused by Draupadī in the *svayaṃvara* on grounds of his caste (*Ādiparvan* 1828*.9), Yudhiṣṭhira did not object. It is clear that invoking such beliefs in his mind as 'the superiority of the ruling dynasty needs to be maintained', does not encapsulate a pre-applicational content from which we can extract this action. The suggested rule or belief is posterior to the actual acts of connivance and not the other way round.

Let us shift to those deeds which can more palpably be ascribed to Dharmarāja's own agency. Following Droṇa's command to take revenge on Drupada (*Ādiparvan* 128.2) meant killing ordinary men in the battlefield (*Ādiparvan* App. 78.53pr–56pr), and shows that the meanings of predicates, viz., *dhārmika* (*Ādiparvan* 114.7), *dhṛti*, *sthairya*, *udāratā*, *anṛśaṃsya*, customarily ascribed to Yudhiṣṭhira (*Ādiparvan* App. 80.3pr) are to be flexible enough to accommodate these acts. Protecting the well-being of subjects is the duty of a monarch, and indeed it is said that during the reign of Yudhiṣṭhira there was fair realization of taxes, absence of any kind of oppression, smooth administration, safety and security, and truthfulness on the part of the subjects. Being righteous to everyone without discrimination, he was looked upon as a father figure by his subjects (*Sabhāparvan* App.16.4 pr, *Sabhāparvan* 145*.1pr). What is the exceptional ethical code that Yudhiṣṭhira might have adopted when he invited the *niṣāda* family, set fire to the Jatugṛha (house of lac), and left them to be charred to death beyond recognition? (*Ādiparvan* 136.4). Perhaps, it is something of the following form: 'few persons can be sacrificed for the security of the monarchs and thus for the greater good for the majority'. Whether 'greater good' can sustain or absorb this killing is not inscribed into the code prior to the act, but later fed into it. Here, again, the general rules are evidently feeding from the particular instances and not containing them in their reservoirs.

The marriage of Draupadī to the five Pāṇḍavas in accordance with Kuntī's command (*Ādiparvan* 182.2) presents a complex interplay of many factors. Here, there are two arguments working in two directions, both seeking to derive the legitimacy of this marriage. As all the Pāṇḍavas were overpowered by their passion for Draupadī (*Ādiparvan* 178.12), one possible rule of action would be the principle of preserving the fraternity among all the brothers. The more important and interesting twist that the argument takes is when it seeks to derive moral rightness of the action from the fact that it seems just to him and his mother. His mother cannot utter a command which is violable; his own mind cannot turn to what is sinful (*Ādiparvan* 187.29). Again, in the standard doctrine, such cognitions or representations are manifestations of their unconscious 'just' *saṃskāras*. These *saṃskāras* were further traced back to their past births, wherein Draupadī and the Pāṇḍavas were deities and were pre-ordained to be married in their next birth (*Ādiparvan* 189.47). Such a story hauled up from the previous birth does not even have the semblance with a significant application of the theory of *saṃskāras*, attempting to withstand the force of the Wittgensteinian critique. Yudhiṣṭhira's assertion, i.e., *sūkṣmo dharma mahārāja nāsya vidmo vayaṃ gatim* (*Ādiparvan* 187.28), should be taken as how the *meaning* of '*dharma*' (and not *dharma* itself) associated with mono-andry creeps on subtle and unpredictable paths as the meanings of 'man' and 'woman' shade into deities and the present birth spills back into the past.

This phenomenon of 'all' in the major premise fleshing out bit by bit from the particular conclusions betrays the non-foundational character of logic itself; it is not peculiar to the case of deducing human actions. We do not appreciate this in case of stock syllogisms like 'all men are mortal, Ram is a man, and therefore Ram is mortal'. But take examples like: 'All facts are concatenation of simples, That it rained in Delhi on 20 August 2010 is a fact, Therefore that it . . . 2010 is a concatenation of simples'. To take another one: '[A]ll objects can be conceived under different aspects, This chessboard is an object, Therefore this chessboard can be conceived under alternative aspects like 32 black squares and 32 white squares or as colours black and white and a schema of squares (This argument is based on an example from Wittgenstein 1984, Section 47). Here, evidently, the concepts of facts, simples, concatenation, or how to conceive different aspects of an object flesh out through particular instances; the latter are not implicitly contained in the former. The premises of a logical deduction put up the stance of adding predicates to subjects in a linear fashion; actually, the subjects are shaped anew, bit by bit, through every predication. The traditional charge of circularity brought against logic feeds on an imagery — that of rules, definitions and quantifiers tying down an infinite mass of particulars under a closed and completed circle, and then extracting each individual application one by one from its hidden reserve. For Wittgenstein, on the other hand, logic does not encapsulate its applications in a closed circle, but carves out newer and newer circles with each application. The rules of action figuring as the major premises in each of the mentioned syllogisms carve out a new circle with each particular action (Wittgenstein 1956, Part II, Section 2; Part II, Section 3).

In the context of two consecutive games of dice in the *Sabhāparvan*, the vacuity of the general principles of action comes up again through multilayered contradictions between the following statements of Yudhiṣṭhira:

(*a*) Being summoned to both the games of dice, he says that the whole universe is at the will of the creator and under the control of fate (*Sabhāparvan* 51.25, 14). In other words, he says that it is due to fate or providence that he is destined to lose his kingdom, whether he plays or not.
(*b*) He further says that once challenged to a game of dice, he, as a monarch, should always observe his duty to rise up to the challenge (*Sabhāparvan* 56.16).
(*c*) In a subsequent conversation with Bhīma, he says that he plays out of greed, in order to win the kingdom from the Kauravas (*Āraṇyakaparvan* 35.2).
(*d*) In a later conversation with Draupadī, he states that he *always* (i.e., without exceptions) performs actions in a *niṣkāma* fashion (*Āraṇyakaparvan* 32.2, 3).
(*e*) In another conversation with Bhīma, he admits that his playing the dice has brought about a disaster and he should have been prevented by Bhīma (*Āraṇyakaparvan* 35.16).

First of all, (*a*) contradicts (*b*), for if obeying Dhṛtarāṣṭra's command to play dice is determined by fate then taking up the challenge cannot be a moral duty, for morality patently involves freedom. Again, (*c*) contradicts (*d*), for they express conflicting motives. (*a*) contradicts (*c*) because if he comprehends that he is destined to lose his kingdom his motivation to snatch the kingdom from the Kauravas becomes somewhat inexplicable. (*c*) manifestly contradicts (*d*), the former being a confession of doing a *sakāma* action, while the latter, a declaration that admits of no exception. All this shows that Yudhiṣṭhira's plunging into the game of dice — sometimes characterized as controlled by *daiva*; sometimes, as determined by his own *saṃskāras* (either passion for dice or greed for the kingdom); sometimes, again, as a moral duty of a monarch; sometimes, as morally (justly) preventable (by Bhīma); and sometimes as *niṣkāma* and sometimes as *sakāma* — could not have been contained in any pre-actional foundation. No ad hoc rule of action that may have been deployed in this case has any predictive power; it is just concocted with a vacuous universal garb.

The concept of *dyūta* or gambling itself shows how semantic indeterminacy breaks through the power of a logical mechanism supposed to entail one's actions. The concept of game was taken by Wittgenstein as the perfect example, wherein a supposedly fixed and unitary essence was first externally ruptured by new fibres coming in and dropping out of old fibres; and then the fibres themselves rupturing from within. (This is clearly suggested by Wittgenstein 1984, Section 66, in his statement that skill in chess does not detach itself to recur as skill in tennis.) There is no way to distill the concept of game in terms of 'fair competition', 'attack and counter-attack', or 'sheer skill without any element of luck', that will decidedly exclude gambling from its purview. Wittgenstein's observations on this specific instance of gambling (ibid.: 33) shows that however Yudhiṣṭhira may have verbally defined the term 'game', sharpened their features, engaged in a mental act of intention or silent speech to draw a boundary around the 'decent' and 'honest' games, he could not have laid hold upon a verbal or a mental foundation to cut out dice or *dyūta*. As Śakuni exhorted: 'Deceit (*nikṛti*) cannot be fixed as the essence of dice for in this game; deceit is attacked by a counter-deceit, and the expert players who know the secrets of winning and losing, who are skilled in baffling the deceitful arts can withstand or absorb all deceit' (*Sabhāparvan* 52.4). When Yudhiṣṭhira still objected that counter-deceit is itself deceitful (*Sabhāparvan* 52.6–10), Śakuni argued that it is the characteristic of every contest that a man with superior knowledge, power or skill approaches it with the desire of vanquishing the opponent. They are the celebrations of superiority which are by no means dishonest or deceitful (*Sabhāparvan* 52.11).

We now know how to handle the situational codes that Yudhiṣṭhira might have adopted in his attempts to pump out the secret strategies of killing the great heroes (Bhīṣma, Droṇa and Kṛpācārya) who were fighting on the Kaurava side. (These requests are placed in the *Bhīṣmaparvan* [41.40, 42; 41.56.; and 41.69, respectively].) The tortuous conflict that Yudhiṣṭhira underwent in choosing between the two motivations — one of killing his kin and the other of losing his legitimate kingdom breaks out in his conversation with Kṛpācārya (*Bhīṣmaparvan* 41.69) and also, to some extent, in his camouflaged lie to Droṇa (*Droṇaparvan* 164.106). A relevant question that arises at this juncture is whether such moral dilemmas imply that one engages in two mutually compatible judgments on the class of actions — one on their prima facie desirability and the other on the prima facie undesirability — before he arrives at the unconditional all-out judgment on the absolute desirability of the action he performs. This is suggested by Davidson with respect to deliberation or choice between conflicting desires, though not with specific reference to moral dilemmas (Davidson 2001; Evnine 1991: 56–57). For him, wants or desires are prima facie judgments on the desirability of an action, while intentions or intentional actions have the form of unconditional judgments. We can accept this view subject to two reservations: first, Wittgenstein's reflections on intentions show that they cannot be confined within the formal closure of an isolated judgment (whether conditional or unconditional); and, second, any argument that might have been deployed to move from the prima facie judgments to the unconditional ones, will not operate within the foundational mechanism.[9]

Yudhiṣṭhira, in his prolonged conversation with Arjuna, confesses that he is completely overpowered by Karṇa; whether awake or asleep, he hallucinates Karṇa everywhere; his entire universe is pervaded by him (*Karṇaparvan* 46.19, 20). The way Yudhiṣṭhira indulged in a graphic imagination of Karṇa's slain and mutilated body betrays an intense voyeurism — visually feasting on the mangled body of his arch-enemy. (*Karṇaparvan* 46.36). This is a paradigmatic example of a *sakāma karma* — perhaps of the *rājasika* variety — where the extreme lust for the end gives rise to a plethora of turbulent emotions. Angst, fear, sense of shame and humiliation (at being captured and released by Karṇa in the battlefield) (*Karṇaparvan* 46.22), intolerance, the 'fire of vindictiveness fanned by the wind of mortification' (*Karṇaparvan* 46.48) — all these tear up the action into false fragments. Interactions with Karṇa, if carried out in the *niṣkāma* fashion, would have absorbed all undesired consequences into the action itself, submerging all the emotions into a peaceful equanimity (*Gītā* II.48, discussed in Section 1.4). The patently foundational device that Yudhiṣṭhira had been deploying in this *sakāma* interactions with Karṇa becomes explicit in his statement that he, for the past 13 years, had been avidly looking for the final *phala*, viz., the killing of Karṇa, resting assured that the auxiliary causes (*daiva*) in the person of Arjuna will function at proper time (*Karṇaparvan* 680*.3). Incidentally, Yudhiṣṭhira had already made arrangements with Śalya to be the charioteer of Karṇa so that he (Śalya) can contrive schemes of detracting him from his optimal performance, knowing fully well that such an act is blatantly immoral. (*Udyogaparvan* 8.27). Once the desire for *phala* splits it from the action itself and seeks to extract it from external foundations, failure or *aprāpti* leads to unhealthy emotions and perverse abuses hurled at Arjuna (*Karṇaparvan* 48.1–3). All these actions constitute Yudhiṣṭhira's character and penetrate into the so-called 'virtuous' core. They are not occasional, sporadic and peripheral manifestations of some certain ignoble *saṃskāras* lying weak and dormant beneath the more dominant and easily retrievable upper layer of the virtuous ones.[10]

---

9 While B. K. Matilal rightly points out that there cannot be any 'perfect organization of one's life-plan' in a way that precludes all dilemmas and conflicts (Ganeri 2002), he seems not to appreciate that the ad hoc means and situational codes also do not have the power of unique entailment.

10 One can, however, say that all such exercises are futile because the author/s of the epic were by no means unfolding the characters in a spontaneous style; rather, they were deliberately contriving and/or interpolating anomalies and inconsistencies in each character as a dramatic device to introduce variations, abrupt changes in the direction of the plot, or create anti-climatic situations. One can accept this only to take it back to the basic insight that the literary techniques of dramatizing a narrative are themselves not abrupt, nor are they mechanical extractions from a pre-conceived reservoir. The author's architectonic conception of a character fleshes out, bit by bit, through the dramatic or un-dramatic actions.

Let us not enter into the exemplary virtuous deeds of Dharmarāja Yudhiṣṭhira; they are overwhelming in number and heavily laden with commentaries. We just need to appreciate in keeping with our present mode of treatment that all his noble deeds lose their charm and grandeur once they are frozen into the reservoir of syllogism. A few of these instances from the *Āraṇyakaparvan*, the *Mahāprasthānikaparvan* and the *Svargārohaṇaparvaṇ* are his exercise of the 'just' choice in reviving Nakula when he could have opted for Bhīma and Arjuna (*Āraṇyakaparvan* 297.71, 73), rescuing Duryodhana from being killed by the Gandharva king Citrasena (*Āraṇyakaparvan* 235.12–14), sacrificing the bliss of heaven for the sake of a dog (*Mahāprasthānikaparvan* 3.7, 11) accepting the torture of hell to be with his kin (*Svargārohaṇaparvan* 2.52). Yudhiṣṭhira is not extracting the desirability of each action from a general principle of morality, whether or not his arguments have the appearance of a foundational operation. To recall his statement, he will not enter into heaven leaving the dog behind since it is his vow never to give up a person who is terrified, devoted, destitute, weak and in need of protection (*Mahāprasthānikaparvan* 3.11). In such arguments, Yudhiṣṭhira is not operating with pure predicates or bare properties and attaching them to bare individuals, so to speak. Rather each case of predication applied to a new instance in the minor premises and conclusion newly reshapes the individual (the individual dog in this instance). As already noted, it is in this sense that the universal quantifier 'all' in the major premises fleshes out bit by bit through each particular predication.

Concluding Remarks

If, non-judgmentally, we just *describe* Yudhiṣṭhira's actions without any universality — claiming a view that simply fleshes out (and does not *explain*) an action in terms of specific beliefs and desires, without expelling the fruit of the action from the ambit of the action itself — it becomes easier to understand how someone like Yudhiṣṭhira — sincere, honest, authentic, well-brought up, self-critical but with the normal dose of human frailty — could aspire to act for the sake of the action alone, while engaged in worldly works, in a sorry world where neither divine parentage nor divine friendship guarantees happiness as a reward of virtue, but the action at best becomes its own fruit. He does not always succeed. But he could try. So could we.

References

Aranya, Shreemat Svami Hariharanda (ed.). 1369 (Bangabda). *Karmatattva* (Bengali). Madhupur: Kapil Math.

Bandyopadhyay, Sibaji. 2009. 'Translating *Gītā* II.47 Or Inventing the National Motto', *Studies in Humanities and Social Sciences*, 16(1–2): 31–94.

Bhaduri, Nrisinga Prasad. 1998. *Krishna, Kunti Ebong Kaunteya* (Bengali). Kolkata: Ananda Publishers.

Bhattacharya, Shreemat Haridas Siddhantabagish (trans.). 1392 (Bangabda [Bengali Era]). *Mahābharāta*. Kolkata: Bishvabani Prakashani.

Bhattacharya, Sukhamoy and Saptatirtha Shastree. *Mahabharater Charitabali* (Bengali). Kolkata: Ananda Publishers.

Bose, Rajshekhar (trans.). 1394 (Bangabda). *Mahabharata: Saranubada*. Kolkata: A.C. Sirkar & Sons Pvt Ltd.

Cioffi, Frank. 1991. 'Wittgenstein on Freud's Abominable Mess', in A. Phillips Griffiths (ed.), *Wittgenstein Centenary Essays*, pp. 169–92. Cambridge: Cambridge University Press.

Dancy, Jonathan. 1985. *An Introduction to Contemporary Epistemology*. Oxford: Basil Blackwell.

Davidson, Donald. 2001. *Essays on Actions and Events*. Oxford: Clarendon Press.

Dutta, M. N. (trans.). 2001. *Mahābharāta*. New Delhi: Parimal Publications.

Evnine, Simon. 1991. *Donald Davidson*. Cambridge: Polity Press.

Ganeri, J. (ed.). 2002. *Epics and Ethics: The Collected Essays of B. K. Matilal*. New Delhi: Oxford University Press.

Glock, Hans-Johann. 1996. *A Wittgenstein Dictionary*. Oxford: Basil Blackwell.

Hiriyanna, M. 2005. *Outlines of Indian Philosophy*. New Delhi: Motilal Banarsidass.

Lal, P. 1980. *The Mahabharata of Vyasa*. New Delhi: Vikas Publishing House.

Radhakrishnan, S. (trans.). 1949. *The Bhagavadgītā*. London: George Allen & Unwin.

Scheer, Richard K. 1991. 'Wittgenstein's Indeterminism', *Philosophy*, 66(255): 5–23.

Sukthankar, V. S. (ed.). 1943. *The Mahābharāta*. Pune: Bhandarkar Oriental Research Institute.

Swami Venkatesananda. 2005. *The Yogasutras of Patanjali*. New Delhi: Motilal Banarsidass.

Wittgenstein, Ludwig 1984. *Philosophical Investigations*, trans. G. E. M. Anscombe. Oxford: Basil Blackwell.

———. 1981. *Zettel*, ed. G. E. M. Anscombe and G. H. Von Wright; trans. G. E. M. Anscombe. Oxford: Basil Blackwell.

———. 1980a. *Culture and Value*, ed. G. H. Von Wright and Heikki Nyman. Oxford: Blackwell.

———. 1980b. *Remarks on the Philosophy of Psychology*, vol. 1, ed. G. E. M. Anscombe and Von Wright; trans. G. E. M. Anscombe. Oxford: Basil Blackwell.

———. 1980c. *Remarks on the Philosophy of Psychology*, vol. 2, ed. G. H. Von Wright and Heikki Nyman; trans. C. G. Luckhardt and M. A. E. Aue. Oxford: Basil Blackwell.

———. 1976. 'Cause and Effect: An Intuitive Awareness', trans. Peter Winch, *Philosophia*, 6(3–4): 409–25.

———. 1969. *On Certainty*, ed. G. E. M. Anscombe and G. H. Von Wright; trans. D. Paul and G. H. Von Wright. Oxford: Blackwell.

———. 1967. *Lectures and Conversations in Aesthetics and Psychology*, ed. C. Barett. Berkeley and Los Angeles: University of California Press.

———. 1965[1929]. 'A Lecture on Ethics', *Philosophical Review*, 74: 3–12.

———. 1956. *Remarks on the Foundations of Mathematics*, ed. G. H. Von Wright; trans. G. E. M. Anscombe. Oxford: Basil Blackwell.

PART II
Aesthetics

Aesthetics of the *Mahābhārata*

Traditional Interpretations

Radhavallabh Tripathi

> Though the Mahābhārata describes a society distracted by deceit and intrigue and though the story is reeking with war and the spirit of war, the author clearly declares himself against the politics of power and looks upon the state not as an organisation of force but as a partnership in *dharma*. The modern apostles of the doctrine that the state is an end in itself with no higher duty than to maintain itself, will not find support for their views in it. The view that the end of the state is to organise and establish dharma, that its powers are strictly limited by unalterable laws which it can only enforce, has a greater appeal to he cultivated conscience of our times. The author refuses to be stampeded by transient moods and agitations of the time but approves of the principle that righteousness exalteth a nation.
>
> — S. Radhakrishnan (2003: xi–xii)

In the tradition of Sanskrit literature, each text generally begins with spelling out its purpose and order of chapters including an index of contents. In this way, a text defines its own category and themes at the very outset. The author of the *Mahābhārata* also adheres to this norm. It is said in the beginning of this great epic that 'the characteristics of this text have been defined here itself' (*Ādiparvan* 1.48).

In this process of defining itself, the following generic and specific terms have been used in the *Mahābhārata*: *upajīvya*, *itihāsa*, *ākhyāna* or *ākhyānavariṣṭha*, *kāvya*, *pañcamaveda*, and *bhāratadruma*. These terms also present the concept of the *Mahābhārata* as an epic poem.

In the tradition of *alaṅkāraśāstra* (literary theory in Sanskrit) the *Mahābhārata* has been defined as a *lakṣyagrantha* (a sourcebook for the *lakṣaṇa*s or theories and definitions) and an *ārṣakāvya* (a *kāvya* or poem composed by a *ṛṣi* or seer). This essay examines the significance of these categorizations in understanding the nature of the unique aesthetic experience that the *Mahābhārata* leads us into.

Mahābhārata as *Upajīvya*

The term *upajīvya* means that which sustains, enlivens or functions as a source. The *Mahābhārata* claims that it should be classed as an *upajīvya kāvya*: 'This text will become an *upajīvya* for all the great poets, like Parjanya (rains, god of rain) for all the beings' (*Ādiparvan* 1.92).

Curiously enough, the term *upajīvya* has not been referred to in well-known Sanskrit dictionaries like *Amarakośa* and *Śabdakalpadruma*. The latter, however, includes *upajīvikā* and refers to *upajīvya* as its synonym (*Śabdalalpadruma*, vol. 1: 252). *Vācaspatyam* provides exhaustive notes on *upajīvya* and *upajīvikā*. Whereas the latter is defined just as a source of livelihood that sustains, *upajīvya* has been treated as a broader concept. It has been explained as the substratum, i.e., some thing that is taken recourse to, for existence of knowledge, for livelihood and other things. It is *prayojaka* (motivator) of *svasattā* (one's own existence) and *prayojaka* of *svajñāna* (knowledge of the self) (*Vācaspatyam*, vol. 2: 1207).

Considering the aforementioned explanation of *upajīvya*, we can say that the creators of the *Mahābhārata* visualized it as something that would sustain the traditions of knowledge and the society. The significance of the term *upajīvya* has been missed in the present studies on the *Mahābhārata* and the authors writing histories of Sanskrit literature have mostly referred to the *Mahābhārata* as an *upajīvya kāvya* only to bring out its impact on the literary tradition. An *upajīvya kāvya*, as envisaged in the *Mahābhārata* itself, would also set norms to be followed, establish trends and set traditions. The *Mahābhārata*, therefore, proclaims its role as an *upajīvya kāvya* in the following manner: 'This *ākhyāna* has become an *upajīvya* for all the good poets, just as a good lord becomes an *upajīvya* for all the servants desirous of progress' (*Ādiparvan* 2.241).

The *Mahābhārata*, as an *upajīvya kāvya*, not only presents the worldview, paradigms and standards for the Indian way of life, but also serves a source of literary criticism. The *ācārya*s (masters or theorists) of *alaṅkāraśāstra* have, therefore, rightly chosen the term *lakṣyagrantha* for the *Mahābhārata*. Ānandavardhana, a great savant of literary theory, remarks: 'The connoisseurs have been finding the attestation of the literary theories in the *lakṣya*s like the *Rāmāyaṇa* and the *Mahābhārata*' (*Dhvanyāloka*, *vṛtti* on 1.1).

The *Mahābhārata* in this way also spells out the criteria of literary analysis to be applied to itself. In fact, it was basically through the process of the composition of the *Mahābhārata* that the whole scenario of literary theory in the first millennium CE underwent a revolutionary change. The theory of *śāntarasa* and, finally, *śānta* as a *mahārasa* (greatest of the *rasa*s) or *mūlarasa* (basic *rasa*) could be conceived because of the *Mahābhārata*.

It has been suggested in the text as well as in the commentaries on it that the *Mahābhārata* encompasses everything that sustains or nourishes a nation, or everything that should be cherished by it. This all-embracing nature of the text is also upheld in the oft-quoted maxim: *yanna bhārate tanna bhārate* ('that which is not in *Mahābhārata*, is not to be found in this country of Bhāratavarṣa'). Again, by the way of self-appraisal, the *Mahābhārata* also declares: 'Whatever has been said here with regard to the four goals of human life can be found elsewhere, but whatever has not been said here will not be found anywhere else' (*Ādiparvan* 56.33).

Mahābhārata as *Itihāsa*

Both the *Rāmāyaṇa* of Vālmīki and the *Mahābhārata* are regarded as *itihāsa*s. The term *itihāsa* is generally translated as 'history'. But it is not exactly analogous to the concept of history. While defining itself as *itihāsa*, the *Mahābhārata* also clarifies the idea of an *itihāsa*. An *itihāsa* is supposed to be as eternal as the Vedas. One of the vedic *saṁhitā*s proclaims: 'Just like the four Vedas, the *itihāsa*, *purāṇa*, *gāthā and nārāśaṃsī* also came out from the Supreme Being' (*Atharvaveda* XV.6.11). The Upaniṣads also treat *itihāsa* on a par with Veda itself (*Bṛhadāraṇyaka Upaniṣad* IV.1.2).[1] The particle *iti* ('thus') in *itihāsa* denotes its capability of leading to a clear perception. Abhinavagupta, in his commentary titled *Abhinavabhāratī* on Bharatamuni's *Nāmyaśāstra* (I.15), gives a twofold interpretation to the term *itihāsa*. *Iti* denotes the visualization through direct perception — the past being visualized as if it is happening in the present. There is a stray verse quoted in *Vācaspatyam* providing the standard definition of *itihāsa*: 'The *itihāsa* comprises an account of past happenings and also preaches the way for the attainment of the *puruṣārtha*s (four goals of human life)' (vol. 1: 924).

An *itihāsa* text thus presents a continuum of past, present and future. It is both prescriptive and descriptive. It is supposed to define the *puruṣārtha*s and also the way for their attainment. The emphasis in this view of an *itihāsa* text is on the description of what ought to be, rather than on what was or has been and, as an *itihāsa*, the *Mahābhārata* is a poem of 'being and becoming'.

Applying the criterion for qualifying as an *itihāsa* to itself, the *Mahābhārata* claims that it is not just a documentation of the practices that have prevailed and are likely to continue, but also unravels the mysteries, records whatever is valuable, and creates a repository of knowledge systems (*Ādiparvan* 1.45–48).

With its discourse on the four goals of human life, an *itihāsa* text attains the status of an *āgama* (scripture). The *Mahābhārata* proclaims that 'it is the essence of the *itihāsa* that would form the best of the *āgamas* as it is imbrued with subtle meanings (*sūkṣmārtha*) and major concepts (*pradhānārtha*)' (*Ādiparvan* 2.31–33).

In this tradition, *itihāsa* is to be treated on a par with the Vedas, and is regarded as an important discipline to be studied like the Vedas. The *Mahābhārata*, in fact, equates itself with the Vedas (*Ādiparvan* 1.19). *Lokavṛtta* or the circle of society at large is said to be the subject for treatment in *itihāsa* (*Nyāyabhāṣya* IV.1.61).

The concept of *itihāsa*, in this way, incorporates cultural narrative of epic dimensions, a grand discourse as well as history of ideas, history of philosophy, together with cosmology. And all this should be visualized to make it relevant to a contemporary audience, as suggested by Abhinavagupta.

The tradition of the *alaṅkāraśāstra* classifies the *Mahābhārata* as an *ārṣa mahākāvya* (an epic composed by a seer). Viśvanātha was the first to use this term

---

[1] *Upanitṣaṁgraha*, 111.

for the *Mahābhārata* (*Sāhityadarpaṇa* VI.304). An *ārṣa mahākāvya* is imbued with the vision of a seer. Having visualized the past, present and future of a country and the continuum of time in a flux, the seer presents the destiny of a nation and society and enables us to see it.

Mahābhārata as *Ākhyāna*

Ākhyāna means a narrative. It formed an essential subject in the curriculum of ancient *gurukulas* or *āśramas*. The Upaniṣads mention *ākhyāna* as one of the disciplines to be studied, along with the Vedas and the Vedāṅgas (six disciplines required for the study of the Vedas). *Ākhyāna* actually formed a part of the curriculum in the Upaniṣadic period (*Chāndogya Upaniṣad* VII.2.4).

The *Mahābhārata* describes itself as an *ākhyāna* and *ākhyānavariṣṭha* (greatest of the *ākhyānas*) (*Ādiparvan* 1.16). It further says that a person does not become wise unless he studies this *ākhyāna* (*Ādiparvan* 2.235).

Ākhyāna stands in close relationship with *upākhyāna*, which can be defined as an epic within the Epic, or a discourse within a grand discourse. Technically, as Bhoja puts it, an *upākhyāna* is a tale retold by one of the characters of an *ākhyāna* for enlightenment of another character, whereas an *ākhyāna* has been defined as a grand narrative to be presented by way of recitation of a text, songs and *abhinaya* (*Śṛṅgāraprakāśa* XI.331). Invariably, it has a relationship with the four Vedas: it is supposed to substantiate the Vedas. It is a narrative recording the achievements and history of an important dynasty. Teaching of the *ākhyāna* was regarded as necessary as the teaching of the Vedas and Vedāṅgas. As the *ākhyāna* forms a part of the collective memory of a community or society, it is told and retold again and again and the literary tradition subsists on it. As the *Mahābhārata* itself proclaims: 'Poets have been telling the *ākhyāna* of the *Mahābhārata* earlier, others are narrating it now-a-days and still some others will narrate it in future' (*Ādiparvan* 1.24; 2.390). Further, an *ākhyāna* is supposed to substantiate the Vedas, and the study of Vedas in itself is incomplete unless the *ākhyāna* is not included as a part of the curricula (*Ādiparvan* 2.235).

The *ākhyāna* was also an important part of Vedic rituals. Vedic rituals had two features: invocation of the divine and representation of the human creativity. The latter included recitation of *gāthās* (a lyrical form) and *nārāśaṁsīs* (heroic tales), as well as that of *ākhyāna*. A later Vedic text, *Aitareya Brāhmaṇa* (XXXIII.6.18), records the Śunaḥśepa *ākhyāna* or the story of Śunaḥśepa which was to be recited by the *hotṛ* priest during the performance of the *Rājasūya yajña* or royal consecration.

In the *Aśvamedha yajña* or horse sacrifice, the horse having been sent out for *digvijaya* (conquest of various kingdoms in all the directions), various *ākhyānas* named *Pāriplava ākhyānas* (series of stories) were recited continuously for a year at the site where the ritual was initiated. The recitation of one *ākhyāna* was to be completed in 10 days, and thus, in each *Aśvamedha*, a total of 36 *ākhyānas* were recited. The *Rāmāyaṇa* of Vālmīki (I.11.21, 12.1) records a gap of one year after the horse was left to wander during the course of the *Aśvamedha* performed by king Daśaratha, but does not specify the activities that went on in the *yajñamaṇḍapa* (pavilion for the sacrifice) till the horse returned. The *Aitareya Brāhmaṇa* (III.25.1) also mentions the *ākhyānavids* (narrators well versed in *ākhyānas*) who can recite the Sauparṇa legend.

Mahābhārata as *Kāvya* and *Veda*

Kāvya, in general, is a literary composition. The authors of the *Mahābhārata* conceived the text as a *kāvya*. The *Mahābhārata*, while defining itself as a *kāvya*, claims that it is a *kāvya* which even the *kavis* (poets) would find difficult to comprehend (*Ādiparvan* 1.97–98). Thus, the word *kāvya* would not just mean an ordinary poem in this context; it is to be treated on a par with the Vedas or *mantras*, and a *kavi* is not just an ordinary poet, but a seer. Describing the *Mahābhārata* as a *kāvya*, the authors of the epic claim: 'This poem is embellished with pious words, with human and divine conventions, it is enjoined with various meters and it is dear to the scholars' (*Ādiparvan* 1.26).

The *Mahābhārata* is also called the 'fifth Veda' or *Kārṣṇya Veda* (a Veda created by Kṛṣṇadvaipāyana Vyāsa) (*Ādiparvan* 3.20). The application of the term 'Veda' to the *Mahābhārata* is not merely a eulogy. The tradition provides the logic of conferring the status of the 'fifth Veda' to the epic. The study of *itihāsa* was taken up by the *Sūtas* in the same way as learned *Brāhmaṇas* recited the Vedas. The *itihāsa* was to be recited before an assembly of *dvijas* (twice-born) (*Anuśāsanaparvan* 90.26). The 88 sages led by Śaunaka are described as devout listeners of the *itihāsa* and *purāṇa* being narrated by a *Sūta*. The invariable link between the Vedas and the *Mahābhārata* is established by Yāska, the author of *Nirukta* (treatise on etymology) who adjusts some of the portions of the Vedas as *itihāsa* and *ākhyāna*. Kauṭilya too uses the term *Itihāsaveda* (*Arthaśāstra* I.3.2) and prescribes it as a part of the curriculum to be studied by a King. Manu also prescribed the daily study of *itihāsa* and *ākhyāna* (*Manusmṛti* III.232).

Tree as Metaphor for *Mahābhārata*

The authors of the *Mahābhārata* itself view the poem as a tree (*bhāratadruma*). The metaphor is extended to make the *Karṇaparvan* analogous to flowers, plucked and spreading their fragrance in the *Śalyaparvan*, and finally yielding the great fruit in the *Śāntiparvan*, with the *Mausalaparvan* forming the end of the tree of *Mahābhārata* (*Ādiparvan* 1.106–107, 120).

The two main characters of the epic are also visualized as two different trees: the tree of *manyu* (wrath) on one hand, and the tree of *dharma* on the other, represented by Duryodhana and Yudhiṣṭhira respectively. 'Duryodhana is a great tree created out of wrath, Karṇa is its trunk, Śakuni its branches, Duḥśāsana its fruits and flowers, and the weak king Dhṛtarāṣṭra its root. Yudhiṣṭhira is a great tree created out of *dharma*, Arjuna is its trunk, Bhīma its branches, the two sons of Mādrī its fruits and flowers, and Śrīkṛṣṇa, the *Brahman* (Supreme Being), and the *Brāhmaṇa*s (those who have knowledge of *Brahman*) its roots' (*Ādiparvan* 1.65, 66). This metaphor of the whole epic poem as a tree is in consonance with the traditional perception of literature. Bharatamuni, while defining the relationship between the diverse components of poetry, explains them beautifully through the metaphor of a tree: 'Just as a tree grows out of a seed, and from the tree come out the flowers and fruits, in the same way, *rasa* is the foundation and from *rasa* all the *bhāvas* (emotional states) find an arrangement' (*Nāṭyaśāstra* VII.38). Abhinavagupta, commenting on this stanza, says: 'A *kāvya* is tree, the performance by the actors is the flower and the relish of its *rasa* by the spectators is fruit'. In our cosmic view also, the Universe is viewed as a tree.

A beautiful verse in praise of the *Mahābhārata* is traditionally recited before the recitation of the *Bhagavadgītā*. It imagines the epic as this unblemished lotus blossom that the words of Vyāsa, the son of Parāśara, constitutes. "The intense fragrance of that flower is the deep meaning of the *Gītā*. Various stories and sub-stories are its petals. And this lotus blossoms as we address Lord Kṛṣṇa Hari) through discourse by Him and about Him. Good and wise people buzz around this lotus like bees, drinking daily and repeatedly the nectar from its heart. May this *Mahabharata*-lotus destroy the dirt we gather in this degraded age of Kali'. This metaphor captures both the purity and the perfume, the aesthetic relishability (nectar, *rasa*) and the ethical attractiveness of this epic poem, which makes honest wise men addicted to the honey it bears.

Mahābhārata as a Text of *Śāntarasa*

Contrary to the views of many Western scholars and modern critics,[2] the *Mahābhārata* is viewed as a homogenous text in the Indian literary tradition. Also, there is a unity of design that is envisaged in the terms used to describe this epic. In this way, the concepts of the *upajīvya kāvya*, *itihāsa*, *ākhyāna* or *ākhyānavariṣṭha*, *kāvya*, *Pañcamaveda* or *Kārṣṇyaveda*, and *Bhāratadruma* are logically linked together. There is unity in its structure and design because the whole text culminates in the realization of the *puruṣārtha*s and finally the fourth *puruṣārtha*, i.e., *mokṣa* (salvation). To understand the aesthetics of the *Mahābhārata*, we have to take into

[2] Modern orientalists failed to appreciate the *Mahābhārata* as a coherent homogeneous poem. M. Winternitz went to the extant of calling it a 'literary nonsense'. To quote him: 'The Mahabharata as a whole is a literary nonsense. Never has an artist's hand tried — and it would have been really impossible — to unite the conflicting elements into a unitary poem. Only theologicians and commentators without poetic leanings and clumsy copyists have at last welded together into a disorderly mass the actually non-combinable parts coming down from different countries' (Winternitz 1987: 305).

consideration the concept of *rasa* (aesthetic experience) and its relationship with *puruṣārtha* (aspirations of human life). Each *rasa* should culminate in one of the *puruṣārtha*s. Even *śṛṅgāra* (erotic) *rasa* not only yields *kāmapuruṣārtha*, but may also lead to the attainment of other *puruṣārtha*s, viz., *dharma* or *artha*. Bharatamuni, therefore, defines three types of *kāma*: *dharmakāma*, *arthakāma* and *mokṣakāma*. (*Nāṭyaśāstra* XXII.96). Ānandavardhana, in his *Dhvanyāloka* (IV *udyota*), says that *śānta* is the dominant *rasa* in the *Mahābhārata*. He also holds *śāntarasa* as a vehicle for salvation. Abhinavagupta establishes the supremacy of *śāntarasa* by arguing that it is a vehicle for *mokṣa puruṣārtha*, and *mokṣa* is the supreme amongst all the four *puruṣārtha*s (ibid.).

If the purpose of whole poem is the realization of *mokṣa*, then *śānta* ought to be its dominant *rasa*. The logic of the whole poem culminating in the experience of *śānta* can be better understood when we consider the concept of *rasa* according to Ānandavardhana and Abhinavagupta. The *rasa*s like *vīra* (heroic) and *raudra* (terrific) do occur in the *Mahābhārata*, but *bībhatsa rasa* (disgust) becomes more conspicuous than these.

Bharatamuni identified four *rasa*s as the *mūla* (basic) *rasa*s: *śṛṅgāra*, *vīra*, *bībhatsa*, and *raudra*. Out of each of these, four subsidiary *rasa*s are generated. Thus, *hāsya* (comic) is born out of *śṛṅgāra*; *adbhuta* (wonder) out of *vīra*; *bhayānaka* out of *bībhatsa*; and *karuṇa* (pathetic) out of *raudra*.

This concept of basic and subsidiary *rasa*s has its own logic as the four basic *rasa*s are invariably linked with the four *puruṣārtha*s, i.e., *śṛṅgāra* to *kāma*, *vīra* to *dharma*, *raudra* to *artha*, and *bībhatsa* to *mokṣa*. The *bībhatsa rasa* is of two types: *kṣobhaja* (generated by anguish) and *udvegī* (born out of uneasiness). The former leads to disillusionment which clears the path to salvation.

Through the aesthetics of the *bībhatsa rasa*, therefore, the spectator or reader undergoes the experiences of anguish, uneasiness and disgust which may finally make him liberated from the mundane and the earthly. Abhinavagupta is right in suggesting that the experience of the *bībhatsa rasa* would thus lead to *śānta* and to salvation. The *kṣobhaja* type of *bībhatsa* is also called pure (*śuddha*) and leads to liberation (*mokṣa*).

The aesthetics of the *Mahābhārata* does not rest on *tanmayībhavana* (rapture). It is just opposite of the aesthetics of ecstasy. It is the aesthetics of distance and detachment. The text itself accepts that it is not about pleasure and happy times. It claims that it is going to describe something sad and awful. Vyāsa, at the very outset of the narrative, approaches Satyavatī, his mother, and tells her that most unhappy times are approaching:

> Gone are the times of happiness
> the terrible times are nearing in,
> each coming day is going to bear
> more and more horror
> and the youth of earth
> has already been exhausted (*Ādiparvan* 119.6).

It is true that the *Mahābhārata* presents the deepest moments of crisis in history and in human life raising perennial questions of existence. But there is this warning note which resounds again and again in its texture. The sense of utter waste persists. After emerging victorious in the great war, Yudhiṣṭhira says: 'The whole world appears empty and hallow and no longer pleases me. They are all gone — the friends and kin — and my army is wasted away' (*Śāntiparvan* 26.2–3). Arjuna, the great hero of the *Mahābhārata* war, loses face in a pathetic debacle at the hands of petty robbers and is unable to rescue the ladies of the Yādava family. But the *Mahābhārata* does not end in this utter dejection and sense of helplessness. The deep anguish and disgust that the heroes like Yudhiṣṭhira and Arjuna feel paves the way for *śānta rasa* and *mokṣa*.

Therefore, the tradition does not hold the *Mahābhārata* as an epic of genocide, as it is viewed by the modern scholarship.[3] Also, neither is it understood as a tragedy ending in utter dejection, again quite unlike the way it is understood by the critics of today.[4] We find that rising from the feeling of dejection, both the great heroes, Yudhiṣṭhira and Arjuna, approach Bhīṣma and Vyāsa respectively and receive the final discourse on *dharma* and the way to salvation. The saga of struggle between two branches of the same dynasty is invested with a higher purpose of life and fulfillment of aspirations of human beings. There is no feeling of joy and sensuous pleasure at the end of the narrative. Ironically enough, both Ānandavardhana and Abhinavagupta, two of the greatest masters of *rasa–dhvani* system in the *alankāraśāstra*, therefore, agree that the *Mahābhārata* has a *virasāvasāna* (an ending devoid of *rasas*). Ānandavardhana says that this ending sans *rasa* produces a feeling of dejection. But this leads to renunciation as well at the same time. Therefore, the keynote of the *Mahābhārata* lies in *mokṣa*. Vyāsa, a person of supreme intelligence, with a view to save the humanity drowned in illusion, imparting the light of knowledge himself, says: 'Just as the world order without an essence, goes disarray, the feeling of renunciation takes over' (*Śāntiparvan* 168.4). Ānandavardhana hints at two levels of *rasa*-realization here: *samanaska* (with attachment) and *vimanaska* (without attachment, dispassionate). There is *rasa* through empathy in former; the latter involves aesthetics of distance and disillusionment.

Commenting on Ānandavardhana's thesis, Abhinavagupta says: 'Annihilation of each other by the people of Vṛṣṇi race, the calamity inappropriately befalling on the Pāṅḍavas and the killing of Kṛṣṇa by a hunter — through all these episodes, the *Mahābhārata* has an ending that is devoid of rasa' (*Dhvanyāloka* IV.5).

Not only does Ānandavardhana hold the *virasāvasāna* as the culmination point of this great epic, but he also says that the *Mahābhārata* is a *śāstra* and

[3] 'One of the themes is repeated, large scale but inconclusive human destruction. The business at Kurukshetra is just one in a series of near genocides' (Brodbeck and Black 2007: 8).

[4] 'It is not Śānta but Duranta — the tragic sense — that prevails in MB' (Sharma 2009: 33).

has been brought to end with complete disillusionment or detachment because a *śāstra* (scripture) should be in a form of a discourse on some *puruṣārtha*. The *Mahābhārata* has *mokṣa* as the *puruṣārtha* and *śānta* as its dominant *rasa*. Despite tremendous emotional scenes, there is *vimanaskatā* or annihilation of all pleasurable sensations.

Ānandavardhana also informs that there has been a tradition of interpreting the *Mahābhārata* in this way. Its author, the great and wise Vyāsa, wrote it with an intention of rescuing the people from the abyss of ignorance in which they were weltering, and leading them to emancipation.

All other *puruṣārthas* are subservient to *mokṣa* and all other *rasas* subsidiary in relation to *śānta rasa*. The opponents of this theory would possibly raise the question: how can one decide that only *mokṣa* and *śānta rasas* are conspicuous in the text, when the text itself declares in the very beginning that all the *puruṣārthas* are to be delineated in it. Ānandavardhana says that there is an inherent focus on *mokṣa* in the text and it is not proclaimed directly, but suggested by the very presence of Śrīkṛṣṇa as the *sanātana tattva* (eternal element). The very feeling of a sheer 'colossal waste' and uselessness of all human efforts would generate the inclination towards renunciation.

The fact that the author of the *Mahābhārata* has named one of the *parvans* as *Śāntiparvan* is a strong evidence for corroborating the theory of Ānandavardhana and Abhinavagupta. The understanding of the *Mahābhārata* requires a paradigm different from the prevailing norms of aesthetics in the later tradition of Sanskrit literary theory.

References

Aitareya Brāhmaṇa. 2006. New Delhi: Rashtriya Sanskrit Sansthan.

Atharvaveda. 1994. New Delhi: Nag Prakashak.

Bahadur, Raja Radhakanta Dev. 2006[1848]. *Śabdakalpadruma*, 5 vols. New Delhi: Rashtriya Sanskrit Sansthan.

Brodbeck, Simon and Brian Black (eds). 2007. *Gender and Narrative in the Mahābhārata*. Routledge Hindu Studies Series. London: Routledge.

Chakravarti K. K. (ed.). 2009. *Text and Variations of the Mahābhārata*. New Delhi: Indira Gandhi National Centre for Arts (IGNCA).

Dandekar, R. N. (ed.). 1990. *The Mahābhārata Revisited*. New Delhi: Sahitya Akademi.

Dwivedi, Rewaprasad (ed.). 2011. *Śṛṅgāraprakāśa*. New Delhi: Indira Gandhi National Centre for Arts (IGNCA).

Īśādidaśopaniṣadaḥ. 1978[1964]. New Delhi: Motilal Banarsidass.

Krishnamoorthy, K. (ed.). 1992. *Nāṭyaśāstra with Commentary Abhinavabhāratī by Abhinavabhagupta*, vol. 1. Varodara: Oriental Institute.

Kulkarni, V. M. and T. Nandi (ed.). 2003. *Nāṭyaśāstra with Commentary Abhinavabhāratī by Abhinavabhagupta*, vol. 3. Varodara: Oriental Institute.

Narang, S. P. (ed.). 1985. *Modern Evaluation of the Mahābhārata*. New Delhi: Nag Prakashak.

Nyāyabhāṣya. 1925. Varanasi: Chowkhambha Sanskrit Series.

Radhkrishnan, S. 2008. 'Foreword' to V. Raghavan (trans.), *The Mahābhārata Condensed in the Poet's Own Words*, pp. xi–ii. Chennai: Kuppu Swami Shastri Research Institute.

Raghavan, V. (trans.). 2008. *The Mahābhārata Condensed in the Poet's Own Words*. Chennai: Kuppu Swami Shastri Research Institute.

Sāhityadarpaṇa, with Locana and Vijñapriyā Commentaries. 1981[1919]. New Delhi: Bharatiya Book Corporation.

Sharma T. R. S. (ed.). 2009. *Reflections and Variations on the Mahābhārata*. New Delhi: Sahitya Akademi.

Shastri, Jagdishlal (ed.). 2000. *Manusmṛti*. New Delhi: Motilal Banarasidass.

———. 1980[1970]. *Upaniṣatsaṃgraha Containing 188 Upaniṣads*. New Delhi: Motilal Banarasidass.

Shastri, T. Ganapati (ed.), *Arthaśāstra*. 1984[1923]. New Delhi: Bharatiya Vidya Prakashan.

Shiromani, Vishveshvar Siddhanta (ed). 1998. *Dhvanyāloka*, with Hindi Commentary. Varanasi: Gyan Mandal Ltd.

Tarkavachaspati, Taranatha. 1990. *Vācaspatyam*, 6 vols. Varanasi: Chowkhambha Sanskrit Series Office.

Vyas, R. T. (ed.). 1992. *Vālmīki Rāmāyaṇa*, Critical Edition. Vadodara: Oriental Institute.

Winternitz, Maurice. 1987[1981]. *History of Indian Literature*, vol. 1, trans. V. Srinivas Sarma. New Delhi: Motilal Banarasidass.

Karṇa in and out of the *Mahābhārata*

Nrisinha Prasad Bhaduri

An Illicit Comparison about an Illicit Character?

It would have better if this essay had remained unwritten. It undertakes a comparison which its author does not consider legitimate. Like its topic, Karṇa, a son born out of wedlock from an inter-species union between a god and a virgin human female, the essay could be said to have been 'conceived in sin'. As I started writing this chapter, I had no knowledge of whether writing this essay would do me any good (*iṣṭa sādhanatā jñāna*) or whether it is within my capacity to accomplish (*kṛti sādhyatā jñāna*) the intended task of writing.

In this essay, I try to compare the depiction of Karṇa in the *Mahābhārata* with that in other non-Sanskrit texts. One kind of comparison inevitably leads to speaking ill or well of either of the objects of comparison. Which Karṇa is superior as a literary character: the Karṇa of Vyāsa, the Karṇa of Kashiram Das, or the Karṇa of Rabindranath Tagore? One of the most important factors here is language, for what we call a character in a work of literary art is made primarily of the words of a language. While Karṇa in the original *Mahābhārata* is dealt with in the Sanskrit language, with its plethora of epithets and adjectives and subtlety, suggestiveness and 'curvature' (*vākrokti*) of speech, Karṇa out of this epic's context is quite different in other regional languages, especially as we have him in Rabindranath Tagore's Bengali verse-play *Karṇa–Kuntī Saṃvād* ('The Dialogue between Karṇa and Kuntī') (1899). Moreover, Tagore's treatment of Karṇa is drenched in the sentiment of pathos. This predominance of a single sentiment, I am afraid, makes the Tagorian Karṇa lack the complexity of the *Mahābhārata* epic character, or the epic totality of a tragic hero. Again, who are we to lament the 'loss of totality' in a new literary creation? The appropriation of a particular trait to the exclusion of others in a transcreated version depends on the particular intention and imagination of the poet-(trans) creator. Poets, we are told, are unconstrained (*nirankuśa*) creatures. Besides, whether the poet's intention is always relevant in determining the meaning of texts it is not even uncontroversial. Rather, it is especially contentious in case of a text like the *Mahābhārata* whose authorship is nearly as shrouded in mystery as was the birth of Karṇa, the unlucky warrior son of Sun god called 'son of a lowborn horse-carriage-driver' all his life.

Tagore drew upon a specific event of Karṇa's life from the *Mahābhārata* and a specific sentiment of the multilayered mind of an anti-hero. Understandably, it becomes difficult to identify him with the effect of that recreated emotion, superimposed on him. Tagore's poetic power attuned the reader to the sentiment of Karṇa's deprivation, the seed of which was latent in Karṇa's epic psyche. But then, in order to locate Karṇa in the total context of the epic, it is imperative to understand how Karṇa gradually turned into an anti-hero and developed a consuming ambition to achieve his goal.

Glamour that Attracts Pity

Karṇa is probably a unique character in the *Mahābhārata* who arouses our pity and admiration at the same time. He is so dazzlingly rich in inner strength that we feel like blurting out 'Poor Karṇa!' The feeling of deprivation wrought by his having been cast away by his mother at the time of his birth and his final fateful encounter with Arjuna when his chariot wheel got stuck to the earth — both cause tears to roll down many a cheek. Again, his life-long struggle that paved the way for him to become a counter-hero, his innumerable dashing and daring feats, and his unflinching friendship with and loyalty to Duryodhana earned him huge appreciation even from his enemies. Although this appreciation and *encomia* showered on him ultimately culminate into a striking sense of pathos, it is noteworthy that the sentiment of pathos is more due to the recreated Karṇa myth in various regional *Mahābhārata*s, especially the one written in Bengali by Kashiram Das in the sixteenth century AD and the transcreation of *Karṇa–Kuntī Saṃvād* by Tagore. All these versions of the *Mahābhārata* recreate the character of Karṇa in a manner that denies the epic totality which binds together the complexities of the royal court and the heroic flare of a life-long struggler. The picture is made even more wholesome (in its credibility) by the epic because it does not hold back or erase the moments when petty selfishness and common indecency of a lowly man do sometimes intrude into his character.

Every *Mahābhārata* character has a focal spot of vulnerability of its own. But if the character is great in itself — negatively or positively — s/he is bound to have multiple such vulnerable spots. In case of Karṇa, his so called blemish of being born out of wedlock, his bond of friendship with Duryodhana and his sporadic acts of selfless munificence — factors often foregrounded in the regional *Mahābhārata*s — combine to give him a larger-than-life persona. But, it should also be remembered that the motif of the 'abandoned child' is a commonplace one in the *Mahābhārata* (as in many other pre-modern texts). After their births, most solar heroes are forsaken: Kṛṣṇa is taken to the cowherd foster parents; Karṇa to the story-teller charioteer Adhiratha; Bhīṣma is left on the banks of Gangā; and even Moses was abandoned among the bulrushes. The 'abandonment' motif has the inbuilt capacity to evoke pity and awe as well as to magnify the majesty of heroic isolation. It gives to the protagonists' daring exploits a special glitter and gloss. The same is the case with Karṇa. Playing upon the motif of early abandonment by the biological mother, the *Mahābhārata* construes a psychic profile of a man whose every characteristic — boastfulness, headstrongness, martial skill, vulgarity, charitable disposition, and, above all, the urge to emerge as an anti-hero — are all *rooted* in the 'original' slight suffered by him. The *Mahābhārata* portrays Karṇa as a 'natural' *outsider*, a man perennially 'homeless', a rebellious refugee. And, it is he who becomes the most important person among Duryodhana's four confidants — so important that he was blamed by Gāndhārī as one primarily responsible for bringing total ruin to the royal race of the Kurus (*Strīparvan* 14.16). Therefore, if we choose Vyāsa's *Mahābhārata* as our point of departure, it is of utmost importance that we pay heed to the sense of smarting and smothering felt by Kuntī that even outstrips those felt by Karṇa. These agonies of the war-ravaged mature Kuntī re-invoke the psychological crisis undergone by the adolescent Pṛthā when she brought into the world her first-born 'solar' child.

The 'Unconscious' and the 'Subconscious' in Karṇa's Mother

On the eve of the Kurukṣetra war, Kṛṣṇa came to the capital of the Kauravas on his ultimate peace-mission. On the evening before the final day of the peace-parley, he met Kuntī. Kuntī asked Kṛṣṇa about her sons-in-exile, but overwrought by the treatment meted out to her by her father and in-laws, she had more to say about them: 'Kṛṣṇa! I have been abused by my father and insulted by my in-laws' (*sāham pitrā ca nikṛtā śvaśuraiś ca parantapa*) (*Udyogaparvan* 90.64).

Kuntī's wrath against her in-laws is understandable. She explained to Kṛṣṇa the reasons for her grievance against her father (*pitā*) — and, the *pitā* was no less than Āryaka Śūra, a scion of the Yadu race, who headed the oligarchic state of Mathurā (and from whose name, according to Megasthenes, was derived the name of the region *śourasenai*).

Kuntī further said to Kṛṣṇa: 'My father had given me away for adoption to his cousin and friend Kuntibhoja and that too when I used to play with balls and toy-elephants' (*vālām mām āryakas-tasmai kriḍantim kandu-hastikam* (*Udyogaparvan* 90.63). This clearly shows that Kuntī was conscious of being given away when the change in guardianship took place. Doubtless, psychological growth of an adopted child is perforce *materially* different from that of the normal child. Analyzing the developmental logic of adopted children, scholars have concluded that adoption after six months of birth 'is sufficient to warrant it being categorized as a late placement' and the late placement may lead to a series of grief-reactions in the mind of the adopted child.

To sum up, Kuntī hinted at the comforting security she enjoyed at her father's place and its subsequent *loss*; she also made it abundantly clear that the pain of being forsaken by her loving parents was something that she had never overcome. We do not know much about her initial shock and disbelief, nor do we know about her bouts of depression or the afflictions of withdrawal she might have periodically suffered in her new surroundings. But this much is certain that she nurtured a deep resentment against her father which eventually exploded. Kuntī said: 'I don't blame myself, nor do I impute any fault to Duryodhana, but I accuse my own father who had given me away like a gift of wealth' (*pitarantveva garheyam nātmanam na suyodhanam* (*Udyogaparvan* 90.62).

However, we are at liberty to infer that in case of Kuntī, the impetus to abandon her pre-marital son came from the psychological mindscape of a person who had never outgrown the *trauma* of being forsaken. Driven by adolescent curiosity, Kuntī sought union with the Sun god. But when the god approached her and went for almost a forced union, Kuntī showed a deep concern for her chastity and concern for the unborn baby.[1] The god 'took care of' both her concerns: Kuntī's virginity was restored by the providential power of the god and the protection of her future son was also arranged for by another divine act. Kuntī was assured that her yet-to-be born child would be provided with a golden shield on the chest and two golden earrings — both divine ornaments that would protect him from death (*Āraṇyakaparvan* 306.8–21).

So, those who always feel like lamenting the misfortune of Karṇa should keep in mind that Kuntī's union with the Sun god was not just a feast of *Eros*. Rather, this provides us with an occasion to remember that the coy but curious maiden did not readily submit to the male sexual overture and she reminded her partner of the likely loss of the social status of the offspring. What she feared most was that she would be compelled to 'disown' her child. So, in the *Mahābhārata*, Karṇa's birth is constituted by a double *lack* — implicated in the wound of rejection Karṇa carried within himself and the similar wound that his mother too bore.

Concerns of a Virgin Mother

Kuntī took much trouble to conceal the signs of pregnancy. After having procured divine assurance regarding the protection of her unborn child earlier, she placed the newborn in a casket and let the container adrift along Gangā.

A man unknown to Kuntī found the casket floating on Gangā. He took the child out of it and brought the babe home as a way of consolation for his barren wife. (In terms of patriarchal calculus) the gift signified the 'greatest' gift that any husband could bestow upon the wife: the 'gift' of a son. The foster-parents saw the golden shield bound to the child's chest and the two golden earrings adorning the ears. Seeing those marks of wealth, they named him Vasuṣeṇa. At that time Kuntī got married to Pāṇḍu, the king of Hastināpura. She never told her husband about the sexual liaison she had entered in her adolescent days. That secretiveness did not stem from the fear that the fact that she had lost virginity prior to marriage would mar her marital life. Rather, it was out of concern for the *prestige* of her biological father, foster-father and husband — her remaining tongue-tied in relation to her first-born was rooted in the socio-psychic complex of an adopted female. Nevertheless, although displaced to a distant place after marriage, Kuntī kept track of her forsaken child with the help of her trusted spies (*carena viditascasit pṛthayā divya-varmabhṛt* (*Āraṇyakaparvan* 308.15).

Karṇa's foster-father was *Sūta* by caste. *Sūta* is, by definition, an offspring of a *Brāhmaṇa* maiden and a *Kṣatriya* male. According to various scriptural texts, including the *Manusaṃhitā*, one of professions of the *Sūta* is that of the charioteer (*sūtānām aśva-sārathyam*). The *Mahābhārata* too refers to it. For example, while addressing Karṇa in a derogatory manner Bhīma asked the former to hold the reins of the horses befitting a charioteer (*kulasya sadrsa-sturnam pratodo grhyatam tvaya*) (*Ādiparvan* 137.6).

Karṇa thus received the training and imbibed the impressions, aphoristically called *saṃskāra*, of a *Sūta* family. This caste-hybridity means valorization of *Kṣatriya* heroism along with a deep sense of regard for the *Brāhmaṇa*. So, this conflicting double ambition was integral to his 'way of being'. The manifold connotations of the word *saṃskāra* cannot be captured in one word — neither does it simply stand for caste traits, nor creed, nor conscious mindset, nor class behaviour, but rather the conglomeration of all the internal and external impressions that a human being receives, adopts and internalizes in his psyche as well as demeanour. The intermingling of two castes is not the moot point in case of Karṇa's mental make-up either. For the inter-caste mingling of two persons belonging to higher social ranks, i.e., a *Kṣatriya* man and a *Brāhmaṇa* woman in this case, did not quite demean the offspring, the *Sūta*. The *Sūta* enjoyed the privileges of a high social rank in the Vedic as well as the post-Vedic times of the *Mahābhārata*.

However, there still remains the problem of culturally induced social conditioning of castes and creeds. It is logical to expect that any inter-caste social mobility would cause 'disturbance' in the individual psyche structured by economic stratification, political ordering and cultural practices including dressing and culinary habits. One does not have to be a casteist to observe that culturally and economically induced differences are bound to affect inter-caste social behaviours. Even today we come across umpteen examples of inter-caste love/arranged marriages going sour after a point. And, in each case, it is the socially privileged upper-caste person who begins the process by flinging accusations — example, miserliness, unhygienic food habits, encouraging objectionable associations — against the so-called lower-caste (male or female) spouse. The one figure in the *Mahābhārata* who pointed that this malady of asymmetry was far too entrenched to be remedied even by cohabitation was the astute *Kṣatriya* Yayāti. When Devayānī, the daughter of a *Brāhmaṇa*, insisted on marrying him, Yayāti said, given that the two upper castes have distinct notions of 'purity' and 'propriety', the commingling of a *Kṣatriya* male with a *Brāhmaṇa* female was injudicious (*Ādiparvan* 81.20).

Bhīṣma, perhaps, the wisest man of *Mahābhārata*, underlined the *saṃskāra* ingrained in Karṇa when he pointed to Karṇa's lamentable habit of fleeing from the battle field at crucial times and his self-indulgent attitude towards dastardly acts (Mbh.)

'Hence, Bashful Cunning': Anxiety and Sneakiness of a Homeless Hero

Karṇa learnt the techniques of arms from three illustrious teachers — Kṛpācārya, Droṇācārya and Paraśurāma. Kṛpācārya was famous for giving primary lessons of arms to both Kauravas and Pāṇḍavas and we believe Karṇa also joined his class as an outsider interested in the same educational course. Incidentally, when Droṇācārya started his school in Hastināpura at the behest of Bhīṣma, the whole batch of Kṛpācārya's students, including Karṇa, was transferred to his school. Karṇa's schooling may have other serious implications, but one thing is clear from the *Mahābhārata* that Duryodhana was known to Karṇa long before the official bout of arms and the bond of friendship between the two was already firm in their childhood (*sa sakhyamakarodbālye rājñā duryodhanena ca*) (*Śāntiparvan* 2.8).

In Droṇācārya's school, Karṇa soon realized that Arjuna, the third Pāṇḍava, was turning out to be a better warrior than he was and was enjoying special words of praise and encouragement from Droṇa. In Karṇa's estimate, that smacked of favouritism. Karṇa, himself a very good student, thus developed a sense of resentment towards Arjuna. This crippling inferiority complex was like a fodder for the furtherance of Duryodhana's enmity towards the Pāṇḍavas.

His jealousy and antagonism towards Arjuna was such that Karṇa tried several times to kill the former in his adolescent days. To do so he was badly in need of a fatal weapon. In those days, *brahmāstra* or the 'ultimate weapon' was probably something that did not require much mastery but could nonetheless wreck massive havoc and destruction. The individual possession of the *brahmāstra*, therefore, had the role of being a 'deterrent'— a symbol of 'balance of power' and not meant to be used in direct encounters. In appreciation of the pupil's achievements, Droṇācārya gifted a *brahmāstra* to Arjuna. Droṇācārya's gift made Karṇa even more hostile towards Arjuna. He approached Droṇa and urged him to bequeath the same favour to him so that he could be on equal terms with Arjuna during warfare (*arjunena samo yuddhe bhaveyamiti me matiḥ*) (*Śāntiparvan* 2.10). While making the request, Karṇa did not forget to remind Droṇācārya of the teacherly virtue of being impartial to all students. Droṇācārya, however, was unmoved, for he was fully aware of Karṇa's jealousy towards Arjuna. Besides, he also knew how eager Karṇa was to put an end to Arjuna's life (*daurātmyancaiva karṇasya viditvā tamuvāca ha*) (*Śāntiparvan* 2.12). So, he said to Karṇa: '*Brahmāstra* is not for a common man; only he, who can control his senses, has the right to handle it'.

Karṇa then approached Paraśurāma, the warrior incarnate who had eliminated the *Kṣatriya* rulers a number of times. And, Paraśurāma, one archetypical representative of Brahmanical orthodoxy, had a peculiar method of recruiting disciples from the higher ranks of society. To obtain what he desired, Karṇa presented himself as a Bhārgava *Brāhmaṇa*, the renowned class to which Paraśurāma himself belonged.

However, Karṇa's impersonation was revealed very soon. Outraged by the scandal of false identity, Paraśurāma cursed Karṇa that at times of great crisis sudden amnesia would screen Karṇa's consciousness and he would forget how exactly he should use the arms at his command. The moment he heard the fatal curse Karṇa did not linger; he returned post-haste to Duryodhana and declared: 'I am fully trained in the art of weapons' (*duryodhanamupāgamya kṛtāstro'smīti cābravīt* (*Śāntiparvan* 3.33) Karṇa, of course, did not reveal all the facts to Duryodhana. But Paraśurāma's curse remained operative — Karṇa could not recall the nomenclature of *brahmāstra* during his last battle with Arjuna and his chariot-wheel got stuck in the earth at the crucial hour. Our conjecture is, the poet of the *Mahābhārata* had deliberately inserted the episode of Paraśurāma's curse on Karṇa — the angry *Brāhmaṇa*'s words afforded a shield-like cover to Arjuna's unethical attack on Karṇa when they met for the last time on the battlefield of Kurukṣetra.

It is noteworthy that not one of Karṇa's early 'misdeeds' is to be found in the regional *Mahābhāratas*. The same applies to various transcreated versions centred on Karṇa. Karṇa's childhood camaraderie with Duryodhana, their shared feeling of spite and anger towards the Pāṇḍavas, Karṇa's calculated moves to belittle the worth of Arjuna, etc. — none of these 'items' features in works that highlight the hero's subjective *angst*. But, surely, to omit them is to commit the fatal error of making totalistic claims based on partial information. The transcreators speak loudly of the pathos which at the last instance is predicated on the sense of *loss* felt by a child abandoned by his mother. But, in particular, it is they who do not bother to go into the complications involved in the virgin-psychosis of an unwed mother. In most of the later adaptations of the epic, Karṇa appears dramatically on the stage — we meet him for the first time in the weapon-tournament and that too at a time when Arjuna had already proved his excellence in the art of archery. However, given his long-standing animosity towards Arjuna and the Pāṇḍavas, his dramatic entry can easily be construed as a sort of pre-meditated strategy conceived in consultation with Duryodhana. It is further borne by the provocative attitude that Karṇa displayed towards the tournament — his cursory nod to Droṇa and Kṛpācārya, his boast that he could any day outsmart Arjuna, etc., were calculated to undermine the gravity of the event. And then, Karṇa dealt a severe blow to Arjuna's pride by proving he was worth his words. Duryodhana went into ecstasy which further inflamed Duryodhana's cousins and their associates. Duryodhana said to Karṇa: 'You are most welcome, my friend! Do please place your foot upon the heads of your enemies' (*durhrdam kuru sarvesam murdhni padam-arindama*) (*Ādiparvan* 136.16). Thereafter, Karṇa challenged Arjuna to a duel. There was another dimension to this tense-ridden scene. Sitting behind screens, Kuntī was witnessing the tournament. Seeing that two of her sons were about to begin a fight she fainted. And, nobody really understood what actually ailed her.

Next, spicing his remarks with crudities, Kṛpācārya intervened. To stop the duel — since he thought that Arjuna might lose it — Kṛpācārya struck at the most vulnerable spot of Karṇa's psyche. He asked Karṇa about his parentage. Kṛpa said: 'Arjuna is a prince, scion of a royal family; therefore, only those of royal lineage are entitled to get into a fight with him'. The words struck Karṇa like a bolt of lightning. Karṇa's enthusiasm and vigour rapidly evaporated. The *Mahābhārata* poet captured the moment with an exquisite piece of simile. He compared the face of Karṇa with a lotus in bloom whose beauty was being washed away with incessant rains (*babhau varsambu-viklinnam padmam agalitam yatha*) (*Ādiparvan* 136.34). Duryodhana then, promptly enthroned Karṇa as the king of Angadeśa. The indebted Karṇa promised to do everything for Duryodhana. The latter was overjoyed at having discovered a new hero.

The one person who was delighted by Duryodhana's gesture was Kuntī. Of course, she desisted from expressing her feelings openly. The guilty conscience that had so long raged in her heart abated to some extent when she saw her premarital son anointed the ruler of Angadeśa. And, Rabindranath Tagore, the twentieth-century transcreator, took the cue for his *Karṇa–Kuntī Saṃvād* from this passage of the *Mahābhārata* — while reminding Karṇa of the incident Tagore's Kuntī spoke freely of the feelings she had undergone then.

Tagore, however, avoided the intricacies of rivalry between the two heroes. His verse-play, instead, was built solely on the theme of conciliation between the mother and her estranged son. With the express intention of convincing Karṇa that Duryodhana's good deed had indeed been like a balm of solace on her guilty heart, Tagore's Kuntī said:

> Blessed is that lad Duryodhana, who crowned you prince of Anga. Yes, I praise him! And as you were crowned, tears streamed from my eyes rushing towards you. Next, Adhiratha, the charioteer, entered the arena, bubbling with joy. And you — in your royal gear and in the midst of the curious crowd milling all around — bowed your only-just anointed head, and saluted the feet of the old charioteer. You addressed him "Father". Cruelly, contemptuously, the friends of the Pāṇḍavas smiled. But right then who blessed you as a hero, O you jewel amongst heroes, was I, the mother of Arjuna.

In the *Mahābhārata*, after having been crowned king of Angadeśa, Karṇa felt very charged; he renewed his offer of duel to Arjuna. But, just at that moment, Adhiratha, the foster-father of Karṇa entered the stage. Karṇa lowered his bejewelled head at his sight and touched his feet (*karṇobhiṣekārdra-śiraḥ śirasā samāvandata*) (*Ādiparvan* 137.2). It was as if to prove that there were no causal connections between *conditions of birth* and *acquiring of heroic traits*, Karṇa made a public display of his respect for his charioteer father. The show was inciting enough to make Bhīma cut a derisive remark. He asked Karṇa to throw away his arrows and bow and instead hold the reins of horses the way his forefathers had done. Duryodhana retaliated by questioning the parentage of Pāṇḍavas. The wrangling was concluded by Duryodhana with the declaration: 'Karṇa was never born of a lowly parentage; can a doe give birth to a tiger? This is my last word: if you still have doubts, please come forward and have a duel with him'.

The fight that was imminent did not take place because by then the sun had set. But Karṇa's enthusiasm, combined with that of Duryodhana's, made it apparent to all that a new hero had appeared among them. Duryodhana, with his hundred brothers and other supporters, made a torch-light procession keeping Karṇa in the front (*dīpikāgni-kṛtalokas-tasmād rangād viniryayan*) (*Ādiparvan* 137.20). Everyone returned home after the jubilation. But Yudhiṣṭhira, the eldest of the Pāṇḍavas, remained pondering over the whole eventful day and reached home convinced that he was no match for Karṇa. The *Mahābhārata*-poet depicts Karṇa's character with multiple brush-strokes. At places, he is shown to be humbled by the exacting experiences of public censure and at others revengeful, aggressive and even impolite. It should be noted that Karṇa, the crowned king of Angadeśa, did not take charge of the country assigned to him. Instead, he dabbled in Hastināpura-politics and went on to further Duryodhana's scheme of self-aggrandizement.

The duty of conducting training in arms for Yudhiṣṭhira was vested in some royal power in state administration by Dhṛtarāṣṭra. And, Yudhiṣṭhira was proving to be an adept pupil and was gaining popularity amongst the subjects. Obviously, this popularity fuelled Duryodhana's ire. He hatched a plot to burn the Pāṇḍavas in a house of lac at Vārṇāvata. It surely is shameful that Karṇa — the man regarded as one of the stellar heroes of the *Mahābhārata* — soiled himself by joining the conspiracy (*duḥśāsanaśca karṇaśca duṣṭam mantram amantrayan*) (*Ādiparvan* 141.1). But, what is of importance to note is that the transcreated versions of the Karṇa-myth methodically avoid or ignore Karṇa's crooked doings — the heinous acts performed at the behest of Duryodhana and Śakuni.

The plot, however, failed to materialize. The episode surrounding the mystery of the house of lac was followed by the episode of Draupadī's matrimonial feast, the *svayaṃvara*. And there too Karṇa was thwarted. The question of parentage and royal inheritance again came up when Draupadī declared in the open assembly that she would not accept one who was born of or brought up by a man of charioteer-class (*nāham varayāmi sūtam*) (*Ādiparvan* 188.23) as her husband. Many scholars take Draupadī's declamation as an explicit instance of exclusionist caste-consciousness. It was because of this resounding statement that Karṇa refrained from participating in the competition. However, Bengali *Mahābhārata*s willfully suppress Draupadī's curt declaration and innovate the miracle of Kṛṣṇa's *sudarśana-cakra* (discus) instead. In the newly fabricated story, we learn, the target was covered by the Kṛṣṇa's discus, thus obstructing the motion of Karṇa's arrow.

So, in the view of Kashiram Das, the author of the sixteenth-century Bengali *Mahābhārata*, Karṇa was a victim of destiny and not of caste discrimination. Perhaps, it was because the poet himself belonged to a so-called lower caste that he could not stomach Draupadī's refusal of one of the most deserving suitors on grounds of caste.

Measure for Measure

Nonetheless, we are of the opinion that Draupadī's public statement is an indispensable element in the overall narrative structure of the epic. The episode of *svayaṃvara* seems to have been concocted to seek out Arjuna from the morass of the house of lac confusion. Since the time king Drupada of Pañcāla was humiliated by his arch enemy Droṇācārya, he was determined to woo Arjuna to his side. The *Mahābhārata* relates that Drupada manufactured the machine of *mīnacakṣu* (fish-eye) with the intention of locating Arjuna (*Ādiparvan* 184.29). He was certain that only Arjuna would succeed in piercing the fish-eye. He had no idea about Karṇa,; thus, when Karṇa was about to hit the mark, Draupadī skillfully fulfilled her father's mission by her announcement. Karṇa, however, never forgot or condoned Draupadī's insult. It served as a secret but inexhaustible fodder for his hatred against his foes at the time of the Great War.

Duryodhana's futile attempt to burn the Pāṇḍavas and the latter's success in procuring a coveted wife as well as a faithful ally in the Pañcālas altered the scenario. This led him to hatch newer plans by which he could subdue the Pāṇḍavas. The 'hero' in Karṇa was often repulsed by his friend's fondness for deceit — he was all for declaring war against the Pañcālas. Even if the genuine worth of Karṇa got revealed at such moments, he finally succumbed to the pressures of real-politic and was embroiled in the bog of trickery and perjury made manifest by Śakuni and Duryodhana.

Again, due to pressures of real-politic, Kuru king Dhṛtarāṣṭra was forced to appease the Pāṇḍavas. In deference to the Pāṇḍava–Pañcāla marital alliance, the blind king agreed to give away a part of his kingdom with Indraprastha as its capital. The royal splendour of the Pāṇḍavas began with the elaborate arrangements of the *Rājasūya* sacrifice, a ritual designed to enhance the political prowess and administrative control of other kingdoms.

The glamour of the *Rājasūya* and the rising glory of Pāṇḍavas made Duryodhana even more jealous and furious. The *Mahābhārata* informs us that while the ultimate counter-product of the *Rājasūya* was the Kurukṣetra war, the game of dice initiated by Śakuni was its immediate fall-out. But once the game was won by Śakuni, Karṇa became hyperactive. We do not, for sure, know — and the *Mahābhārata* poet does not spell it clearly either — whether Karṇa approved of the trickery in the game of dice. But given that he did not protest and gradually got himself enmeshed in the subsequent proceedings of the game, it seems that he was certainly, even if reluctantly, a party to it. Towards the end of the game, Yudhiṣṭhira was lured into betting on Draupadī by Śakuni. In accordance with practice, before placing her as the stake, Yudhiṣṭhira described Draupadī's stunning beauty to affirm the costliness of the stake. And then chaos broke out. Draupadī was won by a simple throw of dice by Śakuni and the whole of Kaurava assembly geared up into action. Draupadī was forcibly dragged into the assembly, praying helplessly for justice.

This was the time when the great Karṇa slid into the mean Karṇa. The epic war-hero changed into a common man, libidinal and revengeful. When Draupadī was being heckled by Duḥśāsana and the upper part of her garment pulled, Karṇa burst out into laughter (*jahāsa karṇo'tibhrsam saha duḥśāsanādibhiḥ*) (*Ādiparvan* 65.44). We know what this laughter meant. It verged on a sexual derision, a lusty taunt, and was expressive of his resentment for having been slighted by Draupadī during the *svayaṃvara*. The laughter was the reaction of Karṇa's shattered dreams. He could neither forget Draupadī's disparaging remark about his lowly origin nor could he tolerate her sexual relations with five husbands. He took Draupadī's polyandry as a proof of her insatiable sexual appetite. Lending (moral) support to Duḥśāsana's molestation of Draupadī he shouted: 'Women-folk indeed enjoy the scratch — the scratch of many male partners (*ipsitaśca guṇāḥ striṇām ekasya bahubhartṛtā*) (*Ādiparvan* 202.8). Herself a harlot, Draupadī enjoys the beds of five husbands which amounts to the act of prostitution; so, what is the harm, if another pulls her garments off'. Karṇa indeed dishonoured womankind in general.

We should note here that while devising the fraudulant dice-game, neither Śakuni nor Duryodhana consulted Karṇa. In fact, he was not even properly informed. But neither was Karṇa discomfited when in course of the game the Pāṇḍavas were cheated. He rather relished the all-round collapse of his arch-enemies. Karṇa was happily seated in the royal assembly along with Duryodhana and was the first to break into raucous laughter when Draupadī was staked. That 'laughter' does bespeak of 'perversion'. But, what must not be ignored is the *history* of the 'perversion'; the tortuous making of a psyche *fractured* by double-rejection, one by the mother and the other by the desired woman.

Draupadī was dragged into the royal assembly at Duryodhana's behest. But the excess which Duḥśāsana made of it by calling her a maid (*dāsī*) — a *dāsī* could be sexually exploited by a buyer or a winner with impunity — invited the excess of Karṇa. Karṇa particularly relished this address; laughing loudly he thanked Duḥśāsana (*karṇastu tadvākyam atīva hṛṣṭaḥ/sampūjayamasa hasan sasavdam*) (*Sabhāparvan* 67.45).

Karṇa, however, could not carry on in this vein for long. Words of protest started to pour in. Vikarṇa, one of Duryodhana's brothers, questioned Yudhiṣṭhira's right to stake Draupadī after he had lost himself to Duryodhana in the betting game. The argument was embarrassing and it was expected that Duryodhana himself would prevent Vikarṇa from pursuing it further. But surprisingly, it was Karṇa who asked Vikarṇa to stop and dismissed whatever he had said by adding the disparaging note: 'It's rather awkward when a child gets so presumptuous as to don the garb of a philosopher'. Karṇa made the matter worse by besmirching Draupadī's honour. He said to Vikarṇa: 'No injustice has been done to this wretched woman; everyone knows that monogamy is the norm as far as women are concerned; but this one has five; verily, she is a whore (*vaudhakīti viniścita*) (*Sabhāparvan* 68.35). So, why are you surprised, my boy! We have brought a public-woman to the assembly; it is immaterial whether she comes naked or in single attire' (*Sabhāparvan* 68.36).

It was Karṇa and not Duryodhana who had ordered Duḥśāsana to collect the clothes of the Pāṇḍavas and strip Draupadī (*pāṇḍavanarica vāsāṃsi draupadyaśca samahara*) (*Sabhāparvan* 68.38). The Pāṇḍavas somehow digested the insult by taking off their turbans, turban being the symbol of warrior-heroes. On the other hand, goaded by Karṇa, the crude Duḥśāsana was bent upon removing Draupadī's upper garment.

This outrage by Karṇa even outstrips the earlier one when he had suggested that instead of being dragged to the assembly hall, Draupadī should be taken from the inner quarters of the palace. Suitably provoked by Karṇa's second command, Duryodhana gave a public demonstration of his ardour: he bared his left thigh and showed it to Draupadī. Duryodhana's tacit support of the thesis that Draupadī was nothing more than a common whore further tickled Karṇa (*abhyusmayitvā rādheyam*) (*Sabhāparvan* 71.12).

We think we are now in a position to argue that Duryodhana was not the sole person responsible for Draupadī's molestation. Karṇa has to bear at least the same measure of responsibility as Duryodhana. The incident gave a dangerous turn to the internal politics of the Kauravas and subsequently became the instrumental cause (*nimitta kāraṇa*) of the Kurukṣetra war. Recall how Gāndhārī cried out standing before the corpses of the battlefield; she felt that the devastation had been caused by Karṇa and Duḥśāsana (*karṇa-duḥśāsanabhyaca vṛtto'yam kurusamkṣayaḥ*) (*Strīparvan* 14.16).

From Vainglory to Unblemished Glory

Poets like Kashiram Das or Rabindranath Tagore and critics like Buddhadev Bose have willingly skipped some of the embarrassing details relating to Karṇa in order to serve their poetic interests. More precisely, the later poets blacked out the obnoxious aspects of Karṇa's character so that they could emotionally capitalize on the tribulations of a child forsaken at birth. Kuntī's hesitation to meet Karṇa and her pronounced feeling of guilt for having abandoned her first-born was the primary focus of Tagore. Thus, the dialogue penned by him is suffused with sentimentalism.

In the original *Mahābhārata*, the *Sabhāparvan* marks a climax — a climax of cunning pertaining to the anti-heroes of the *Mahābhārata*. After this, it petered off. Karṇa, who showed scant respect for the elders and incessantly indulged his indulgent friend Duryodhana, remained silent for some days. He found no one in the capital worth his rivalry. To bestir the dying wind Karṇa, proposed to Duryodhana that he build a royal camp near the forest-abode of the exiled Pāṇḍavas and pounce upon them with weapons. The plan was later revised and given the look of being a harmless sport. Karṇa said to Duryodhana:

> The entire world is now in your palm. The feudal kings are waiting upon you with gifts and tributes. But what is the worth of this wealth if you can flaunt it before the destitute Pāṇḍavas. I think you should go to Dvaitavana right now along with your queens and servants all bedecked with jewels and you should parade them in front of the Pāṇḍavas till Arjuna bleeds to death out of shame and Draupadī repents her marriage with five beggars. Draupadī heaving a long long sigh will certainly cheer you up (*kim nu tasya sukham na syāt/ . . . sa ca nirvidyatampunaḥ*) (*Āraṇyakaparvan* 236.20–21).

Duryodhana heartily accepted Karṇa's plan and went to the forest with the excuse that he was going there to execute the duty of supervising the cow-breeders appointed by Dhṛtarāṣṭra. The plan, however, utterly failed. Duryodhana, Karṇa and their entire band of soldiers were beaten by Gandharva Citrasena, a divine friend of Arjuna. Karṇa fled from the battlefield and Duryodhana was captured. He was released later due to Arjuna's grace. When Duryodhana was wailing in his defeat and was reluctant to return to Hastināpura, Karṇa pleaded for his safe retreat. The pleading makes conspicuous both his weakness and vaingloriousness. He said:

> It is the duty of your subjects [in this case the Pāṇḍavas] to save the life of their king. So, the slaves have done their jobs. Come on, Duryodhana! Do not get hurt. Pāṇḍavas have been enslaved long before (*preṣyatam purvam āgataḥ*) and the slaves have released their master. There is nothing more to it. Do not brood over it.

Such utterances are unbecoming of a warrior-hero like Karṇa, a warrior who in terms of martial skill could be compared with Arjuna, Bhīṣma, Droṇa, and Aśvatthāmā. It is remarkable in this connection, that in later Sanskrit literature and in medieval and modern Bengali literature, Karṇa is known by the proverbial *Veṇīsaṃhāram* utterance, 'One's birth in a good family is controlled by Providence, but all manly powers are one's own' (*daivayāttam kule janma madayāttam pauruṣam*). But all this seems to be mere tall talk, particularly if we read it in the context of his repeated defeats in various wars. Karṇa was defeated when he accompanied Duryodhana to attack the Matsya country in a bid to seize the herds of cows owned by king Vīrāṭa. Karṇa again had to flee from the battlefield as he had to do in the earlier battle. But more than these defeats which a *Kṣatriya* war-hero might incur in life, we feel astounded by his crafty behaviour when he suggested to Duryodhana that the latter should find out the whereabouts of the Pāṇḍavas who were living one year in disguise in compliance with the terms of defeat in the second game of dice. Karṇa gambled on the fact if the Pāṇḍavas were traced, then in keeping with the terms of defeat they would be compelled to live in exile for another spell of 12 years.

At the end of it all, *Mahābhārata*'s Karṇa turns out to be self-defeating, so much so that in matters dealing with trickery and treachery he was surpassed only by

Śakuni. Later poets, including modern ones, tried their level best to salvage Karṇa from the morass of corruption to which the epic condemns him.

Karṇa's proverbial trait of magnanimity, i.e., gifting anything to any *Brāhmaṇa* was a creation of the famous Sanskrit dramatist Bhāsa in the second or third century AD. The same theme was picked up by Kashiram Das in his Bengali *Mahābhārata*. From the original *Mahābhārata*, we learn that after performing the *Vaiśṇava Yajña* in the *Āraṇyakaparvan*, Karṇa had taken the vow of making gifts to *Brāhmaṇa*s whenever solicited. We are inclined to believe that the story of Karṇa's ever-bountiful nature had been fashioned by the *Mahābhārata* poet to give credence to the poetic moment at which Karṇa gave away his golden armour and earrings as a *dāna* or gift to Indra who had approached him in the guise of a *Brāhmaṇa* and then cheated him of his life-support. Bhāsa wrote his famous one-act play *Karṇābharam* based on this episode. Karṇa's munificence reached its height in the Bengali transcreation of Kashiram Das — a text in which the institutionalized form of *dāna*, as outlined in the *Dharmasāstra*s or 'Law Books', gets fleshed out through Karṇa's action.

Nevertheless, Karṇa remained vainglorious to the bitter end. And as far as slighting others was concerned, he spared none — from the old and experienced people of the Kuru clan to preceptors of any rank, everyone had to bear his cutting caustic remarks. An instance of this is his quarrel with Droṇācārya in the *Virāṭaparvan* of the *Mahābhārata*. When during the one-year period of 'living in disguise', Arjuna faced the Kaurava army in the form of Bṛhannalā, the eunuch, Droṇa guessed his true identity. At this Karṇa became very impatient and ridiculed Droṇa by saying: 'This man gets utterly confused even when he hears the neighing of war-horses'. Karṇa asked Duryodhana to push back Droṇa to the rear post of the army (*tathainam pṛṣṭhāth kṛtvā*) because he felt certain, all said and done, Droṇa was no better than those garrulous Puṇḍits who devote themselves to hair-splitting analyses of trivial things such as 'purity' or 'impurity' in the affair of partaking of food (*paresam vivara-jriane manuṣya-cariteṣu calanna-saṃskāra-doṣesu paṇḍitastatra śobhanaḥ*) (*Vīrāṭaparvan* 47.31–32). After casting this vile aspersion on Droṇa, Karṇa boasted about himself: 'If Arjuna does come, I am here; I am no less a warrior than him' (*ahancāpi nara-śreṣṭhād arjunānnāvaraḥ kvacit*) (*Vīrāṭaparvan* 48.8).

Karṇa's harsh words for Droṇa instigated an immediate quarrel with Droṇa's son Aśvatthāmā. The situation became so ugly that Karṇa even threatened to kill Aśvatthāmā. Karṇa said: 'I am a little shy of killing you; were you not a *Brāhmaṇa* by caste, I would have killed you by this time'. In response, Aśvatthāmā pulled off his sacred thread and thumped the ground signalling that he was ready for fight. Duryodhana and Bhīṣma intervened; only when reminded of the imminent war, were the two angry young men assuaged.

We have excerpted this acrimonious exchange from the *Vīrāṭaparvan* only to show how Karṇa's audacity reared its head on many occasions but seldom managed to make good the bragging claims. In the last case, he had to even flee away from the battlefield; when he rejoined the battle, he, along with others, was struck senseless by Arjuna's arrows. Karṇa never outgrew his narcissistic arrogance. At places, his haughtiness beggars belief. One illustrative episode is in the *Udyogaparvan.* Yudhiṣṭhira sent an emissary to the Kuru court asking for the share of kingdom due to the Pāṇḍavas. Even while the emissary was addressing Duryodhana, Karṇa butted in to say: 'Do not threaten us with the war-cry; if you do, Duryodhana will not give you even a small slice of the earth (*duryodhana bhayādvidvanna dadyāt pādam antataḥ*). And if you still think of war, remember my ultimatum, you will not be granted a single slice of land' (*Udyogaparvan* 21.12).

These circumstances led Bhīṣma to intervene. But he could not understand why Karṇa was talking so much. Although Bhīṣma could not tolerate the aggressive attitude of Drupad's emissary, he still could not accept Karṇa retorting on Duryodhana's behalf. Bhīṣma began teasing Karṇa by reminding him of his countless defeats at Arjuna's hand. To rub it in further, he said: 'You were the first victim of Arjuna's wrath in the Vīrāṭa country and your turban [the symbol of heroism] was taken away for the decoration of [Vīrāṭa's daughter] Uttarā's dolls'.

Vyāsa Churns the Ocean and Tagore Drinks the Poison: Ambrosia for the Vernacular Karṇa

Duryodhana, however, stuck to Karṇa. Karṇa distanced himself from old warriors, particularly Bhīṣma, the grandsire whom he personally detested. Insulted by Bhīṣma, he laid down his arms and refused to fight under the grandsire's leadership. Fearing that people might confuse his heroic ventures with those of Bhīṣma's, he did nothing that could contribute to the increase of Bhīṣma's fame. Karṇa said forthright to the old man: 'I will take up arms only after your demise (*naham jivati gangeyeyotsye rajan kathancana*) (*Udyogaparvan* 167.29). *Mahābhārata*'s Karṇa is truly a bundle of contradictions: although not born into a *Sūta* family, he was reared in a *Sūta* household; taking himself to be the progeny of a *Kṣatriya* man and a *Brāhmaṇa* woman, he unconsciously imbibed *Kṣatriya*-like arrogance and *Brāhmaṇa*-like indifference to martial defeat. This was exactly how Bhīṣma viewed him.

Let us now turn to the crucial moment. Kṛṣṇa failed in his peace-mission, but thereafter gave a lift to Karṇa in his chariot and engaged him in a one-to-one talk. After the preliminaries, Kṛṣṇa came to the point of the imminent war and wanted Karṇa to fight for the Pāṇḍavas. Kṛṣṇa said: 'You are, in fact, Pāṇḍu's son (though) borne by Kuntī before her marriage (*Pāndor hi putro'si dharmataḥ*); you should join your brothers; Yudhiṣṭhira, Bhīma, Arjuna and others will serve you like servants; and last but not the least, Karṇa, you will get the chance of sleeping with Draupadī'.

It is here that we get a glimpse of the Karṇa who is noble and not an opportunist. In keeping with the best traditions of epic-heroes, he refused to succumb to

Kṛṣṇa's adducing. Friendship for Duryodhana and fondness for the foster-mother outweighing all other considerations, Karṇa rejected the proposal of switching sides on the eve of the war. He said to Kṛṣṇa: 'I know everything, Kṛṣṇa! I know everything, but how can I forget my mother who fed me with the first stream of her milk (*sadyaḥ kṣiram avatarat*) how can I forget her who used to cleanse my refuse in my childhood days' (*sa me mutra-puriṣañca pratijaraha mādhava*) (*Udyogaparvan* 141.6).

There is ample proof in this conversation with Kṛṣṇa that Karṇa was well aware of the psychological make-up of his immediate younger, Yudhiṣṭhira, i.e., Karṇa asked Kṛṣṇa not to divulge his secret to Yudhiṣṭhira, for then he might forsake the plan of war and give up his claim to kingship. Karṇa seemed to have had his finger on the pulses of all his younger brothers; and it is this pleasing feeling of brotherhood which has been brilliantly captured by Tagore in *Karṇa–Kuntī Saṃvād*: 'Why did I have to hear from Arjuna's mother's throat my own mother's voice? Why did my name ring in her mouth with such exquisite music — so much so that suddenly my heart rushes towards the five Pāṇḍavas, calling them brothers'.

Tagore's *Karṇa–Kuntī Saṃvād* is a reworking of the *Mahābhārata*'s *Karṇa–Kuntī Samāgama* ('The Meeting of Karṇa and Kuntī'). The sun had set then; as Kuntī approached him, we believe, Karṇa recognized her gait and so harshly introduced himself as: 'I am the son of Rādhā, the son of Adhiratha, I welcome you (*rādheyo'ham adhirathiḥ karṇastvam abhivadaye*) (*Udyogaparvan* 145.1). This is outright refusal of Kuntī's claim to 'motherhood'. Tagore retains this attitude in his poem; disjoining the *taddhita* suffix in the words *rādheya* and *adhirathi* he forms a compound or *samāsa*: *adhiratha-sūta-putra rādhā-garbha-jāta*. In the *Mahābhārata*, whenever Kuntī tried to bring home the reality of her motherhood to Karṇa, he said: 'I cannot really accept it' (*na caitad śraddadhe vākyam*) (*Udyogaparvan* 146.4). Karṇa also talked about *dharma* and *a-dharma* here — the ethics and non-ethics — and at last blatantly charged Kuntī of having meted out to him the worst possible treatment, a treatment that only a faithless mother was capable of meting. He said: 'Even the most virulent of my enemies had not done such damage to me as you have done' (*tvat-kṛte kinnu pāpiyaḥ śatruḥ kuryan-mamahitam*) (*Udyogaparvan* 146.6). 'You have never been affectionate to me; you have not performed the duties of a proper mother; but now you have come selfishly to secure your own good' (*sa ma samvodhasyadya kevalatma-hitaisini*) (*Udyogaparvan* 146.8). 'Moreover, what would others say about this reunion. Would not they mock, how is it, dear! Just at the eve of war you discover who your own brothers are! So far they had no brotherly presence in your life and now suddenly they make their appearance (*abhrata viditaḥ kinicit yuddhakāle prakāśitaḥ*) (*Udyogaparvan* 146.10). Then again what would be the reactions of the warriors if I now join the Pāṇḍavas. They will take me for a coward, a man who deserts the field out of fear for Bhīma or Arjuna'.

The aforecited lines from the Sanskrit *Mahābhārata* indicate adequately the surge of human emotions befitting an epic-hero. But Karṇa's stern retorts are mellowed in Tagore. Since Tagore's aim was to describe only the final meeting of two separated souls — a mother and a son — he had the clear advantage of omitting all the earlier evil doings of Karṇa. Hence, even his harsh words to Kuntī become poetically melodious in Tagore's rendering. Tagore, the poet of poets, transcreated a superb poetic piece out of the epic mass of crudeness, revenge and violence. Tagore's Karṇa is a modern man, crying out claiming our sympathy especially because he is a social rebel, provoking our outrage at the unfairness of cosmic injustice and wringing out of us a negative amazement at Kuntī's partiality towards her 'legitimate' son Arjuna and her heartlessness towards her first-born yet another time. It is impossible to summarize 'critically' or re-describe the pure profound pathos of this modern Karṇa except in Tagore's own words.

The limited purpose of this short essay was, without diminishing the greatness of Tagore's emotional artistry, to remind the comparativist that the Karṇa in Vyāsa's *Mahābhārata* is more real, total and multifaceted than the modern vernacular Karṇa. To that extent the 'original' anti-hero still affords us the potential perhaps for more post-modern drama. We should not forget, after all, Bharata's remark: 'No drama can be born of a single aestheticized emotion' (*na hi ekarasajam nāṭyam bhavati*) (*Nāṭyśāstra* I).

References

Pancānan Tarkaratna (ed.). 1908 (Śakābda 1830). *Mahābhārata*, Kolkata: Bangabāsī.

Tagore, Rabindranath. 2011. 'The Meeting of Karṇa and Kunti', in Rabindranath Tagore, *Selected Poems: Rabindranath Tagore*, trans. Sukanta Chaudhuri. Oxford University Press.

PART III
Ethics

Care Ethics and Epistemic Justice

Some Insights from the Mahābhārata[1]

Vrinda Dalmiya

Why the *Mahābhārata*?

Care ethics appeals to intimate personal connections rather than formal contracts as the basis of moral life. The central notion of caring is parsed as 'intolerance of ignorance' according to Annette Baier (1982). After all, we clearly do not care if we are indifferent to what someone needs. Less obviously, caring also implies an awareness of why we want to address those needs in the first place. To care is to make something which might not be naturally valuable, important to us. But if the object we care for matters, it also begins to matter *whether we care* for it or not. Caring, therefore, involves a '*caring* about caring'. 'Mattering', however, is a desire to acquire more knowledge about that which matters. So, to care about anyone entails getting clearer on what the object of care is like *and* on the nature and reasons for that caring itself. In this way, care is deeply intertwined with knowing, at least, two levels: knowing the cared-for and knowing the roots of our caring for the cared-for.

While it is generally conceded that we must know the cared-for in order to successfully care for her, there is controversy over whether care includes the iterative moment of caring for caring and thereby involves knowing the nature of our cares. And even when first-order caring (for persons and objects) is understood to include the second-order ratiocination about the caring, there is not much analysis about the nature of the *thinking* involved in this step. Carol Gilligan characterizes the care perspective as 'joining the heart and eye in an ethic that *ties the activity of thought to the activity of care*' (1982: 149; emphasis mine). But even she leaves the 'activity of thought' as an un-analyzed given. My excursion into the *Mahābhārata*[2] is motivated by these specific concerns within contemporary discussions of the care perspective.

---

[1] A version of this essay was presented at the Spring School on *Mahābhārata Today* held at the Indian Institute of Advanced Study, Shimla (April 2010). I would like to thank members of the audience for their comments. I am particularly grateful for discussion with Sibaji Bandyopadhyay, Arindam Chakrabarti, Anirban Das, Peter DeSouza, Bodhisattva Kar, and Kanchana Natarajan.

[2] All references to the *Mahābhārata* are from Kinjawadekar (n.d.).

I do not claim that the *Mahābhārata* develops a consistent ethic of care, nor do I assert that since care ethics is (arguably) a feminist theory, the text is a feminist text. Rather, I enter the 'tropical rainforest' of the epic and follow some of its twists and turns for insights regarding two questions: must our commitment to the objects of desire (or care) include an inquiry into the nature of those desires? And what is the nature of the *inquiry* that goes hand in hand with caring? The *Mahābhārata*'s general intertwining of 'living well' with 'knowing well' can be illuminating for answering both these questions.

To anticipate my answers: with regard to the first question, Indra's dialogue with a parrot (in the *Anuśāsanaparvan*) and with Yudhiṣṭhira (in the *Mahāprasthānikaparvan*) foregrounds the concept of *anukrośa* (literally, 'crying after'). I analyze the use of *anukrośa* in these two episodes to reinforce a self-reflexive cognitive moment in care.[3] Thus, the *Mahābhārata*'s stand is that caring for someone does involve a second-order caring for/knowing about that first-level caring. With regard to the second question, the dialogues of sage Kauśika with an 'ordinary housewife' and a butcher (in the *Āraṇyakaparvan*) foreground the transformation needed for being a 'good knower'. I argue that the epistemological maturing of Kauśika establishes that knowing involves an active search for ignorance.[4] My claim is that this vision of knowledge found in the *Mahābhārata* — where the will to know is to cultivate an ability to not know — is productive for caring.

Of course, putting these two claims together creates an interesting paradox. If caring involves knowing and knowing is a search for ignorance, then caring is both an intolerance of and an investment in ignorance. This tension is negotiated in this chapter by falling back on the *Mahābhārata*'s idea that epistemic and ethical lives coalesce in particular notions of character or virtue. I articulate a specific virtue of 'relational humility' — a dynamic between self-ascribing ignorance and other-ascribing knowledge — as being this foundational disposition or character trait necessary for both good living and good thinking. Relational humility shows us how (and why) knowing is infused with an active recognition of not-knowing. Hence, caring, too, must accommodate ignorance in some form even as it refuses to tolerate it: in fact, *accepting ignorance in one sense is absolutely essential for rejecting it in another* for caring to be successful.

The discussion concludes by exploring how relational humility as a 'virtue of truth' is also a virtue of epistemic justice. But I go on to discuss whether this can become a general 'virtue of social justice' in ways that its protagonists in the *Mahābhārata* — Kauśika, the parrot, Yudhiṣṭhira, and Indra — might not have been interested in themselves. Thus, even though the caring/knowing self in the *Mahābhārata* fails to be a feminist subject striving to rectify injustices of oppression,

---

[3] The argument for this was spelled out in Dalmiya (2001).

[4] I have explored this connection in Dalmiya (2007).

yet interesting ideas about political subjectivity can be derived by reading the epic against the grain.

Living Well: Yudhiṣṭhira, the Relational Self and *Anukrośa*

According to some contemporary scholars, the concept of *anukrośa* in the *Mahābhārata* gestures towards non-cruelty, and the allied notion of *ānṛśaṃsya* is said to destabilize the violence/non-violence dichotomy (Bandyopadhyay 2010). However, to the extent that being non-cruel amounts to not causing harm or, at least, willingness to explore the least harmful of options in complex relational contexts, one can pursue *anukrośa* as the voice of ethical care. In this context, note Gilligan's elucidation of care as that which 'expands from the paralyzing injunction not to hurt others to an injunction to act responsively toward self and others' (1982: 149). Such responsiveness is the essence of the *Mahābhārata*'s notion of non-cruelty. The plausibility of the comparison between *anukrośa* and care further rests on the relational self being central to both perspectives. But a close reading shows that *anukrośa* is the self-conscious and *reasoned* construction of a relational self. Thus, it can underscore that caring also must involve a reflective exploration of connections that make us who we are.

In the first, lesser known story in the *Anuśāsanaparvan* (13.2), Indra questioned a parrot who refused to leave the dying tree that had served as its home and take refuge in (literally) greener pastures. The parrot defended its decision by the reply: 'I was born in this tree and have lived here all my life. This tree has camouflaged me from hunters and has nourished me with its fruit. I cannot leave it now. It is cruel not to be sympathetic to those who are loyal. Why are you trying to weaken my bond with the tree (*anukrośa*) by sympathizing with me?' (*Anuśāsanaparvan* 5.22–24). In the more familiar dialogue between Indra and Yudhiṣṭhira in the *Mahāprasthānikaparvan* (17.3), the latter insisted on taking with him a hapless dog that had followed the Pāṇḍavas on their 'final journey' to heaven. He thus expressed his resolve: 'O Indra, I think the sin of abandoning one who is loyal is greater than many other sins put together. I cannot leave the dog behind' (*Mahāprasthānikaparvan* 3.11). In these episodes, the unconventional and apparently absurd stances of the parrot and Yudhiṣṭhira are ultimately applauded and both become ethical exemplars for their 'intelligence and *anukrośa* for all creatures' (*Mahāprasthānikaparvan* 3.18).

What is significantly similar between *anukrośa* and the contemporary care perspective is that both the parrot and Yudhiṣṭhira emphasized bonds they had with others and the *experience of these emotive ties* in reaching their respective decisions. They also structured their moral dilemmas as a struggle within relations which they had not entered into contractually. The parrot after all, was born in that particular tree, and Yudhiṣṭhira did not ask or, may be, even want the dog to tag along with him. Yet, both agents asserted themselves to be irrevocably 'in-relation' to the tree and dog, respectively. Construction of such relational selfhood as the root of ethical agency is reminiscent of how moral decisions are reached in care ethics.

However, even though the parrot and Yudhiṣṭhira made *anukrośa* central to their decisions, their decisions are lauded only *after a reflective dialogue* with Indra. One could conjecture then that moral excellence in the text is tied not to the content of the choice but to the manner in which it is made. When the parrot pleaded with Indra, 'Why are you trying to weaken my bond (*anukrośa*) with the tree under the guise of sympathizing with me?', we have someone aware of the possibility of a different (tree-independent) life and someone who even feels the attraction of this alternative and yet chooses an identity in-relation-(to-the-tree) after conscious deliberation. It is to be remembered also that Indra applauded Yudhiṣṭhira for his '*intelligence* and compassion'. The engagement of both our subjects with a contrary position represented by Indra indicates a reflective and imaginative role-playing with the caring relation that is ultimately chosen. Thus, *anukrośa*-based connection in the *Mahābhārata* is not simply awareness of the needs of the direct cared-for (the tree and the dog), or a 'crying after' in empathizing with those needs, but includes an epistemic vigilance about the desire to meet those needs. Our ethical agents actively explore 'what would it be like to be connected in a particular way', and play with various improvisations of relational identities before owning one of them. First-order *anukrośa*-pulls felt by the parrot and Yudhiṣṭhira are subjected to critical analysis before they are endorsed. *Anukrośa*-as-care is thus clearly embedded in *thinking* about the nature of the caring relation itself.

Now, deliberation in constructing relational selfhood can help counter an important objection to the care perspective. Since individuals are formed by relational webs and these networks often constitute oppressive power structures, it is often feared that caring selves cannot be liberated selves. Autonomy, therefore, becomes a contentious issue for care ethics. Surprisingly however, we find that the parrot and Yudhiṣṭhira did not follow conventions blindly. It remains fascinating that Yudhiṣṭhira, who had earlier passed a moral test by defining the 'Moral Path' as a convention — that which is 'followed by great or great many people' (*Āraṇyakaparvan* 313.17) — was rewarded for taking a deliberate stand at the end of his life *against* Indra, the greatest of elders. Can the *Mahābhārata* episodes, then, be read as allowing the termination of connections deemed unhealthy even as they endorse relational selfhood? Can caring about caring in the fashion of the *Mahābhārata* refashion autonomy within a relational ontology?

A positive answer seems forthcoming. Since acting on *anukrośa* is not an automatic good in the *Mahābhārata*, there is scope to abandon its dictates in any particular case. This could happen because an investigation of our affective responses reveal that we diminish ourselves by acting on them and that some connections are not in our best interest. Even though the parrot and Yudhiṣṭhira were not led to this conclusion, the reflective discourse encouraged by Indra's questions could well motivate a withdrawal from problematic first-order cares. In the *Bhagavadgītā,* for example, we see Arjuna being dissuaded *away* from his affective response not to fight because of the complicated connections of his kinship with, loyalty to and love for individuals in the Kaurava army. The *Mahābhārata* protagonists, therefore, exemplify how *thinking* about the nature of our spontaneous carings can rule out coerced carings. By digging into alternatives before settling for the connections we are happy to live with, we embark on a quest for authenticity. Which caring bonds we let go, which we prioritize and how we function within them — all involve the process of active self-making. Such 'feeling in control and right in your skin' (Meyers 1992: 125) is a form of self-governance. Hence, a reflective caring about caring becomes a conscious choice to be the particular relational selves that we are.

Unfortunately, such reflective authenticity cannot take us too far. Marina Oshana has shown how autonomy understood as psychological histories of reflective consistency is too 'internalist'. She compares Harriet and Wilma, two hypothetical agents each of whom rationally chooses to be other-regarding caregivers. Harriet lives in an environment that does not value this choice and, in living out her decision, finds herself constantly compromised. But Wilma's social context is one in which institutions support caregiving and caregivers. Here, as Oshana points out, Wilma lives a fulfilling and authentic life while Harriet fails to be autonomous 'not because she wants to be subservient, but because she is subservient. Her lack of autonomy is due to her personal relations with others and *to the social institutions of her society*' (1998: 90; emphasis mine). After all, nourishing children requires access to funds even if the caregiver is not a wage earner herself, and if she is, her own well-being while performing caring functions is linked to how flexible her workplace is, for example, in granting family/sick leaves that enable her to attend to her cared-for. Caring straddles the private/public and household/market divides; so, cleaning up the 'personal' by ensuring consistency is not sufficient for its success.

According to the 'externalist' understanding, then, no amount of inner deliberation could make either the parrot or Yudhiṣṭhira autonomous in their caring choices. Even when they reflectively 'chose' to defy entrenched codes of behaviour personally, it is not clear whether our *Mahābhārata* characters ended up like Oshana's Harriet or like Wilma. The crux of the matter lies in the nature of the social institutions within which caring is embedded. Thus, for second-order reflection to be autonomy-ensuring, we would have to see whether the thinking (involved in an endorsement of our carings) can also ensure corresponding social changes to support those decisions. Summarily put, does the epistemological vision found in the *Mahābhārata* enable socio-political interventions to back up personal choices to care? Do we have a kind of *thinking* here that can do justice to the *materiality* of care? To explore these issues, we are led to considering what knowing is, in the *Mahābhārata.*

Knowing Well: Kauśika and Relational Humility

The learned sage Kauśika was meditating under a tree when a bird defecated on his head. Enraged by this rude interruption, Kauśika cast a withering look at the culprit and the poor bird shrivelled under his gaze and fell down dead. Filled with remorse, Kauśika realized that his much famed 'learning' amounted to nothing and embarked on a quest for 'real' knowledge.

Kauśika's journey brought him to the doorstep of an 'ordinary housewife' who ended up ignoring her guest while she tended to her husband. Incensed with rage once again — this time, by the woman's apparent impoliteness — Kauśika threatened to harm her with his powers. The housewife calmly held her ground. 'Excuse me', she said, 'I am no bird' (*Āraṇyakaparvan* 206), indicating mysteriously that she *knew* of the incident that had brought the sage to her doorstep. It was clear to Kauśika that he was in the presence of someone who was cognitively extraordinary even though the housewife herself emphasized the 'ordinariness' of her life. Being suitably impressed, Kauśika took her advice of going to Mithilā to learn from a butcher. In the unlikely surroundings of a slaughter house and through the words of a low-caste butcher, Kauśika, the Brahmin, learnt the 'Law' (*dharma*) (*Āraṇyakaparvan* 206–14).

This episode has been analyzed in terms of the content of the message imparted by the Dharmavyādha (literally, 'virtuous butcher') (*Āraṇyakaparvan* 206.44).[5] The virtuous butcher, according to Sibaji Bandyopadhyay (2010), literally embodied a mediation of the violence/non-violence dichotomy that played itself out on the larger historical canvas in the split between the Brāhmaṇic and Śramaṇic traditions. My purpose, however, is to move away from this substantive reading and look at the formal structure of the narrative. The story is a framework wherein an ordinary woman and a lowly butcher displace a Brahmin as an epistemic exemplar. My focus is on what facilitated this radical shift and on *what enabled* Kauśika to learn from these marginal figures in the first place. The content imparted to Kauśika — *what* he learnt — becomes less important now. For readers, the episode holds up not only the ordinary housewife and the butcher as cognitively exemplary, but also Kauśika himself who came to recognize their cognitive excellence. What does *Kausika* model for us? How can we become 'good knowers' like him? To explore this, let us break down the process whereby Kauśika attained epistemological maturity into the following steps:

(*a*) Experience of shame.
(*b*) Considering emotional incontinence as a mark of epistemic inadequacy.
(*c*) Self-ascription of ignorance, i.e., the realization that he did not possess knowledge.

[5] I have given an interpretation of the episode which is different from the one I am suggesting here. See Dalmiya and Alcoff (1993).

(*d*) His search for teachers.
(*e*) The search leading him to individuals at the social margins, i.e., to others who were marginalized by:

  (*i*) the public–private dichotomy (a wife), and
  (*ii*) the upper-caste–lower-caste and theory–techne dichotomies (a butcher).

(*f*) Other-ascription of knowledge, i.e., the recognition that the wife and butcher knew (what he did not).

Thus analyzed, Kauśika's transformation began when he shamefully confronted his moral fall and linked it to a cognitive limitation. But this did not lead him to a Cartesian-style meditation of individual epistemological-purification, a cynical skepticism, or a defeatist acceptance of unavoidable human error. Rather, Kauśika went in search of teachers who were able to give him what he was looking for. The key to Kauśika's eventual epistemic success was, thus, a shift from realizing that *he* did not know to acknowledging that certain *others* did know. This shift was made possible because of a deep characterological transformation which is the acquisition of what I call the virtue of 'relational humility'. Unravelling this disposition, thus, becomes an entry point to grasping what good knowing is in the *Mahābhārata.*[6]

Kauśika became 'humble' insofar as he found himself lacking (in knowledge). But this humility is 'relational' because it is accompanied by a parallel ascription of cognitive power to others. This is different from mere humility or the stance 'I do not know' and also from straightforwardly acknowledging epistemic authority in the stance 'you know'. Rather, relational humility indicates an organic relation between the two whereby I say 'I thought I knew but *you* tell me where I have gone wrong'. Becoming a 'good knower' is, therefore, acquiring the ability to grasp one's own ignorance and hollow out one's own epistemic agency *while* acknowledging and enriching the cognitive authority of others. As a character trait, relational humility is a quality of the individual. However, it cannot be manifest without referencing other people. In being essentially 'other-regarding' in this way, the virtue of relational humility is very different from virtues like mere humility, self-control or patience which can be exemplified in isolation.

This complexity of relational humility as an epistemic virtue is best understood by what is called the non-overestimation model (Richards 1988), used to explain mere humility. A modest person, according to this model, is not someone who underestimates or devalues her own worth. Rather, she is one who *knows* her limits. Recognition of one's limit, however, is also a gesture to the reality of something

[6] Of course, there is no 'one' view of knowledge in the *Mahābhhārata.* I explore the strand exemplified in the Kauśika story.

beyond that boundary. Even as I meditate on what my knowledge illuminates about the world, I am also aware of its shadowy underside that remains in the dark. I grasp the object *as unknown* in reflecting on the extent to which it is known (Mohanty 2000). In the context of epistemic practice, this means that the more we understand where knowledge ends, the more we can acknowledge the vastness of what lies beyond. Not only do the contours of this 'beyond' gradually come into focus as the contours of my knowledge, but it also becomes a space that *others can know* even though I can only grasp it vaguely *as the unknown*. *My* ignorance signals the possibility of knowledge for *others*. And self-ascribing such ignorance (a de-authorizing of myself) amounts to epistemically authorizing these others.

When sustained by such a virtue of relational humility, truth-seeking is clearly a social affair and suggests an emerging, novel relation between not-knowing and knowing. Acknowledging ignorance is no longer opposed to accessing objective facts. Rather, it is an *awareness* of concealed parts of reality *as* hidden. Thus, my ignorance gestures to possible agents for whom these parts are *not* concealed. Relational humility works with these twin trajectories of epistemically receding oneself while bringing others to the forefront. Without the former, granting a voice to others simply leads to a cacophonous multiplicity of epistemic perspectives. Without the latter, we end up in a passive and stagnating acceptance of human fallibility. In a healthy community of knowers, hitherto ignored perspectives progressively come to light and are taken seriously *because* of the slackening of the stranglehold of the centre. Self-ascription of ignorance, therefore, becomes the heart of continued cognitive growth in a community.

Another interesting feature of Kauśika's relational humility is that the 'others' he granted authority to are improbable or surprising as knowers. Housewives and butchers do not typically come to mind when we think of knowledge, yet the story resolutely humbles the 'learned' sage in relation to them. Kauśika's relational humility, therefore, allowed him to consider *marginalized others* as knowers and thereby made it a *virtue of epistemic justice*. To understand this, let us turn to some of the harms and injustices of marginalization in epistemic life.

In most societies, certain identities are routinely constructed as being unfit for epistemic agency. Such individuals suffer from 'credibility deficit' and are not taken seriously as conveyors of information. Miranda Fricker (2007) who uses this term, traces credibility deficit to prejudicial stereotypes regarding identity construction. Women, for example, are considered to be overly emotional, partial and prone to exaggerations, and individual women become unbelievable given this understanding of femininity. Similarly, butchers are considered epistemically unreliable because of their association with impurity and mechanical skill in a trade when knowledge is understood as a pure, abstract and theoretical endeavour. Prejudices also nurture 'credibility excess' or the upgrading of authority simply because of group membership. The cultural construction of masculinity with its links to reason, for example, makes individual men authoritative as sources of knowledge even when there might be evidence to the contrary. Parallely, in a caste-ridden society that associated knowledge with Brahminhood, Kauśika was automatically considered 'learned' even though he was clearly not worthy of that respect. The notions of credibility deficit and credibility excess, therefore, alert us to forms of 'identity power' whereby someone is 'wronged specifically in her capacity as a knower' (ibid.: 20).

Credibility deficit harms its recipients by denying them the important avenue of self-expression as epistemic agents. Such exclusion becomes all the more problematic when the claims presented by these individuals resist or critique received wisdom and can ground social change. The harm of credibility excess is more nuanced. Of course, it gives *a priori* credence to views that might not deserve to be taken seriously. But it also blocks the epistemic growth of individuals by depriving them of honest feedback and criticism. What is clear is that both credibility deficit and credibility excess are disadvantages that prevent people from reaping benefits of participation in epistemic community.

In light of the aforementioned, Kauśika's act of 'learning' from a housewife and butcher clearly becomes a move to overturn both *their* credibility deficit and *his own* credibility excess. The skilled-in-killing butcher trumps the professional intellectual even in academic discussion and debate when the Brahmin 'learns' from him. Kauśika's relational humility thus becomes a means of correcting the prejudicial workings of what, according to Fricker, is identity power. By shifting received patterns of inter-subjective epistemic inter-actions, it redistributes epistemic power in general and becomes a device for righting the (epistemic) wrongs in a community. The practice of truth-seeking based on relational humility thus makes inquiry intrinsically an involvement with issues of fairness.

Of course, drawing the epistemic virtue of relational humility from the Kauśika episode goes against the grain of the narrative. At one level, the story merely underscores the instrumental importance of ethics for cognitive life: truth eludes immoral beings. At another level, the episode emphasizes very conservative identity constructions. The housewife proudly upholds traditional gender roles and the message imparted by the butcher reinforces conventional moral codes and distribution of labour of the times. To retrieve radical epistemic agency from the story, we need to go beneath its overt content and focus on the form through which its (very traditional) message is articulated. The plausibility of this reading is also strengthened by other sections of the *Mahābhārata* wherein we encounter concepts very similar to what we have cast as the relational humility of Kauśika.

The *Śāntiparvan* (162.15, 17), for instance, surprisingly lists *hrī* and *tyāga* amongst the 13 marks of truth. Truth, it is to be remembered, is the goal of an epistemic community. To explain that in terms of quintessentially moral ideas of *hrī* and *tyāga* indicates that epistemic life is to be in an ethical relation with oneself and with others. *Tyāga*, of course, is renunciation or 'giving up'. It is also elucidated as renouncing attachment or *sneha*. *Hrī* is translated as 'modesty' or 'humility'. More richly, the modesty of *hrī* is said to consist in 'securing the *good of others* without regret or pride'. Now, taken as marks of truth, these two simple ethical configurations can model the epistemic virtue of relational humility in the following manner.

To the extent that ascribing the status of being a knower is a 'good', granting epistemic authority to others is part of *hrī*. And to the extent this is done 'without regret or pride', it suggests a willing letting go of our own epistemic authority. Such withdrawal is also reinforced by *tyāga* read as renouncing of attachment (*sneha*) to our own views. Thus, epistemic life based on *tyāga and hrī* in the *Śāntiparvan*, encompasses the two movements in relational humility — the self-receding from epistemic authority by claiming ignorance, and giving it to others in ascribing knower-hood to them. Notably the text says that a person with *hrī* is '*dhīmān*' or 'one with *understanding*' (*Śāntiparvan* 162.15). Clearly then, a reading that makes an 'ethical person' with certain moral virtues (with *hrī*) an intelligent 'epistemic agent' (*dhīmān*) is also sanctioned by the text.

Living Well and Knowing Well: Limits of the Parrot, Yudhiṣṭhira and Kauśika

Badrinath Chaturvedi (2006: 183) notes how the *Mahābhārata*, by relating cognition to character, goes against received philosophical wisdom of separating epistemology and ethics. The argument of the previous section identifies the virtue of relational humility as the character trait foundational to cognition. However, what is the relation between relational humility and the good life *once the latter is articulated in care ethical terms*? To what extent could Kauśika's epistemic orientation help the parrot and Yudhiṣṭhira in their *anukrośa*-based visions of living well?

Before delving into this, we should be clear that caring involves knowing at two levels: first, the ground level of grasping needs of the object of care and second, knowledge of the nature of our first-level caring — of why we want to meet those needs at all. Now, if knowing is construed in terms of relational humility, then the *Mahābhārata*'s epistemological vision can affect caring in two ways. Let us explore these in turn.

Relational humility can play an important role in knowing the cared for. First-order care must resist slipping into paternalism. Noddings (1984) and Tronto (1993), therefore, have emphasized a 'reciprocity' condition to guard against the caregiver projecting her own needs as those of the cared-for. The reciprocity here does not mean that the *cared-for* must begin to care for the caregiver, but rather that she *respond to* or *receive* the care. This may or may not take the form of verbal feedback but is the state of acknowledging what the care means for the cared-for: it might well amount to criticizing, commending and pointing out what the efforts of the caregiver have achieved and where it has failed. Giving the cared-for a voice in this way ensures shared control and secures a mutuality between the caregiver and cared-for when identifying the needs to be met by the caring relation.

Relational humility can ensure such mutuality. In order to have any impact, the cared-for must not simply be able to show/speak her mind but her input must be *listened* to. For this, the caregiver must be relationally humble. She must not only give credence to the feedback, but in order to change her caring behaviour accordingly, she must be willing to relinquish her own perspective. A father, for example, may think that his daughter is wasting her life working in a retail job and needs to move on to a graduate programme at a prestigious college. He proceeds to do whatever he can to enable this: he lectures her on the advantages of life of the mind, bombards her with college brochures and sets aside funds for tuition. His daughter, however, does not want to continue with academic life and is sullen, resentful and hostile. For a genuine reciprocity in Noddings' sense, the father must not only carefully watch his daughter's responses and encourage her to articulate her vision of the future, but must be willing to let her point of view persuade him away from his own. This is possible only if the father accepts that he might not know what she needs and is open to being surprised. The twin faces of relational humility — admitting that we do not know while acknowledging that the other does — can be said to undergird the reciprocity condition of care. The *Mahābhārata*'s analysis of knowing, therefore, enables the kind of non-paternalistic care spoken of by its feminist advocates.

In spite of this, it is noteworthy that the tree and the dog were silent in the *Mahābhārata* episodes that we have referred to earlier — they did not express themselves nor tell our protagonists what they wanted. The narratives set up the parrot and Yudhiṣṭhira as classic paternalist caregivers who claimed to know the needs of their respective cared-fors without any dialogue with them. But of course, this is an unfair criticism. Upon our reading, the point of these episodes is to illustrate the *second-order reflection* of caring about caring. There is nothing in the stories themselves to rule out a prior dialogic exchange (with their respective cared-fors) before the parrot and Yudhiṣṭhira move onto reflectively endorsing those cares by dialoguing *with Indra.* But the question now is whether such reflection, when based on relational humility, can help the parrot and Yudhiṣṭhira. Can relational humility be a catalyst for institutional change so that caregivers who choose to care thoughtfully can be truly empowered?

It seems not, given an externalist notion of autonomy. Kauśika's interrelationality is confined to the *inter-subjective* conceived of as the purely personal. He granted epistemic status to individuals who happened to be marginalized no doubt, but he approached them as discrete, ahistorical subjects. He did not, for example, speculate on the socio-economic processes that adulated him as 'learned' but denied the housewife and the low-caste butcher the status of knowers. Even though prejudicial constructions of credibility deficit and credibility excess were resisted by Kauśika, there was no move to link the two. Similarly, when the parrot and Yudhiṣṭhira eventually thought through their caring choices (with Indra), they 're-made' themselves relationally no doubt, but the units of the relation still remained ahistorical atoms: the dog, Yudhiṣṭhira, and Indra — and their dialogue — are not situated in a social space of meanings constituted by oppressions and resistance. The inter-subjective thinking here is not one with a history, for the dialogic partners meet each other *as* and *only* as self-contained individuals and not as richly embedded social units. Even though 'living well' is relational, the *Mahābhārata* focuses on personal growth and virtuosity in meeting personal 'needs'. The connections forged in this way lose the multiple and inter-sectional inter-relationalities of historical co-constitution.[7] What is missing in the Kauśika story is a transition from epistemic justice to *social justice* or a movement from the ethical to the *political* — to an inter-historicity that sees subjects as co-constituted by structures of privilege and exclusion.

Ignorance, Shame and Political Subjectivity: Going Beyond the *Mahābhārata*

Even though Kauśika himself did not take the step, it would be interesting to explore whether relational humility could ground a robust political agency in a different historical climate. The argument for this would hinge on a thicker notion of relational humility derived from a closer analysis of the virtue of mere humility. I revisit the non-overestimation model mentioned earlier — this time through its analysis by A. T. Nuyen (1998) — to attempt such a reformulation.

According to Nuyen, the 'non-overestimation' of worth which is the heart of being humble comes from a 'realistic' assessment of ourselves. It urges us to juxtapose achievement with its context and work towards equity or proportionality. For example, the unique circumstances of a crime can mitigate the punishment considered to be just. Similarly, the unique circumstances of accomplishments can reduce the reward/approbation they merit. To be realistic about our successes, therefore, we need to actively examine and give credit to the factors that enable them. 'Invariably', Nuyen points out, 'the examination of the particular circumstances will have a deflationary effect on one's accomplishment' (ibid.: 106) and cause us to be humble.

Now, Nuyen leaves vague the nature of the 'circumstances' that have such deflationary effects on judgments of worth. But subjects are embedded in history and success is determined, at least in part, by the privileges and limitations of their location. A *realistic* self-estimation of our epistemic worth must, therefore, take into account structural features — the advantages and disadvantages that we enjoy because of our social positioning. Such systemic awareness can alert us to two features. The more we realize how much our success owes to contingencies of our positionality, the less proud we become of them. But the formations which privilege

[7] I am relying heavily here on Colin Danby's critique (2004) of the care literature as being wedded to a 'modernist' ontology in spite of its paying lip service to inter-connections.

us also simultaneously disable others. Thus, to the extent we grasp the roots of our social luck we also grasp the exclusions that are necessary to maintain the inequalities that such luck is based on. This introduces the relationality of domination and oppression. In this way, a 'realistic' assessment of our achievements produces a materially grounded humility and a relationality which is explicitly politicized through awareness of power. Epistemic injustices can now be consciously linked to larger socio-cultural imperialisms.

The play of ignorance and knowledge in the relational humility of such embedded and historicized subjects is configured slightly differently from what we see in Kauśika but remains formally similar. The relationally humble person now is one who realizes that he *could have been ignorant* had he not had the social advantages that he now does. He sees how privileges associated with his location contribute to his epistemic success. But to the extent that he grasps this fact, he also realizes that others, who are now not accomplished, *could have easily been so* had they not been excluded from certain opportunities. Thus, we have a subjunctive ascription of ignorance in ourselves that goes hand in hand with a subjunctive ascription of knowledge in others. The 'humility' here comes with awareness that inequalities of opportunities exist and that I could easily have been ignorant and others could have been knowledgeable, had there been a different and just world. Social inequalities, therefore, are the root of my success — realizing which I am humbled. But they are also the root of the failures of others — realizing which I understand that they could well have succeeded in a different world.

Once again, Kauśika, and thereby the musings of the parrot, Yudhiṣṭhira and Indra stop short at an individualized inter-relationality. The focus on individual character-building in the *Mahābhārata* seems to preclude discourses of a genuinely socialized ontology. Subjects are imagined as self-contained atoms and much faith is put on the expansion of individual consciousness to secure connection. Individuals in this framework are conceptualized with personal vices like pride and rage to be rectified by personal virtues like humility and compassion. The resulting relationality generates a very thin sense of the 'social' (Danby 2004) that misses the realities of oppression.

Before giving up on deriving historicized subjectivities and hence a more complex form of relational humility from the Kauśika story, it might be productive to visit the experience of shame, which started his transformative journey in the narrative. Though shame (as in the narrative itself) is usually seen as an individual response to an individualized failure, the concept might be capacious enough to accommodate more politicized sensibilities. The core of shame is the apprehension of oneself as somehow diminished. But this felt inadequacy is deeply relational and presupposes a normative background. I judge myself negatively because I think others judge me to have violated received norms. When feeling shame, I become, as it were, my own spectator who has *caught myself failing*. Of course, Kauśika felt shame because he realized that he had not met the standards of being a good

Brahmin where the category is defined in terms of possessing personal virtues. But he/we can be 'shamed' in more ways than by individualized character flaws.

Once we see ourselves as co-implicated in struggles for domination and resistance, we can be shamed by our histories — by recognizing our complicity in patterns of oppression. This is not an individual-lapse-based shame. It is rather a historical embarrassment — a we-shame if you will — at an unjust world and our complicity in maintaining it. I am diminished now because of my acknowledged membership of groups that have historically perpetrated undeserved exclusions, which in turn, has given me unearned privileges. This is the shame of my unwittingly enjoying social luck sustained partly by the ensuing bad luck of others. But to feel diminished in this way is to implicitly acknowledge a normative grid that requires equality and justice of us. We shrink now because we realize that the world is *avoidably* unjust and so we have failed the stricture on us to make it a more equal place.

In a cognitivist framework of emotions, negative affective experiences can be a 'profound mode of disclosure both of self and situation' (Bartky 1990: 85). This can be a grasp of the complex expectations and the norms of behaviour in place, as well as of deviations from them. It can be a grasp that the world *ought* to be just but is not, that we are at the receiving end of such injustice, or that we are responsible for perpetuating it. But an affective grasp of such facts need not be articulable in a language. Thus, in experiencing shame, we can become 'aware' of inequalities and of the fact that in failing to fight these we have failed to live up to a justified expectation.[8] But this affective grasp can remain pre-discursive and not make it to the level of explicit belief. We can inchoately hold ourselves to a pre-vision of a future state of equality and this pre-theoretical awareness of the normativity of justice could well contain seeds for robust social critique and politicized interventions that eventually make their way up to conscious articulation.

What then was Kauśika ashamed of? The narrative *expresses* it as the failures of rage, pride and incontinence. But it is to be noted that affective experience can hold more content than what is available for articulation. Maybe Kauśika non-discursively did grasp the normativities of social justice — that he, as a member of a privileged class, had failed to live up to, that he had done nothing to redress the systemic imbalance of power between himself on the one hand and the housewife and butcher on the other. After all, the *Śāntiparvan* (162.8), too, speaks of *samatā* (equality) as a mark of truth. Maybe in a different time, in a different place, Kauśika's angst could receive an articulation in terms of his having failed to bring about *samatā*. Maybe in an atmosphere where structural analysis is more prevalent, Kauśika's relational humility, too, would have been cashed out differently. In such a time and place, the ignorance that Kauśika ascribed to himself and the form

---

[8] I speak here of the shame of the privileged. The shame of the marginalized have political consequences in a different way. See Bartky (1990).

of thinking it would initiate could be empowering and autonomy-conferring by engaging with the material conditions that make true self-governance possible. His shame then would have a material basis, as would his resulting relational humility. In this way, the making of relational personhood in the *Mahābhārata* could well bleed into remaking social institutions.

Conclusion: Ignorance and Caring

Our excursion into the *Mahābhārata* makes encounter with ignorance constitutive of knowing. To the extent that caring involves knowing, it too must live with the self-ascription of not-knowing. But caring, as the central notion of care ethics, is concerned with action. In parsing care as involving self-ascription of ignorance, have we not parsed it out of the ethical domain itself? After all, can we act responsibly if we are constantly reminding ourselves of what we do not know? The *Mahābhārata*'s conception of knowledge when juxtaposed with care leads to a paradox: caring involves knowing and knowing involves ignorance, and so caring is the incoherent notion of both knowing and not-knowing.

The conundrum quickly disappears once we remind ourselves that the ignorance of relational humility is not a simple *not-knowing* but an awareness of the object *as not-known*. This establishes the relational fact that *my* ignorance can be supplemented by knowledge of *others who do know* those aspects of the object that I do not. But it also gestures to the relational fact that every act of exposure is simultaneously an act of apprehending the *hidden*, or what lies behind and beyond what is exposed. The beam of a search light makes us aware of the murky terrain beyond what it illuminates, even as it lets us know what is there in the region it lights up. By acknowledging a hidden underside to what is known, the object acquires a life beyond our knowledge: this reinforces a metaphysical realism about objects of knowledge and of care — they are not reduced to what is claimed to be known about them. Thus, to the extent that knowing reveals concealments through its disclosures, we can grant an 'excess' to objects of knowledge/care. This transcendence can then become the source of epistemic surprises and political resistance. Discourses of care have often bled into discourses of romantic mergers, of love and, hence, of possession. An articulation of the object of care in terms of ignorance can prevent caring from degenerating into missions of appropriation.

The general intuition here is that embracing ignorance does not disrupt care as the basis of action but actually enables politically robust caring interactions. Ethico-political life is an encounter with genuine others. But a radically different other always escapes full representation. Thus, the knowledge that caring is based on must be *allowed to fail*: it must steer clear of certainty and must acknowledge its own limits. This is because respectful and non-appropriating encounters with objective others is a 'witnessing of the *impossibility* of her appearance in the context of anything demarcated as knowability' (Davis 2002: 155). It is rather a witnessing of her as not-known through my ignorance.[9]

The notion of thinking in Kauśika's story might carve a style of acting that steers a middle course between paralysis and arrest of all action on the one hand, and imperialist interventions on the other. What we get is action based on open-endedness, ambiguity, uncertainty, and self-doubt. The *Mahābhārata*'s overall moral vision is famous — or notorious — for such open-endedness. The butcher's message to Kauśika is a constant problematizing of received codes of conduct. His technique is of pointing out endless contradictions in what is considered 'good' like non-violence. His refrain *tatra kim pratibhāti me* ('what do I make of this?' or 'what appears to me in this regard', *Āraṇyakaparvan* 208.16–38)[10] reinforces the requirement of self-doubt and the impossibility of theoretical closure even about entrenched moral values. Such endless deferral in the absence of certainty is an invitation to constantly re-think. This, in turn, is sustained by cultivating an 'ability to not-know' which suggests a mode of acting within an ever-shifting horizon wherein others can find their own voice.

Ethical life based on such contingency is emphasized by both protagonists from the *Mahābhārata* and the representatives of the care perspective in Gilligan's study. Remember Yudhiṣṭhira's famous saying, 'Wise men disagree, traditions conflict, the real nature of *Dharma* is hidden in the cave' (*Āraṇyakaparvan* 313.17). This important gloss on the Ethical Way has been variously interpreted by Classical commentators. But from our perspective, why not now see it as echoing the angst of Gilligan's experimental subject, Amy (who is considered to be the paradigmatic voice of the care perspective), when she says: 'If both the roads went in totally separate ways, if you pick one, you'll never know what would happen if you went the other way — that's the chance you have to take, and like I said, it's just really a guess' (Gilligan 1982: 32)?

References

Baier, Annette. 1982. 'Caring about Caring: A Reply to Frankfurt', *Synthese*, 53(2): 273–90.

Bandyopadhyay, Sibaji. 2010. 'A Critique of Non-violence', *Seminar*, 608: 1–16.

[9] Colin Danby (2004) gives a fascinating argument, linking the temporal dimension of care work to a Post-Keynsian analysis of an open-ended future. This suggests another way of reconciling caring with not-knowing which has not been explored here.

[10] Interestingly, in the Critical Edition the line is *tatra kim pratibhati te*, meaning 'what do *you* make of this?' or 'what appears to *you* in this regard?', which shifts the burden of doubting to the interlocutor.

Bartky, Sandra Lee. 1990. 'Shame and Gender', in Sandra Lee Bartky, *Femininity and Domination: Studies in the Phenomenology of Oppression*, pp. 83–98. New York: Routledge.

Chaturvedi, Badrinath. 2006. *The Mahābhārata: An Inquiry in the Human Condition*. New Delhi: Orient Longman.

Dalmiya, Vrinda. 2007. 'Unravelling Leadership: "Relational Humility" and the Search for Ignorance', in P. Hershock, M. Mason and J. Hawkins (eds), *Changing Education: Leadership, Innovation and Development in a Globalizing Asia Pacific*, pp. 297–321. Hong Kong: Comparative Education Research Center and Springer.

———. 2001. 'Dogged Loyalties: A Classical Indian Intervention in Care Ethics', in Joseph Runzo and Nancy M. Martin (eds), *Ethics in the World Religions*, pp. 293–306. Oxford: One World.

Dalmiya, Vrinda and Linda Alcoff. 1993. 'Are "Old Wives" Tales Justified?', in Linda Alcoff and Elizabeth Potter (eds), *Feminist Epistemologies*, pp. 217–44. New York: Routledge.

Danby, Colin. 2004. 'Lupita's Dress: Care in Time', *Hypatia*, 19(4): 23–48.

Davis, Dawn Rae. 2002. '(Love is) the Ability of Not Knowing: Feminist Experience of the Impossible in Ethical Singularity', *Hypatia*, 17(2): 145–61.

Fricker, Miranda. 2007. *Epistemic Injustice: Power and Ethics of Knowledge*. Oxford: Oxford University Press.

Gilligan, Carol. 1982. *In a Different Voice: Psychological Theory and Women's Development*. Cambridge, MA: Harvard University Press.

Kinjawadekar, Pandit Ramchandrashastri (ed.). n.d. *The Mahābhāratam* (with Nilkantha's commentary). New Delhi: Oriental Books Reprint.

Meyers, Diana T. 1992. 'Personal Autonomy or the Deconstructed Subject? A Reply to Hekman', *Hypatia*, 17(1): 124–32.

Mohanty, J. N. 2000. 'Knowledge and Ignorance', in *Concepts of Knowledge: East and West*, pp. 212–22. Kolkata: Ramakrishna Mission Institute of Culture.

Noddings, Nel. 1984. *Caring: A Feminine Approach to Ethics and Moral Education*. Berkeley, CA: University of California Press.

Nuyen, A. T. 1998. 'Just Modesty', *American Philosophical Quarterly*, 35(1): 101–9.

Oshana, Marina A. L. 1998. 'Personal Autonomy and Society', *Journal of Social Philosophy*, 29(1): 81–102.

Richards, Norvin. 1988. 'Is Humility a Virtue?', *American Philosophical Quarterly*, 25(3): 253–59.

Tronto, Joan C. 1993. *Moral Boundaries: A Political Argument for an Ethic of Care*. New York: Routledge.

Who Speaks for Whom?

The Queen, the Dāsī *and Sexual Politics in the* Sabhāparvan

Uma Chakravarti

Amongst all the major 'characters' in the *Mahābhārata*, Draupadī dominates the popular imagination in India where she, in my view, overshadows both Arjuna and Kṛṣṇa, even though they are the protagonists of the famous conversation that forms the text of the *Bhagavadgītā*. The episode of her humiliation in the *sabhā* of Hastināpura stands at the centre of the *Mahābhārata* and moves events forward to their tragic denouement. It is the absolute core of the moral crisis that the *Mahābhārata*, as a text, epitomizes in a series of wrongs that are depicted in it: the abandonment of Karṇa by his mother Kuntī to hide her pre-marital liaison, the lie uttered by Yudhiṣṭhira that leads to the defeat and death of his guru Droṇ ācārya, the killing of the unarmed Karṇa by Arjuna while he was pulling the wheel of his chariot out of the mud it was stuck in — whatever be the interpretation of the *dharma* by which these acts are justified. Indeed all these wrongs, committed, as they are, by the Pāṇḍavas who won the war, as the more righteous of the two sides in a battle represented as one that was between the forces of evil and the forces of good, lend themselves to ambiguity. Only the humiliation of Draupadī at the hands of the Kauravas occupies the moral high ground — the utter indefensibility of the sexual violence against her in the *sabhā* makes this one act *the casus belli* of the fratricidal war, a war that virtually finishes off all the *Kṣatriya*s, save a few. The dynasty itself is destroyed before the divine intervention of Kṛṣṇa revives the dead embryo of Parikṣita, to ensure that the Bhārata lineage somehow keeps going.

Given the investment that almost everyone reading/hearing/engaging with the text today has in the matter of 'Draupadī in the *Sabhāparvan*', any discussion of the episode from a slightly different standpoint is fraught with difficulties since we all are already pre-disposed to reading Draupadī's humiliation through the text's own lens. Nevertheless, I will attempt a different reading of the episode, since I think there is enough room to look at the episode, especially the question that Draupadī asks in the *sabhā* which finally buys the freedom for all Pāṇḍavas, from my perspective on the *implications* of the question, rather than the question itself. In doing so, I will build on the very insightful works of a range of scholars,[1]

[1] See, for example, Mehendale (1985, 1990); Hiltebeitel (1980, 1981, 2000, 2001); and Falk (1977), among others.

who to my mind, have, however, left some things unsaid and some critical questions unasked.

The *Sabhāparvan*

Any reader/listener of the *Mahābhārata* tale is also engaged with the simultaneous task of critically evaluating its main protagonists. In the case of Yudhiṣṭhira, the evaluation leads most people to ask: why did he stake Draupadī? This implies that his staking of his brothers is not so loaded. This, in turn, inevitably leads them to ask the next question: why did he play the game of dice at all? We may recall the advice about four things that are to be avoided by kings because they lead to a clouding of judgment: hunting, womanizing, drinking, and gambling (Buitenen 1975: 145). In Yudhiṣṭhira's case the dicing is even more difficult to condone because he is represented as the *dharmarāja* of his time, as the one who becomes a model king for all time. However, the matter is not so simple; as J. A. B. van Buitenen argues quite forcefully, Yudhiṣṭhira had no choice but to play, not after he had staked his claim to the status of the imperial monarch and decided to perform the *Rājasūya* (Buitenen 1973: 4–6).[2] In the introduction to his translation of the *Sabhāparvan,* he tells us why Yudhiṣṭhira had no choice and since I am inclined to agree with him, especially because it illumines the infamous stripping episode for me, let me summarize his argument first.

For Buitenen, the *Sabhāparvan*[3] is the pivotal *parvan* in the larger structure of the *Mahābhārata*: the narration of events here move in quick succession and have their own underlying structure in that they are closely related, almost as cause and effect, even though each of them may appear to have a discrete and episodic character in the arrangement of the different segments of the *parvan.* Buitenen unravels the structure through the implications of these discretely arranged units, beginning with the performance of the *Rājasūya* by Yudhiṣṭhira, leading, next, to the dicing game; why Yudhiṣṭhira *must* dice is accounted for within the framework of the Vedic *Rājasūya* ritual that he, as king, performs. Buitenen argues that the *Sabhāparvan* is an epic dramatization of this Vedic ritual wherein dicing is

2 Buitenen argues that the events of the *Ādiparvan* — which culminated in the division of the kingdom into two with the Kurus staying on in Hastināpura and the Pāṇḍavas headed by Yudhiṣṭhira being 'adjusted' in Indraprastha — could simply have ended the rivalry between the two branches of the Bhāratas/Kurus, closing the *Mahābhārata* narrative. Instead a whole new set of rivalries are set in motion that unfold in the *Sabhāparvan* (Buitenen 1973: 3–6).

3 The *Sabhāparvan* events could well be closely associated with the way the term *sabhā* was understood in early times. R. S. Sharma suggests that *sabhā* denoted an association of kin, clan and family; it was therefore a kin-based assembly, in which the members debated various issues, played dice and offered sacrifice. In fact, in the *Ṛgveda, sabhā* is a dicing and gambling assembly (Sharma 1959: 105–7).

mandatory after the *abhiṣeka*, the consecration of the king, is performed. While Buitenen draws from the work of J. C. Heesterman (1955, in Buitenen 1973: 28), other scholars too have examined the *Rājasūya*. Kumkum Roy, for example has argued that dicing is as integral to the *Rājasūya* as chariot racing is to the *Vājapeya* ritual, both having incorporated popular practices within new ritualized contexts. The *Rājasūya* itself is conceptualized as an explicitly status-conferring ritual, a way of defining *rājya*, or kingdom, and a means of acquiring *ādhipatya* or lordship and, more pertinently, *sāmrājya* or overlordship (Roy 1994: 27, 83, 107, 201, 205, 285).

Clearly then, the *Rājasūya must* trigger off a chain of events, and the dicing game that follows the *Rājasūya must* take place in order to complete the claim for overlordship, and the Kauravas *must* challenge that claim, given that they see themselves as the senior branch and the legitimate heirs of the Kuru kingdom.[4] The dicing was therefore inevitable and, as a *Kṣatriya* claiming overlordship, Yudhiṣṭhira had no option but to play. It is significant that in the *Mahābhārata*, the *Rājasūya* and the dicing are preceded by the killing of Jarāsandha, whose hegemony was accepted until then by many kings (Buitenen 1975: 57) and only thereafter could Yudhiṣṭhira's claim to suzerainty make sense to others in his times (ibid.: 15). Buitenen adds further that in the *Sabhāparvan* account, the action/ritual is split and set in two different *sabhās*: the *Rājasūya* and the *abhiṣeka* take place in Indraprastha, the seat of the Pāṇḍava kingdom, but the dicing takes place in Hastināpura. Significantly, the 'ritual' of dicing, now set in a new venue, works to introduce a degree of uncertainty in the legitimacy of the claimants:

> When the claims of rivals within one ruling lineage were as insolubly complex as here, the only answer was to decide by lot . . .
>
> The authors [of the *Mahābhārata*] have seized upon the dicing rite of the vedic ceremony as a ritually legitimate, even prescribed way of swinging the doubt from the Yudhiṣṭhira's apparently unassailable position to the claims of the Kauravas. With a masterly stroke of composition the dead letter of the vedic game is dramatically revived (ibid.: 29).

Thus, not only was Yudhiṣṭhira required to play, his overlordship was not yet accepted; suzerainty certainly was contested, and that too by the rivals *within* the clan.[5]

---

[4] Buitenen argues that the conflict between the cousins is about entitlement to a single kingdom, as is evident in the dual locations of the rituals: the *Rājasūya* in one and the dicing in another. There is a single assembly and the house acts as a unit: both sets of cousins participate in the ceremonies in Indraprastha; later, the scene of action shifts to Hastināpura for the dicing game and continues to evoke a single kingdom which will vacillate between Hastināpura and Indraprastha (Buitenen 1970: 76).

[5] Once this inevitability is accepted, Yudhiṣṭhira is not the 'statue with the clay feet, the paragon of virtue with the sudden tragic flaw', as Buitenen comments. He also points

Let us now look at the game of dicing as it proceeds. Again, one is struck by the choice of players. The ritual of the dicing in the *Rājasūya* is played between two parties and not two individuals (Buitenen 1975: 29). As claimant of overlordship, Yudhiṣṭhira, perhaps, must necessarily play, but on the part of the challengers there appears to be some latitude in who will play as long as it is clear on whose behalf the dice is being thrown and his right of ownership over what is staked. So, Śakuni plays on behalf of Duryodhana, but it is the latter who will pay for the stake. As the game begins and it becomes clear that Śakuni will play on behalf of Duryodhana, Yudhiṣṭhira protests somewhat mildly at this arrangement and there is a suggestion that kings should settle their conflicts like real *Kṣatriya*s through means other than dicing. This mild intervention makes no difference and the game begins.

The number of throws is set in two lots of 10 throws each, 20 in all. The stakes progressively move upward, directly related to the order of 'dispensability' in terms of kingdom and kingship: first, the two parties stake wealth in the form of priceless gems, chariots, elephants, a mix of inanimate and animate objects, going on to *dāsī*s (female slaves who are bejewelled we are told) and *dāsa*s, chariots with skilled charioteers making up to 10 stakes. At this half-way point, Vidura tries to halt the second set of stakes to be made because he is fearful/aware that as the items to be staked are moving higher in terms of value, sooner or later the kingdom will be staked and he urges Dhṛtarāṣṭra to stop the game. Since Vidura fails to persuade Dhṛtarāṣṭra, the dicing continues and soon enough the kingdom with all its inhabitants — except the *Brāhmaṇa*s — are staked.

Losing that too, Yudhiṣṭhira moves on to stake the Pāṇḍava princes (all the sons of Draupadī), then his brothers, moving from the youngest to the oldest — and all are lost by the 18th throw. Finally, Yudhiṣṭhira stakes himself and loses. The last throw is still left and thus arrives the critical moment of the entire game: the staking of Draupadī, doubling up in her persona as Srī, standing for the king's wife as well as symbolizing sovereignty, inseparable from the earth/kingdom, possession and control, which gives the king his claim to sovereignty.

Draupadī in the *Sabhā*

If the throws of dice in the game are almost frenetic in the intensity of timing, the sequence of events that lead to the staking of Draupadī are almost surreal: when 19 throws are over and all are won by Śakuni, he suggests that there is one more 'possession' that Yudhiṣṭhira can *still* wager: 'his precious queen'; this way, the king can win himself back, along with Draupadī if she is staked and if Yudhiṣṭhira succeeds in winning the final throw. Immediately, as if on cue with no ifs and buts, Yudhiṣṭhira goes into an unreal dreamlike moment, describing

out that the text itself does not condemn Yudhiṣṭhira for his gaming, in this segment of the text (Buitenen 1975: 28–29).

Draupadī graphically in terms of different body parts, interspersed with elements evoking her Srī-like persona, along with qualities of mind and heart, especially her non-cruel nature, *ānṛśamsya*, which Hiltebeitel has interpreted marvellously for us (2001:177–244). Scholars have also noted the more frequent references to Draupadī as Pāñcāli, which also stands for a doll, in this segment of the text alluding to the play of forces working upon her in the sabhā at Hastināpura (ibid.: 260). The description of Draupadī over, the dice is thrown and proclaimed as won by Śakuni to shouts of horror from a section of the *sabhā* with Vidura collapsing in agony, but to joyous cries from the Kuru 'party'. Dhṛtarāṣṭra is 'elated', desperately hoping that Duryodhana has won, hoping that Srī will now reside with *his* progeny, returning the earlier undivided kingdom and sovereignty to his side.

The real drama then begins: Duryodhana demands that Vidura bring Draupadī, the beloved wife of the Pāṇḍavas whom they honour, into the *sabhā*:

> Let her sweep the house and run our errands
> What a joy to watch! With the serving wenches [*dāsīs*]! (Buitenen 1975: 138)

The word *dāsī* occurs with frequency thenceforth till the battle over Draupadī is over; it has been introduced earlier when Yudhiṣṭhira stakes all his beautifully adorned *dāsīs* at the beginning of the game. For Duryodhana, Draupadī has already become *his dāsī* after this last throw and he must, therefore, assert his mastery and control over her, making her act according to his commands.

But there are obstructions: Duryodhana's first instruction to Vidura to bring Draupadī into the *sabhā* is thwarted. Vidura objects, countering Duryodhana's attempt to demonstrate his control over Draupadī by raising the legal question that will ultimately hang over the assembly once it is posed by her: Was the stake a valid one? It is framed somewhat more hesitantly by Vidura and is not posed to the *sabhā* but to Duryodhana: Kṛṣṇā/Draupadī could not have been reduced to the *dāsī*dom, in his view, as she was staked when the king was no longer *his own master* (ibid.), leaving the implications of that position unstated but highly suggestive. Duryodhana contemptuously dismisses Vidura's opinion by totally disregarding it: as a *dāsīputra* (son of a *dāsī*), it seems that Vidura does not count and this may also be one reason why it is he who is asked by Duryodhana to bring Draupadī to the *sabhā* even though there were other potential candidates present and willing to execute this job. Thwarted by Vidura's non-compliance,[6]

[6] There is something poignant about Vidura's refusal to be party to the humiliation of Draupadī, something Bhīṣma is so complicit in. It is as if Vidura's own antecedents as the son of a *dāsī* he knows what the life of a *dāsī* is and so does not want Draupadī to be reduced to that position — to a position similar to that of his mother, a woman who won her freedom by sexually servicing Vyāsa when Ambikā asked her to sleep with Vyāsa instead of her.

Duryodhana finds someone else to do his bidding. He proceeds to command Pratikāmī, an usher/charioteer (*sūta*), to bring Draupadī in.

Somewhat hesitantly, but having little option as he too is in the pay of his master, Pratikāmī goes to Draupadī, the Queen of the Pāṇḍavas, and tells her that Yudhiṣṭhira, intoxicated by the dice, has lost her to Duryodhana. Addressing Draupadī as Yājñasenī (a patrnonymic derived from Yajñasena, another name of her father Drupada), Pratikāmī tells her that he must, therefore, take her to the house of the Dhṛtarāṣṭra to perform her chores (as a servile woman) in his household:

> Come enter the house of Dhṛtarāṣṭra
> To your chores I must lead you, Yājñasenī! (Buitenen 1975: 140)

An outraged Draupadī chastises the usher Pratikāmī for his temerity to speak to her, as he does, as if she were already and indisputably now a slave, and demands to know if there was nothing else left for the king to stake. No *rājaputra* (prince), she claims, would do what Yudhiṣṭhira *appears* to have done. The usher confirms that it was when there was nothing else left for the king to stake that Ajātaśatru, the 'invincible one' (a neat piece of irony here), who had already staked all his brothers and himself, then staked her.

Armed with this information about the sequence of stakes — all her other husbands, and not just Yudhiṣṭhira, have lost their mastery over themselves — Draupadī frames her question specifically to Yudhiṣṭhira which the usher must take back to the *sabhā*: 'Whom did you lose first, yourself or me?' She frames it thus even though she *knows* quite well what came first: clearly this rhetorical question is meant to raise the legality of the stake and get Yudhiṣṭhira to think about the 'lawfulness' of his act — the *dharmik*-ness of it — now that the momentary madness which gripped him seems to be over. She tells Pratikāmī, addressing him pejoratively as *sūtaputra*, that once he has got an answer he can return to take her with him — presumably to Dhṛtarāṣṭra's residence to live out her servile status.

Pratikāmī returns to the *sabhā*; slightly reframing Draupadī's question, he states it more precisely to Yudhiṣṭhira and the *sabhā*:

> 'As the owner of whom did you lose us' so says Draupadī',

and then adds more faithfully:

> 'Whom did you lose first? Yourself or me?' (ibid.).

Yudhiṣṭhira does not stir, and the text adds that it is as if he had lost 'consciousness'. As other scholars have noted Yudhiṣṭhira remains in this 'speech-less' 'consciousness-less' condition till the end of the 'disrobing–hair-pulling–sexual-assault' phase of the narrative is over (Hiltebeitel 2001: 243). But Draupadī has succeeded in buying time: she has formulated her question in a way that 'opens up two points that might work for her' (Hiltebeitel 2001: 242). She has thus staged an indirect confrontation with Yudhiṣṭhira for his act of staking her: but the question holds more than what it states formally. Through this question, Draupadī indirectly addresses the *sabhā*; forces it to think about Yudhiṣṭhira's wager of her as a question of law, of *dharma*; and expects the *sabhā* to treat it as such. She is able to introduce the possibility of a difference of opinion into a matter that earlier seemed to be clear, thus bringing doubt into certainty.

What she implicitly asks is: as a slave himself, who had lost his status as a master before he staked her, Yudhiṣṭhira no longer has mastery over her; therefore, she is free from the power of her husband/master. Perhaps, she is also suggesting that therefore she could be regarded as having returned to her pre-marital *Kṣatriya* princess status — as the daughter of a king if not the wife of a king, and in such position she cannot be staked and, therefore, enslaved.

While Duryodhana is surprised at her question, since until then everyone present had seemed to assume that Draupadī had lost her status as a free woman, he now recognizes that she herself does not agree to this position and he 'tacitly admits' that the question is justified (Mehendale 1985: 183). It also gives him an opening to catch Yudhiṣṭhira in the wrong and work the situation to his own advantage. So, Duryodhana decides to ask her to come into the assembly and pose it in person to all the people assembled there.

Giving herself over now to 'fate', Draupadī is brought into the ante chamber of the *sabhā*, clad in a single garment, in her menstruating condition, weeping, to stand before Dhṛtarāṣṭra. Since the usher will not bring her any further, Duḥśāsana is ordered by Duryodhana to bring her into the main *sabhā* where the Pāṇḍavas are. Duḥśāsana goes across to Draupadī and tells her:

> Come Pāñcālī, you are won. Look upon Duryodhana without shame. You shall now love the Kurus . . . You have been won in the law (Buitenen 1975: 141).

Duḥśāsana is suggesting that as someone who has been won 'lawfully', Draupadī must change sides and be the woman/queen/slave of the Kauravas; her time of stay with the Pāṇḍavas is over.

Cornered, Draupadī runs for shelter towards the women, but Duḥśāsana now grabs her by her hair — the very hair that had been anointed earlier when she had performed her ritual functions as the queen at Yudhiṣṭhira's *abhiṣekha*, so the text tells us. For the Kurus, the queen, representing earth, kingdom and Srī or sovereignty, can be forcibly wrested to change sides, if she resists. By this act, the Pāṇḍavas were 'unmanned', leaving Draupadī unprotected amidst her protectors, as the text reports.[7] When she tells Duḥśāsana that she is in her monthly courses,

[7] This is the title of the famous solo theatrical performance of the *Sabhāparvan* episode by Shaoli Mitra (2002): *Nathabati Anathabat* translated as *Five Lords, Yet None a Protector*.

is clad only in a single garment, and cannot be taken into the *sabhā* in that condition, Duḥśāsana taunts her:

Be in your month, Yajñasena's daughter,[8]
Or wear a lone cloth or go without one
You've been won at the game and made a slave,
And one leches with slaves as the fancy befalls (Buitenen 1975: 143).

While Duryodhana for the moment is willing to address the ambiguous status of Draupadī, even if he does so for tactical reasons, Duḥśāsana simply addresses her as *dāsī*. It is this location that Draupadī protests: she is not a *dāsī*, she cannot be made a *dāsī*; the Kurus have gone too far, they have violated all limits: the laws and the ways of the *Kṣatriyas* have been overridden in the very presence of the elders. Castigating not only Droṇa and Bhīṣma, but also Yudhiṣṭhira as the son of Dharma, and darting furious glances at her husbands, Draupadī protests her public humiliation even as Karṇa, Śakuni and Duryodhana cheer Duḥśāsana on, while others are distressed but do not protest. Draupadī's question is yet unanswered by the moral leaders who stand on the side of the Kauravas.

Not surprisingly, and in keeping with his uncertain moral stances and his inability to take decisions, the great elderly statesman Bhīṣma takes recourse to the position that *dharma* is subtle, a position that will tie him up in knots but will make him complicit in Draupadī's continuing sexual humiliation. Quite in keeping with his character, he explicitly brings in established patriarchal ideologies/laws to refract the question from its master/freeman agential power-to-act dimension, by framing his argument thus:

(*a*) A man without property [which Yudhiṣṭhira now is, as one reduced to a *dasa*] cannot stake another's property, so in a sense the stake is ambiguous;
(*b*) But wives are counted among the goods of their husbands, so in a sense the stake is valid (ibid.).

In both formulations, Draupadī is *already* reified. She could have been staked as property of Yudhiṣṭhira while he was free, but he was not; so, there is an ambiguity in his staking. As a wife, Draupadī is reified as she is a thing to be included in the total goods of the husband; so, there is an ambiguity there too. Thus, for Bhīṣma, the patriarchal law is: the husband is permanently the master of his wife, even if he is enslaved. Even so, matters are more complicated for Bhīṣma, as always. So, he brings in a new dimension to his state of confusion: since Yudhiṣṭhira never utters

[8] It is significant that she is being described as Yajñasena's daughter, born out of a sacrificial fire, suggesting her ritual persona as Srī.

a falsehood, and he had acknowledged that he was won; therefore, he was won fairly. But, in any case, the riddle is too much for him!

Draupadī is not convinced that any of the stakes including Yudhiṣṭhira's were won through fair play, and she does not accept the free choice argument either. Defending Yudhiṣṭhira's staking of herself, she points out that he staked her only when he had nothing else left, but she is still questioning the validity of its acceptance by the Kurus and, more significantly, of the fact that the suggestion emanated from the Kuru side — therefore, they led the stake, which is suspect in terms of procedure. And so, she repeats her appeal to the Kuru elders to answer the question she has posed, but alas apparently to no effect.

Duḥśāsana uses the moment to grasp Draupadī by the hair and drags her into the hall, proclaiming that one can lech with *dāsīs*, and laughing at that humbling of Draupadī, the Queen of the Pāṇḍavas (Buitenen 1975: 142–43).

Unable to stand the humiliation of Draupadī, reduced to the status of a *dāsī* by the stake, Bhīma berates Yudhiṣṭhira for using his mastery over her through such an act, an act that the worst common gambler would not be guilty of even with the 'whores' (*bandhakīs*) in their country, suggesting the extreme level of reification in the staking of Draupadī (ibid.: 144).[9]

By staking Draupadī, who had *chosen* the Pāṇḍavas as a young girl, she has now been placed in a position whereby the Kauravas could humiliate her and this Bhīma could not allow. (We can see shades of the battle over Srī, embodied by Draupadī in this passage, between the Pāṇḍavas and the Kauravas, and the attempt to forcibly take over Srī without fighting a war and winning her, as true *Kṣatriyas* would be expected to do.) The potential of this rebellious moment bursting upon the Pāṇḍavas, through internal dissensions, is not lost upon Arjuna who appeals to Bhīma not to fall prey to the plans of the enemy. The elder brother's authority is supreme in his view and must not be challenged.

This unexpected passage in the text captures tensions between the brothers, not only over Draupadī but also challenging the normative codes of authority in the hierarchy of the elder and the younger in the brahmanical texts. Extending such tensions, Vikarṇa the youngest of the Kaurava brothers, speaks up on behalf of Draupadī, exhorting the assembly to resolve her question: whatever the diversity of opinion, she must get an answer from the *sabhā*. Vikarṇa brings in a fresh dimension to the legality of the stake, especially when the staker himself has lost his capacity to uphold the *dharma* through a loss of his own agency as one already enslaved. Apart from all the other faults in his staking of Draupadī, Yudhiṣṭhira had staked Draupadī when he had already gambled away *his own freedom*. In that case, how could the stake be regarded as valid? And with this statement of the very

---

[9] We should note that it is Bhīma who first uses the term *bandhakī* or whore in alluding to the unrighteousness of staking Draupadī. It is picked up and turned around by Karṇa to attack Draupadī later in the fiery verbal duels in the dicing sequence.

'rightness' of the act of staking articulated in terms of its technicality rather than its ethicality, the balance of the arguments tips in favour of Draupadī.

An enraged Karṇa, who has not forgotten his own humiliation in the *sabhā* of the Pañcāla king Yajñasena at Draupadī's *svayaṃvara*[10] where she had explicitly rejected Karṇa's temerity to aspire for her hand since he was not a high-born *Kṣatriya* but a lowly *sūtaputra*, now takes over the legal battle. As a member of the Kuru *sabhā*, Karṇa puts forward his answer to the question posed by Draupadī: in his view, it was not necessary to stake her independently — he is going beyond the validity of the 20th stake; instead it is the 17th throw that he is building his argument on — as Yudhiṣṭhira had staked 'all he owned' and Draupadī is part of all he owns, that is, all wives are the possessions of their husbands (Buitenen 1975: 145). Karṇa is thus returning to the arguments of Bhīṣma and extending it further.

But, having dealt with the legal issues, or in a sense the technicalities of *dharma*, Karṇa moves to the ethico-moral dimensions of *dharma*, especially the lowliness of the act of bringing Draupadī into the *sabhā* in her menstruating condition, clad only in a single piece of cloth. He denies any form of dharmic protection to Draupadī that a chaste and virtuous lady would normally be entitled to. Citing the 'divine' law of a single husband for a woman, Karṇa vilifies her for flouting that law as *she* 'submits' to 'many men', which makes her a whore (ibid.: 146). Taking her into the assembly in a single piece of cloth, or even with none was not adharmic. Further, as a possession of the Pāṇḍavas, and the Pāṇḍavas themselves being won lawfully, she too was, like the rest of the Pāṇḍavas, reduced to servitude. Therefore, they should *all* be stripped without any exceptions.

All the Pāṇḍava men strip themselves without further ado (ibid.). But Draupadī clearly does not — she has never accepted her *dāsī* status and does not agree with it even now. Duḥśāsana then forcibly tries to execute Karṇa's suggestion to him (Duryodhana is passive at this point with the active protagonists on the Kuru side being Karṇa and Duḥśāsana). The stripping of Draupadī begins but cannot be completed as she keeps being clothed miraculously, even as the *sabhā* watches in wonder. Bhīma swears vengeance on the evil Duḥśāsana, and the people assembled at the *sabhā* berate the Kauravas led by Dhṛtarāṣṭra for not answering Draupadī's question.

Despite one more intervention by Vidura, Draupadī's question remains unanswered and, therefore, by implication, the slave status of Draupadī holds, as determined by the vocal Kauravas. Karṇa makes that position explicit; he tells Duḥśāsana:

> Take this *dāsī* Kṛṣṇā to the house! (ibid.: 148).

---

[10] Technically *svayaṃvara* implis self-chosen groom. It was a form of marriage common among the *Kṣatriyas* wherein a bride chose her groom from among a number of *Kṣatriya* princes assembled for the occasion. It was often linked to a contest set up by the father which practically overrode the actual decision to choose a particular groom by the bride.

Draupadī's enslavement is to be translated into a reality; Karṇa clearly revels in Draupadī's slave status, hitting back at her insult to him at her *svayaṃvara* for not being a *Kṣatriya* and yet seeking to participate in a tournament that excludes the 'low-born'.

Duḥśāsana begins to drag Draupadī, who once more tries to interrupt the offending actions she has been subjected to. She draws the attention of her elders to the extraordinary humiliations and violations she, even as she is the daughter-in-law of the Kurus, is being subjected to. She asks: is she, the wife of the Pāṇḍavas, the sister of Dhṛṣṭadyumna, the friend of Vāsudeva, and the one whose birth *matched that of* Yudhiṣṭhira, a slave, or is she free? Can she be won? The assembled *sabhā must* answer, she demands.

With the drama of stripping and the miraculous covering of Draupadī over, but her question still hanging over the assembly, posed once more by her and now couched in terms of her class status and position as 'good' woman, Bhīṣma too is forced to address the question once more. Again, the problem with *dharma*, though sovereign, is that it is too subtle, mysterious and grave, at least for him. It is no doubt a bad time for the Kurus whose end is near, particularly since the great guru Drona is struck with paralysis. But instead of trying his hand at answering it, Bhīṣma smartly passes the question on to Yudhiṣṭhira, the acknowledged authority on *dharma* but technically on her side, both as husband and as a Pāṇḍava. He is, therefore, not inherently tainted as the Kurus would be. Though it was he who staked her, Yudhiṣṭhira can still provide an answer on the legality of the stake and of Draupadī being won, which, in turn, would decide whether she was enslaved 'rightly' or not.

With Yudhiṣṭhira still rendered speechless, Duryodhana makes his last move: he argues that the rest of the Pāṇḍavas should decide the matter among themselves by stating that Yudhiṣṭhira is not her master and cannot override *their shared* mastery over her and thus release her from her servitude. Of course, he knows that if the Pāṇḍavas did so, it would make Yudhiṣṭhira a 'liar' — someone who acted unlawfully in staking her — but, nevertheless, would release her. If Yudhiṣṭhira decides the question of who has mastery over Draupadī, she would be in a position to make her own choice between Yudhiṣṭhira and the rest of the Pāṇḍava brothers. If Yudhiṣṭhira were to do that, Bhīma himself would be able to act, be released from his own forced inaction and thereby save Draupadī from her impending doom.

Karṇa adds to the Kuru salvo: he returns to the theme of who has legal power over Draupadī by proclaiming:

> There are three who own no property: the student, the slave and the dependent woman. The wife of a slave you are his now, my dear:
>
> A masterless slave wench, you are now slave wealth!

Come in and serve us with your attention:

That is the chore you have left in this house.
Dhṛtarāṣṭra's men and not the Pārthas
Are your masters, o *rājaputrī*! (Buitenen 1975: 150).

Karṇa's position is: if Yudhiṣṭhira is a slave, and no one seems to be denying that, then as the wife of a slave she is now *his*, i.e., Duryodhana's property. As a masterless *dāsī* with her 'master' Yudhiṣṭhira's own enslavement, she must automatically yield to the control by the new 'master'. It is the Dhṛtarāṣṭra's sons, not the Pāṇḍavas who are now her masters though she be a *rājaputrī* (daughter of a king). She is to be wife-cum-slave and, so, she can choose a new 'husband' from among those on the winning side, one who would be more mindful of her importance so as not to gamble her away.

Karṇa states:

Licence with masters is never censured
That is the slave's rule: remember it! (ibid.)

Thus, as Karṇa argues, all Draupadī's former husbands are themselves slaves in any case. So, she too should accept her status:

Become a slave, come inside Yājñasenī!
The ones who are won are no longer your men (ibid.: 151).

Bhīma's rage takes over once more; he says that Karṇa is too small a man, the *sūtaputra* that he is, for him, as a *Kṣatriya* prince to argue with, and in any case the law of serfdom has silenced him and his brothers, but above all he is held back because, sadly, it was Yudhiṣṭhira himself who put her on stake, and *that* is what holds him back. *That* is the power that cripples his own selfhood, holding back his power to act. It is as if Bhīma is saying: 'as a slave I am bound to compliance, but why, my lord, Yudhiṣṭhira, have you done this to her, the innocent Draupadī, the Srī who chose *us*, only to be given away to the enemy?' (ibid.).

With this opening provided by Bhīma's acknowledgment of being prevented from acting for the moment, Duryodhana gets his opportunity to make a final closing gesture indicating the takeover of all the Pāṇḍavas and their possessions, including their queen/wife. Making a sign of his mastery over Draupadī, as also the final 'unmanning' of the Pāṇḍavas, Duryodhana exposes his left thigh to Draupadī in full view of Bhīma (ibid.). This clear sexual gesture whose full meaning I leave for the moment, makes clear that Duryodhana is now treating Draupadī *as a dāsī*, and in doing so he has answered/decided her legal status: she is his sexual partner whether she is a *dāsī* or not, whether Yudhiṣṭhira is her master or not. He also goads the Pāṇḍava brothers to, even at this late point, reject the mastery of Yudhiṣṭhira over them, as that will make their beloved Draupadī free, releasing her from the *dāsī*-dom to which Yudhiṣṭhira has condemned her. The sexual gesture, intended to insult Draupadī, is also designed to goad the brothers to revolt.

Now, for the first time since he had earlier held back Bhīma's near successful revolt, Arjuna speaks. He acknowledges the legality of their being reduced to servitude because Yudhiṣṭhira was still a free man then. But Draupadī? That is another matter. After all, whose master is he who has lost himself? In a sense, Arjuna is finally repeating Draupadī's question as well as challenging the validity of Yudhiṣṭhira's wager of Draupadī. And so, it is back to square one, to the question Vidura first raised, of the very legality of her *dāsī*dom: Draupadī's interrogation of the certitude of her slave status still hangs over the *sabhā*.

The impasse is finally broken when ill omens are heard and Dhṛtarāṣṭra is terrified enough to terminate the legal and dharmic wrangles ending the sexual violence against Draupadī and the humiliation of the Pāṇḍavas and their queen/wife. Dhṛtarāṣṭra offers two boons to Draupadi with which she indirectly buys back her own freedom: first, she asks for Yudhiṣṭhira's freedom and, then, the freedom of her other husbands. She explicitly states the meaning of servitude for the people around her:

> If you give me a boon, I choose this: the illustrious Yudhiṣṭhira . . .
>
> shall be no slave! Do not let these little boys . . . say of Prativindhya [Draupadī's son by Yudhiṣṭhira] . . . here comes the son of a slave!'
>
> He has been a king's son, as no man has been anywhere. Spoiled as he is he shall die when he finds that he has been a slave's son! (Buitenen 1975: 153).

With her second boon Draupadī seeks the release of her other husbands and, therefore implicitly, their sons too will not be stigmatized as the sons of *dāsas*. With the freedom of her husbands secured, by implication, Draupadī herself is free and the question she posed to the assembly is no longer relevant.

In a neat little reversal, Karṇa applauds Draupadī's wit but this too is a way of humiliating the Pāṇḍavas. For the *sabhā*, the dharmic crisis is over. But, another question now hangs over *us*: Could Draupadī have been legally enslaved; can she, the daughter of a king, a *Kṣatriya* by blood and political status, the wife of a king whose birth she matches, a Srī-incarnate, and a ritually anointed queen be dharmically enslaved, reified as a possession, denied of agency and the power of choosing? Can *she* be reduced to the position of a sexual slave?

The Meaning of Servitude

The Draupadī-in-the-*sabhā* episode has been subjected to multiple interpretive readings by a host of scholars all of which have expanded our understanding of the philosophical and symbolic meanings of the acts of hair-pulling and disrobing, as also of the apparent loss of consciousness displayed by Yudhiṣṭhira. I will use this body of interpretations as they have been important in unravelling different strands of the complex processes at work in this episode. For purposes of the thrust of this essay, I will mark the strands that help me to interpret hair-pulling, disrobing, sexual gesturing, and verbal duels at the symbolic/philosophical levels. But moving on from them, I will also explore the Draupadī-in-the-*sabhā* episode at the level of the mundane: the questions and notions of class and servitude implicated in the dramatic developments in the *sabhā* post the dicing game which have been of less importance to most, though not all, of the earlier readings.

There are four axes/threads that are significant for my reading of the *Sabhāparvan*: the question of validity of the stake that Draupadī raises which will decide whether she has indeed been reduced to the status of a slave (which has been recounted in the previous section but requires a further analysis); the meaning of hair-pulling, the meanings of disrobing; and the meaning of the sexual gesture Duryodhana makes to Draupadī. All four are, in a fundamental sense, connected but have lain in mythic memory as discrete entities. There is a need to bring them together.

Mastery, control and possession over goods, land and people is the hallmark of the *Kṣatriya*s as a 'class' and of kingship in particular. At its other end stands the *dasa* — I am consciously refraining from bringing in the *dāsī* at this stage of the discussion — who has no possessions — indeed, he is barred from having them, has no mastery over anything, and no agency or sense of self — not merely in a philosophical but also in a material sense, is subject to the will of his master, and cannot speak or act independently. This is powerfully articulated by a *dāsa* in the Buddhist texts:

> Here is Ajātasattu, the king of Magadha
> He is a man,
> and so am I
> But the king lives in the full enjoyment of the five pleasures of the senses —
> a very God methinks,
> and here am I, a slave working for him,
> rising before him and retiring later to rest,
> keen to carry out his pleasure
> anxious to make myself agreeable in deed and work,
> watching his very looks (*Dialogues of the Buddha*:163).

The king and the slave represent the two poles of the 'self': full control over oneself and over others, doing as one likes, fulfilling every desire, a virtual God at one end; and loss of control, servility depicted by assuming the mien of one who is in the total control of the king, required of the slave, at the other. In Greece, the master–slave dichotomy was honed to be the epitome of the free, sovereign self at one end in the form of the master, and the non-being-ness of the slave on the other: the polar opposites are represented in the form of citizens and slaves (Anderson 1974: 21). In the *Mahābhārata*, it appears that the two poles are represented by the *Kṣatriya*/king at one end and the *dāsa* at the other. Stories of slavery, servitude or near-servitude and the loss of 'freedom' seem to be more closely associated with *Kṣatriyas*/kings in the *Mahābhārata* than with any other social group. Why is this so? There was a clear indication that a *Brāhmaṇa* cannot be reduced to slavery; rather he enslaves others, according to the *Manusmṛiti* (Bühler 1984: 326). We may also note that when Yudhiṣṭhira stakes his kingdom with all its people in the 18th stake, the *Brāhmaṇa*s are specifically excluded (Buitenen 1975: 135). The *Vaiśyas* and the *Śūdra*s were already 'subjects' and so, perhaps, there was little value in further eroding their freedom. The *Kṣatriya*/king would then be the archetypal figure in representing the free self and the loss of that self through the workings of power, or of 'chance'.

The question for me, then, is: is there a deeper level of meaning in terms of power and agency being wagered in the dicing, especially in the loss of the kingdom and of the self of the king in the build-up of the sequence of losses? Yudhiṣṭhira has lost his self not merely as a man, but as a *Kṣatriya*, as a king with power and control over others.

The Nala episode both bears my argument out and suggests the working out of its embryonic themes with much greater force in the *Sabhāparvan*. Nala, like Yudhiṣṭhira, finds himself in a situation where he is clouded by a compulsive desire to play the dice. Nala is possessed by Kali, an evil force sent by the gods to try and destroy Nala, since he is chosen by Damayantī at her *svayaṃvara* over a host of other contenders. Angered at this, Kali says to his cohort Dvāpara: 'I shall take possession of Nala, and unseat him from his kingdom, and he shall not have the pleasure of [Damayantī]. You must enter into the dice and give me assistance' (ibid.: 330).

After entering the body of Nala, Kali goes to Nala's brother, Puṣkara, and works on him saying, 'Come and dice with Nala, and win the [kingdom]'. Puṣkara challenges Nala to a game of dice and Nala, as king, cannot refuse the challenge. So, he plays and keeps on playing, despite warnings by Damayantī and entreaties of his people, quite unable to resist its maddening power over him. Finally, he loses all, including the kingdom and himself. But unlike Yudhiṣṭhira, he stops short of staking Damayantī, his queen. Significantly, in the Nala story too, the king loses the kingdom to a brother; so, this, too, is a fratricidal contest. Nala's real self has been taken over by Kali till Nala recovers it with the help of a snake beholden to Nala, who, in turn, poisons Kali. Finally, Nala wins back the kingdom after challenging Puṣkara to another game of dice, a challenge that the latter accepts happily hoping to win Damayantī, who is now explicitly placed as a wager by Nala, who, in this last and final round, is free unlike Yudhiṣṭhira. Restored to his real self, Nala wins the game and is reunited with Damayantī. But in the interim years during which he was no longer the king, Nala has been stigmatized, humiliated and reduced to some form of servility as he goes to work king Ṛtuparṇa to earn his living. So is Damayantī who becomes the 'chambermaid' of a queen. And thus, both the wife/queen and the kingdom are restored to Nala as the rightful owner of the realm, its possessions and its queen.

Also significant is a detail of the final parts of the contest between Nala and Puṣkara; the latter says that he only likes to play the dice *within* the family and when he loses the final all-or-nothing round with Nala, he is reduced to slavery, a status that Nala generously does not enforce. The possessed self, the self as detached from its owner, and the free and autonomous self in the case of a king — all seem to be closely linked.

Draupadī's question about the validity/legality or rightness of the sequence of stakes, and its formulation 'as the owner of whom did you stake us' has a social relevance beyond the metaphysical/philosophical explanations that are sometimes offered. Who is a slave, and who can be reduced to it? Can the queen be reduced to slavery after the king has become one when his mastery over her as king/husband has ceased, or is she enslaved/reduced to servitude with him if she chooses to accompany him into his servitude as Damayantī does. The status of an anointed queen/wife of the king as Srī-like or Srī-incarnate also hovers over these narratives without resolution. So, in the Draupadī-in-the-*sabhā* episode, is Draupadī challenging the validity of the wife being staked, the queen being staked or Srī being staked, or does her question contain all three elements in it. The brothers, for example, accept the right of the eldest brother to stake them as we have already said; the only controversy even for them is whether Draupadī should have been staked. They can be enslaved but can Draupadī? Especially if the text tells us that she is Srī, not merely an ordinary *Kṣatriyānī?* Do the Pāṇḍavas not see that? Why are they allowing the Kauravas to turn *her* into a *dāsī* so that she is reduced to a mere possession, to be subjected to the whims of chance, not won through valour, forcibly controlled through 'un-*kṣatriya*' conduct, and then reified such that she is subjected to multiple forms of sexual humiliation which is the defining condition of *dāsītva*?

Let us look at the three sexual gestures that follow from the Kaurava claims that Draupadī is a *dāsī*, not a queen, or even a *kṣatriyani* after Yudhiṣṭhira has lost her, and that she should come into the *sabhā* to be taken over as a *dāsī*, a claim that they dramatically make, by asking, first, a *dāsīputra* and, then, a *sūtaputra* to bring her in. When neither of the two is willing, or able to 'turn' her into a *dāsī*, the Kauravas enforce their mastery by dragging her by hair into the *sabhā*, in the first of the sexual gestures against her *as a dāsī*. Scholars have noted the connection between hair, sexuality and fertility. Hair-pulling is an act of defilement, touching it by anyone except the husband especially so, and is compared to Dhṛṣṭadyumna's pulling of Droṇācārya's hair (Falk 1977: 101). Hair-pulling is thus a sexual gesture, and a sign of sexual control. The violation of Draupadī is already a sexualized violation. So, the stage is already being set for other forms of sexual humiliation which though 'normal' in the case of *dāsī*s are clearly outrageous in the case of Draupadī whose hair has been anointed as part of the rituals of king-/queen-ship.

The second explicit gesture of establishing sexual control over Draupadī-as-*dāsī* is Duḥśāsana's act of stripping her in the *sabhā* at the suggestion of Karṇa, who says quite explicitly that she is a *bandhakī*, i.e., she is not a virtuous woman since she sleeps with more than one man. Karṇa also suggests that the Pāṇḍavas too be stripped. At this, the five brothers strip the upper cloth *(uttariya)* off themselves, voluntarily and without force, and sit down (Buitenen 1975: 146). It is then that Duḥśāsana forcibly tries to strip Draupadī. We have already been told that she is in a single cloth which, we presume, she is wearing to cover both the lower and upper part of her body because only then will the act of stripping have any meaning comparable to that of the Pāṇḍavas, who too have been asked to strip. There seems to be a symbolic meaning to the act of stripping as the marker of the new status of a slave to which all the Pāṇḍavas, and Draupadī too, have descended according to the Kauravas. We may recall that when Nala lost his kingdom to his brother, he too left his kingdom in a single piece of cloth, as did Damayantī (ibid.: 332). The bare-chested lower orders are thus distinguished from their masters who alone have a right to cover the upper part of their bodies.[11] Stripping may then have a meaning akin to branding of slaves in certain cultures.[12] In the nineteenth century this was the meaning of the breast cloth controversy of the Shanars in Kerala when they demanded the right of their women to cover their breasts,[13] a privilege restricted to the upper-caste women, who alone were presumed to have modesty. Honour, virtue and modesty are the monopoly of the upper castes; conversely the lower orders are excluded from claiming such values.

The stripping of Draupadī is part of the claim of the Kauravas that she is now a *dāsī* and with this explicitly sexualized gesture they are establishing that she is now their sexual property and they can do to her what they will.

That sexual control over *dāsī*s is the norm with the *Ksatriya*s is also explicitly stated in the proceedings of the *sabhā* and numerous other examples from the text bear this out. The *dāsīs* of Ambikā (Buitenen 1973. 236) and Sudeṣnā (ibid.: 232) are palmed off by their mistresses to deal with smelly and crotchety *Brāhmaṇa* sexual partners whom they are required to sleep with to reproduce sons for the dynasty. To escape this forcible sexual intercourse, which as *Kṣatriya* wives they cannot otherwise refuse, they substitute their *dāsī*s for themselves, as the former cannot refuse anyway. Similarly, during Gāndharī's long pregnancy Dhṛtarāṣṭra is served well by his *dāsī* who gives birth to his son Yuyutsu (ibid.: 245). The text also tells us that when Devayānī marries Yayāti and goes over to his house with her retinue of maids that includes the erstwhile *Kṣatriya* princess Śarmiṣṭhā, now reduced to servitude, she makes Yayāti promise that he will not exercise his privileges of

---

[11] This is the interpretation for the entire stripping episode provided by Mehendale (1990) who explicitly substitutes a social explanation for a metaphorical one.

[12] For branding as a method to identify slaves, see Patterson (1982: 59).

[13] Summarized from a description in Kooiman (1989: 148*ff.*).

lordship over Śarmiṣṭhā by sleeping with her (ibid.: 185–89) . That lordship over slaves includes sexual control over them is also clear from the sexual assault upon Draupadī in her disguise as Sairandhrī, by Kīcaka, brother-in-law of the Matsya king Virāṭa — an attack that Yudhiṣṭhira seems to take as an occupational hazard of her new status as a chambermaid, but which Bhīma does not accept with such ease since he is not reconciled to Draupadī's status as a *dāsī*.[14] Damayantī, too, explicitly seeks immunity from normal *dāsītva* conditions when she becomes the chambermaid of a queen: the mistress must not display her before strange men and if anyone seeks to violate her he must be punished (Buitenen 1975: 343). The Buddhist texts too make clear that the master of a household has easy recourse to his *dāsīs*, even when the mistress of the household does not like it, and so the *dāsī* faces a double dose of violence, first from the master and then from the mistress who beats the *dāsī* up for sleeping with *her* lord (Chakravarti 2006: 89).

To return to the *Sabhāparvan*, we find that the attempt at establishing sexual control over Draupadī fails yet again as the stripping cannot be completed with many layers of cloth miraculously appearing upon her body and Duḥśāsana falling into an exhausted heap of cloth. There is a renewed round of discussions on Draupadī's question about her post-stake status and, again, while she resists her *dāsī* status and the rest of the *sabhā* debates the niceties of the situation, the Kauravas attempt to take the lead once more.

Faced with an aborted exercise of inflicting *dāsī*-dom upon Draupadī through his aide de camp brother Duḥśāsana's two assaults upon her, and also faced once more with the unresolved question of her status, Duryodhana acts directly, and not though Duḥśāsana, to provide decisive evidence of his mastery over Draupadī as his *dāsī*: he bares his left thigh to her, looking at her invitingly, smiling conspiratorially at Karṇa who is completely convinced that Draupadī *is* a dāsī (Mehendale: 1990: 286), and openly taunting Bhīma. The exposure of left thigh is an explicit sexual gesture since the left thigh is a phallic symbol.[15] We are also told that the left thigh is reserved for wives and lovers in the account of Gangā and Pratīpa when she wrongly sits on his right lap and seeks to seduce him. Pratīpa points out that it is the left lap that is meant for wives and mistresses; the right lap, on the other hand, is reserved for children and daughters-in-laws and thus she is passed on to Pratipa's son, Śantanu, in marriage (Buitenen 1973: 218). Thus, by baring his left thigh, an explicitly sexual gesture, Duryodhana seeks to assert the final loss of control by the Pāṇḍavas, the erstwhile sexual partners of Draupadī, over her and simultaneously marks their 'unmanning' by him. It is a gesture that seeks to

---

[14] Perhaps, what is significant is the fact that the name 'Sairandhrī', which Draupadī chooses to adopt during her one-year incognito stay with the Pāṇḍavas in the Matsya kingdom, actually means a slave or maidservant. Hence, as a synonym of *dāsī*, the pseudonym is quite unlike the ones adopted by the Pāṇḍavas, and its selection be a conscious decision by her as a reminder to her husbands of her humiliation.

[15] We know this from the interpretation of the gesture by Sutherland (1992).

assert the new sexual ownership of Draupadī by the Kurus, to lech with as is to be *expected* with dāsīs.

In concluding this paper, let me return to the meaning of Draupadī's question to Yudhiṣṭhira, to the Kauravas and to the *sabhā*. Has she legally and dharmically been actually reduced to servitude; has she become a *dāsī*? She has by the very posing of the question refused such an interpretation of her status being imposed upon her by the Kauravas, and which the Pāṇḍavas are not in a position to challenge as they have already been reduced to servitude and, therefore, lost their agential power to act, as we argued earlier. But as a temporarily freed person — freed from Yudhiṣṭhira's control over her — she has returned to her status as a *Kṣatriya* woman. As we have seen, when Dhṛtarāṣṭra offers her a series of boons by which she frees first Yudhiṣṭhira from his slave status and then the other brothers (the slave status is for real: Draupadī does not want her children too to be enslaved or be known as the sons of slaves), she stops after the second boon and explicitly states that as a *Kṣatriyānī* she is entitled only to two boons, and in case as free men her husbands will rebuild their futures. She has never accepted her *dāsī*-dom and has never stepped out of her status as a *Kṣatriya* princess though she may no longer be the queen.

Only one question still remains to be asked: whom does Draupadī speak for when she poses her question to the *sabhā*? Does she speak for all women, for women as a 'class' that calls into question 'two kinds of male lordship: that of kinship and family. and that of the dharmic politics of kingship in the *sabhā*'?[16] Is Draupadī the ultimate feminist of textual traditions? Quite the opposite: she speaks for herself and she carefully limits the question to the legal validity of the stake, never even denying Yudhiṣṭhira's right to stake her. It is her own refusal to be a *dāsī* that leads her to ask the question in the way she does, framing it in a narrowly bounded way that works fully within a framework that accepts the master's right of lordship over his *dāsīs*, to do as they please. She never for a moment erases the difference between *Kṣatriya* princesses and *dāsīs*; she never once says, 'you cannot do what you are doing, this violation of a woman's personhood, to any woman!' Her question is not *the* woman's question, it is the *Kṣatriyānī*'s question, a question that divides women into those who have rights and others who don't. She files a 'class action suit' as Hiltebeitel (2002: 120) has suggested but, as he himself points out, only on behalf of daughters and daughters-in-law (in this case perhaps only *Kṣatriya* daughters and daughters-in-law) which excludes those who are not regarded as entitled to families — to husbands, sons and daughters — as *dāsīs* (Chakravarti 2004: 91). It is not a question that will give all women dignity and demand that as a right that must be upheld by a dharmic king in an 'ideal' kingdom. In the case of *dāsīs*, only one kind of male lordship applies and that lordship takes for granted the rights of *Kṣatriya* men over them: their labour

[16] See Hiltebeitel (2000: 120) for such a reading of Draupadī's question to the *sabhā*.

and their sexuality which is part of the *dharma* that kings uphold. In sum, she has filed a 'class-ed' action suit, one that is confined to her class as the *Kṣatriyānī*, the Srī incarnate, the Queen of the kingdom. If she had spoken for all women, not just for herself, or for herself as a *dāsī*, she would have asked a different question, a question that might be along the lines of Dopdi's act of resistance to the police officer/king in her domain in Mahashweta Devi's text the import of which is: 'what can you do to me except "counter" me', that is, kill me. Even that cannot kill the spirit of her resistance (Spivak 1997).

It has been argued that the *Mahābhārata* is a series of precisely stated questions posed imprecisely and, therefore, never conclusively resolved (Buitenen 1973: 29). In keeping with this spirit, my question stated precisely is: why did Draupadī not ask the question that spoke also for the *dāsī*? Can we ask such a question today? And who will ask it?

References

Anderson, Perry. 1974. *Passages from Antiquity to Feudalism*. London: Verso.

Bühler, G. (trans.). 1984. *The Laws of Manu* in *The Sacred Books of East*, vol. 25, ed. F. Max Müller. New Delhi: Motilal Banarsidass.

Chakravorti, Uma. 2006. 'Of Dasas and Karmakaras: Servile Labour in Ancient India', in Uma Chakravarti, *Everyday Lives, Everyday Histories: Beyond the Kings and Brahmanas of 'Ancient' India*, 70–100. New Delhi: Tulika.

Chakravorty Spivak, Gayatri. 1997. *Breast Stories*. Kolkata: Seagull.

Falk, Nancy. 1977. 'Draupadī and the Dharma', in Rita M. Gross (ed.), *Beyond Androcentrism: New Essays on Women and Religion*, 89–114. Missoula: Montana.

Heesterman, J. C. 1955. *The Ancient Indian Royal Consecration*. The Hague: Mouton.

Hiltebeitel. Alf. 2001. *Rethinking the Mahābhārata: A Reader's Guide to the Education of the Dharma King*. Chicago: University of Chicago.

———. 2000. 'Draupadī's Question', in Kathleen M. Erndl and Alf Hiltebeitel (eds), *Is the Goddess a Feminist? The Politics of South Asian Goddesses*, 113–22. New York: New York University Press.

———. 1981. 'Draupadī's Hair', *Purushartha*, 5: 179–214.

———. 1980. 'Draupadī's Garment', *Indo-Iranian Journal*, 22(2): 97–112.

Kooiman, Dick. 1989. *Conversion and Social Inequality in India*. New Delhi: Manohar.

Mehendale, M. A. 1990. 'Once Again Draupadī's Garments', Bulletin of the Deccan College Research Institute, 50: 285–90.

———. 1985. 'Draupadī's Question', *Journal of the Oriental Institute of Baroda* 35(3–4): 179–94.

Mitra, Saoli. 2006. *Five Lords, Yet None a Protector* (*Nanthabati Anathabat*), trans. Nabaneeta Dev Sen. Kolkata: Stree.

Patterson, Orlando. 1982. *Slavery and Social Death*, Cambridge, MA: Harvard University Press.

Rhys Davids, T. W. (trans.).1973. *Dialogues of the Buddha*, vol. 1: *Digha-Nikaya*. London: Pali Text Society.

Roy, Kumkum. 1994. *The Emergence of Monarchy in North India, Eighth to Fourth Century B.C.* New Delhi: Oxford University Press.

Sharma, R. S. 1959. *Aspects of Political ideas and Institutions in Ancient India*. New Delhi: Motilal Banarsidass.

Sutherland, Sally. 1992. 'Seduction, Counter Seduction and Sexual Role Models: Bedroom Politics in the Indian Epics', *Journal of Indian Philosophy*, 20(2): 243–51.

Buitenen, J. A. B. van. 1975. *The Mahabaharata II: The Book of the Assembly Hall & III: The Book of the Forest*. Chicago: Chicago University Press.

———. 1973. *The Mahābhārata I: The Book of the Beginning*. Chicago: Chicago University Press.

———. 1972. 'On the Structure of the *Sabhāparvan* of the *Mahābhārata*', in J. Ensink and P. Gaeffke (eds), *India Maior: Congratulatory Volume Presented to J. Gonda*, 68–84. Leiden: E. J. Brill.

Moral Doubts, Moral Dilemmas and Situational Ethics in the *Mahābhārata*[1]

Prabal Kumar Sen

The standards of morality as preached in the *Mahābhārata* recognise both the absolute and relative nature of morality (Dasgupta 1961: 225).

In the *Mahābhārata* we see directly a dynamic moral tradition employing its immersed critical principles in a process of genuine development (Ganeri 2007: 92).

The tradition in India was extremely self-conscious about moral conflicts and disputes about ethical principles, commitments and priorities; and mental emotions, love, passion and self-control. This becomes crystal clear once we look at the great epics and other narrative literature . . . the *Dharmaśāstra*s supply only a skeletal account of the *dharma*s. The epic stories and narrative literature add flesh and blood to this skeleton. The richness and the ambiguity of the concept of *dharma* are interwoven with the narrative at every step (Matilal 2002: 39).

Indian ethical theorizing was done . . . not by first formulating an all-comprehensive theory, and then testifying it by applying it to concrete situations. Rather, it grew through reflecting on concrete cases, and seeking solutions to the ethical problems they posed. Therefore, it is always put forward that being morally well and living well in the world were something like the two sides of the same coin (Prasad 2008: 169).

I

A few explanatory words about the title of my essay are necessary. I have used the expressions 'moral doubt', 'moral dilemma' and 'situational ethics' for translating the Sanskrit expressions *dharmasaṃśaya*, *dharmasaṃkaṭa*/*dharmapāśa* and *āvasthikadharma*/*āpaddharma* respectively, insofar as they are related to moral problems. I am aware of the fact that the term *dharma* means much more than morals *alone.* It can certainly stand for rituals, the conduct of people belonging to specific groups of the society (e.g., *rājadharma*, which specifies how a king should administer his kingdom), or the conduct of a person at a specific stage of his life (e.g., *yatidharma*, which specifies how a mendicant or *sannyāsin* should lead his life), which may not always be connected with any moral issue. Thus, questions such as how many ministers a king should appoint, how he should select his advisors,

[1] I am grateful to Sri Nrisinha Prasad Bhaduri for his valuable suggestions.

how much tax he should impose on his subjects, or what sort of diplomacy he should adopt under some specific circumstance, are not problems in which a moral philosopher might find any genuine interest. Likewise, questions such as what should be in the possession of a *sannyāsin*, or how many times in a day he should take his meals, and in what quantity, are not, strictly speaking, problems of moral philosophy. Certain other conducts recommended by the *Dharmaśāstras* do not also come under the purview of moral philosophy. Thus, there are scriptural injunctions to the effect that before taking meals, one should wash one's hands, feet and face, or that one should take meals facing the eastern direction, which are obviously not connected with moral issues. One failing to obey these injunctions may be considered guilty of transgressing the scriptures, but I am sure that no one will accuse that person of doing something that is morally reprehensible. I do not deny the 'ambiguity and richness of the concept of *dharma*' to which B. K. Matilal has drawn our attention, but for the sake of convenience, I shall restrict here the use of the term *dharma* to 'morals'.

II

We are far removed from the times in which the *Mahābhārata* was composed. During the long period of time that has elapsed since its composition, our social conditions have undergone some significant changes. With the advent of scientific knowledge, many of the beliefs that were well entrenched earlier have now been discarded, and our attitudes to certain things have undergone radical changes. No one, for example, thinks that monarchy, which is extolled in the *Mahābhārata*, is the only possible form of government. We have come into contact with various other religions and cultures and, as a consequence, many social practices that were earlier prevalent in India have been discarded, or at least subjected to serious scrutiny. Under such circumstances, dealing with moral issues discussed in the *Mahābhārata* may raise a few eyebrows. Why should one, after all, spend time and energy on such an ancient work that might have become outdated and irrelevant for solving current problems? But in my opinion, such an attitude is as biased as the attitude of suspicion or intolerance that some people exhibit towards things that are new. Just as a thing does not become useless or unworthy of attention simply because it is new, one need not indulge in a wholesale rejection of whatever is old. Indeed, many passages of this timeless epic that have captured our imagination for so many centuries seem to be equally applicable to the contemporary society and its problems. Thus, the exercise undertaken here need not be considered as wastage of time. Besides, a discussion of the *Mahābhārata* passages dealing with moral issues does not amount to an uncritical acceptance of the views expressed therein — indeed, there is much in the teachings of this epic that is prone to be rejected outright by many of us. What is needed, therefore, is an unbiased examination of the relevant doctrines that we find in the epic, and I will try my best to do that.

III

In the *Mahābhārata*, scriptures as well as reasoning have been recommended as means of knowing *dharma* and *adharma*, *kartavya* and *akartavya*. This attitude is also found in the *Dharmaśastras* which are now often regarded as extremely reactionary and oppressive in outlook. It is certainly a fact that in such works, much importance has been given to the Vedas and the works based on the Vedas. For instance, it has been stated in *Manusaṃhitā* that if a 'twice-born' person condemns such texts with the help of reasoning, then he should be excommunicated by the good people, since such vilification of the Vedas is an act of sacrilege; and whoever indulges in it is a non-believer (*nāstika*) (XII.105–6).

At many places, the *Mahābhārata* also displays a similar attitude. For example, it maintains that the scriptures (especially the Vedas) are the ultimate authority in matters regarding *dharma* and *adharma* (*Āraṇyakaparvan* 32.9, 197.39, 200.2).

But such passages need not be considered instances of wholesale rejection of the role of reasoning in deciding the distinction between *dharma* and *adharma*. Thus, even the *Manusaṃhitā*, which now faces much criticism for many of its obscurantist views, emphasizes at times (XII.105–6) the role of reasoning in deciding what is *dharma* and what is *adharma*.

In the aforementioned verses, it is clearly stated that one who wants to purify *dharma* should be well versed in the three *pramāṇa*s (means of acquiring *pramā*, or certain knowledge), viz., perception, inference and the various *śāstras*. Only when one examines the instruction of *dharma* by sages in the light of reason that is not aimed at contradicting the scriptures, can one comprehend the true nature of *dharma* and not otherwise. Kullukabhaṭṭa, one of the well-known commentators of the *Manusaṃhitā*, displays a similar attitude in the second introductory verse of his commentary:

> *mīmāṃse bahu sevitāsi suhṛdastarkāḥ samastāstha me*
> *vedāntā paramārthatattvaguravo yūyaṃ mayopāsitāḥ* /
> *jātā vyākaraṇāni bālasakhitā yuṣmābhirabhyarthaye*
> *prāpto'yaṃ samayo manūktavivṛtau sāhāyyamālambyatām* //

This verse clearly shows that along with *Vyākaraṇa* (grammar) that deals with the derivation of words, *Mīmāṃsā* that deals with the interpretation of Vedic sentences and *Vedānta*, i.e., the *Upaniṣads* that instruct us about the ultimate reality or truth, *Tarka* (i.e., the science of reasoning) is also helpful in the task of explaining the nature of *dharma* and *adharma*. The role of *yukti* (i.e., reasoning) in such matters has also been acknowledged in the *Bṛhaspatismṛti* (I.114).

In the *Mahābhārata* also, especially in the *Śāntiparvan*, we find disputes on what is to be done in a particular situation; in such cases, the persons involved in disputes invariably give some arguments in favour of their respective views.

Thus, it is only proper that we look at some of the passages in the *Mahābhārata* that deal with moral doubt, moral dilemma and situational ethics, and judge them impartially in the light of our experience and reasoning. It is true that the *Mahābhārata* maintains that the duty of the king is to ensure that the people belonging to different *varṇa*s do not deviate from their respective duties. It also reiterates *ad nauseum* that the Brahmin is superior to the three other *varṇa*s, and that consequently, they must be obeyed and honoured under all circumstances. Additionally, it sometimes makes pronouncements that now appear to be outrageous and obnoxious. But there are, in my opinion, many passages whose appeal is eternal and universal. Avoiding the extreme courses of wholesale acceptance and wholesale rejection, we may accept what is reasonable and discard what is outdated, unreasonable or evidently biased in some way or other.

IV

Moral doubt (*dharmasaṃśaya*) arises when one is not sure as to whether a certain course of action is in accordance with the norms of morality or not, and, accordingly, whether it should be adopted or avoided. This is not a matter of simple ignorance (*jñānābhāva*) about *dharma*. If I am totally ignorant of something, then not only cannot I entertain any definite opinion about it, I cannot also doubt it, or even be inquisitive about it. In order to have some *definite* view about something, my cognition of that thing must be characterized by certitude (*niścayatva*). When such a cognition is veridical, my opinion about it is also correct, otherwise the latter is incorrect. When I know with certitude the existence of something, or only the general features of that thing, but am ignorant of its specific or distinguishing properties, I may have a desire to know the exact nature of that object. This desire to know that something gives rise to inquisitiveness about the specific features of that object. If the general features are such that they have been found in the past to be associated with some properties or features that are opposed to each other, then the awareness of these general features evokes the memory of those contradictory features. This leads to doubt (*saṃśaya*) in the knower, who, so to say, 'oscillates' between these mutually opposed alternatives that are simultaneously ascribed to that object and cannot decide which one of the alternatives is true. But once one of these alternatives is definitely ascertained, the doubt concerned ceases to exist. It is here that a basic question may be raised: since *dharma* and *adharma* have been discussed at length in the Vedas and *Dharmaśāstra*s, why should one have any doubt about *dharma* and *adharma?*

One possible reason is the bewildering variety of *dharma*s enumerated in the scriptures. There were some *dharma*s which were to be observed by all persons, irrespective of the social group (*varṇa*) or the stage of life (*āśrama*) to which they might belong. These are called *sādhāraṇadharma*s and are also specifically said to be mandatory for everyone. Thus, in the *Śāntiparvan* (60.7–8ab), speaking the truth, sharing one's wealth with others, giving up anger, being tolerant (i.e., forgiving the lapses of others), maintaining fidelity to one's spouse (by begetting children only through one's lawful wife), espousing purity, non-violence and straightforwardness, and taking care of one's dependents have been declared to be the *sādhāraṇadharmas* to be observed by everyone.

There is also another long list of such *sādhāraṇadharmas* (i.e., ordinances to be respected by all members of the society) in the *Śāntiparvan* (285.23–24) itself: disavowal of cruelty and violence, absence of carelessness, sharing of wealth, performance of *śrāddhas* (funerary rites), hospitality towards guests, truthfulness, forsaking anger, remaining satisfied in one's spouse, purity, abjuring jealousy, self-knowledge and forbearance.

However, a little reflection shows that some of these *dharmas* (e.g., begetting children through one's own spouse, taking care of dependents, sharing of wealth, etc.) could be observed only by those who belonged to the second *āśrama* (i.e., those who were householders, married and could have owned some property), while the others were to be observed by all people, irrespective of the *āśramas* to which they might belong.

In another chapter of the *Śāntiparvan* (37.7), there is a list of nine characteristics of *dharma* enumerated by Vyāsa. The verse containing this list reads as follows:

> *adattasyānupādānaṃ dānamadhyayanaṃ tapaḥ* /
> *ahiṃsā satyamakrodhaḥ kṣamejyā dharmalakṣaṇam* //

Here, it is stated that non-taking of anything that has not been given by the owner of that thing (i.e., not stealing or forcibly taking away something that belongs to others), charity, study of scriptures (especially the Vedas), practice of austerities, non-violence, truthfulness, absence of anger, forbearance, and performance of sacrifices/worship of deities are the markers of *dharma*. But here, too, there are some activities that could not be performed by all and sundry. Study of scriptures was permitted only to the *traivarṇikas* (i.e. *Brāhmaṇas*, *Kṣatriyas* and *Vaiśyas*); it was specifically prohibited for the *Śūdras*. The same is true of the performance of Vedic sacrifices (*yajñas*). But even among the *traivarṇikas*, only the householders (*gṛhasthas*) were eligible to perform sacrifices; those belonging to the three other *āśramas* were not entitled to do so. In addition to such *sādhāraṇadharmas*, there are also (*a*) *varṇadharmas* that are specifically recommended for people belonging to a certain caste or social group (*varṇa*); (*b*) *āśramadharmas* that are specifically recommended for people in a certain stage of their life (*āśrama*); (*c*) *kuladharmas*, i.e., familial obligations; (*d*) *kulācāras*, i.e., practices that were customarily current in the family to which a person belonged; (*e*) *lokācāra*, i.e., customary or conventional morality; and (*f*) *deśācāra*, i.e., regional practices, whereby certain activities were permitted (or, even expected to be performed) as per local customs. One was expected to owe allegiance to all these *dharmas* scrupulously. According to Vyāsa (*Śāntiparvan* 37.14), anyone who neglects or gives up any one of these *dharmas* ceases to be *dhārmika* (i.e., one who lives according to *dharma*).

It is not always possible to keep track of all these multifarious duties that one is required to perform. In some cases, deciding whether a certain action is obligatory or not may not be a mean task. Moreover, while following a certain course of action, one may doubt whether he is doing what is right for him. In such cases, one may have doubts as to its validity. This becomes quite possible in the case of *deśācāra*. Marrying the daughter of the maternal uncle was prevalent in the southern parts of India, and as per the diktat of the *Dharmaśāstra*s, this practice would be *dharma* for the residents of those areas. But the Northerners considered this practice to be obnoxious. Suppose someone who originally belonged to the northern parts of India decided to migrate and settle in the southern part of India. In view of the fact that he was residing then in the southern parts of India, would he be justified if he married the daughter of his maternal uncle, or should he have stuck to the practices that were followed by his forefathers? Would *deśācāra* prevail over *kulācāra* in this case, or not? In such cases, one can have a genuine doubt about the course of action to be followed, since convenient and readymade solutions to such problems are not always available.

Another source of moral doubt is the plethora of scriptures that lay down *dharma*s and *adharma*s and that are not unanimous on all matters. In a dialogue between Gālava and Nārada reported in the *Śāntiparvan* (276.8–10), Gālava complained that due to the multiplicity of scriptures, it was very difficult to decide one's duties. Had there been only one scripture, then there would be only one definite course of action to be followed in a certain circumstance. Since there are so many scriptures, what is good for us has actually become 'hidden'.

At the beginning of the commentary of this chapter, Nīlakaṇṭha points out that there are many *śāstra*s, which may again be either Vedic or non-Vedic. Among the Vedic *śāstra*s, *Pūrva-Mīmāṃsā* and *Vedānta* are mainly based on Vedic injunctions, while the *śāstra*s like *Nyāya*, *Vaiśeṣika*, *Sāṃkhya*, etc., are mainly based on arguments. Among the non-Vedic *śāstra*s, the Cārvākas depend on arguments, while the Buddhist and Jaina *śāstra*s are based on the instructions of Buddha and Mahāvīra respectively. Each of these *śāstra*s claims that it *alone* can show the path to liberation and that the other *śāstra*s cannot do so. This naturally created confusion among the people, who could not always choose between them.

Matters become worse when in the same treatise, we find diktats that are mutually contradictory. For example, in the *Prāyaścittīya* section of the *Śāntiparvan* (35.30), Vyāsa states that an adulterous wife should be abandoned, because such abandonment purifies her and consequently, her husband does not become guilty of ignoring his duties.

But in the anecdote of Cirakārin, the son of Ahalyā and the sage Gautama, recorded in the *Śāntiparvan* (258.36), Cirakārin states that in a case of adultery, the man involved is guilty, and not the woman. The same view is subsequently expressed by his father Gautama, as is evident from the verses 258.42 and 46cd. Now, when two great sages like Vyāsa and Gautama thus express views opposed to each other, one may justifiably be in doubt regarding the course of action to be followed in such cases.

It is rather surprising to note that in the *Mahābhārata* itself, even the same character, in some cases, made at least apparently incompatible pronouncements about *dharma*. For example, in the *Viduravākya* section of the *Udyogaparvan* (37.7), Vidura, who was acknowledged as an expert on *dharma*, told Dhṛtarāṣṭra that one should behave with a person in accordance with the manner in which that person behaved with others. Accordingly, one should behave in a deceitful manner with a deceiver; and in an honest manner with an honest person. But subsequently, in the same section (39.58), Vidura told Dhṛtarāṣṭra that one should win over an angry person by absence of anger; a dishonest person by honest dealing, a miser by charity, and a liar by truthful speech.

What Vidura stated here does not seem to be consistent with what he had said earlier. Moreover, even if we grant for the sake of argument that what he had said earlier is reasonable, it still remains a fact that the practical application of the principle stated earlier may not be easy, because ascertaining the real nature of a person could be a difficult job. Different persons behave in different ways and first appearances can be deceptive. People who are actually nasty and dishonest may masquerade as nice and honest persons, while persons who are actually true gentlemen may appear as uncultured and uncouth. Before forming an opinion about the real nature of a person, we should properly observe him/her, and then alone come to a conclusion. After stating this important fact, some verses in the *Vyāghragomāyusaṃvāda* section of the *Śāntiparvan* (112.61–63) cite some good examples of the dangers of depending upon first impressions. The sky looks like a dome that has a blue surface and glow-worms look like sparks of fire, but the sky has no surface, nor are the glow-worms sparks of fire. Hence, even what is perceived should be believed only after a thorough examination so that one does not have to repent afterwards. Such warnings are useful, but they also make us apprehensive about passing any facile judgment on *dharma* and *adharma*, and indicate the factors that are sometimes responsible for moral doubts (*dharmasaṃśaya*).

Another source of doubt regarding *dharma* is the fact that sometimes, what apparently seems to be a case of *adharma* can turn out to be in reality a case of *dharma*, and vice versa. Again, sometimes, what seems to be *dharma* turns out to be a genuine instance of *dharma*. Only wise people, by virtue of their superior intellect, can properly distinguish between instances of *dharma* and those of *adharma*. This was told to Sañjaya by Yudhiṣṭhira in the following verse of *Udyogaparvan* (28.2):

yatrādharmo dharmarūpāṇi vibhrat
dharmaḥ kṛtsno dṛśyate' dharmarūpaḥ /
tathā dharmo dhārayandharmarūpaṃ
vidvāṃsastaṃ saṃprapaśyanti buddhyā //

The commentators of the *Mahābhārata* have interpreted this enigmatic verse in different ways. Nīlakaṇṭha states in his *Bhāratabhāvadīpa* that when a crooked person, in order to cause the death of someone, indulges in *Śyenayāga*, which is a form of *abhicāra* (i.e., a sacrifice made for malevolent purposes, recommended in the Vedas), he actually indulges in *adharma*, since it results in the death of someone. But to ignorant persons, it may seem that what he is doing is *dharma*, since it is, after all, a ritual like *Agnihotra* which is certainly an instance of *dharma*. Again, when liberated persons like Dattātreya, who are totally devoid of both attachment and aversion, behave like lunatics, ignorant people may think that what they are doing is *adharma* although their activities are, in fact, instances of *dharma*. In the case of sages like Vaśiṣṭha, the activities that appear to be instances of *dharma* are also actual cases of *dharma*. According to Haridāsa Siddhāntavāgīśa, however, this verse begins with describing something which is apparently a case of *adharma*, but, upon closer examination, turns out to be a case of *dharma*. In one case, killing a notorious robber, as an act of killing a human being, seems to be a instance of *adharma*, but is, actually, an instance of *dharma*, since it results in saving innocent people from the torture by that robber. The second case is that of malevolent rituals like the *Śyena* sacrifice which results in the death of someone. The third case is that of rituals like prayers held three times a day (*sandhyāvandanā*), which appear to be and actually are instances of *dharma*.

Once we admit in view of what Yudhiṣṭhira had said to Sañjaya in the aforementioned *Udyogaparvan* verse, we will also have to admit that in many cases, it becomes extremely difficult to decide whether a certain course of action is justified in a certain circumstance. The *Mahābhārata* states repeatedly that it is extremely difficult to ascertain the nature of *dharma* — it is ever elusive. For instance, in the *Rājadhārmānuśāsana* section of the *Śāntiparvan* (128.6), Bhīṣma told Yudhiṣṭhira that the nature of *dharma* is extremely subtle and very few people grasp its nature, though it is, in principle, possible to ascertain *dharma* with the help of scriptures, the conduct of good people and the use of one's intellect. Again, in the *Rājarṣivṛtta* section of the *Śāntiparvan* (130.19–20), Bhīṣma told Yudhiṣṭhira that grasping the nature of *dharma* is as difficult as finding the feet of a snake. One has to find *dharma* through a painstaking search, just as a hunter finds the deer it has shot with an arrow by following the trail of the deer's blood.

Thus, mere scriptural knowledge may not always enable someone to decide what is *dharma* and what is *adharma*. In the *Pativratākauśikasaṃvāda* section of the *Āraṇyakaparvan* (197.39, 41), the devoted wife (*pativratā*) told Kauśika that even through the scriptures are the final authorities on *dharma* and even though Kauśika has studied the Vedas and leads a pure life, he has not grasped the true nature of *dharma* which is subtle and, on that account, extremely difficult to comprehend.

In the *Dvijavyādhasaṃvāda* section of the *Āraṇyakaparvan* (200.2), Dharmavyādha also told Kauśika about the subtle ways of *dharma*, which can be known from the Vedas and which has various branches that grow in different directions:

śrutipramāṇo dharmo'yamiti vṛddhānuśāsanam /
sūkṣmā gatirhi dharmasya bahuśākhā hyanantikā //

Perhaps, this inscrutable nature of *dharma* made Yudhiṣṭhira enquire about the nature of *dharma* on so many occasions. Everyone agreed that Yudhiṣṭhira never deviated from the path of *dharma*. In the *Āraṇyakaparvan* (31.9), Draupadī stated that the intellect of Yudhiṣṭhira followed *dharma*, just as the shadow of a person accompanied him. When Bhīṣma, lying on the bed of arrows, was requested to give his advice on *dharma* and other related matters, he chose as his interlocutor Yudhiṣṭhira, who, in Bhīṣma's opinion, would not give up *dharma* under any circumstance (*Śāntiparvan* 55.2,7). In the *Āraṇyakaparvan* (32.2–5), Yudhiṣṭhira himself told Draupadī that he followed the path of *dharma* by his very nature, and not for enjoying the good results that the observance of *dharma* might produce. Yet, in the *Yakṣayudhiṣṭhirasaṃvāda* section of the *Āraṇyakaparvan* (App. 32.67), Yudhiṣṭhira told the Yakṣa that the real nature of *dharma* was 'hidden in a cave' (*dharmasya tattvaṃ nihitaṃ guhāyām*). In the *Dharmalakṣaṇa* section of the *Śāntiparvan* (251.1), Yudhiṣṭhira told Bhīṣma about the doubt regarding *dharma* that was so pervasive and asked him about the nature of *dharma*, as well as the means of attaining it.

Why should a person like Yudhiṣṭhira, who always abided by *dharma*, enquire so often about the nature of *dharma* and the means of knowing it? One possible reason for this may have been indicated by Yudhiṣṭhira himself in a verse in the *Yakṣayudhiṣṭhirasaṃvāda* section of the *Āraṇyakaparvan* which we have already quoted in part. There is, however, some dispute about the exact reading of the first hemistich of this verse. The verse, placed in the appendix of the critical edition of *Mahābhārata*, reads as follows:

tarko'pratiṣṭḥaḥ śrutayo vibhinnā
naiko ṛṣiryasya mataṃ na bhinnam /
dharmasya tattvaṃ nihitaṃ guhāyāṃ
mahājano yena gataḥ sa panthāḥ // (App. 32.65–68)

Among the commentators, Nīlakaṇṭha reads the first hemistich in the following manner:

tarko'pratiṣṭhaḥ śrutayo vibhinnā
nāsau munirmataṃ yasya na bhinnam /

On the other hand, Haridāsa Siddhāntavāgīśa prefers the following reading:

vedāḥ vibhinnā smṛtayo vibhinnāḥ
nāsau munirmataṃ yasya na bhinnam /

Some editions, however, have the reading: *tarko'pratiṣṭhaḥ śrutayo vibhinnā nasau ṛṣir yasya mataṃ na bhinnam*, and still others admit the reading: *naiko ṛṣir yasya mataṃ pramāṇam*.

But whatever be the proper reading of this disputed verse, one thing is quite clear: scriptures like the Vedas and the *Smṛtis*, from which we should ascertain *dharma*, are not unanimous on all points. Nīlakaṇṭha and Haridāsa Siddhāntavāgīśa themselves have also cited examples of such conflicting scriptural passages in their commentaries. The sages who were supposed to be experts on *dharma* have not interpreted the scriptures in the same way, or even codified *dharma* in the same way in their treatises. *Tarka*, i.e., argumentation is not also of much help, since any argument may, in principle, be refuted by a counter-argument.

The last line of this verse (*mahājano yena gataḥ sa panthāḥ*), which is supposed to provide the answer to the question of the Yakṣa and which means, 'the path to be adopted is that which is followed by the common people', poses, in its turn, another problem. Here, 'path' obviously stands for the course of action to be followed. When accredited sources of knowledge like scriptures, reason and opinions of sages, for various reasons, fail to be our guide, how can the behaviour of common people be a reliable guide in deciding what one should or should not do? Does this sentence indicate that during his sojourn in the forests, Yudhiṣṭhira came to realize that the attempt at grasping the nature of *dharma* and *adharma* was as hopeless as the attempt at reaching the horizon and that the only safe course was to follow the common people and thereby, at least, avoid public censure? But in that case, unless we assume that Yudhiṣṭhira was a consummate hypocrite, how can we explain the fact that even after the Kurukṣetra war, he was questioning Vyāsa, Bhīṣma and others about the nature of *dharma*? Another possible answer may be that Yudhiṣṭhira had trust in the collective wisdom of people, who had an intuitive feeling about what was morally right and what was morally wrong; this collective wisdom accounts for the degree of unanimity in different societies regarding the goodness or badness of actions. No sane person will ever say that murder or arson is morally defensible, not would (s)he say that helping a needy person or looking after a sick person is morally reprehensible. The day-to-day conduct of ordinary human beings is mostly determined by such a moral awareness (which may be either innate or inculcated by long experience and tradition). That is why they do not have to consult scriptures every now and then for deciding which action is right and which one is not. This has been stated in a verse that is traditionally ascribed to Vyāsa:[2]

idaṃ puṇyam idaṃ pāpaṃ ityetasmin padadvaye /
ācaṇḍālaṃ manuṣyānamalpaṃ śāstraprayojanam //

For developing such a sense, one does not require acquaintance with scriptures so much, as one requires virtues like simplicity, honesty, selflessness,

---

[2] This verse has been ascribed to Pārāśarya, i.e., Vyāsa by Kumārila Bhaṭṭa in his *Ślokavārttika*, section on *Autpattikasūtra*, verse no. 3.

straightforwardness, and compassion or mercy. In the absence of such virtues, even a great scholar of *Dharmaśāstras* may have a distorted view of *dharma*. It is extremely difficult to throttle this basic sense of good and bad, justice and injustice, right and wrong. Even a hardened criminal, while performing a misdeed, is aware of the fact that what he is doing cannot be morally justified even though he may not admit it publicly. Sometimes, such people even have remorse or repentance for their misdeeds, of which at least they themselves are witnesses. The following statement of Dharmavyādha in the *Āraṇyakaparvan* (198.51) draws our attention to this fact:

> *pāpaṃ kṛtvā hi manyeta nāhamasmīti pūruṣaḥ* /
> *taṃ tu devā prapaśyanti svasyaivāntarapūruṣaḥ* //

Thus, the collective wisdom of common people may be of *some* help to us in deciding what we should or should not do in a certain situation. May be, Yudhiṣṭhira wanted to emphasize this fact when he identified the 'path' as that 'by which the majority goes'.

One may, however, try to explain Yudhiṣṭhira's inquisitiveness about *dharma* in a different manner. It may be due to the fact that the ambit of *dharma* is so vast that no single person can understand it in its entirety, and questioning others can certainly be helpful. Besides, in view of the bewildering variety of different types of *dharma* that have been enumerated earlier and are not always compatible with one another, it often becomes difficult for us to choose a course of action that can take into account all these varieties. Another tentative answer can be that even though *dharma* is usually claimed to be *sanātana*, i.e., eternal and immutable, it is, in fact, subject to gradual change over time, as is evident from the fact that some social practices like levirate (*niyoga*) that were formerly permissible were subsequently prohibited by the authors of *Dharmaśāstras*. In such a situation, one cannot always decide whether a course of action that was earlier taught to be in accordance with *dharma* is still permissible or not. Another possible reason may be the fact that *dharma* is supposed to sustain and promote social order and harmony (*dhāraṇād dharma ityāhuḥ*, *Śāntiparvan* 110.11), and it is not always easy to foresee whether a certain course of action will definitely satisfy this condition. One may also say that Yudhiṣṭhira, inspite of all his virtues, lacked self-confidence and, consequently, wanted to be assured every now and then by others that he was on the right path.

V

Dharmasaṃśaya (i.e., moral doubt) should be distinguished from *dharmacchala*/*dharmapāśa*/*dharmasaṅkaṭa* (i.e., moral dilemma). In the case of *dharmasaṅkaṭa*, one is not in doubt about what one should or should not do. Rather, one is placed in a predicament because one is compelled to choose between two courses of actions both of which are recognized by the agent to be equally obligatory and are also, at the same time, mutually incompatible and irreconciliable. At that moment, the agent does not have any rational ground for choosing between the two alternatives and, hence, becomes unable to take any decision. Such a situation is evidently painful for any person who is conscientious and dutiful. There are many instances of such moral dilemmas in the *Mahābhārata*.

One example is the story of king Śibi narrated in the *Śyenakapotīya* section of the *Āraṇyakaparvan* (131.10–12). A pigeon, chased by a hawk, came to Śibi and asked for shelter. As a king, Śibi was duty bound to offer protection to anyone who sought refuge (*śaraṇāgata*), and as a householder, it was his duty to ensure the well-being of a guest in every possible manner. But thereafter, the hawk that was chasing the pigeon came to the court of Śibi and requested him to hand over the pigeon. The hawk pointed out that by the law of nature, the pigeon was its rightful prey and Śibi had no right to deprive the hawk of the pigeon. No creature can survive when deprived of its natural food, and by offering protection to the pigeon, Śibi was virtually forcing the hawk to die of starvation, even though the hawk had not harmed Śibi in any way. To cause the death of an innocent creature would be a prime case of *adharma*. The hawk further pointed out to Śibi that an act which is normally regarded as *dharma* ceases to be so when it comes into conflict with another *dharma*. An action is *dharma* only when it is in conformity with other *dharmas*. When two obligatory actions become opposed to each other, one should assess their relative importance and then choose the duty that is more pressing or important.

But if Śibi had granted the hawk's request, then, too, he would have committed an act that would be *adharma*, since he would be guilty of two misdeeds — (*a*) breaking the promise that he had made to the pigeon, and (*b*) failing in his duty to provide safety to a creature that had asked for protection. Placed in such a predicament, Śibi chose to protect the pigeon and satisfy the hawk by offering his own flesh to the latter in lieu of the pigeon.

The second instance of moral dilemma chosen by me is from *Bhagavadgītā* which forms part of the *Bhīṣmaparvan*. It pertains to Arjuna who at the very beginning of the Kurukṣetra war decided not to fight (*na yotsye*), since it suddenly dawned upon him that by participating in this war he would commit a grave crime in being the cause of the death or injury of his elders like Bhīṣma and Śalya, teachers like Kṛpa and Droṇa, and other relatives like Duryodhana, Jayadratha, etc. He was then reminded by Śrīkṛṣṇa that as a member of the *Kṣatriya varṇa* and a responsible member of the Pāṇḍava army, he was duty bound to participate in the war which alone could earn for the Pāṇḍavas their rightful share of the kingdom that had been usurped by Duryodhana and his cohorts. The option of going to war was adopted by the Pāṇḍavas and their allies after a long discussion, in which Arjuna was also a participant. Hence, withdrawal from war at that critical juncture would have been almost an act of betrayal. Thereafter, Arjuna confessed to Śrīkṛṣṇa that he was *dharmasammūḍhacetā*, i.e., totally confused and unable to decide upon a course of action. Only after much persuasion and encouragement from Śrīkṛṣṇa could Arjuna overcome his hesitation and participate in the war.

The third instance of moral dilemma is found in the *Droṇaparvan*. Before the Kurukṣetra war started, Droṇa had confessed to Yudhiṣṭhira that he would give up fighting only if his son Aśvatthāman were killed in the war. After a few days of becoming the general of the Kaurava army, Droṇa began to kill a large number of Pāṇḍava soldiers. No warrior in the Pāṇḍava camp could resist Droṇa, and the defeat of the Pāṇḍavas became a distinct possibility. In order to stop this massacre, Śrīkṛṣṇa asked Yudhiṣṭhira to go to Droṇa and tell him that Aśvatthāman had been killed. In order to save Yudhiṣṭhira, who had till then never uttered a falsehood from the sin of telling a damn lie, Bhīma killed an elephant called Aśvatthāman and then told Droṇa that Aśvatthāman has been killed. Droṇa, however, did not believe Bhīma. Then, at the insistence of Śrīkṛṣṇa, Yudhiṣṭhira loudly uttered the words, 'Aśvatthāman has been killed', and then added, almost inaudibly, the two words 'the elephant', which were drowned or submerged in the noise of the battlefield. Trusting that Yudhiṣṭhira would not deviate from the path of *dharma* under any circumstance, Droṇa took his words to be true and gave up his weapons, whereupon he was killed by Dhṛṣṭadyumna, the Pāṇḍava general (*Droṇaparvan* 164.97–110). Here, Yudhiṣṭhira agreed, after much persuasion by Śrīkṛṣṇa, to uttering a lie that had put on 'the cloak of truth' (*satyakañcuka*). Prior to that, an honest man like him must have had a moral dilemma: should he have stuck to his vow of always telling nothing but the truth and watched the wholesale massacre of his own army, or should he have done something that would avert the defeat of his army, even though the means adopted by him would be at least devious, if not downright dishonest? This misdeed of deceiving his teacher haunted Yudhiṣṭhira even after winning the war, which is evident from his words of repentance in the *Śāntiparvan* (27.13–17).

The fourth example of moral dilemma again pertains to Arjuna and appears in the *Karṇaparvan*. When Yudhiṣṭhira, who was not properly guarded by his brothers, came face to face with Karṇa, a battle ensued between them. Yudhiṣṭhira was no match for Karṇa in the art of war, and very soon, he was at the mercy of Karṇa who let him go scot-free, since he had promised earlier to Kuntī that apart from Arjuna, he would not kill any of the Pāṇḍavas. When Yudhiṣṭhira went back to the camp, Arjuna came to know what had happened in the battlefield, and went to Yudhiṣṭhira to inquire if everything was alright. Yudhiṣṭhira, who was still smarting under the utter humiliation at the hands of Karṇa, scolded Arjuna for not being able to provide protection to his elder brother and fulfill his promise of killing Karṇa. In the heat of the moment, Yudhiṣṭhira also told Arjuna that he should hand over his *Gāṇḍīva* bow to Śrīkṛṣṇa and become the charioteer of the latter (*Karṇaparvan* 48.14–15). This placed Arjuna in a quandary because he had earlier taken a vow to kill anyone who would ask him to hand over the *Gāṇḍīva* bow to somebody else (*Karṇaparvan* 49.9–12). In order to keep his vow, Arjuna unsheathed his sword and proceeded to kill Yudhiṣṭhira. Śrīkṛṣṇa, however, made him understand that keeping a vow under all circumstances was not justified, especially if it were a childish vow, the observance of which would result in fratricide (*Karṇaparvan* 49.18–23). Here, Arjuna must have been in a dilemma because as a *Kṣatriya*, he was expected to keep his vow and, at the same time, was not supposed to kill his own elder brother. Once again, Śrīkṛṣṇa came to the rescue of the Pāṇḍavas by telling Arjuna that his promise could be kept if he simply insulted Yudhiṣṭhira, because for honourable men insult is even worse than death (*Karṇaparvan* 49.65–69).

The last example of moral dilemma chosen by me is given in the story of Cirakārin, son of sage Gautama and his wife Ahalyā, narrated in the *Śāntiparvan*. Cirakārin always delayed in taking any decision and acting upon it, whereupon the sarcastic epithet 'Cirakārin' (i.e., one who is slow in doing everything) was given to him. Once, attracted by the beauty of Ahalyā and with evil intentions, Indra, the king of *deva*s, came to the hermitage of Gautama as a guest. While Gautama had gone elsewhere, Indra assumed the form of Gautama and had sexual intercourse with Ahalyā. When Gautama came to know about this incident, he was naturally infuriated and left for the forest after commanding Cirakārin to kill Ahalyā. This order of his father put Cirakārin in a dilemma because on the one hand, he was duty bound to obey his father and on the other hand, he could not, in any circumstance, commit the sin of killing a woman who was also his mother. Hence, his filial duties towards Gautama and Ahalyā were equally binding on him (*Śāntiparvan* 258.9– 12). Placed in such a quandary, Cirakārin went on thinking about what to do, and this enabled Gautama, who later repented the harsh command given by him, to be reunited with his wife. (*Śāntiparvan* 258.42–49, 57–59).

At this point, a question about the very possibility of moral dilemmas may be raised. Some moral thinkers are of the opinion that the very admission of such a possibility would result in the impossibility of any consistent theory of morals because no consistent moral theory can allow a situation where the moral agent is compelled to choose between two equally obligatory but mutually incompatible duties. Any moral theory that allows such a possibility must itself be inconsistent. According to these thinkers, such so-called moral dilemmas occur when the moral agent, either due to some wrong notion about morality or some emotion or ignorance, entertains the wrong notion that he has to choose between two mutually opposed obligations both of which are *equally* binding upon him. Proper information or clear thinking would reveal that the one or other of these two alternatives is not binding on him. But in that case, there can be no *genuine* moral dilemmas that admit of no solutions. In some cases, people may also fail to do what they ought to do because of their infatuation for someone or animosity towards someone. A good example of this can be the case of Dhṛtarāṣṭra who knew perfectly well that what Duryodhana and his cohorts had done to the Pāṇḍavas was palpably wrong and unjustified, and yet, due to his blind affection for his sons, he was unable to do what he should have done (i.e., make Duryodhana return to the Pāṇḍavas their rightful share of the kingdom). This becomes evident in the *Āraṇyakaparvan* (5.16–18), wherein Vidura advised Dhṛtarāṣṭra to make peace with the Pāṇḍavas by restoring to them their share of kingdom. This made Dhṛtarāṣṭra extremely annoyed and he accused Vidura of being partial towards the Pāṇḍavas. Dhṛtarāṣṭra even accused him of duplicity and crookedness and told him that he might stay in the Kaurava court or leave it according to his wish because even after being sufficiently honoured by Dhṛtarāṣṭra, Vidura continued to plead on behalf of the Pāṇḍavas. Thereafter, Dhṛtarāṣṭra left the royal court, after saying that Vidura was like an unfaithful wife who deserts her husband who has treated her well (*Āraṇyakaparvan* 5.19). Afterwards, however, Dhṛtarāṣṭra repented and sent Sañjaya to bring back Vidura who had meanwhile gone to meet the Pāṇḍavas.

In the *Udyogaparvan* (40.28–30), Dhṛtarāṣṭra himself asked Vidura for his advice and, after listening to him, frankly confessed that even though he wanted to do justice to the Pāṇḍavas, his attitude would change radically whenever he came in contact with Duryodhana. He then went on to blame his fate for his predicament which was, in fact, due solely to his weakness of will. Dhṛtarāṣṭra was placed in this predicament because even though he knew that as the head of the Kuru family, it was his duty to ensure that no injustice was done to the Pāṇḍavas, due to his blind attachment to Duryodhana, he also felt that it was also his duty to protect the interests of Duryodhana at all costs, even if that resulted in palpable injustice to the Pāṇḍavas. But if only he had the capacity to shake off this irrational attachment, he would have understood that while it was certainly his duty to safeguard the *legitimate* interests of his sons, it was *not* his duty to support his sons when their actions were evidently wrong. Thus, all the so-called moral conflicts or dilemmas arise either from *mistakenly* considering some non-obligatory action as obligatory, or from our *inability* to assess the relative importance of two courses of action, both of which may be obligatory even though one of them actually overrides the other, and thus wrongly considering them to be *equally* obligatory.

In our opinion, such an attitude towards moral dilemmas as displayed by some moral thinkers seems to exhibit some sort of snobbish insensitivity to the predicaments in which an ordinary mortal may be placed from time to time. A person may be placed in a situation where one *has* to decide upon a course of action, and yet, all the options open to him/her at that time may appear to be equally unacceptable. Unlike Cirakārin, such a person does not have at his/her disposal all the time in the world for pondering over the problem, the possible solutions and the basis on which one of the latter may be chosen — nor can (s)he simply desist from acting in any way whatsoever. His/her situation may be compared with that of a hapless fawn chased by a band of hunters, who finds a steep mountain in front, a deep lake on the left and a forest-fire on the right and hence can neither go somewhere, nor stay in the same place, as has been described in the following floating verse:

puro revāpāre giriratidurārohaśikharo
dhanuṣpāṇiḥ paścācchabarakavaro dhāvati muhuḥ /
saraḥ savye'savye davadahanadāhavyatikaro
na gantuṃ na sthātuṃ hariṇaśiśurevaṃ prabhavati //

One usually acquires the ideas about moral norms from some prototypes of socially acceptable behaviour to which the members of a society are normally exposed from their childhood, and during this period of learning, what is usually demanded of them is unqualified obedience to what is being taught — one is not expected to question or challenge the basis on which these prototypes are chosen. Such uncritical acceptance tends to generate the feeling that one simply has to follow this or that dictum blindly, otherwise one would be doing something immoral or reprehensible. Now, if it so happens that as per such accepted norms, a person becomes obliged to take two courses of action simultaneously, which are such that the performance of one of these acts would automatically preclude the performance of the other, then such a person is placed in a quandary from which there is no easy way out. If moral dilemmas are always due to ignorance, mistake, bias or muddle-headedness, then the solution of any such dilemma would consist simply in identifying which one of the two conflicting courses of action is *really* morally obligatory for the agent concerned. Once this can be done, the other course of action would simply cease to be obligatory, and thus, at least one of the proverbial horns of the dilemma would be broken. But things are not that simple.

Let us consider once again the story of king Śibi in the *Śyenakapotīya* section of the *Āraṇyakaparvan*. Therein, the hawk also told Śibi that there cannot be any genuine conflict between two *dharma*s. If some course of action runs counter to some other action that is definitely an instance of *dharma*, then the former is to be declared a case of *adharma*. When there is nevertheless some apparent conflict between two *dharma*s, one has to decide which one of them has more 'moral weight' (*guru*), and choose *that* as his duty so that the conflict disappears.

But such things are easier said than done. When two conflicting courses of action appear to be equally obligatory, then there is no rule of thumb by which one can decide which one of them is really obligatory for him/her. Following Matilal, two examples of such situations from *Rāmāyaṇa* and *Mahābhārata* and the manner in which they were resolved may be mentioned here. In the *Uttarakāṇḍa* of *Rāmāyaṇa*, it is stated that when Rāma was talking to Kālapuruṣa, other persons were prohibited from entering the room where the discussion was being held. Rāma had promised that he would banish any person who would happen to enter that room. As bad luck would have it, the sage Durvāsas, famous for his ill-temper, arrived in the palace and sought an audience with Rāma. If his request was not honoured, then there was every chance of Durvāsas hurling some terrible curse on the royal family or the inhabitants of Ayodhyā. In such an emergency, Lakṣmaṇa was compelled to enter that room and announce the arrival of Durvāsas. Rāma then faced a genuine dilemma. On the one hand, if he had to keep his promise, then he would have to banish Lakṣmaṇa who was compelled by his concern for others to enter that room and whose expulsion from the country would be extremely unfortunate. On the other hand, if he allowed Lakṣmaṇa to stay in Ayodhyā, then Rāma would be guilty of breaking his promise which, as a man of honour, he was not supposed to do. In the *Mahābhārata*, too, we find Arjuna placed in a similar predicament when Yudhiṣṭhira, being angry with Arjuna, asked the latter to hand over the *Gāṇḍīva* bow to Śrīkṛṣṇa because Arjuna had promised earlier that he would kill any person who would utter such a statement. But the two dilemmas were solved in radically different ways in these two epics. In *Rāmāyaṇa* (VII.106.9), we find Rāma banishing Lakṣmaṇa in accordance with his promise. If he had any qualms in this matter, then they were removed by the verdict of the sage Vaśiṣṭha who said that a promise that had been made must be honoured at all costs, even if that entailed the banishment of one's own brother because if people tended to break their promises, then *dharma* itself would disappear from earth. But in the *Mahābhārata*, Arjuna was advised by Śrīkṛṣṇa to insult Yudhiṣṭhira instead of killing him on the specious ground that insulting a person is as good as killing him (*Karṇaparvan* 49.65–69).

Thus, in one epic, observance of a promise *in toto* was declared to be *dharma* as it was of supreme importance, whereas in the other epic, abstaining from fratricide was considered to be more important and the observance of promise was virtually turned into a caricature. When we find two equally famous warriors and their advisors acting in diametrically opposed ways, even though they were placed in similar predicaments, can we say that one can, after all, always decide which one of the conflicting duties is *guru* (more weighty), and which one of them is *laghu* (less weighty)? Thus, unless we can hit upon some dependable and uncontroversial means of solving these dilemmas, our problems will remain intact — we will not be able to wish them away.

VI

Let us now see how far the epics themselves can help us in finding ways that may help one to decide upon some course of action if (s)he happens to be the victim of *dharmasaṃśaya* or *dharmasaṅkaṭa*.

In the *Vyāsavākya* section of the *Śāntiparvan* (36.20), *dharma* has been declared by Vyāsa to be situational (*vyāvasthika*). If *dharma* varies due to variation in the situation, then one may very well be in doubt about *dharma*. Vyāsa has, however, given some hints about the ways in which such doubts can be removed. If there is any doubt regarding the obligatoriness of some action, then the collective decision about it taken by 10 scholars of Vedas or three scholars of *Dharmaśāstra*s should be taken as final. It may be mentioned here that the *Manusaṃhitā* (XII.111–12) also speaks of such a *pariṣat* or body of scholars. The decisions reached by such a body should not be flouted. This body may contain three or 10 scholars. The difference here is that Manu suggests that in addition to the scholars of Vedas and *Dharmaśāstras*, there should be experts in the sciences of argumentation, interpretation and etymology, as also members of the first three *āśramas*. The policy of not depending on the judgment of any single person seems to be a sound one. It may be expected that if all these members are competent and honest, then the decisions handed out by them are likely to be dependable.

VII

Situational ethics has been discussed primarily in the *Āpaddharma* section of the *Śāntiparvan* (though not all the chapters of this section deal with ethical issues). In the words of S. K. Belvalkar, the editor of the *Śāntiparvan*, *Āpaddharma* literally means 'duties of the king in abnormal times of stress and struggle' (1966: clxxi), which are to be adopted in circumstances wherein 'a king would be justified in transcending the commonly accepted ethical maxims in the interest of the still higher demands of the welfare of the State and of the whole humanity' (ibid.: ccxi). In fact, the necessity of such departures from the commonly accepted moral norms by even persons other than kings has been stated by many characters in different *parvans* of the *Mahābhārata*.

The most compact formulation of the basic principle underlying the adoption of *Āpaddharma* comes from Vyāsa in the *Rājadharma* section of the *Śāntiparvan* (37.8):

> *ya eva dharmaḥ so'dharmo'deśe'kāle pratiṣṭhitaḥ* /
> *ādānamanṛtaṃ hiṃsā dharmo vyāvasthikaḥ smṛtaḥ* //

In this verse, Vyāsa points out that whether a certain action is an instance of *dharma* or *adharma* depends on the situation or circumstance in which that action takes place. What is *adharma* (e.g., stealing, telling a lie and violence or killing) in a normal situation may be *dharma* in an abnormal situation. Likewise, what is *dharma* (e.g., telling the truth) in a normal situation may be *adharma* in an abnormal situation (wherein telling the truth would be harmful to an innocent person).

In the *Āpaddharma* section of *Śāntiparvan*, we also find several anecdotes wherein some concrete cases are given for illustrating this view. One of them is the *Mārjāramūṣikasaṃvāda* which illustrates how two creatures, one of whom being the mortal enemy of another, could enter into a temporary truce for mutual benefit. A mouse used to live in a burrow at the feet of a huge banyan tree in a forest, and a cat used to live in the branches of that very tree. A hunter began to set a snare in that area and one night the cat was trapped in that snare. Seeing the cat in this condition, the mouse which had begun to look for food without any fear started eating the piece of flesh that had been placed as a bait in the snare. But the mouse suddenly noticed the presence of two other mortal enemies — a mongoose that was on the ground and an owl that was sitting on the branch of a nearby tree. The mouse sized up its situation and concluded that the only way it could save itself was to ask the entrapped cat for shelter because like the mouse, the cat was also in great danger and, since the mouse could also help the cat by gnawing though the ropes of the snare, it ought not to harm the mouse if it valued its own life. The cat agreed to the request of the mouse and asked the latter to cut the snare as soon as possible. The mouse, however, began to cut the strings of the snare very slowly and told the cat to have some patience, since the snare would certainly be cut before the arrival of the hunter. Towards the morning, the disappointed mongoose and owl went away and, as soon as the hunter arrived there, the mouse cut the last string in the snare so that it could enter its burrow and the cat could climb the tree at the same time. After the departure of the disappointed hunter, the cat repeatedly requested the mouse to come out of the burrow since they had now become friends, but the mouse declined to come out in spite of such entreaties. It told the cat that friendship and enmity are not permanent — they are formed according to one's self-interest. Hence, there are times when a friend can become an enemy and an enemy can become a friend (*Śāntiparvan* 136.134–35). The friendship between the cat and the mouse was formed earlier since both of them were endangered, and with the cessation of that danger, the resultant friendship also came to an end (*Śāntiparvan* 136.156). While this story is instructive in matters of diplomacy, it does not deal directly with any moral issue. It, however, illustrates the maxim that in abnormal situations, one may have to adopt some policy which one may not even dream of in a normal situation. But it is easy to see how this principle of expediency can also be extended to decisions that involve moral choice.

Another instructive story found in the *Āpaddharma* section is *Caṇḍālaviśvāmitra-saṃvāda* which describes how taboos regarding food can be ignored during times of distress. It also states the conditions under which even theft is permitted. At the juncture of *tretā* and *dvāpara* aeons (*yugas*), there was a draught that lasted for 12 years, and the normal life of people was totally disrupted by the resultant famine. Even the sages left their hermitages and began to wander around in search of food, having given up their daily chores like study of scriptures or practice of penances. During these trying times, sage Viśvāmitra, who had come to a village inhabited by *Caṇḍāla*s (who were considered to be untouchable, since against the stipulation of scriptures, they ate the meat of dogs and hence were called *śvapaca* or *śvapāka*), failed to get any food by way of alms. Weakened by the enforced fasting for a long time, he fainted near the door of a *Caṇḍāla* household. At night, on regaining consciousness, he found that in the house some portions of a dog's carcass that even the *Caṇḍāla*s had considered to be inedible. Viśvāmitra thought that his first duty was to save his own life even by eating this prohibited meat because life was always preferable to death, and for that, whatever was needed had to be done. After all, one could be on the path of *dharma* only when one was alive (*Śāntiparvan* 139.59). Accordingly, Viśvāmitra decided to steal the dog-meat. He also remembered the scriptural rule that in such cases of stealing for the sake of survival, one should first choose the household of someone who is inferior in caste and that in such cases, taking something without the consent of its owner did not amount to theft (*Śāntiparvan* 139.37–39).

When Viśvāmitra entered the *Caṇḍāla* household for stealing the dog-meat, the owner of the house, who was asleep, woke up and was about to kill Viśvāmitra whom he took for a common thief. Viśvāmitra revealed his identity to the *Caṇḍāla* who was extremely surprised to find a sage like Viśvāmitra trying to steal dog-meat from the house of a *Caṇḍāla* — an act that was extremely improper on several counts. First, it was an act of stealing which was *adharma*. Second, what was being stolen was the flesh of dog, which was a strict taboo for Viśvāmitra. Third, the flesh was from so despicable a limb of the dog that even the *Caṇḍālas* refrained from eating it. Fourth, the flesh was being taken from the house of an untouchable *Caṇḍāla* which was also supposed to be out of bounds for a sage like Viśvāmitra. The *Caṇḍāla* maintained that if he allowed Viśvāmitra to take this flesh, then both he and Viśvāmitra would be committing something sinful, and accordingly, he implored Viśvāmitra to seek some other food. But Viśvāmitra was insistent on eating this flesh because in his opinion, since he had not been able to procure any other food even when he tried his best and since he had to survive, he had no other option open to him. He would certainly be comitting *adharma* by stealing dog-meat and eating it, but he could later perform penitential acts or expiation (*prāyaścitta*) or practise severe penances (*tapas*) for removing the sin that would accrue from the act of theft or the eating of some forbidden food. After much argumentation, Viśvāmitra told the *Caṇḍāla* that the latter was not authorized or competent enough to instruct Viśvāmitra about *dharma* and *adharma*, whereupon the *Caṇḍāla* did not prevent him any more from taking the piece of dog-meat (*Śāntiparvan* 139.24–88). Viśvāmitra saved his life by eating this flesh after consecrating it and offering it to the deities (see 12.357*.5).

In both the stories that we have recounted, one point has been highlighted again and again — one's first duty is to protect one's own life, even if that has to be done by some unusual or questionable means. A person who is alive can, after all, atone for his misdeeds, but in the absence of life, the very performance of *dharma* becomes impossible. This very point was emphasized by Viśvāmitra in his answer to the *Caṇḍāla* (*Śāntiparvan* 139.58–59, 61–62). A similar story is also found in *Chāndogyopaniṣad* (I.10.1), and the message conveyed there is the same — in times of distress, certain codes of conduct may have to be transgressed for one's own survival.

Incidentally, it may be noted that in the *Śāntiparvan*, Bhīṣma said that when in distress, a *Kṣatriya* king could forcibly take things from others for building up his treasury, just as people dug up land for making a pond because the real strength of the *Kṣatriya* depended on his wealth. Bhīṣma essentially argued that the *Kṣatriyas* were the protectors of people and, hence, had a right to usurp the property of others by force when such actions were necessary. Once they assumed power, they could then be generous to those from whom they had earlier extracted wealth. The only rider here is that the *Kṣatriya*s should not appropriate anything that belonged to mendicants and the *Brāhma* (*Śāntiparvan* 128.11–12,16, 21–22, 27).

In this way, even though abstaining from stealing or plundering (*adattāsyānupādānam*) figures prominently in the list of *dharma*s, both these misdeeds were allowed under abnormal conditions. The same principle applies to the virtue of truthfulness as well. One should speak the truth so long as it does not harm the genuine interest of somebody. This has been exemplified in the story of Kauśika that was related by Śrīkṛṣṇa to Arjuna in the *Karṇaparvan*. Kauśika, a mendicant, had taken the vow of always speaking the truth so that he could go to heaven after his death. One day, some persons who were chased by some robbers came to Kauśika and requested him not to reveal to the robbers the place where these persons were hiding. But when the robbers came and asked Kauśika about the place where these fugitives were hiding, Kauśika, in accordance with his vow, told them the truth and, as a result, these people were killed by the robbers. After his death, Kauśika, who was thus responsible for the death of these innocent persons, was sent not to heaven but to hell. After narrating this story, Śrīkṛṣṇa pointed out that while keeping one's promise and telling the truth are certainly admirable virtues, there are occasions when it is better to break one's promise or to tell a lie (*Karṇaparvan* 49.27–53). In the *Mahābhārata*, one often comes across detailed lists of such occasions. Thus, in the *Āraṇyakaparvan* (198.69), Dharmavyādha told Kauśika that non-violence and truth-telling are beneficial to all and that non-violence, which is the highest virtue, is based on truth-telling:

ahiṃsā satyavacanaṃ sarvabhūtahitaṃ param /
ahiṃsā paramo dharmaḥ sa ca satye pratiṣṭhitaḥ //

But subsequently (*Āraṇyakaparvan* 200.3–4), Dharmavyādha also said that one should tell lies when someone's life is at stake, as well as during marriage:

prāṇātyaye vivāhe ca vaktavyamanṛtaṃ bhavet /
anṛtaṃ ca bhavet satyaṃ satyañcaivānṛtaṃ bhavet //
yadbhūtahitamatyantaṃ tatsatyamiti dhāraṇā /
viparyayakṛto'dharmaḥ paśya dharmasya sūkṣmatām //

In the *Droṇaparvan* (164.99), while urging Yudhiṣṭhira to tell Droṇa the lie that Aśvatthāman had been killed, Śrīkṛṣṇa told Yudhiṣṭhira that one does not incur the sin of telling a lie when it is told for saving the life of someone — indeed, in such cases, a lie becomes superior to a true statement:

sa bhavāṃstrātu no droṇāt satyājjyāyo'nṛtaṃ bhavet /
anṛtaṃ jīvitasyārthe vadanna spṛśyate'nṛtaiḥ //

Vyāsa gives a longer list of permissible lies in the *Śāntiparvan*, wherein it has been stated that one should tell a lie for saving the life of oneself or of somebody else and in the interest of one's teacher. Likewise; one should tell lies to women; and for the purpose of marriage:

> *prāṇatrāṇe' nṛtaṃ vācyamātmano vā parasya vā* /
> *gurvarthe striṣu caiva syādvivāhakaraṇeṣu ca* // (*Śāntiparvan* 35.25)

Bhīṣma also said in the *Śāntiparvan* that there are cases wherein telling a truth amounts to telling a lie, and vice versa:

> *bhavet satyaṃ na vaktavyaṃ vaktavyamanṛtaṃ bhavet* /
> *yatrānṛtaṃ bhavet satyaṃ satyaṃ vāpyanṛtaṃ bhavet* // (*Śāntiparvan* 110.5)

Here, no ready-made list of permissible cases of telling lies is given — Bhīṣma simply said that such cases have to be decided by the application of reason:

> *tādṛśo' yamanupraśno yatra dharmaḥ sudurvacaḥ* /
> *duṣkaraḥ pratisaṅkhyātuṃ tarkeṇātra vyavasyati* // (*Śāntiparvan* 110.9)

Afterwards, however, Bhīṣma said in the same chapter that one should tell lies (*a*) when one's life is endangered, (*b*) in matters concerning marriage, and (*c*) for saving one's property:

> *prāṇātyaye vivāhe ca vaktavyamanṛtaṃ bhavet* /
> *arthasya rakṣaṇārthāya pareṣāṃ dharmakāraṇāt* // (*Śāntiparvan* 110.18)

In another subsequent chapter of the *Śantiparvan*, Bhīṣma enumerated *five* cases of false statements, the utterance of which does not incur any sin. These are false statements that are made either (*a*) in jest, or (*b*) to women, or (*c*) during marriage, or (*d*) in the interest of one's teacher, or (*e*) for saving one's own life:

> *na narmayuktaṃ vacanaṃ hinasti na strīṣu rājan na vivāhakāle* /
> *na gurvarthe nātmano jīvitārthe pañcānṛtānyāhurapātakāni* // (*Śāntiparvan* 159.28)

Here, however, we may pose some pertinent questions. In *Śāntiparvan* 35.25, Vyāsa said that one should tell a lie for saving the life of oneself, or of somebody else. The question that arises is: does this phrase 'somebody else' apply to all and sundry, including even criminals like murderers, rapists and arsonists? If so, then is an eye witness of such crimes, when asked to testify in a court of law, supposed to deny having seen such an incident, so that the life of even the justifiably accused person is saved? This, however, would make the award of punishment to such criminals virtually impossible, and this is certainly not desirable. Again, the blanket mandate that one *should* tell lies (and not that one *may* tell lies) in matters of marriage, and also in dealings with women seems to be downright obnoxious. In the first of these cases, one becomes morally justified in foisting an unworthy spouse on another person; and in the second case, women are denied the very right to truthful speech from others; which is, after all, quite consistent with the extremely misogynous attitude expressed in some ancedotes related by Bhīṣma in the *Śāntiparvan*. One of them is the story about the sage Aṣṭāvakra and 'Northern Direction' (Uttarā Dik) in the form of an old woman, while the other is the story about the sage Nārada and the celestial nymph Pañcacūḍā, where we have a most unflattering account of women as a class. In both these stories, women are depicted as untruthful, fickle and unreliable creatures, who remain faithful to their husbands only so long they are kept under strict control, and who are also insatiable nymphomaniacs always craving for sexual intercourse with any available man, so much so that on seeing a handsome man, their vaginas turn moist due to secretion caused by carnal desire. Women are also supposed to combine in themselves the dangers posed by a sword, a razor, a viper and poison. No wonder, such despicable creatures do not deserve the right to truthful speech from others! What is most reprehensible here is that in both these stories, this obscene harangue against women has been put in the mouths of two female characters (viz., Uttarā Dik and Pañcacūḍā), so that such canards can have the stamp of authenticity.

It is stated and often reiterated in the *Mahābhārata* that non-violence (*ahiṃsā*) is the highest form of virtue (*paramo dharmaḥ*); and yet, it also admits that in some cases, violence is consistent with principles of *dharma*. It is stated in clear terms that the best form of death that a *Kṣatriya* can desire is death in a battlefield — for a *Kṣatriya*, nothing could be more detestable than dying in a sick-bed, being covered with excreta (*Śāntiparvan* 98.23–31). It is also often stated that *Kṣatriya*s who die in war go to the heaven because the wounds that they suffer in a war absolve them of all sins (e.g., *Śāntiparvan* 98.9–14). This means, however, that war is considered to be almost an act of *dharma*. In the *Śāntiparvan*, Bhīṣma tells Yudhiṣṭhira that a warrior who creates a river of blood in the battlefield is indeed a *dhārmika* (121* in the *Śāntiparvan* 55.16). In the *Udyogaparvan* (139.29–51), while speaking to Śrīkṛṣṇa, Karṇa compared in detail the impending and inevitable war with a vedic sacrifice. Earlier, Duryodhana also had compared war with a sacrifice (*Udyogaparvan* 57.12–13). In the *Śāntiparvan* (25.26–27, 26.28), Vyāsa also compared war with a sacrifice.

In the *Śāntiparvan* (29.10–11, 33.2–3, 55.14–16), while trying to cheer up Yudhiṣṭhira, who was repentant for causing the death of so many people, Vyāsa, Śrīkṛṣṇa and Bhīṣma told him by way of consolation that all the warriors who had died in the Kurukṣetra war had gone to heaven; and hence, there was no point in grieving over their death. Vyāsa told Yudhiṣṭhira that in the war between the *deva*s and the *asura*s, which went on far a long time, the *deva*s took possession of heaven after turning the earth into an ocean of blood. This war was, like the war in Kurukṣetra, a battle between cousins; and Yudhiṣṭhira, who had won the battle, should now rule the kingdom instead of being dejected (*Śāntiparvan* 28.58, 34.13–21). Thus, violence in a battlefield is, according to the *Mahābhārata*, inevitable as well as desirable. Though it has been stated in the *Mahābhārata* that a victory that is achieved without war is superior to a victory that comes through war (*Udyogaparvan* 26.1, 69.22; *Śāntiparvan* 95.1), we do not see how war could be avoided if every *Kṣatriya* wanted to die in a battlefield.

Another form of violence that is permitted in the *Mahābhārata* is the killing of animals as an inseparable part of many Vedic sacrifices and the annual offerings (*śrāddha*) to the manes. Though Vedic sacrifices like *Agnihotra*, *Darśapūrṇamāsa*, etc., did not involve any killing of animals, such killing was an integral part of sacrifices like *Nirūḍhapaśubandha*, *Jyotiṣṭoma*, *Vājapeya*, *Aśvamedha*, etc. In the annual ritual known as *Māṃsāṣṭakā*, eight types of meat were offered to the manes (*pitṛvarga*), and no meat could be obtained without killing animals. Animals were killed by kings during hunting (*mṛgayā*) as well. The Pāṇḍavas themselves survived on hunting during the 12 years they had to spend in forests. Since a lot of people were accompanying them, hunting turned out to be so extensive that the Pāṇḍavas had to move from one forest to another, so that the wild animals did not become totally extinct. Here, we find an activity that is not a religious ritual, and yet results in violence to often innocent creatures. At that time, there was perhaps always a conflict in the society between those who supported the killing of animals in rituals and those who opposed it. The *Mahābhārata* itself relates a story where the king Vasu was requested to mediate in a quarrel between the sages and the *deva*s regarding the desirability of killing animals in a sacrifice. While the sages opposed this practice, the *deva*s favoured it. Vasu supported the *deva*s, whereupon he was cursed by the sages; the *deva*s, on the other hand, tried to make amends to Vasu by arranging for an offering known as *Vasudhārā* that was to be offered to Vasu on all auspicious occasions (*Anuśāsanaparvan* 116.54–56). The practice of killing animals in rituals came in handy for those who wanted to support the eating of meat (*Āraṇyakaparvan* 198.18). In the *Dvijavyādhasaṃvāda* section of the *Āraṇyakaparvan*, Kauśika expressed surprise at the fact that Dharmavyādha, who was so knowledgeable about *dharma*, was involved in a cruel profession like selling meat. In answer, Dharmavyādha said that this profession ran in his family and he could not abandon *kuladharma* and take up some other profession (*Āraṇyakaparvan* 198.14–15, 20). He also pointed out that he did not kill the animals — he only traded in the meat of animals killed by others (*Āraṇyakaparvan* 198.31). He said further that he himself did not eat any meat, while the meat supplied by him could be offered to the deities, forefathers and other people who wanted to eat meat (*Āraṇyakaparvan* 199.3–5). It is here that Dharmavyādha pointed out the intimate connection between Vedic sacrifices and killing of animals. He stated that had the sacrificial fire not been desirous of meat, there would have been no killing of animals. Likewise, had there been so scriptural sanction of *aṣṭakāśrāddha*, then animals would not be killed for offering their meat to the manes. Dharmavyādha also told Kauśika that according to the scriptures, plants, creepers, birds and beasts are consumed as food by others; thus, eating meat is in accordance with *dharma*. Besides, the animals killed in sacrifices after being consecrated by *mantras* also go to heaven. Thus, there is nothing wrong in the consumption of meat (*Āraṇyakaparvan* 199.8–10). Dharmavyādha then pointed out that no person or creature can survive without doing some harm to other creatures. Even mendicants, who profess non-violence, are compelled to commit violence, though they try to keep it to a *minimum* (*yatnādalpatarā bhavet*), and once we realize this, we would also realize that no one can be totally non-violent in the true sense of the term (*Āraṇyakaparvan* 199.13, 19–28).

Bhīṣma, who has emphasized on many occasions the fact that it is better to perform sacrifices with corn, milk, etc., so that no creatures are killed (*Śāntiparvan* 255.30–34, 37–38; 264.3–5, 19; *Anuśāsanaparvan* 116.53), nevertheless said elsewhere that the animals that are consecrated by sprinkling water on them after uttering appropriate *mantras* and are then killed go to heaven; thus, by killing animals in a ritual, one actually does favour to these victims (*Śāntiparvan* 264.9,13–15). Vyāsa has also expressed a similar opinion (*Śāntiparvan* 35.28). It has also been stated that animals were created as objects of offering in the sacrifices (*Śāntiparvan* 260.29). Accordingly, one does not incur any sin by causing the death of these consecrated animals or by eating their meat (*Anuśāsanaparvan* 116.38, 56). He thus virtually conceded the point that ritual killing of animals does not amount to violence. Bhīṣma also supported the practice of hunting, though his arguments in defence of this practice were a bit different. He started by almost equating hunting with the practice of killing animals in a ritual. He claimed that the great sage Agastya had consecrated the wild animals; thus, eating the meat of hunted animals is comparable to eating meat offered in a ritual and thus fit for consumption. His second argument was that hunting is a risky affair because in many cases, the hunters get killed by wild animals. Thus, the meat obtained in hunting, which has been obtained by the hunter by putting his own life at stake, can be eaten by him since like war booty, it rightfully belongs to him (*Anuśāsanaparvan* 117.16-19). Just as Dharmavyādha pointed out that no one, including even the mendicants (*yatayaḥ*), can be completely non-violent; Bhīṣma also pointed out that even for the lonely sage who lives in a forest, it is impossible to abandon violence completely (*Śāntiparvan* 128.28). Thus, violence that deserves to be condemned or avoided becomes identical with *vṛthāhiṃsā*, i.e., killing animals outside a ritual, or causing unnecessary suffering to other creatures (*Anuśāsanaparvan* 116.42–45, 50).

The last instance of unavoidable violence discussed in the *Mahābhārata* pertains to punishment that had to be meted out to criminals and other offenders. In the *Śāntiparvan*, there is a dialogue between Satyavat and Dyumatsena reported by Bhīṣma to Yudhiṣṭhira, who had asked Bhīṣma as to how a king can protect his subjects and be at the same time non-violent. If violence is *adharma* and non-violence is *dharma*, then how can a king, who punishes those who deserve to be punished, be non-violent? If, on the other hand, in order to be non-violent, he refrains from punishing wayward elements, then how can he maintain law and order? Satyavat had argued that capital punishment should not be imposed on anyone because killing a person would certainly be a case of *adharma*. To treat such punishment as *dharma* would result in a blatant contradiction. Dyumatsena, however, replied that if capital punishment were not imposed on hardened criminals like robbers and murderers, then the incidence of crime would increase and normal life in society would be totally disrupted. In the *Kali* age, when *adharma* is on the rise, what other means can be employed for restraining the criminals? In response, Satyavat said that when capital punishment is imposed on a criminal, the other members of his family are adversely affected, even though they may be innocent. Making innocent persons suffer is not justifiable under any circumstances. Hence, attempts should be made at reforming the criminals instead of putting them to death. It is not impossible for an offender to become a better person. If the offender is killed, then this possibility of self-improvement will be denied to him, which is certainly unjust. Instead of killing people, punishment may also be imposed by threatening, imprisonment, branding or disfigurement through mutilation of some limb. If, after committing the first offence, the offender feels remorse and promises before an assembly of priests that he would never commit such a crime in future, then he should be released after a stern warning. If, however, the person persists in committing major offences, then some severe punishment must be given to him. Dyumatsena was not, however, in favour of such leniency. He pointed out that the king should ensure that laws laid down by him are not flouted. If capital punishment is abolished, then there will be total chaos in the society. In the earlier ages like *satya*, *tretā*, etc., people were law-abiding by nature, and even verbal censure (*dhigdaṇḍa*) by people or reprimand (*vāgdaṇḍa*) by authorities would be enough to keep them in check. Thereafter, imposition of fine or confiscation of property (*ādānadaṇḍa*) was enough as penal measure. But in the *kali* age, some incorrigible criminal elements cannot be dissuaded from committing serious crimes even though capital punishment (*prāṇadaṇḍa*) is in vogue. Hence, the system of punishment proposed by Satyavat is utopian and unpractical (*Śāntiparvan* 259.2–22).

VIII

When moral rules are admitted to vary in different circumstances, there is always the possibility that one might thereby end up with sheer opportunism. It is not difficult for a clever but unscrupulous person to find some convenient excuse or other for justifying actions that are palpably immoral under the pretext that such actions *were not* performed under normal conditions, or were performed with some noble intention (like saving the life or property of someone), or were performed so that one's promises are kept. Whether the moral doctrines preached in the *Mahābhārata* open up the path to such cynicism and opportunism is a moot question, and many eminent scholars have tried to show that this is not the case. Thus, S. K. Belvalkar states in his introduction to the *Śāntiparvan*:

> In the *Āpaddharma*, the topic is discussed with apt illustrations, as to the circumstances under which a king would be justified in transcending the commonly accepted ethical maxims in the interest of the still higher demands of the welfare of the state and of the whole humanity. Illustrations of such exceptional departures are supplied not only by the *Āpaddharma* text in appropriate places, but also by the actions and advice of Śrīkṛṣṇa at crucial moments in the Kaurava-Pāṇḍava fight, which forms the central theme of the Great Epic.
>
> And yet it is worth noting that the author of the Epic is particular in pointing out that such exceptional lapses from the strictest code of morality *pro bono publico* always make their authors — not excluding even Śrīkṛṣṇa himself . . . suffer their inevitable consequences (1966: 202–3).
>
> From the abstract discussion and interesting concrete illustrations of the "Āpaddharma" policy . . . the impression is likely to be that the epic is advocating an all-round policy of "End justifying the Means". In order to prevent such a misunderstanding, the author of the Epic emphasizes the importance of virtues like self-control (Ch. 154) . . . Austerity (Ch. 155) . . . and Truth (Ch. 156); also the great danger from vices like Avidity (Ch. 152, 157) . . . Passion (Ch. 152), Wickedness (Ch. 158); and in the case of any lapses, the need for atonement (Ch. 159). This naturally saves the author of the Epic from willful advocacy of any crooked and immoral policy (ibid.: 199).

Caturvedi Badrinath also makes two similar comments:

> The prudence literature in the *Mahābhārata* displays at the same time the awareness that, understanding neither self-interest nor the importance of time and place with which it is connected, most people might as easily misinterpret the maxims of prudence. In order to prevent prudence from turning into a lack of principles, the talk of 'time' and 'place' into a lack of scruple, every prudence maxim is balanced by its opposite. But self-interest is still kept as the basis of that balance. For example, the advice against speaking unpleasant truth, if taken too literally, or taken too far, may turn against one's best interest, for there *are* occasions when the unpleasant truth must be spoken (2007: 159).
>
> [T]he *truth is relative* argument may easily degenerate into opportunism, and what is palpably wrong and untruthful sought to be justified on one ground or another, in bad faith. It is for this reason that the *Mahābhārata* places the conditionality of ethical norms and social *dharma* is defined as the force which sustains people and secures the good of all living beings" (ibid.: 190).

The opinions expressed here are, to a large extent, unexceptionable. But one can certainly question as to whether such departures from 'normal' moral laws that we encounter in the *Mahābhārata* were really *pro bono publico*, or merely for the sake of obtaining some selfish end like victory in a bloody war. Both the Kauravas and Pāṇḍavas were guilty of such transgressions, and they did not really cross out each other. It is a fact that the Kauravas, led by Duryodhana, adopted blatantly unfair means for harming the Pāṇḍavas. Their machinations started with giving poisonous food to Bhīma and then throwing the unconscious Bhīma in a river after tying him up with ropes. The attempt to kill the Pāṇḍavas along with their mother by setting fire to the 'house of lac' at Vāraṇāvata was another such heinous act. Depriving the Pāṇḍavas of their kingdom and possessions by a devious game of dice was another such act. But the worst part was perhaps the manner in which Draupadī was sought to be humiliated in an attempt to disrobe her in the Kuru court. Even after such bitter episodes, the Pāṇḍavas were willing for a peaceful settlement because as per the agreement reached after a second game of dice which was also lost by Yudhiṣṭhira, the Kauravas had to return to the Pāṇḍavas their share of the kingdom, after the latter had undergone exile in forest for 12 years and incognito life in some secret hiding without being discovered (*ajñātavāsa*) for one more year. However, even after the stipulated period of exile, Duryodhana refused to return to the Pāṇḍavas their share of kingdom on the pretext that they had been discovered before the stipulated time of one year of incognito residence in a secret hiding; he also declared that he would not yield even that much of the kingdom that could be pierced by the tip of a needle. Duryodhana went even to the extent of conspiring to capture Śrīkṛṣṇa who had gone to the Kuru court as an emissary of the Pāṇḍavas. Thereafter, war between the two parties became inevitable. Before the beginning of the war, both parties agreed that the rules that one should observe during a war would be scrupulously observed, and that no underhand means would be adopted. Such an undertaking was specifically given on both the sides by Bhīṣma and Arjuna respectively (*Udyogaparvan* 194.10, 195.15; *Bhīṣmaparvan* 46.19). But such rules were frequently violated by both the parties. For example, even though the consensus was that no weapon of divine origin (*divyāstra*) should be employed against an ordinary warrior who lacked such weapons (*Udyogaparvan* 195.15), Bhīṣma nevertheless used *brahmāstra* for killing Uttara, the young son of king Virāṭa, who could not be defeated by using conventional weapons. Again, when Abhimanyu, the young son of Arjuna, entered the *cakravyūha* (an array of soldiers in the form of a wheel which is very difficult to penetrate), seven veteran warriors, viz., Droṇa, Aśvatthāman, Kṛpa, Karṇa, Bṛhadbala (or Duḥśāsana, according to some editions), Kṛtavarman and Jayadratha, attacked him *simultaneously*, and went on injuring him with weapons, even though he had lost all his weapons. Defenceless Abhimanyu was thus killed in an 'unequal war' (*asamayuddha*) which was supposed to be against all civilized norms of warfare. The worst of such horrible incidents is found in the *Sauptikaparvan*, wherein Aśvatthāman, who wanted to take revenge for the unethical manner in which his father was killed, watched an owl attacking some sleeping crows at night and killing them all; and decided to act in a similar manner by attacking the Pāṇḍava camp at night, killing the inmates while they were asleep. Kṛpa and Kṛtavarman tried at first to dissuade him, but ultimately accompanied Aśvatthāman to the Pāṇḍava camp where he massacred the unsuspecting Pāṇḍava army.

But such contraventions of the war ethics were committed by the Pāṇḍavas as well. For example, while fighting with Bhīṣma, who could not be killed by anyone on earth, Arjuna placed Śikhaṇḍin, the hermaphrodite (*napuṃsaka*) offspring of Drupada, between himself and Bhīṣma because Bhīṣma had taken the vow that he would never use weapons against a hermaphrodite. Thus, while Arjuna shielded by Śikhaṇḍin went on piercing the body of Bhīṣma with his arrows, the latter could not hurt Arjuna with his weapons, since those weapons might have injured Śikhaṇḍin. Consequently, the battle between Arjuna and Bhīṣma became simply one-sided; and after some time, Bhīṣma fell down on the ground, lying on 'a bed of arrows' (*śaraśayyā*). In this devious manner, Bhīṣma, the first general (*senāpati*) of the Kauarava army was prevented from taking any further part in this war. Again, as has been stated before, the Pāṇḍavas took the help of a despicable lie for preventing Droṇa, the second general of the Kauravas, from participating in the battle; and when Droṇa had given up his arms, he was killed by Dhṛṣṭadyumna, the general of the Pāṇḍava army, and this heinous action was condemned even by Arjuna. It seems to us that Yudhiṣṭhira subsequently felt remorse for having lied to Droṇa precisely because Droṇa had specifically asked Yudhiṣṭhira to speak the truth, and in answer, Yudhiṣthira had uttered a falsehood dressed up in a 'cloak of truth' (*satyakañcuka*). According to a recent work, this is why Aśvatthāman holds Yudhiṣṭhira morally responsible for the murder of Droṇa: 'Yudhiṣṭhira is responsible, because Droṇa trusted him; and by trusting him, as it were, put himself in Yudhiṣṭhira's care. Yudhiṣṭhira did not protect Droṇa, a person he had made dependent on him for his protection' (Ganeri 2007: 71).

Karṇa, the third general of the Kauravas, was killed by Arjuna when he was trying to move his chariot, the wheel of which had sunk into the earth. Before that, the armour and earrings with which Karṇa were born and the presence of which prevented him from being killed by anyone were taken from him by Indra who had gone to Karṇa in the guise of a Brahmin asking for those two items as gifts, since it was well known that Karṇa never refused the prayer of any person who asked him for something. Again, while Bhūriśravas (who was in the Kaurava camp) was on the verge of killing Sātyaki (who was on the side of Pāṇḍavas) in a one-to-one fight, Arjuna cut off the arms of Bhūriśravas from behind, whereupon the defenceless Bhūriśravas was killed by Sātyaki. Such a cowardly act was not expected of Arjuna, who was supposed to be the best warrior on earth. Finally, in the mace-fight (*gadāyuddha*) between Duryodhana and Bhīma, which took place after almost all the major figures in the Kaurava camp had been killed in the Kurukṣetra war, Bhīma broke the thighs of Duryodhana with his mace, even though hitting the adversary below the belt was strictly forbidden in a mace-fight.

What is worth noting in such cases is that almost all the improper acts done by the Pāṇḍavas were performed at the behest of Śrīkṛṣṇa who was supposed to be *Parabrahman* ('The Supreme Reality') that had assumed an incarnation for the establishment of *dharma*. After being defeated in the mace-fight through a deceitful trick, Duryodhana accused Śrīkṛṣṇa of planning and instigating all the misdeeds committed by the Pāṇḍavas (*Śalyaparvan* 60.23–38). As one would expect, Śrīkṛṣṇa denied all such allegations and told Duryodhana that the latter was in no position to lecture others on morality, and that there was nothing unfair in adopting tricks for defeating an enemy who was superior in strength. He told Duryodhana that the latter was simply enjoying the just deserts of his evil deeds, and that no one else was responsible for the sad plight in which he now found himself (*Śalyaparvan* 60.39–46). He also told the Pāṇḍavas, who felt ashamed by the accusations of Duryodhana, that such tricks in warfare were employed also by the *devas* against the *asuras*, and that the employment of such tricks and stratagems was approved even by respectable and honest people (*Śalyaparvan* 60.62). (It may be mentioned here that even in the *Udyogaparvan*, when Duryodhana claimed that he was not guilty of any misdeed [*Udyogaparvan* 125.1–9], Śrīkṛṣṇa had enumerated all the heinous acts committed by Duryodhana and his associates [*Udyogaparvan* 126.6–18].) If one were to believe Śrīkṛṣṇa, then one would have to admit that there was no moral lapse on the part of the Pāṇḍavas when they deviated from the norms of warfare in accordance with *dharma* (*dharmayuddha*). In the next section, we will try to decide how far such a claim can be sustained.

IX

The behaviour of Yudhiṣṭhira after the Kurukṣetra war makes one thing amply clear — he was appalled at the extensive destruction and loss of life caused by the Kurukṣetra war and sincerely repentant for the moral lapses of the Pāṇḍavas during the war. His feeling of guilt was so overwhelming that he was ashamed to meet Gāndhārī and Dhṛtarāṣṭra after his victory in the war. Due to the personal losses that he had to suffer (like the death of Bhīṣma, Droṇa, Drupada, Virāṭa, Dhṛṣṭadyumna, Śikhaṇḍin, Abhimanyu, and the five sons of Draupadī), the victory achieved by him also seemed to him an empty one and devoid of all charm. The extent of his remorse for being somehow responsible for such loss of life can be guessed from the fact that he declined to ascend the throne and expressed the desire for retiring to the forest where he could lead the life of a mendicant and strive for achieving emancipation from the cycle of rebirth (*Śāntiparvan* 1.13–28, 7.31–35, 32.10-11, 76.15–17, 77.1–25). His brothers, as also Draupadī, took him to task for such an attitude. His brothers went to the extent of saying that had Yudhiṣṭhira earlier expressed his lack of interest in the kingdom, they would not have fought this war, which had resulted in such a huge loss of life on both sides. Bhīma, out of frustration, compared Yudhiṣṭhira with a stupid person who toils hard for digging a well and then leaves the place, after being covered with dirt and sweat, without even washing himself in the water of that well (*Śāntiparvan* 10.7–9). After much persuasion from his near and dear ones, Yudhiṣṭhira could somehow control his grief. But he continued to be in a state of depression, even though people like Śrīkṛṣṇa, Vyāsa and Bhīṣma (who was still lying on the 'bed of arrows', and waiting for a more propitious time for leaving his mortal body) tried to console him by saying that he should not be ashamed of his deeds, or feel responsible for the terrible destruction caused by the Kurukṣetra war because Duryodhana, guided by his greed, envy and pride, had created a situation in which the war had become inevitable. If the misdeeds of Duryodhana were allowed to go on unchallenged, then there would have been a miscarriage of *dharma*, and the Pāṇḍavas would have been accused of cowardice. Bhīma, Vyāsa and Bhīṣma also told Yudhiṣṭhira that if he nevertheless felt any pangs of conscience for the violations of war ethics, then he could perform *Aśvamedha* (horse sacrifice) which would absolve him of all sins that he might have accrued through his unethical acts during the war (*Śāntiparvan* 16.26, 34.26, 35.6). Thereafter, Yudhiṣṭhira did perform the *Aśvamedha* sacrifice and ascended the throne. After the completion of the sacrifice, however, something very strange happened. A mongoose, whose eyes were blue and half of whose body was golden, came to the place where the sacrifice was being held. Thereafter, it rolled on the ground in the arena of the sacrifice and then declared that the merit (*puṇya*) earned by Yudhiṣṭhira through this sacrifice was not equal even to the merit earned by a Brahmin who had given, during a terrible famine, some barley meal (*yavasaktu*), the only food at the disposal of his entire family, to a guest who had asked for food. On being questioned about the basis on which he made such an audacious pronouncement, the mongoose replied that the guest was none other than Dharma himself in disguise, who had come to test the piousness of the Brahmin and who took the Brahmin along with his family to heaven as a reward for this remarkable act of charity and selflessness. The mongoose, who lived in the house of this Brahmin, was attracted by the smell emitted by the few grains of barley power that had fallen to the ground, and as soon as his body touched those particles, half of his body became golden. This was due to the virtue or merit earned by the Brahmin. The mongoose then stated that since then, he had been visiting places of great sacrifices with the hope that due to the merit earned by those rituals, the other half of his body could also become golden; but even after the visit to the site where Yudhiṣṭhira was performing the *Aśvamedha*, his desire has not been fulfilled. Thereafter, the mongoose disappeared.

Two pertinent questions may be raised here. Yudhiṣṭhira's performance of the *Aśvamedha* sacrifice assumed the role of an expiatory or penitential act (*prāyaścitta*), which was supported to purify a sinner. While advising Yudhiṣṭhira to perform *Aśvamedha*, Vyāsa stated that Paraśurāma, who had massacred the *Kṣatriya*s mercilessly 21 times, had also performed the *Aśvamedha* so that he could atone for his cruel deeds, and as a result, he was absolved of his sins (*Śāntiparvan* 36.6). This clearly shows that such sacrifices primarily served the purpose of expiation. Now, why should a person, who has not done anything sinful, and who is confident of innocence, decide to perform a ritual which is penitentiary in nature? Second, even though the *Aśvamedha* sacrifice was performed, why did the mongoose declare that the merit earned by Yudhiṣṭhira could not match even the merit earned by the poor Brahmin who had given, during a famine, the last morsel of food at his disposal to a hungry guest? Does this not suggest, at least indirectly, that the *Aśvamedha* performed by Yudhiṣṭhira had not yielded the desired result? If that be so, then what could plausibly explain this fact?

The fact that Yudhiṣṭhira, who claimed on several occasions that he never consciously deviated from the path of *dharma*, nevertheless agreed to perform *Aśvamedha*, shows clearly that inspite of all the consolations provided by Śrīkṛṣṇa, Vyāsa and Bhīṣma, he was painfully aware of the fact that many of the acts of the Pāṇḍavas during the Kurukṣetra war were blatant transgressions of war ethics, even though they were *compelled* by the circumstances to act in such a manner for ensuring their victory against a numerically superior army at the disposal of a ruthless and crooked enemy like Duryodhana. The answer to the second question is more difficult to find — we are trying to give here only a tentative answer.

In the *Prāyascittīya* section of the *Śāntiparvan* (36.37–46; see also 148.22–33), Vyāsa has opined that one can remove one's sins through sincere repentance, through the resolve of not committing such misdeeds and by performing instead morally good deeds in future, visiting places of pilgrimage, giving gifts to Brahmins and performing expiations or penitentiary acts . But expiations are effective only when the sinful act is committed unknowingly, and the sinner, besides being sincerely ashamed and repentant for his lapses, also believes in the efficacy of the expiatory ritual. Expiations cannot purify sinful persons who are wicked by nature, who doubt the efficacy of rituals and who habitually commit misdeeds without subsequently feeling any shame or remorse (*Śāntiparvan* 36.41–43). That the *Aśvamedha* sacrifice recommended to Yudhiṣṭhira by Vyāsa, Bhīṣma and others was looked upon as an act of expiation is clear enough because the suggestion for performing it was given while stating that Yudhiṣṭhira *could* get rid of the sins that he *might* have incurred during the Kurukṣetra war, by undertaking expiations or penitentiary acts (*Śāntiparvan* 16.26, 34.26, 35.5). But even the performance of the *Aśvamedha* sacrifice did not totally purify him, as can be seen from the pronouncement of the strange blue-eyed mongoose. Unlike the Brahmin who had given during a prolonged famine his last morsel of food to a hungry guest, Yudhiṣṭhira was not immediately transported, along with other members of his family, by Dharma to heaven — he could reach it after a long interval, during which he had to rule cheerlessly over his kingdom, suffer in silence the tragic death of his elders (like Dhṛtarāṣṭra, Gāndhārī, Kuntī, and Vidura) in a forest fire as also the demise of Balarāma and Śrīkṛṣṇa, and finally undertake a long and arduous journey during which he had to endure the loss of Draupadī and all his brothers. Besides, he had the mortification of seeing Duryodhana in heaven and also experiencing the hell, before he could cast aside his mortal body and become a resident of heaven. Had he been totally purified of his sins by the performance of the *Aśvamedha*, he would not have to pay a visit to hell, even through it was of a very short duration.

In a recent work, Yudhiṣṭhira has been held to be guilty of not only deceiving Droṇa, but also himself, since he thought that by adding the rider 'the elephant', he could avoid the sin of uttering a falsehood; and it was this self-deception that was even more damaging:

> Yudhiṣṭhira might have preserved his moral integrity and saved himself from shame, had he followed the counsel either of Kṛṣṇa or Arjuna, but in opting instead for Bhīma's slippery double deceit (hiding both the truth and the fact of deception), he displays the moral weakness with which he is often associated . . . . In lying to himself about his lie, Yudhiṣṭhira reveals himself as having neither the clear moral pragmatism of Kṛṣṇa, nor yet Arjuna's unwavering moral integrity. We will learn from the *Mahābhārata* itself that if deception *per se* is in certain cases morally permissible, deceiving oneself is always destructive of the soul (Ganeri 2007: 62, 64).

The question that may now be raised is: why was not Yudhiṣṭhira totally absolved of his sins by his acts of piety and righteousness? He was, after all, by nature a follower of *dharma*, he was overwhelmed by remorse and regret for the misdeeds committed during the war, and he also had full faith in the efficacy of the rituals recommended in the scriptures. To us, the answer seems to be that the misdeeds of the Pāṇḍavas were *not* committed unknowingly. They knew very well that such acts were morally wrong, though, perhaps, unavoidable during a war wherein victory was of paramount importance, and might have to be obtained at any cost.

It is also worth noting that most of such unethical acts were performed as per the advice of Śrīkṛṣṇa who did not seem to have any moral qualms at all, and who could invariably come up with some excuse or other for justifying such deviations from the codes of war ethics. For him, the end always justified the means, however ignoble that might be. Of late, B. K. Matilal (2002: 91–108) has discussed in detail to what extent his activities can be justified; and while I agree with my respected teacher on some issues, I also feel compelled to differ from him on a number of them. Many of the strategies and tricks suggested by Śrīkṛṣṇa were pre-meditated, as is evident from his own pronouncements on many occasions (*Droṇaparvan* 155.27–29, 156.5–30; *Śalyaparvan* 60.56–62, 372*). The tricks that he had used for causing the death of Droṇa, Karṇa, Jayadratha, and Duryodhana may be sought to be justified on the ground that these warriors had also violated the war ethics on numerous occasions; and some of them (e.g., Karṇa, Jayadratha and Duryodhana) had behaved with the Pāṇḍavas and Draupadī in a despicable manner even before the war. Thus, Śrīkṛṣṇa was simply ensuring that such persons were, so to say, paid back in their own coins. But there are some definite instances wherein such a pretext or justification is inadmissible, and the ruthless manipulator in him is fully exposed. One such instance is found in the *Droṇaparvan* wherein we find Śrīkṛṣṇa dancing with joy after Ghaṭotkaca, the son of Bhīma and the demoness Hiḍimbā, was killed by Karṇa with the unfailing weapon known as *ekāghnī śakti* that had been given to him by Indra in lieu of his armour and earrings with which he was born and which protected him from being killed by anyone (*Droṇaparvan* 155.2–3). Karṇa had planned to use this *ekāghnī śakti* (which could be employed for killing only one person) against Arjuna who was his foremost rival in archery. Ghaṭotkaca had come to assist the Pāṇḍavas in the battle which continued on that occasion even at night when Alāyudha, a demon who had joined the Kaurava army, caused extensive damage to the Pāṇḍavas through various tricks that are known to the demons. Ghaṭotkaca succeeded in killing Alāyudha and also struck such terror in the Kaurava army that Duryodhana was afraid of an imminent defeat, whereupon he prevailed upon Karṇa to kill Ghaṭotkaca by using the *ekāghnī śakti*. When asked about the causes of such joy at a time when others were grieving for Ghaṭotkaca, Śrīkṛṣṇa told unabashedly that he was happy for two reasons. First, Karṇa had lost his inborn armour, earrings as well as the *ekāghnī śakti* and thus become doubly vulnerable to Arjuna. Second, Śrīkṛṣṇa had himself planned to kill Ghaṭotkaca, since due to his demonic nature, Ghaṭotkaca was opposed to the Brahmins and their rituals like Vedic sacrifices. Since he had been killed by Karṇa, what Śrīkṛṣṇa had intended to bring about had been achieved (*Droṇaparvan* 156.24–28, 157.40–43). Now, the first reason adduced here may be unexceptionable from a purely strategic point of view. But the second reason was so outlandish that even Yudhiṣṭhira, who usually agreed with Śrīkṛṣṇa on almost all issues, felt compelled to protest against this baseless accusation after recounting the various earlier occasions on which the Pāṇḍavas had been helped by Ghaṭotkaca (*Droṇaparvan* 158.26–32). Śrīkṛṣṇa did not have even a kind word for Ghaṭotkaca who had come to fulfill his filial duties towards Bhīma in a totally selfless manner because he did not have any claims to the throne in Hastināpura or Indraprastha, nor did he expect any share in the war-booty that might be available to the victors. Such was his allegiance and devotion to the Pāṇḍavas that even at the time of death, he adopted some magical means for expanding his body so that a large number of Kaurava soldiers were crushed under his carcass (*Droṇaparvan* 154.55–61). But none of these things were of any importance to Śrīkṛṣṇa who looked upon the brave and selfless Ghaṭotkaca as merely an expendable means which could be used to keep Arjuna safe from the deadly *ekāghnī śakti*. Elsewhere, too, he had boasted that it was he who, through the agency of Droṇa, had caused the great archer Ekalavya to lose the thumb of his right hand (*Droṇaparvan* 156.17–21). Apart from the fact that the relevant incident in the *Mahābhārata* does not record the involvement of Śrīkṛṣṇa in any way, the question that remains is: was the cruel and inhuman treatment meted out to the Niṣāda prince Ekalavya, who had done no harm to the Pāṇḍavas in any way, morally justified? If not, then what can we say of a person who boasts of having engineered such a heinous act? Ekalavya had come to Droṇa for lessons in archery, but the latter declined to accept him as a student. Even after this refusal, Ekalavya considered Droṇa as his teacher, and after installing an earthen statue of Droṇa for worship in his household, he went on practising archery; and through sheer talent and incessant practice, he achieved such skill in archery that the disciples of Droṇa became both surprised and envious. On enquiry, Droṇa came to know that even though he had not accepted Ekalavya as a disciple, the latter, nevertheless, had considered Droṇa as his preceptor and had immense reverence for Droṇa; whereupon Droṇa told Ekalavya that if the latter considered himself to be the disciple of Droṇa, then he should pay to Droṇa the fee payable to a teacher (*gurudakṣiṇā*) at the completion of training. When Ekalavya asked about the fee payable to Droṇa, the latter asked for the right thumb of Ekalavya as *gurudakṣiṇā*; Ekalavya complied with this order without even a murmur. This vile act of Droṇa is nothing short of utter deception and treachery, since he had taken advantage of the unconditional feeling of allegiance, respect and trust that Ekalavya had towards him. Droṇa had promised that he would make Arjuna the best archer in the world. When Ekalavya turned out to be an even better archer than Arjuna, Droṇa employed this mean trick, whereby the supremacy of Arjuna could be ensured, even though it resulted in depriving the innocent Ekalavya of his remarkable achievement as an archer — an achievement for which Droṇa could not claim any credit because he had *never* given any lessons to Ekalavya. Only a completely callous and amoral person could boast for planning such a mean act of blatant treachery, whereby an innocent person was shamelessly victimized, simply for protecting the self-esteem of a favourite student.

In this context, it may be recalled that the killing of Droṇa made Aśvatthāman extremely angry and determined to avenge this heinous act. He was not angry because his father was killed because in war, a person may get killed by his adversaries. What caused his anger were: (*a*) the dirty trick employed by Yudhiṣṭhira for making Droṇa give up his arms, and (*b*) the manner in which he was killed by Dhṛṣṭadyumna, viz., by beheading Droṇa after holding his lock of hair, and then displaying the severed head. After the failure to avenge this death by using the *nārāyaṇīya* weapon, which was made ineffective by Śrīkṛṣṇa, Aśvatthāman, along with Kṛpācārya and Kṛtavarman as his associates, attacked the Pāṇḍava camp at night after the end of the Kurukṣetra war and killed all the inmates of this camp, including Dhṛṣṭadyumna and the five sons of Draupadī. This entire chain of gory events started with the utterance of a lie by Yudhiṣṭhira who had been instigated by Śrīkṛṣṇa. In a recent work, the question has been raised as to whether the ultimate responsibility for all these tragic events should be ascribed to Śrīkṛṣṇa:

> [I]t will turn out that the vengeance of the real Aśvatthāman is mightier than anything that the Pāṇḍava conspirators had foreseen. Only Arjuna's last-minute intervention will save them from complete annihilation. And we shall have cause to wonder whether or not it was Kṛṣṇa who created this mess, provoking Aśvatthāman into avenging his father, discrediting Yudhiṣṭhira, and putting Arjuna into an impossible moral position from which he would emerge wishing only for death. In the final analysis, is it not Kṛṣṇa upon whose head falls the moral responsibility for this result?

> How, indeed, is Kṛṣṇa's advice here consistent with his own counsel on the eve of the mighty battle, when Arjuna was wracked with doubt about the morality of the war and his own part in it? It is hard to recognize here the 'deontological' Kṛṣṇa, who lectured on the detached action in the *Bhagavadgītā* (Ganeri 2007: 67–68).

Śrīkṛṣṇa was not even consistent in applying the moral doctrines that he preached from time to time. For example, in the *Karṇaparvan* (48.14–15), when Arjuna was about to kill Yudhiṣṭhira for keeping a promise that he had made earlier, Śrīkṛṣṇa dissuaded him from committing fratricide on the ground that protecting a human life was more important than keeping a promise. But in the *Śalyaparvan* (59.4–7), he ensured that Bhīma broke Duryodhana's thighs during the mace-fight between them. Hitting the opponent below the waist was against the rules of mace-fight. When Bhīma actually hit Duryodhana on his thighs with his mace, Balarāma, the elder brother of Śrīkṛṣṇa, and who had taught both Bhīma and Duryodhana the art of mace-fight, was furious with Bhīma and was on the verge of killing him. Śrīkṛṣṇa, however, tried to pacify Balarāma by arguing that unless Bhīma acted in this manner, he would be guilty of breaking the promise that he had made at the Kaurava court during the infamous game of dice, after Duryodhana had bared his thighs and asked Draupadī to sit there, which was an extremely obscene gesture (*Śalyaparvan* 59.11–16). Thus, on one occasion, promise-keeping became secondary when breaking that promise prevented someone from committing fratricide, while on another occasion, promise-keeping assumed supreme importance, even though it involved a blatant contravention of rule (which may be compared with a boxer kicking or stabbing his opponent during a bout of boxing). In short, for Śrīkṛṣṇa, the same sort of action was morally justified when it served one's purpose and unjust or improper when it went against one's interest. This is opportunism at its worst. No wonder, Balarāma was not convinced by the arguments or pretexts given by Śrīkṛṣṇa and left the place in a huff (*Śalyaparvan* 59.17–19, 22–26). In view of the expression *diṣṭyā vardhase* used by Śrīkṛṣṇa in a long speech to Yudhiṣṭhira after Duryodhana fell, Matilal (2002: 102) has opined: 'The Pāṇḍavas won against all odds because of luck, [and] not through the omnipotence of Kṛṣṇa'. However, statements highlighting the implacability of *destiny* and those highlighting *agency* cannot but be at cross-purposes — and, if nothing else, Śrīkṛṣṇa was definitely guilty of this inconsistency.

Sometimes, what Śrīkṛṣṇa said in defence of his acts cannot be supported by the facts as narrated in the *Mahābhārata*. For example, he proclaimed on several occasions that he had to deviate from the standard norms of war ethics in order to bring about the death of warriors like Bhīṣma, Droṇa, Jayadratha, Karṇa, and Duryodhana so that the Pāṇḍavas could be victorious in the war. He argued that such famous warriors could never be defeated or killed through honest means. In his own defence, he even said that such tricks were employed in the past by the *devas* against the *asuras* and that the deployment of such tricks in war was also approved by respectable people (*Śalyaparvan* 60.55–62). Let us, however, recall some incidents from the *Mahābhārata*. In the *Āraṇyakaparvan*, it has been stated that Jayadratha (i.e., the brother-in-law of Duryodhana), who was on his way to a *svayaṃvara*, happened to see Draupadī in the forest hermitage and became enamoured of her. Thereafter, he tried to seduce her and, on failing to do so, abducted her. When the Pāṇḍavas came to know about this incident from their priest, Bhīma chased Jayadratha who promptly dumped Draupadī and tried to escape. Bhīma, however, captured Jayadratha and gave the latter such a severe beating with his bare hands that Jayadratha became almost half-dead. Bhīma spared his life on the order given by Yudhiṣṭhira only on the consideration that his death would result in the widowhood of Duḥśalā, the only daughter of Gāndhārī. On another occasion, Duryodhana and his associates decided to set up a camp with pomp and splendour near the forest-dwelling of Pāṇḍavas who had become paupers after the infamous game of dice. They thought that the Pāṇḍavas, after watching the affluence of the Kauravas, would become jealous and then feel sorry for their own impoverishment. But when Duryodhana and his associates went to the part of the forest where they had planned to set up their camp, they found the spot to be occupied by the army of *Gandharvas* (semi-divine beings). A quarrel broke out between the two groups, which resulted in a battle that Duryodhana eventually lost, ending up as a prisoner of the *Gandharvas*. It was only due to the intervention of Yudhiṣṭhira that Duryodhana was released by the *Gandharvas*. Thus, neither Jayadratha nor Duryodhana can be said to be invincible.

Again, in the *Virāṭaparvan*, when the Kauravas went to the kingdom of Virāṭa for plundering his cattle, a battle ensued between Arjuna (in the form of Bṛhannalā, a hermaphrodite) and the Kaurava army which had almost all the great warriors mentioned earlier. In this battle, Arjuna employed a very powerful weapon, whereupon all these great warriors like Bhīṣma, Droṇa, etc., became unconscious. This enabled Arjuna to recapture the cattle of Virāṭa without killing any of the Kauravas. Thus, both Bhīma and Arjuna were capable of defeating single-handed, all (or at least some) of these warriors without adopting any unfair means. This clearly shows that even though Bhīṣma, Droṇa, Karṇa, etc., were formidable warriors, they were not invincible. Hence, the claim of Śrīkṛṣṇa that none of these warriors could be defeated or killed through honest means is not correct.

Again, in the *Strīparvan* (25.36–42), Gāndhārī accused Śrīkṛṣṇa of not making any sincere attempt to prevent the Kurukṣetra war and also cursed him by saying that in future, the Yādavas (i.e., the clan to which Śrīkṛṣṇa himself belonged) would be exterminated as had been the Kaurava clan . In response, Śrīkṛṣṇa told Gāndhārī that she *alone* was responsible for the destruction of the Kaurava clan (*tavaiva hyaparādhena kuravo nidhanaṃ gatāḥ*). He accused Gāndhārī of not controlling Duryodhana in a proper manner (*Strīparvan* 26.1–6) after remarking that Gāndhārī had unnecessarily cursed that the Yādavas, the clan to which Śrīkṛṣṇa belonged, would also be destroyed because apart from Śrīkṛṣṇa himself, nobody could destroy the Yādavas — be he a human being, a deity (*deva*) or a demon (*dānava*). Hence, Śrīkṛṣṇa would see to it that the Yādavas are exterminated by each other (*Śāntiparvan* 25.44–45). Let us now see how far such statements are consistent with the other narratives in the *Mahābhārata.*

Even a cursory reader of the *Mahābhārata* would know that unlike Dhṛtarāṣṭra who invariably overlooked the misdeeds of Duryodhana, Gāndhārī never supported the evil acts of her errant sons and even tried to dissuade them from acting in such an immoral manner. But her reprimands and advices always fell on deaf ears. In the *Udyogaparvan* (127.39), we find Gāndhārī reminding Duryodhana that no one can be sure of winning a war, which invariably brings in its wake several undesirable consequences. In the *Sabhāparvan* (66.28–35), she strongly denounced the way in which Duryodhana and Duḥśāsana had dishonoured Draupadī and also urged Dhṛtarāṣṭra not to invite the Pāṇḍavas for a second game of dice. In the *Udyogaparvan* (127.9–53), after Duryodhana had left the royal court after refusing Śrīkṛṣṇa's proposal for an amicable settlement with the Pāṇḍavas, Gāndhārī, at the instance of Dhṛtarāṣṭra, called back Duryodhana to the royal court and tried to persuade him to accept the terms of Śrīkṛṣṇa, but Duryodhana did not listen to her and again left the royal court in an uncourteous manner. This she did in the presence of Śrīkṛṣṇa himself. Thus, the persons solely responsible for the arrogance, jealousy and the consequent misdeeds of Duryodhana are Dhṛtarāṣṭra and the associates of Duryodhana like Śakuni and Karṇa — no sane person can put the blame for this on Gāndhārī. Moreover, it is stated in the *Strīparvan* (17.5–7) that when Duryodhana asked for her blessings for victory in the Kurukṣetra war, Gāndhārī said that victory would belong to that side which had abided by the principles of *dharma*. What more could be expected of a person who was, after all, the mother of Duryodhana? Thus, the charge levelled by Śrīkṛṣṇa against Gāndhārī is totally baseless and unjustified.

Śrīkṛṣṇa's claim that the Yādavas could not be killed by anyone other than Śrīkṛṣṇa himself also seems to be an overstatement, if we take into account some of the statements made by him in the *Sabhāparvan* (13.33–53). Therein, he said that he, along with the members of the 18 groups (e.g., Andhaka, Bhoja, Vṛṣni, Kukura, etc.) that constituted the Yādava clan, had to emigrate from Mathurā to Dvārakā, in order to be safe from the attacks of Jarāsandha, the infamous king of Magadha, who was well known for his physical and military prowess. The tyrant Kaṃsa, who was killed by his nephew Śrīkṛṣṇa, was married to two daughters of Jarāsandha who wanted to avenge the death of his son-in-law and accordingly attacked Mathurā. There was also bitter enmity between the Yādavas and two other powerful kings, Kālayavana and Dantavakra. Śrīkṛṣṇa, however, arranged for the safe emigration of Yādavas to Dvārakā through a lot of clever maneuverings and also ensured the death of these three powerful adversaries by means of some superb strategies. In case even the deities (*deva*s) were incapable of killing the Yādavas, why did Śrīkṛṣṇa take so much trouble for ensuring the safety of his own clan?

Śrīkṛṣṇa's claim that he himself would bring about the destruction of the Yādava clan is however, consistent with the account of events in the *Mauṣalaparvan* wherein the destruction of the Yādavas through internecine fighting is described because the iron clubs (*muṣalas*) with which the Yādavas had killed one another were produced when Śrīkṛṣṇa, shocked at the misconduct and drunken brawl of the Yādavas, picked up one among the reeds that had grown around Prabhāsatīrtha, whereupon the other reeds were transformed into *muṣalas* that became the weapon of murder for the Yādavas. Here, too, some questions remain unanswered. Unlike the Kauravas, the Yādavas did not die in the battlefield — they attacked each other when they were dead drunk and thus suffered the most ignominious form of death. Why did Śrīkṛṣṇa, who was supposed to be the incarnation (*avatāra*) of the Godhead the purpose of which was the establishment of the rule of *dharma* (*dharmasaṃsthāpana*), remain a passive spectator while the Yādavas gradually reached the nadir of moral depravity? Why did he not bring them back to their senses and make them worthy members of a clan that had a superhuman persona like him as its protector? Does this indicate that when the members of a clan become arrogant, such moral degeneration among them is inevitable, against which even an *avatāra* becomes ineffective?

What, however, comes as a shock to us is the cruel statement that Śrīkṛṣṇa made at the end of argument in self-defence. He told Gāndhārī that she should not grieve over her sons who were slain in the war because *Kṣatriya* women like her bear sons who are destined to be killed, just as *Brāhmaṇa* women bear sons who are destined to perform austerities, *Vaiśya* women bear sons who have to raise cattle, *Śūdra* women bear sons who are destined to serve others, cows bear male calves who are destined to carry loads and mares bear foals who are destined to run (*Strīparvan* 26.5). Could any one think of words of advice to a woman, who has lost all her sons in a devastating war, more improper, insensitive and inhuman than the ones said by Śrīkṛṣṇa? Does this statement not compare women with domestic animals, whose only value is to give birth to offsprings that would serve some purpose of others? If it be the case that such words, even though blunt and uncharitable, convey an undeniable but unpalatable truth, then why did Śrīkṛṣṇa not remind Draupadī of this unpleasant truth when she demanded that Aśvatthāman be properly punished for killing her sons while they were asleep? After all, like Gāndhārī, Draupadī was also a *Kṣatriya* woman who was doomed to bear sons so that they could be killed by someone! But on the insistence of Draupadī, the Pāṇḍavas began to search for Aśvatthāman, who could not save himself by using even the terrible divine weapon *brahmaśira*. He had to face utter humiliation of having to part with the crest jewel with which he was born and, as per the pronouncement of Śrīkṛṣṇa, of being banished — destined to wander all alone, suffering from his wounds, without water or medicine. But surprisingly, no comparable punishment was imposed on Kṛpācārya or Kṛtavarman who had guarded the gate of the Pāṇḍava Camp and set fire to it from all sides, thus helping Aśvatthāman in killing the unsuspecting Pāṇḍava soldiers while they were asleep. What could possibly explain this show of leniency to these two persons? Kṛpācārya was retained as the teacher of archery for Parīkṣit, the son of Abhimanyu, while Kṛtavarman, who was a member of the Yādava clan, went back to Dvārakā, and even came subsequently to attend the

Aśvamedha sacrifice of Yudhiṣṭhira as an invitee. On such occasions, the behaviour of Śrīkṛṣṇa was enigmatic, to say the least.

In a recent work, we find an interesting observation on the activities of Śrīkṛṣṇa which detects a common pattern in them without attempting any justification:

> Appearances notwithstanding, there is indeed a consistency in Kṛṣṇa's characterization. His role in the great epic, it seems, is to oversee the unfolding of a chain of events that is destined to be; and he intervenes whenever human beings threaten to throw things off course, whether it be because of their moral weakness or indeed because of their moral strength." (Ganeri 2007: 69–70).

One explanation of his activities is that being superhuman, he is not bound by the norm of consistency or the moral rules that govern human conduct (Das 2009: 201). Another line of defence is to suggest that Śrīkṛṣṇa was setting a new paradigm, whereby moral laws became flexible, unlike the rigid moral codes that one encounters in the *Rāmāyaṇa* (Matilal 2002: 34; Ganeri 2007: 92). It has also been suggested that while Bhīṣma exemplifies adherence to the old value system that was gradually becoming outdated, Śrīkṛṣṇa ushered in a new value system (Chakravarti 2006: 55). One may also suggest that these enigmatic activities of Śrīkṛṣṇa point out that for one who had assumed the human body, it was not possible to be perfect. The *Mahābhārata* specifically states that while truth (*satya*) reigns supreme in the realm of *deva*s and falsehood (*anṛta*) in that of *asura*s, there is an intermixture of truth and falsity in the human sphere (*Śāntiparvan* 183.1–4). Hence, a perfectly satisfactory solution to our moral problems cannot always be found in this imperfect world inhabited by imperfect human beings (Matilal 2002: 8). We do not presume to solve this riddle here — perhaps it does not even have any satisfactory solution.

Before we close this section, we may, however, note some apparently bizarre theories that have been expounded in the *Mahābhāratatātparyanirṇaya* (henceforth *MTN*) of Ānandatīrtha (also known as Madhvācārya) and the commentary *Bhāvaprakāśikā* (henceforth *BP*) on it by Vādirājatīrtha, which clearly go against the statements in the *Mahābhārata* itself. The sole purpose of all these theories is to show the supremacy of Śrīkṛṣṇa, who was supposed to be the Supreme Reality (*Parabrahman*). In defense of the manner in which Bhīma defeated Duryodhana in mace-fight, Ānandatīrtha and Vādirājatīrtha have stated that Bhīma, who was the best among the individual selves (*jīvottama*), could have easily defeated Duryodhana by employing fair means, but Śrīkṛṣṇa made him break the thighs of Duryodhana so that he could keep his promise that he had made during the infamous game of dice (*MTN* with *BP*: 847–48). Breaking a promise is a more serious lapse than violating the rules of warfare, and Śrīkṛṣṇa ensured that Bhīma be guilty of the latter rather than of the former. The editor of these texts goes even a step further and states in the editorial note that while both Bhīma and Duryodhana had apparently learnt the art of mace-fight from Balarāma, it was actually Śrīkṛṣṇa who had taught them in the guise of Balarāma, and that Duryodhana, being the worst kind of individual (*jīvāpasada*), was only a pseudo-pupil (*śiṣyābhāsa*). None of these claims, however, tallies with the relevant accounts given in the *Mahābhārata*. Śrīkṛṣṇa himself said before the mace-fight that while Bhīma was superior in strength, Duryodhana was more skillful, since he had devoted more time to practice (*Śalyaparvan* 57.3). Afterwards also, he said that it was impossible on the part of anyone, including Bhīma, to defeat Duryodhana in a fair mace-fight (*Śalyaparvan* 57.4–8). Moreover, Vādirājatīrtha does not explain in the least as to why Balarāma was angry with Bhīma for violating the rules of mace-fight and, in his fury, was even on the verge of killing Bhīma with his plough (*Śalyaparvan* 59.4–7, 17–19, 23–26).

Another strange claim made by Ānandatīrtha and Vādirājatīrtha is that Yudhiṣṭhira had to visit the hell since he doubted the propriety of Śrīkṛṣṇa's advice that he should lie to Droṇācārya, so that the Pāṇḍava army could be saved from total rout. After showing hell to Yudhiṣṭhira, Indra told Yudhiṣṭhira that it was improper on the part of the latter to modify the false statement 'Aśvatthāman has been killed' by the rider 'the elephant'. What was said by Śrīkṛṣṇa, who was the Supreme Godhead himself, was bound to be in accordance with *dharma*; and hence, anyone who doubted the propriety of his advice committed a grave sin (*MTN* with *BP*: 992–93). Thus, according to Ānandatīrtha and Vādirājatīrtha, Yudhiṣṭhira should have, in accordance with the advice of Śrīkṛṣṇa, simply uttered the statement, 'Aśvatthāman has been killed', *without* adding the qualifier 'the elephant'— it was the addition of this qualifying clause that turned Yudhiṣṭhira into a sinner. This claim, like the one mentioned earlier, is not supported by any verse in the *Māhābhārata* — on the contrary, it goes against all the available textual evidence. In the *Droṇaparvan*, it has been said that as soon as Yudhiṣṭhira loudly uttered the word 'Aśvatthāman has been killed', and then whispered the additional words 'the elephant', his chariot, which always moved a few digits above the earth, came down on the ground (*Droṇaparvan*164.107). There could not be a better poetic indication of the fact that for Yudhiṣṭhira, it was a serious lapse, which resulted in the lowering of his erstwhile exalted status as a moral person. Besides, in the *Svargārohaṇaparvan* (3.12, 37), Indra and Dharma explained to Yudhiṣṭhira the three reasons due to which he had to visit the hell, though only for a short time. The first reason was that all kings had to visit the hell for some time, since while ruling over their kingdoms, they were invariably compelled to commit some immoral acts. The second reason was that persons whose merits (*puṇya*) exceeded their demerits (*pāpa*) had to be at first in the hell and then go to the heaven (*Svargārohaṇaparvan* 3.13–14). The third reason, which is most important for the purpose of this study, was that Yudhiṣṭhira lied to Droṇācārya, even though the latter had implored Yudhiṣṭhira to speak the truth (*Svargārohaṇaparvan* 3.15–16). Neither Indra nor Dharma even hinted that Yudhiṣṭhira had to visit the hell for doubting the propriety of Śrīkṛṣṇa's advice and trying to turn his false statement into a true one. We, on our part, fail to understand why erudite scholars like

Ānandatīrtha and Vādirājatīrtha should indulge in such an unnecessary attempt at proving the greatness of Śrīkṛṣṇa, which ultimately becomes counterproductive.

X

We conclude this essay by making some general observations on the moral doctrines propounded in the *Mahābhārata*. The first noteworthy point is that a certain practice or course of action is often recommended simply on the ground that such a practice has been in vogue for a long time. The half-verses, *atrāpyudāharantīmam itihāsaṃ purātanam* and *atraivodāharantīmam itihāsaṃ purātanam* ('in this matter too people cite this ancient anecdote') occur umpteen times in the *Mahābhārata*. Such statements usually precede the narration of some anecdote, where the practice in question has been sanctioned or recommended by some well-known person. In a few cases, some practices are justified on the ground that they have been ordained by scriptures. As examples of these two types of justification, we may cite the case of Śrīkṛṣṇa justifying the use of devious means for defeating the enemy by arguing that even in earlier times, such measures were adopted by the *deva*s against the *asura*s, and that respectable people also approved of such measures; and also the case of Dharmavyādha justifying his own profession by stating that in the scriptures it has been said that organisms like plants, creepers and animals are supposed to serve as food of other organisms, and also that the sacrificial fires are desirous of meat. But there can very well be time-honoured practices that may turn out to be immoral if we refuse to be guided solely by tradition or precedents; in fact, some practices that may be sanctioned by scriptures in one age may be prohibited in another age. Thus, *maṃsāṣṭakā* (the custom of offering meat at the *srāddha* ceremony for the manes), or *niyoga* (levirate) whereby a childless widow could have an offspring by copulating with some person chosen by her elders, were in vogue during the *dvāpara* age. But subsequently, they were prohibited by the authors of *Dharamaśāstra*s during the *kali* age. Thus, the mere fact that some practice has been in vogue for a long time, or has been sanctioned by some scripture does not automatically make it sacrosanct. What is lacking here is the willingness for (or even the possibility of) the examination of some moral issue on purely rational grounds. This may (at least in part) be due to the fact that in matters pertaining to *dharma*, greater emphasis was always put on scriptures (*śruti/smṛti*), prevalent customs (*sadācāra*) and self-satisfaction (*ātmatuṣṭi*) — *reason had only a subservient or instrumental role*, insofar as it helped one to interpret the scriptures in a proper manner or decide upon a course of action when different scriptures gave conflicting views on the same issue, or when the scriptures did not have any ready-made solution to a problem. The *Mahābhārata* is full of instances wherein actions performed on the basis of blind adherence to scriptures or social practices that either resulted or could have resulted in disastrous consequences. Thus, we find Jarāsandha, the infamous king of Magadha, keeping a large number of kings in captivity so that they could be used as sacrificial victims. Such a horrible practice that was sanctioned by some scriptures would have been perpetrated if Bhīma had not killed Jarāsandha at the behest of Śrīkṛṣṇa. Likewise, one of the social practices in vogue among the *Kṣatriyas* was the abduction of a maiden for the purpose of marriage. In accordance with this practice, Bhīṣma abducted Ambā, Ambikā and Ambālikā, the three daughters of the king of Kāśī, so that his step-brother Vicitravīrya could be married to them. By this act, Bhīṣma deprived these three princesses of the freedom to choose their prospective husbands in a *svayaṃvara* that had been arranged by their father who could not match Bhīṣma in military prowess and was thus unable to protect his daughters. Thus, instead of free choice, it was sheer brute force that ultimately decided the fate of these three princesses. On the face of it, such abduction smacks of the practices current among barbarians, where the victorious party in a war automatically became the master of the material possessions as well as the women belonging to the vanquished party. What is noteworthy here is that this brutal and rash act of abduction did not produce any good results. While Ambikā and Ambalikā could somehow meekly accept the inevitable, Ambā did not agree to marry Vicitravīrya on the ground that she had already chosen king Śālva as her husband. On hearing this, Bhīṣma arranged for sending her to Śālva who refused to marry Ambā on the ground that she had been touched by Bhīṣma during the act of adduction. After being thus rejected by Śālva, Ambā requested Bhīṣma to marry her and thereby save her from utter humiliation. Bhīṣma could not agree to this proposal due to his vow of lifelong celibacy. Ambā was thus placed in a tragic situation from which there was no honourable way out, even though she was not responsible for her plight in any way — it was due solely to a cruel social custom that was in vogue among the *Kṣatriyas* at that time. Faced with such unbearable insult and humiliation, Ambā ended her life, but with a vow to avenge in a future birth the sufferings that she had to endure because of Bhīṣma and was subsequently reborn as Śikhaṇḍin who played a vital role in the defeat of Bhīṣma in the Kurukṣetra war. So far as Ambikā and Ambālikā were concerned, their married life came to an abrupt end when Vicitravīrya, who was given to excessive pursuit of sensual pleasures, died prematurely of consumption; and on top of that, both Ambikā and Ambālikā were without any issue at that time. Satyavatī, the mother of Vicitravīrya, was anxious to ensure the continuity of the Kuru dynasty. Consequently, the two widows had to submit to the obnoxious practice of levirate (*niyoga*), whereby at the behest of Satyavatī, the sage Vyāsa (the son born to the sage Parāśara and Satyavatī before her marriage to Śāntanu) was appointed by Bhīṣma for impregnating Ambīkā and Ambalikā. Vyāsa suggested that both these princesses observe some austerities, so that they could be physically and mentally prepared for the physical union with him, but Satyavatī was in too much of a haste to listen to this advice. Hence, when these princesses were sent to Vyāsa, neither of them could tolerate either the terrible appearance of Vyāsa or his stinking body odour — Ambikā closed her eyes in revulsion, while Ambālikā turned pale with fear. Vyāsa declared that as a result of this, the son of Ambikā would be blind, and the son of Ambālikā would be pale in complexion.

This was how Dhṛtarāṣṭra and Pāṇḍu were born. Satyavatī, not deterred by this turn of events, again appointed Vyāsa for levirate — but this time, the princesses arranged to send to Vyāsa a maidservant of Śūdra caste, and the son born from this union was Vidura. What we should note here is that while imposing the practice of levirate on Ambikā or Ambālikā, neither Satyavatī nor Bhīṣma took into account the likes, dislikes or sensitivities of these young and beautiful women — they were treated literally like breeding mares that could be sent to chosen stallions for getting some thoroughbreds. Such incidents are poignant reminders of the fact that blind adherence to social practices without any thought for possible unintended consequences may lead to immense disappointment and suffering.

Another case of blind adherence to practices then current in the society that had led to disastrous results was Yudhiṣṭhira's acceptance of the invitation from Duryodhana for participating in the game of dice, the consequences of which are too well known to be recounted here. Duryodhana exploited Yudhiṣṭhira's addiction to the game of dice, even though the latter was not good at it. Yudhiṣṭhira also had the apprehension that this game of dice might not be a fair one because in the Kaurava court, there were expert dice-players like Śakuni who could use deceitful means for ensuring victory in such a game. Nevertheless, he did accept this invitation. When he was subsequently taken to task for such an improper decision, he answered that if a *Kṣatriya* was invited to a game of dice, then he *could not* decline such an offer. This is almost analogous to the custom prevalent among the knights in the medieval age — if a knight was challenged to a dual, then it would be extremely unchivalrous and cowardly of him if he did not accept the challenge. Yudhiṣṭhira's answer is not, however, a satisfactory one. There was no *moral* compulsion for gambling, as is evident from the subsequent admonitions of Draupadī in the *Āraṇyakaparvan* (31.17–19). Had the participation in the game of dice been morally obligatory on the part of Yudhiṣṭhira, Draupadī, who was well acquainted with the rules of conduct of a king, would not have such strong reservations about the game of dice. In effect, Yudhiṣṭhira was arguing that the option of refusing to participate in a game of dice was not open to him, but this was so simply because he allowed himself to be tied up by uncritically abiding by the practices current among the *Kṣatriya*s. That the participation in a game of dice was not a moral obligation on the part of Yudhiṣṭhira is also evident from the fact that addiction to dice has been declared to be a vice (*vyasana*) in *Dharamaśāstra* texts like *Manusaṃhitā* (VII.47).

Another notable feature of the exposition of morality in the *Mahābhārata* is the diversity of opinions on the same issue. This is perhaps inevitable in view of the fact that in a mammoth epic like the *Mahābhārata*, where we find so many different characters, one should only expect such divergence of views. Another possible source of such incongruity may very well be the numerous interpolations that took place from time to time. Thus, as we have already noted, in the *Prāyaścittīya* section of the *Śāntiparvan*, we find Vyāsa making the pronouncement that even though it is the moral duty of a man to provide sustenance to his wife, the abandonment of an adulterous wife does not amount to dereliction of duty, since such an act maintains the purity of the lineage of a family and also helps in purifying the woman concerned (*Śāntiparvan* 35.30). But in the selfsame *Śāntiparvan*, in the anecdote of Cirakārin, we are told that in a case of adultery, the man involved is guilty and not the woman (*Śāntiparvan* 258.46). Again, in the *Āraṇyakaparvan* (198.19–22), we find Dharmavyādha defending his profession of selling meat by arguing that since this profession ran in his family, he could not give it up; moreover, he did not kill the animals whose meat was being sold — the animals were killed by others, while he merely traded in their meat (*Āraṇyakaparvan* 198.31). He also claimed that the meat sold by him could be used for propitiating the deities, the manes and human beings desirous of meat, and that the animals, whose meat was thus used, would go to heaven (*Āraṇyakaparvan* 199.8–10). The implicature of such a plea seems to be the claim that while killing animals was morally reprehensible, selling the meat of those animals was not an immoral act, or that even if selling meat was morally objectionable, Dharmavyādha was, so to say, condemned by his very birth to take up such a profession. The last claim may be seen to concur with the advice of Śrīkṛṣṇa in *Bhagavadgītā* that the work that one was supposed to perform by virtue of his birth should not be given up even if it was not morally justified (18.48).

But such a view was not endorsed by Bhīṣma, who said in the *Anuśāsanaparvan* (116.3–5, 29, 38–39, 47) that when the meat of an animal was consumed, the moral responsibility for killing that animal had to be shared by (*a*) one who procured the animal, (*b*) one who killed the animal, (*c*) one who skinned the animal and cut it into several parts, (*d*) one who approved of such killing, (*e*) one who traded in the meat, (*f*) one who cooked the meat, and (*g*) one who consumed the meat. The only occasions when no moral guilt accrued to the persons involved in the killing of an animal and consumption of its meat were sacrifices (*yajñas*), offerings to the manes (*śrāddha*) and hunting (*mṛgayā*). Incidentally, it may be noted here that at least one of the claims of Dharmavyādha, viz., that the meat sold by him could be used for propitiating the deities, is not in consonance with Vedic texts like *Taittirīya saṃhitā*, *Taittirīya Brāhmaṇa*, *Śatapatha Brāhmaṇa* or the *Śrauta-sūtras* of Āśvalāyana, Kātyāyana, etc. wherein the ritual of killing the sacrificial animal after its consecration by the priests has been described in great detail. The meat of an unconsecrated animal that is procured from a butcher's shop could not be used in a sacrifice. One wonders why Kauśika, who was supposed to be conversant with Vedic texts and sacrificial practices, did not point this out to Dharmavyādha. I am not, however, sure whether the meat purchased from a shop could be used in *Aṣṭakāśrāddha*.

In the *Mahābhārata,* we also find quite a few instances wherein the same person employed the so-called double standard — one for justifying some action performed by oneself or by someone dear to oneself, and quite an opposite one for castigating the same sort of action when it was performed by some other person. Thus, we find that Śāmba, the son of Śrīkṛṣṇa and Jāmbavatī, tried to abduct

Lakṣmaṇā, the daughter of Duryodhana, when she was about to choose her husband in a *svayaṃvara*. The Kauravas, however, foiled this attempt at abduction and made Śāmba a captive. This enraged the Yādavas, and as their representative, Balarāma came to Hastināpura and demanded that Śāmba be set free. When the Kauravas refused to do so, Balarāma became extremely angry and began to use his plough for displacing Hastināpura from its location, whereupon the terrified Kauravas agreed to the proposal of Balarāma and also arranged for a marriage between Lakṣmaṇā and Śāmba. Thus, a matrimonial alliance was established between the Yādavas and Kauravas, a fact to which Śrīkṛṣṇa's attention was drawn by Duryodhana in the *Udyogaparvan* (89.14; see also *Bhāgavatapurāṇa, Skandha* 10, Chapter 60). It may be recalled that earlier, Śrīkṛṣṇa, too, had abducted Rukmiṇī, the princess of Vidarbha who was betrothed to Śiśupāla, the king of Cedi, by her father Bhīṣmaka and elder brother Rukmī. However, Śrīkṛṣṇa had done so at the request of Rukmiṇī herself, as she did not want to marry Śiśupāla. Here again, the abduction resulted in a quarrel between the Yādavas and the Vidarbha king and crown prince; and the Yādavas, including Balarāma, solidly backed Śrīkṛṣṇa (*Harivaṃśa, Viṣṇuparvan*, chapters 47, 59, 60; *Bhāgavatapurāṇa, Skandha* 10, chapters 52–54). Bhīṣmaka and Rukmī could not, however, reconcile themselves to this situation; and out of spite, they became staunch supporters of Jarāsandha, the arch-enemy of the Yādavas (*Śāntiparvan* 13.21–23). But subsequently, when Arjuna abducted Subhadrā, the sister of Śrīkṛṣṇa, at the suggestion of Śrīkṛṣṇa himself, the other Yādavas became furious and made preparations for capturing Arjuna, so that he could be taught a proper lesson. The most vociferous among the Yādavas was no other than Balarāma who accused Arjuna of betraying the Yādavas who had been the most generous hosts to Arjuna. Balarāma compared this act of treachery with the improper act of breaking a plate from which one had taken one's meals (*Ādiparvan* 212.16–32). He could be pacified only after a lot of persuation by Śrīkṛṣṇa (*Ādiparvan* 213.1–12). Now, what is of interest here is the fact that the Yādavas approved of abduction when it was done by someone like Śrīkṛṣṇa or Śāmba who were among their kinsmen, but they felt insulted if any Yādava maiden was abducted by a person like Arjuna who belonged to some other clan. This, then, is a clear case of adopting double standards.

We do not, however, wish to give the impression that our primary aim is to find fault with all the doctrines about morals that may be found in the *Mahābhārata*. Moral beliefs, like other beliefs, are subject to revisions, and one cannot expect that the moral views that have been expressed in this epic will be admissible for all times to come. Thus, we find in a recent work on ethics: 'loyalty must be always be restrained by the limits of right and wrong, where right and wrong is assessed independently' (Nuttal 1993: 165)

In the *Mahābhārata*, however, we find loyalty and gratitude getting more importance. Bhīṣma, who was personally extremely honest and who publicly censured Duryodhana and his associates for their misdeeds, nevertheless remained on the side of Kauravas due to his loyalty to the Kaurava court wherefrom he had drawn his sustenance. He confessed as much to Yudhiṣṭhira before the beginning of the Kurukṣhetra war:

arthasya puruṣo dāso dāso hyartho na kasyacit /
iti satyaṃ mahārāja baddho'smyarthena kauravaiḥ // (*Bhīṣmaparvan* 41.36)

The same thing holds about Droṇa, Kṛpācārya and Śalya who also made the same statement (*Bhīṣmaparvan* 41.51, 66, 77). In the *Śāntiparvan*, Bhīṣma said that there may be some act of expiation that may purify a person guilty of killing a Brahmin, drinking wine, stealing, or forsaking one's vow, but there was no expiation that could purify an ungrateful person. A person who betrayed his friends or harmed his benefactors was the vilest creature on earth; his carcass was so impure that it was not consumed even by carnivorous creatures or maggots:

brahmaghne ca surāpe ca caure bhagnavrate tathā /
niṣkṛtirvihitā rājan kṛtaghne nāsti niṣkṛtiḥ //
mitradrohī kṛtaghnaśca nṛśaṃsaśca narādhamaḥ /
kravyādaiḥ kṛmibhiścaiva na bhujyante hi tādṛśaḥ // (*Śāntiparvan* 166.24–25)

The *Mahābhārāta* contains many such verses (e.g., *Udyogaparvan* 105.10; *Śāntiparvan* 167.19). Clearly, we have here a society where loyalty and gratitude were given much importance; and which compelled people not to forsake benefactors who might even be guilty of many moral lapses.

Again, in a recent book, we find the following view about war ethics:

> [W]hat counts as morally right in war must differ in many respects from what counts as morally right at other times. However, morality, if it is about the right way of living; and it is when life is most difficult that morality is most needed. Morality might *appear* as a luxury in war because doing what is morally right is more difficult, and it is also more difficult to decide what is morally right — but this is not to say that it is a luxury (Nuttal 1993: 174).

In *Mahābhārata*, however, moral lapses during war like adopting deceit and breaking rules have been justified on the ground that such strategies were adopted by the *devas* against the *asuras*; and that victory against a strong enemy cannot be obtained without underhand means. The trouble is that such an argument is like a double-edged sword — it also justifies the misdeeds of the wily opponents, and we are led to the cynical conclusion that 'war ethics' is only an empty expression.

One of the basic assumptions of ethical doctrines is freedom of choice without which no moral responsiblity can be assigned to anyone. In the *Śāntiparvan*, however, we find some strange doctrines expressed by Vyāsa that seem to strike at the very roots of this assumption. In order to persuade Yudhiṣṭhira, who was in deep sorrow, to ascend the throne and rule his kingdom in a proper manner, Vyāsa told Yudhiṣṭhira that like his forefathers, he should ensure that the *dharma*, which had been expounded by the Vedas and the Brahmins, be properly maintained because the duty of a *Kṣatriya* was to uphold the rule of *dharma*. Vyāsa further advised Yudhiṣṭhira to restrain, punish, or even kill, if necessary, whosoever disrupted this order (*Śāntiparvan* 32.3–6). In this connection, Vyāsa also told Yudhiṣṭhira that such harsh or cruel acts of the king did not make the king a sinner. People performed actions as directed by God, and hence the results of good or bad actions pertained to God, and not to the so called agents of these actions. When a person cut a tree with an axe, the sin incurred here pertained to the person and not to the axe (*Śāntiparvan* 32.12–13). Accordingly, the king should dedicate the results of his acitons to God and remain unaffected by those results (*Śāntiparvan* 32.15).

In this connection, it should be noted that in the *Āraṇyakaparvan* (31.27), Draupadī also maintained a similar view when she said that individual selves, who were ignorant, were also incapable of determining their pleasures and sufferings — being guided by God, they went to heaven or hell. Yudhiṣṭhira rebuked Draupadī for harbouring such a view and accused her of expounding the view of non-believers (*nāstikyameva ca bhāṣase*). But in the *Śāntiparvan*, where an almost identical view was expressed by Vyāsa, Yudhiṣṭhira did not protest in any way. Incidentally, it may be noted that in *Kauṣitakī Upaniṣad* (3.8) we find a view very similar to this. Even if the results of one's actions are thus dedicated to God, can one shake off the moral responsibility of one's actions? Of course, one may bring forward here the doctrine of *niṣkāma karma*, but whether this solves the basic problem remains an open question.

In this connection, the following comments of Rajendra Prasad seem to be extremely pertinent:

> [C]lassical Indian ethics, both practical and theoretical, developed in accordance with the structure of the then classical social order. In this order, every individual or group was not always morally fair to every other individual or group. But still, classical Indian ethics did grow, as any classical ethics did, primarily to enable every member of the order to live a socially cohesive and personally satisfying life . . . To be specific, it developed an organ to provide a theoretical support to the ethics then considered worthy to be practiced. Whenever and wherever such theoretical attempts are made, some theoretical devices are brought in, which generally provide a moral justification in terms of concepts or categories thrown up by, or relevant to, the way or ways in which the particular social order in which they are used, functions . . . when such theoretical devices and the concepts or categories which go with them are used for a long time, they generate, or get congealed into some well-marked normative structure. Then, a mere appeal to the conformity or non-conformity of an action to such a normative structure is considered sufficient to make that course of action morally justified/unjustified. But all such theoretical devices or structures are *not* always used to do only this sort of justification work. . . *Some* of them, and all of them *sometimes* are also used, or are usable, to provide an allegedly, or a seemingly moral justification for some prevalent practices which are not, or cannot be

justified on moral grounds . . . When such things happen, it is generally the case that the theorizers, by and large, belong to a class which occupies a higher status, a position of greater power, in the social organization than the class to which belong the *sufferers* or victims of unfairness or unfair practices; and those who commit the unfair acts, or are the beneficiaries of the unfair practices, come from the former class, the class of superiors, the same class from which the theorizers come as well (2008: 175–76).

This is not to suggest, however, that the ethical doctrines propounded in *Mahābhārata* are nothing but clever ploys for perpetuating inequality and injustice in the society, so that the interests of the social group(s) in power could be protected. To me, it seems that instead of telling us how people *should* behave, *Mahābhārata* shows how different types of people *actually* act and tend to morally defend their own actions. Crooked people would obviously adopt questionable means of self-justification. But in the *Mahābhārata* we also find characters like Vidura, who, more than anyone else, seems to be the very embodiment of righteousness and moral wisdom. Among the numerous stories of deceit and betrayal, greed and passion, cruelty and vengeance, his words to Dhṛtarāṣṭra seem to serve as the beacon light of morality when he says that one should not give up *dharma* in the face of lust, fear, avarice or the desire for living; because *dharma* is eternal, while pleasure and pain are ephemeral (*Udyogaparvan* 40.11–12).

References

Primary Sources

Mahābhārata (Vulgate edition) with the commentary *Bhāratabhāvadīpa* of Nīlakaṇṭha, ed. Ramachandra Shastri Kinjwadekar, Second Reprint, vols 1–6. 1979. New Delhi: Oriental Books Reprint Corporation.

Mahābhārata with the commentary *Bhāratabhāvadīpa* of Nīlakaṇṭha, along with the commentary *Bhāratakaumudī* and a Bengali translation by Mahāmahopādhyāya Haridāsa Siddhāntavāgīśa, 2nd edn, vols 1–43. 1976–93. Calcutta: Visvabani Prakasani.

Mahābhārata (Critical Edition), ed. V. S. Sukhthankar et al., vols 1–18. 1933–66. Pune: Bhandarkar Oriental Research Institute.

Mahābhāratatātparyanirṇaya of Ānandatīrtha (also known as Madhvācārya) with the commentary *Bhāvaprakāśikā* by Vādirājatīrtha, ed. V. Prabhañjanācārya. 1998. Bangalore: Śrī Vyāsa Madhva Sevā Pratiṣṭhāna.

The Pratīka-Index of the *Mahābhārata* (*Mahābhāratastha-Ślokapādasūcī*), ed. P. L. Vaidya, vols 1–6.1967–72. Pune: Bhandarkar Oriental Research Institute.

Manusaṃhitā with the commentaries of Medhātithi, Sarvajñanārāyaṇa, Kullukabhaṭṭa, Rāghavānanda, Nandana, Rāmacandra, Maṇirāma, Govindarāja, and Bhāruci; ed. J. H. Dave, vols 1–6. 1972–84. Bombay: Bharatiya Vidya Bhavana.

Secondary Sources

Agarwal, Satya P. 2010. *Āpaddharma in the Mahābhārata*. New Delhi: New Age Books.
Barlingay, Surendra S. 1998. *A Modern Introduction to Indian Ethics*. New Delhi: Penman Publishers.
Belvalkar, S. K. 1966. 'Introduction', in S. K. Belvalkar (ed.), *Mahābhārata* (Critical Edition), vol. 16. Pune: Bhandarkar Oriental Research Institute.
Bhattacharya, Sukhamaya. 1984. *Mahābhārat-e Caturvarga* (in Bengali). Calcutta: Government Sanskrit College.
Chakravarti, Sitansu S. 2006. *Ethics in the Mahābhārata: A Philosophical Enquiry for Today*. New Delhi: Munshiram Manoharlal.
Chaturvedi, Badrinath. 2007. *The Mahābhārata: An Enquiry in the Human Condition*. New Delhi: Orient Longman.
Das, Gurcharan. 2009. *The Difficulty of Being Good: On the Subtle Art of Dharma*. New Delhi: Allan Lane.
Dasgupta, Surama. 1961. *Development of Moral Philosophy in India*. Bombay: Orient Longman.
Fitzgerald, James L. 2009. '*Dharma* and Its Translation in the *Mahābhārata*', in Patrick Olivelle (ed.), *Dharma: Studies in Its Semantic, Cultural and Religious History*, pp. 249–63. New Delhi: Motilal Banarsidass.
Ganeri, Jonardan. 2007. *The Concealed Art of the Soul: Theories of Self and Practices of Truth in Indian Ethics and Epistemology*. Oxford: Oxford University Press.
Matilal, Bimal K. 2002. *Ethics and Epics*, ed. Jonardan Ganeri. New Delhi: Oxford University Press.
Nuttal, Jon. 1993. *Moral Questions: An Introduction to Ethics*. Cambridge: Polity Press.
Olivelle, Patrick (ed.). 2009. *Dharma: Studies in Its Semantic, Cultural and Religious History*. New Delhi: Motilal Banarsidass.
———. 2005. *Dharmasūtra Parallels: Containing the Dharmasūtras of Āpastamba, Gautama, Baudhāyana and Vasiṣṭha*. New Delhi: Motilal Banarsidass.
Prasad, Rajendra. 2008. *A Conceptual–Analytic Study of Classical Indian Philosophy of Morals*. New Delhi: Centre for Studies in Civilisations.
——— (ed.). 2008. *A Historical-Developmental Study of Classical Indian Philosophy of Morals*. New Delhi: Centre for Studies in Civilisations.
Ramanathan, C. 2008a. 'Ethics in the *Mahābhārata*', in Rajendra Prasad (ed.), *A Historical-Developmental Study of Classical Indian Philosophy of Morals*, pp. 95–118. New Delhi: Centre for Studies in Civilisations.
———. 2008b. 'Ethics in the *Rāmāyaṇa*', in Rajendra Prasad (ed.), *A Historical-Developmental Study of Classical Indian Philosophy of Morals*, pp. 71–94. New Delhi: Centre for Studies in Civilisations.
Sharma, Arvind (ed.). 2007. *Essays on the Mahābhārata*. New Delhi: Motilal Banarsidass.
Vohra, A. *et al.* (eds). 2005. *Dharma: The Categorical Imperative*. New Delhi: D. K. Printworlds.
Vora, D. P. 1959. *Evolution of Morals in the Epics: Rāmāyaṇa and Mahābhārata*. Bombay: Popular Book Depot.
Wujastyk, Dominik. 2009. 'Medicine and *Dharma*', in Patrick Olivelle (ed.), *Dharma: Studies in Its Semantic, Cultural and Religious History*, pp. 409–20. New Delhi: Motilal Banarsidass.

Of Sleep and Violence

Reading the Sauptikaparvan *in Times of Terror*

Anirban Das

The *Sauptikaparvan* is one of the shortest chapters in the *Mahābhārata*. However, it describes one of the most violent moments in the text. A violence that, in order to be discerning, does not really belong to the great war of Kurukṣetra. A violence that is almost an appendage to the narrative of the war. Yet, in a certain sense, it is the quintessential moment of the war. An essence that comes at the end, almost after the end. Like the centre that lies beyond the structure. The centre that is definitionally outside the structure. The violence of this moment enacts, in a concentrated and focussed manner, the meaningless and senseless violence that inheres in the reasons of the war, of the social, of the life itself. We may, through a reading of this chapter in a given mode, learn some aspects of the violence that inheres in our world, our life and our reasons. It is instructive that this chapter which narrates the killing of the entire victorious army of the Pāṇḍavas is named not after the act of killing and aggression. Instead, it bears the name of the unwitting passivity of the massacred. The name points at the state of sleep when terror struck. The word *sauptika* is derived from *supti*, that is, slumber. Or is it the slumber of reason? Not the moment when reason sleeps but the sleep that reason bears, with and in.

A number of disclaimers are in order. First, to state the obvious, when we learn from the *Mahābhārata*, when reading the text we seem to hear resonances of some of our own predicaments; we do not claim that the text predicts the twenty-first century or that it reflects a society similar to our own. Keeping away from the naivety of a mirror-theory for literary depictions, I read some of my concerns into the text. Of course, the text has to be pliant and expansive enough to accommodate that. That, as anyone who has read the *Mahābhārata* in any of its redactions would perhaps agree, is the minimum one can say for the text. Thinking of terror in the twenty-first century, one can read the part of the text that names itself as related to sleep. This text describes the killing of the sleeping Pāṇḍava army at the end of the Kurukṣetra war when the enemy, that is, Kaurava prince Duryodhana, awaits death with broken thighs at the Dvaipāyana *hṛd* (lake). Like the apogee in the chain of vengeance that marks the war as well as the text, the killing of a sleeping army becomes symptomatic of the devious forms of reasoning that went into the making of the war. I will go into that later.

The *Sauptikaparvan* follows the *Śalyaparvan*. The latter ends with Duryodhana's last act as the prince and the leader of the Kauravas. The last three great warriors of the Kauravas, viz., Aśvatthāmā, Kṛpācārya and Kṛtavarmā, came to meet Duryodhana, defeated (in an unfair battle with Bhīma) and waiting to die. Aśvatthāmā broke into a tirade of abuse against the Pāṇḍavas and declared that he would destroy them all. Duryodhana made him the general of the Kaurava army. This seemed a symbolic yet ineffectual move: he was made the general of a three-man army against the mighty Pāṇḍavas who had just vanquished the great Kaurava army (along with its allies) of which these three were a part.

The *Sauptikaparvan* begins with the three warriors first moving south from the battlefield and then changing direction to the east as they feared that the Pāṇḍavas might come after them. The three-men army did not show much sign of the offence it had promised Duryodhana. As Kṛpācārya and Kṛtavarmā went to sleep in the forest where they had reached and settled for the night, the angry Aśvatthāmā remained awake and alert. Then something happened which resonated with Aśvatthāmā's raging mind. It seemed to suddenly reveal the only act he could embark on at that juncture. A ghastly owl arrived and was killing its sleeping preys, the crows in their nests:

> He tore the wings of some and cut off the heads of others with his sharp talons and broke the legs of many. Highly strong as he was, he killed many that fell down before his eyes (*Sauptikaparvan* 1.40–41).*

Having destroyed the victims, the owl went away satisfied. Witnessing this carnage, Aśvatthāmā reached his own conclusions. The lessons that he learnt were of a pragmatic nature. He had promised Duryodhana that he would destroy the Pāṇḍavas. The flipside of this promise was that he was not equal to them in war. He would be defeated if he fought in a fair manner. The inference, obvious for him, was to kill them when they were not ready to fight, to take them unawares. His reasoning was impeccable:

> People generally, as also those well-read in the scriptures, always prefer means which are certain to those which are uncertain. Censure and bad name, whatever this act may engender, ought to be incurred by a person who leads the life of a kṣatriya. The sinful Pāṇḍavas have, at every step, perpetrated very ugly, censurable and deceitful acts (ibid.).
>
> . . . The enemy's forces, even which fatigued, or wounded, or while eating, or when retiring, or when resting within their camp, should be beaten. They should be equally treated when sleeping at dead at night, or when bereft of commanders, or when routed, or when labouring under an error (*Sauptikaparvan* 1.51–52).

---

* All references to the *Sauptikaparvan* of the *Mahābhārata* are from Velankar (1948) and English translations from Dutt (2004) and Lal (2008).

Thus, he resolved to attack and rout the Pāṇḍava forces as they slept in the camp. This was the beginning of a long line of reasoning that the Kauravas followed before they actually launched the attack.

Both Nrisinha Prasad Bhaduri (in his piece on Aśvatthāmā in his Bengali book on the biographies of *Mahābhārata*'s anti-heroes, *Mahabharater Pratinayak* [2009]) and Sibaji Bandyopadhyay (in his Bengali play *Uttampurush Ekbachan: Ekti Bhan* [2002] whose English translation bears the title *The Book of Night: A Moment from the Mahabharata* [2008]) bring out the intricate texture of reasoning that went into the making of this decision. This was not a spontaneous gesture made at the spur of the moment. A tortuous line of logical argument ensued with Kṛpācārya, Aśvatthāmā's maternal uncle and another of the three warriors. Kṛpa tried to dissuade Aśvatthāmā in a number of ways. One of these was to postpone the act by referring to the need to discuss with friends and elders the following morning. He even spoke of his own inability to think clearly due to the sorrows inflicted by the war. On a more general register, he spoke of the role of *daiva* and *puruṣakāra* (translated by M. N. Dutt as 'destiny' and 'manliness' respectively, the latter translated by P. Lal as 'effort') in one's actions. He spoke of Duryodhana's wrong-headed actions leading to disastrous results for them all. And he promised fighting the Pāṇḍavas in the morning along with Aśvatthāmā. But Aśvatthāmā persisted in his decision to attack the Pāṇḍava camp unawares that very night. His was an argument that combined reason and emotion. He spoke of his own inability to rest till he avenged the wrongs perpetrated by the Pāṇḍavas. He reasoned on the basis of his own inability to defeat the enemy in fair battle. Thus, unfair attack emerged as the only possible consequence of the reasons of emotion.

Aśvatthāmā's emotions had distinct traces of a Nietzschean *ressentiment*. This aspect is forcefully brought out in Bandyopadhyay's play (2002); in the short and insightful 'Afterword' by Bandyopadhyay for the English translation of the play (2008); and in the 'Afterword' for an anthology of his essays titled 'A Return to Now' (2012a). Like the Nietzschean notion, Aśvatthāmā's emotions and actions have that nature of being pitted tooth and nail against the dominant and yet structured by the very rules of that dominant. The sign of that structuring is in the ontologizing of terror as the transcendental answer to the pragmatic moves of Kṛṣṇa, the archenemy of the Kauravas. As Bhaduri's biographical reconstruction brings out, Aśvatthāmā's moralizing moves only go on to show his own moral depravity. Yet, depravity may be vaunted, in the Nietzschean vein, as the only possible weapon of the defeated. That weapon, as *The Book of Night* underlines, works in reverse yet in accordance to the law of the dominant. But let us not anticipate our arguments.

Anatomy of an Argument

Ultimately, whether through the force of his arguments or through that of his convictions, Aśvatthāmā succeeds in making Kṛpa and Kṛtavarmā participants in his plan. They set out to fulfil the nefarious task of killing the sleeping Pāṇḍavas.

In 'Terror: a Speech After 9–11', Gayatri Chakravorty Spivak begins with the comment: 'War is a cruel caricature of what in us can respond' (2004: 81). A caricature of response is not a true response. It mimics response. It does not respond itself. To be more exact, it responds in a way that is not a response. Ways of responding to the other's moves or the other's words include anger, shame and disgust. But for that, one has to understand and respect the other as other, as that which is not the self, that which is not derivable from, nor a reflection of the self. War caricatures these responses when it destroys the other, kills the other. It is not awake, not aware of the possibility of the other's response. Non-response can occur in multiple ways. Not always does it take the form of direct negation.

One may argue that war is mimicry in yet another sense.[1] A fair war is never originary. The origin of war lies *elsewhere*, in an earlier violence. War is posited as a response to this prior act. The legitimacy of the 'just' war is in its act of responding, in not being the source of the 'first' violence. This claim, I would suggest, is itself the founding gesture of war's violence. That it is only a response, that it follows an originary act of past aggression in a bid to institute justice, is the reason that authenticates war. War has to posit its own past, produce a temporality of reactions, to legitimate its presence. The *Mahābhārata*, in its very structure of circulations of escalating revenge, weaves this teleological ontology of war.

From Spivak's piece, we learn of two aspects of terror. Terror that slides into something called terrorism as a social movement, acts as an antonym for peace as well as for declared war. Terrorism is not full-blown frontal war. From the viewpoint of the dominant state (the US in the world, the government in the nation-state), terrorism is the irrational, unseen response to the 'legitimate' reasons of the state. One does not know terrorism. It acts without being known. It acts nonetheless. For Spivak, '"terror" is the name loosely assigned to the flip side of social movements — extra-state collective action — when such movements use physical violence' (ibid.: 91).

Spivak is also aware of terror as the name of an affect (the second aspect). Going beyond the governmental move to coalesce the affect and the movement to assert victory in anti-terroristic steps, she speaks of the logical dynamic in which terror is branded mindless. The mindless slumber of terror is analogous to the Kantian sublime, Spivak seems to argue. Strictly speaking, and for the spectator, the Kantian sublime is mindless and stupid. For the sublime, by definition, exceeds intelligibility.

> It names a structure: the thing is too big for me to grasp; I am scared; reason kicks in by the mind's immune system and shows me, by implication, that the big thing

[1] Arindam Chakrabarti, in personal communication, pointed at the possibility of such a reading.

> is mindless, "stupid" in the sense in which a stone is stupid, or the body is . . . I call the big mindless thing "sublime" (ibid.: 94).

She calls terror an 'affect beyond affect'. To reduce Spivak's argument to the bare skeleton of formulae, and to read something of my own into her text, I see here the possibilities of a certain formulation. To reach towards the 'affect beyond affect', one does not try to understand. This is what she calls the 'eruption of the ethical'. This eruption is, for her, 'an interruption of the epistemological, which is the attempt to construct the other as object of knowledge' (ibid.: 83). Terror is not an object of knowledge. It is beyond the structure of epistemology. As such, it can only be touched by the eruptions of the ethical. And these eruptions are only imaginable through a training in 'uncoercive reorganization of desires' that, for Spivak, is the task of a humanities classroom worth its name. Not that this is sufficient. Teaching humanities is not the solution for problems in world politics. Only, in the space of the academia, one can hope to get a glimpse of the situation through imaginations thus organized. Again, this is not a task amenable to an easy formulation. It is the responsiveness to the singularities of moments that can impossibly address such a predicament. Obviously, the notion of the ethical she is alluding to is different from a common-sense view of ethics as moral imperatives. The ethical here is an intendedness to the wholly other that inheres in one's being. Ethics here is an ontological predicament. It is an experience of the impossible in the sense of the inherent impossibility of the radical other. Attention to the singularities, singularities that are underivable from (although inalienable at the same time from) the generality of calculable reason, can — it is not necessary that it always would — reach out to the ethical in this sense. Calculations in the social science mode have something to learn from the humanities' training of desire and imagination. Always to remember, in the latter, this is not a guarantee but a possibility.

Reading the *Sauptikaparvan* in times of contemporary terror may point at some such moments of sublimity. It can be an exercise in the hearing of the unexpected murmurs of the ethical as the terrible. As the three warriors approached the camps of the Pāṇḍavas, they encountered a dreadful apparition. The description of this figure is reminiscent of Śiva, and a little later he would actually turn out to be Śivā himself. When Aśvatthāmā hurled weapons at him, they were all devoured by this figure. All weapons, from the arrows to fiery maces, proved futile. Aśvatthāmā, then, stopped attacking him and started worshipping Śiva, his favourite god. Dreadful figures seemed to attack him. Aśvatthāmā submitted wholeheartedly, offering his life to Śiva. And then he was rewarded:

> For honouring [Kṛṣṇa] and at his request I have protected the Pāñcālas and displayed various sorts of illusion.
>
> By protecting the Pāñcālas I have honoured him. They have, however, been assailed by Time. The lease of their lives is over.

> Having said so to the great Aśvatthāmā, the divine Mahādeva entered Aśvatthāmā's body after giving him an excellent and polished sword (*Sauptikaparvan* 7.62–64).

Was it Aśvatthāmā or was it Śiva himself in the body of the great warrior who started the great carnage? It started with the slaying of Dhṛṣṭadyumna. Avenging the inglorious slaughter of his father Droṇācārya by Dhṛṣṭadyumna, Aśvatthāmā killed him with his bare hands and feet. He did not use any weapon, thus humiliating the enemy even in murder. One by one, the Pāñcāla and the Pāṇḍava warriors were slain. It was a gory, cruel and absolute destruction. To the dying soldiers, Aśvatthāmā looked like a scary *rākṣasa* (demon). His body was covered with blood gushing forth from the murdered. It was dark, thousands of bodies covered up the ground, and the confused army fought among themselves.[2] Those who escaped Aśvatthāmā were slain by Kṛpa and Kṛtavarmā at the entrance of the camp. Finally, all — except the five Pāṇḍava brothers, Kṛṣṇa and Sātyakī who were not there at the camp — were murdered. The camp was set to fire.

The next day, the three warriors conveyed this message to Duryodhana. He died satiated in revenge. The Pāṇḍavas, on hearing the news of the massacre, were stricken with grief. For Yudhiṣṭhira, this signified the futility of it all:

> I have defeated my enemies,
> and am now
> myself defeated.
> . . .
> The losers have won –
> and the winners
> have lost!
>
> We killed brothers, friends,
> fathers, sons, relatives,
> well-wishers and counsellors
> and grandsons –
> and we thought we won.
> But we have lost. (*Sauptikaparvan* 10.9–11)
> . . .
> Foolish indeed is the victor
> who lives
> to regret his conquest.
> What kind of victory is his? (*Sauptikaparvan* 10.13).

Grief was followed by vengeance. As Bhīma went in search of Aśvatthāmā, now hiding from the consequences of his deeds, Kṛṣṇa advised Yudhiṣṭhira and Arjuna

[2] The trope of armies fighting among themselves without seeing each other recurs in the *Mahābhārata* in other occasions. A famous reference to such a situation in a 'modern' text is in 'Dover Beach': 'Where Ignorant Armies Clash by Night' (Arnold 1867).

to follow him. He knew Aśvatthāmā had the deadly weapon of *brahmaśira*. About Aśvatthāmā, Kṛṣṇa had the following to say:

> He is anger-obsessed.
> He is wicked-*atmaned*.
> He is whimsical and crafty.
> He is cruel. He knows how to shoot
> the Brahmaśira missile (*Sauptikaparvan* 12.40).

Seeing the angry Bhīma with Nakula as his charioteer approach him with weapons, Aśvatthāmā let go the all-powerful *brahmaśira*, asking it to destroy all Pāṇḍavas. Interestingly, the infinitely destructive *brahmaśira* was animated in a blade of *īṣikā* grass. The *īṣikā* also played a major destructive role of in the later part of *Mahābhārata*, in the penultimate chapter, the *Mausalaparvan*. There, it was Kṛṣṇa who animated the *īśikā* to destroy his own clan, the Yādavas. Unlike the *brahmaśira* that animated a single blade, in the *Mausalaparvan*, each blade that the Yādavas threw at each other turned into *musala* (club), a deadly weapon. Kṛṣṇa, the god-incarnate, watched ineffectually as his relatives and his friends killed each other. In *Mahabharater Katha*, Buddhadeb Bose has noted how the *Mausalaparvan* reiterates the pointlessness of the Kurukṣetra war, the banality and ineffectuality of violence turned inward. He uses the expressions *biśuddha unmattatā* or 'unalloyed madness' and *chooranta buddhilop* or 'extreme senselessness' (2010: 161). The latter term may also be translated as 'extreme loss of reasonableness'. Yet, one has to remember that this madness flowed from a reason, the loss of reason followed a certain use of reason, as in the 'original' Kurukṣetra war. The little blade of *īśikā* turning into the all-destroying *brahmaśira* may yet be another metaphor for the possible banality of mass destruction, of the menace of synchronic global death in the everyday.[3] One might remember at this point that the Kurukṣetra war itself had brought in the possibility of the synchronicity of death in the sense of an interruption in the diachronic sequence of death across generations. When grandfathers and uncles had conspired together to kill the boy Abhimanyu in an unjust war, the diachronicity of death was already actively disrupted. Yet, it was still a possibility, one among many others, and not an imminent and unavoidable future. A displacement of that unavoidability would soon mark the life-cycle of yet another 'boy' of the future generation, Parikṣit. But let me not move fast in the narrative of my argument.

Arjuna, upon a quick appeal from Kṛṣṇa, did shoot his own *brahmāstra* to counter and neutralize the effects of Aśvatthāmā's weapon. Before he activated the *brahmāstra*, Arjuna did not forget to chant mantras for the well-being of his

[3] For the theorization of the possibility of synchronic death — which interrupts the 'natural' diachronic order of death — following the nuclear armament of the world, see Bandyopadhyay (2009).

brothers and even of Aśvatthāmā and for paying respect to the gurus and the gods. Then, the weapon for the destruction of the Pāṇḍavas and the weapon to make it ineffective remained poised against each other.

> Shot from the Gāndhīva,
> flaming with *maha*-splendour,
> the missile dazzled
> like the all-consuming fire
> of universal dissolution
> at the end of a yuga.
>
> And the weapon discharged
> by Droṇa's radiant son
> burst
> into fearful flames
> like a colossal *maṇḍala*
> of fire.
>
> And suddenly,
> thunder pealed
> thousands of meteors
> fell from the sky,
> and fear gripped
> all living creatures.
>
> Cacophony crackled
> in the sky,
> and lapping flames
> licked the directions.
> The hill-forest-and-plant-
> filled earth trembled (*Sauptikaparvan* 14.7–10).

The two weapons could destroy the universe with their impact. The sages Nārada and Vyāsa positioned themselves between the weapons to prevent such a consequence. They appeared like the *pāvaka* (fire) that saved the world. But, while Arjuna could retract the weapon, Aśvatthāmā could not. Arjuna, after reminding the sages that he had used the *brahmāstra* only to save their own selves from the effects of Aśvatthāmā's *brahmaśira*, withdrew his weapon. As Aśvatthāmā pleaded his inability to take back his weapon, Vyāsa asked him to direct the weapon to the pregnant bellies of the Pāṇḍava women. However, Aśvatthāmā was to give away to the Pāṇḍavas the divine stone (*maṇi*) he wore on his forehead. That would leave him devoid of strength and defence. The *brahmaśira* struck Parikṣit, the fetus in the womb of Uttarā, Abhimanyu's widowed wife. With the sole heir of the Pāṇḍava line dead, Kṛṣṇa used his powers to rejuvenate him in the womb. So, Parikṣit both died and regained his life in the womb. He would later become the king and rule for many years. The terror that had the possibility of exterminating the world with the whole human race thus caused the death of a foetus — though a fetus destined to be the king — and that too, momentarily. Was this death? Or was it something else — a temporary cessation of life — that, by definition, could not be the irrevocable death? Before going into the implications of the event at the end of this essay, one should look closely at the moment of terror that we just passed through.

A Pathology of the Everyday

One can distinguish between terror as an *affect* and terrorism as a *social movement.* Spivak (2004) insists on this distinction. By resisting the affect of terror, by refusing to be terrorized by the terrorist, the (normal and dominant form of) society tries to face terrorism as a social movement. But what is the structure of terror as an affect? What is terror? These very large questions, as everyone knows, are deceptive. Most of the times, they are non-questions. The answers are too general to have a specific content. Yet, sometimes, they produce interesting responses. Bandyopadhyay, in his essay 'Defining *Terror*: A Freudian Exercise' (2012b) has pursued Freud's theorization to come up with one such explanation. He defines 'terror' in the following manner:

> *Terror is that state of the affective state during which the subject expects a known danger threatening from within and/or without to fall suddenly from some unexpected quarter* (ibid.: 441; italics in the original).

This definition tries to spell out the specificity of 'terror' in its relations with the other three 'danger situations' that Freud speaks of: *fright*, *fear* and *anxiety.* Bandyopadhyay prepares a tabular representation of classification where *fright* and *fear* are conditions produced after facing a danger-situation, unexpected and indefinable in the former, and expected and definable in the latter. *Anxiety* is the condition of expectation of danger, not after one faces the situation. Terror combines expectation with the certainty of knowledge and the certainty of danger with the uncertainty of the source. The reaction is that of a combination of preparedness and helplessness, the nature of the perpetrator being abstract yet specific.

The moment of the impending collision of the two weapons is a moment of terror. One knows that destruction is certain and imminent. However, one does not know how it will happen and at what moment. One also does not know the outcome of the clash of the two weapons for certain. Yet, at the moment of terror, does one not have an inkling of hope, hope against the certainty of devastation, hope of the world-destroying encounter resulting in the momentary death (an oxymoron) of the fetus? The unanticipatability of the moment gets translated into the hope of survival. In the text of the *Mahābhārata*, this magical moment is ontologized, and hope gets embodied in the event. Yet, this is not unalloyed survival. It is survival shot through with death, for the economy of revenge marks this very moment of remembrance. The death of the fetus is the symptom of the wound of vengeance that haunts the body of the narrative. Parikṣit, the would-be child in the womb, would be central in the chronicling of the *Mahābhārata* story. In the repeated tellings of the tale of Kurus, Parikṣit's court plays a crucial role. Re-membering is marked by the dis-memberings that the revenge achieved.

Arindam Chakrabarti has written at length on 'the moral psychology of revenge' (2005, 2008). He closely interrogates the 'psychology of revenge', that is, the moral defence upon which that psychology is premised. He questions the idea of getting even with the one who had perpetrated the 'first injustice', of the notion of retributive justice implicit in revenge, and also the idea of 'teaching a lesson' to the aggressor. He stresses upon the fact that structurally the act of revenge can never be equal to the first act of aggression. If its effects are the same (on some imaginary scale), it seems to be less as it lacks the element of being unprovoked. If the act of revenge tries to even out this inequality by increasing its effects, the target of revenge may take this as uncalled for and go in for an increased retaliation. Thus, a spiralling of violence goes on ad infinitum. The act of revenge can never re-store the loss of the earlier act. It simply replaces one loss with another. Thus, Chakrabarti argues against the dominant form of morality in the psychology of revenge. His call is not for forgiveness and forgetting but for a positive resistance (in the sense of an act beyond the structure of the initial aggression) to violence in its remembrance. The argument, at the level of analytical philosophical tradition, is convincing. It shares with that tradition an emphasis on the secure subject as the individual who decides on the basis of moral judgment in a given condition. My point is to remember the constitution of this very subject of action through a structure of events that acts way beyond the empirical contexts of the action. The moral intentions of the subject get skewed by the traces of events that constitute the subject. The will to revenge is a mark of that displacement. As such, an awareness of the dangers of a moral psychology may very well go along with a sense of inability to not act according to it. The acts of Kṛṣṇa may be seen to reflect this inability to deviate from revenge, even when he is aware of the disasters that such an action would bring about, even when he knows about its futility and the escalation of violence it will result in, even in him who for the narrative is a god incarnate. In his essay 'A Return to Now', Sibaji Bandyopadhyay presents this predicament in a specific context:

> We are left wondering: if Kṛṣṇa was forewarned, why did he not prevent the disaster? Why did he only save himself and the other six? Was he then a fatalist? Did the 'Superself' think he was powerless in the face of Fate? That even with the help of 'Superman' Arjuna he could not unsettle a cosmic plan already settled? (2012: 489).

Bandyopadhyay speaks of other possibilities and keeps the question open. I read the 'fatalism' of Kṛṣṇa as a symptom of the structural constitution of the subject. This is not to absolve the subject who takes revenge from the responsibility of his/her action, but to think of the mechanism of interpellation of that very subjectivity. The intentions of the actor are unavoidably marked by the structures of being within which s/he is inserted. The apparent paradox of being responsible for what one cannot do is a predicament that the text of the *Mahābhārata* often enacts.

The awareness of the constructed nature of the subject does not take away the need to address the intentions of the subject. Even when one is attending the mechanisms of subject formation, one has to deal with the dynamic of the subject in the register of its purposive functions. Elsewhere (Das 2010: 1–36), I have discussed this necessity of addressing the intendedness of the subject in the register of ideology along with a tracing of power mechanisms that constitute the subject. Power mechanisms can chart the field of possibilities opened up to the production of the subject. For attending the unanticipatable vagaries of the workings of the subject within that field, one has to bring in the question of ideologies, though in a particular register. This register of thinking of ideologies of the subject even when the secure subject has already been dissolved into its production mechanisms, has been inaugurated at least since Althusser's notion of interpellation. In the present context, to think of the responsibility of the one who participates in the economy of revenge — being always and already inserted into that economy (logically) prior to that participation — it is not enough to invoke the inevitable markings of revenge that constitute her/his being. Chakrabarti's attempts to interrogate the moral psychology of such action have relevance in this context. Spivak talks about the non-coercive reorganization of desires that make possible the task of imagining the terrorist. The violence of terrorism cannot be ended by 'ruthless extermination', she asserts. 'I believe that we must be able to imagine our opponent as a human being, and to understand the signification of his or her action' (Chakravorty Spivak 2004: 93).

This seemingly liberal and humanist call for 'understanding' has some import even in the awareness of the structure of *ressentiment* that marks the being of the 'human'. This 'understanding', as I understand it, is not 'knowing'. It is the imagination to reach out to the 'other'. One has to remember that imagination, here, is also a short-hand term for something not reducible to that name. Imagination is a metaphor for 'figuring': giving figure to the other who is radically different from the self. One has to figure with the tools that one wields, with the tools of the self. Yet, one has to figure the other who is not reducible to, nor derivable from, the self. This is an impossible task. Imagining the terrorist is the impossible task one has to perform if one wants to reorganize the intentions of the self beyond the constructions of revenge. The moment of terror may, not necessarily though, let one have a glimpse of an other beyond the constructions of reason. The terrorist is outside reason. The sublimity of terror has a hint of the outside, a hint which is necessary, if not enough, for the figuration of the terrorist.

Death as a trope is constitutive of terror in more than one sense. In a general sense, death is the trope of a radical futurity underivable from the present. Death, by definition, is the experience one cannot experience, for at the moment of death, there is no experience. This is different from the experience of dying which is varied and depends on the contexts of society across time and space. Thus, death, which is the most certain aspect of one's existence, is also an instance of the unanticipatable. It shares the unanticipatability of the outside to the self. The figuration of death (not that of dying) is an impossible task. One has to encounter some 'unverifiable' generalities in order to be responsible. The nature of this responsibility is complicated. An undifferentiated ethic of responsibility for all others may consist in a non-response to each. This is the act of giving name to a relationship to many that blurs the specificity of each. The relationship to each 'other' is a singularity. In the context of violence and embodiment, the ultimate singularity of the one event, death, reflects the unanticipatability of the *event* — of any event not reducible to the predictions of a prior calculus. In another, more specific, sense, death is an inalienable aspect of terror. Death, the ultimate unknown ('the undiscovered country from whose bourn no traveller returns'), shares with terror the anxiety over the unknown. As in death, so in terror, the attempt to figure the unknown is a crucial part of negotiating with the phenomenon. Terror has in it the unanticipatable anticipation of death. The moment of the two weapons is pregnant with that suggestion. The resolution of the situation is also reminiscent of the taming of that moment into a safer ontology of momentary death of the future king, marked strongly by the dynamic of reproductive heteronormativity. The terror of imminent synchronic death is displaced onto a temporary interruption of the generational line of the Pāṇḍavas. Yet, the resolution that this event enacts is again temporary and contingent. The text of the *Mahābhārata* carries the mark of death forward into the destruction of the Yādavas. The act of Kṛṣṇa saves the moment in the *Sauptikparvan*. It returns as the utter inability to act of that same Kṛṣṇa in the *Mausalaparvan*. The effects of the *īśikā* grass pregnant with the *brahmaśira* are nullified in the former instance. The *īśikā* grass is activated to deadly weapons in the latter. The former event keeps alive the dynasty of the Pāṇḍavas. The latter ends that of the Yādavas. The *Mahābhārata*, as a text, thus forgets nothing.[4] Before going into the related questions of violence, remembering and the relationship to the other, we will dwell a little on the way the *brahmaśira* is deflected onto the womb of Uttarā. In a pragmatic sense, this is a comparatively intriguing and placatory resolution of a dangerous situation. The possibility of the all-encompassing violence that threatened the world has been channellized into the

[4] Buddhadeb Bose (1974) and Sibaji Bandyopadhyay (2010) have commented acutely on the repetition — with displacements characteristic of memory — of the scene of Kurukṣetra in the *Mausalaparvan*.

womb of a single woman. But what made this deflection possible? What economy of gendered (with the connotations of genre and generation) sex-differentiation organized this possibility? There is a calculation in the deflection of violence thus instituted. The fetus can be killed because it is not fully human. The fetus cannot be killed because it carries the ideological burden of reproductive heteronormativity. It has to continue generations. The fetus becomes the target; it, in its male form, can become the target of the all-destroying *brahmaśira* because it carries the burden of human generational continuity. That continuity is the metaphor for humanity in the given context. The female fetus lacks this quality. The female fetus, only because it is female, does not belong to the category 'human'. In a very different context, Derrida has spoken about the inherent anthropocentrism as male-centrism active in the structure of 'sacrifice' in the sense of a 'noncriminal putting to death' (Derrida 1991: 112). The structure of being that is premised upon sacrifice of the 'other', a structure that allows for this killing which is not the killing of the human, is built upon the exclusion of all categories which are not included in the 'human'. The 'animal' is the metaphor for all 'others' that can be so killed. One may, at this juncture, be reminded of how the abortion debate is displaced in certain areas of the global south onto questions of female feticide. In the present context, Parikṣit's death could replace the death of the world because it had the metaphoric capacity to do so. And yet, this death had to be transitory to keep the 'human' line alive. We have already discussed how the *Mahābhārata*'s text re-membered this moment in a latter event of mass destruction of the Yādavas.

Remembering is a dangerous act. It involves the task of imagining the other. This task, as Derrida has shown, takes the form of a certain cannibalism. Eating may be a metaphor to think of the relationship to the intimate other. Penelope Deutscher (1998) refers to Derrida's speech after the death of Paul de Man. Derrida talks about his friend becoming, in and through his speech, an object of the speaker's memories and speculations. The act of speaking *to* and *with* him gives place to that of speaking *of* him. Derrida emphasizes the 'resistance and excess of de Man to his memory'. The mourning for the friend is not speakable or nameable and hence is not contained in the memory of the living. Deutscher speaks of an encryptment of the other within the self. This encryptment is not the same as what she calls the digestive assimilation of the other in mourning. Here, there is a reference to Abraham and Torok's use of Freud's distinction between mourning and melancholia. Here, 'introjection' of normal mourning (that totally interiorizes the dead other so that it is no longer an other) is opposed to 'incorporation' (as a failed mourning where the other 'continues to inhabit me, as a stranger'). Derrida questions this introjection/ incorporation binary. He points at the inevitable remains of the other that constitute the self and changes the issue of mourning to that of an ethics of alterity. Mourning becomes a figure to think the self.

In this notion, introjection of the other is the way in which the other is an assimilated part of the self. The success of mourning is in the act of 'eating' and 'digesting' the other to form the self inalienably in terms of the other. Thus, introjection, which signifies a sort of disintegration of the other into unrecognizable elements appropriated into the self, is also a process that suggests the making of the self in terms of the other. The act of incorporation that maintains the integrity of the other within the self, keeping the other inaccessible in a crypt, is also the process of simple enveloping and not an active engagement with the other. Thus, an active engagement disaggregates the other and a respectful distance does not engage. To quote Derrida:

> We can only live this experience in the form of an aporia . . . where faithful interiorization bears the other and constitutes him in me . . . and then the other no longer quite seems to be the other because we grieve for him and bear him *in us* . . . And inversely: an aborted interiorization is at the same time a respect for the other as other, a sort of tender rejection, a movement of renunciation which leaves the other alone, outside, over there in his death, outside of us (1989: 167, emphasis orginal).

Interrogating Aporias

The aporia reached in terms of the two opposing poles of successful and failed interiorization is not enough to access the complications of the various possible situations. One has to be careful enough to remember this predicament. The fetus in the womb is a figure very near to the encrypted other. Its identity has a certain detachment from that of the (m)other who bears it in her womb. Yet, we have just now accounted the ways in which the fetus remains marked by machinations of a patriarchy that constitutes the mother. Parikṣit's predicament of dying and the inability to die both stem from his markings as the sole heir to the Pāṇḍava clan. The encrypted other is not as distant from the 'self' as it seems to be. Yet, the need to think the processes of othering in terms of eating remains. And with it remains the imperative of reducing the implicit violence in the act, the need to 'eat well'. Thinking of the self as ever always a cannibal self, one knows the impossibility and the inevitability of this cannibalism:

> The moral question is . . . not, . . . should one eat or not eat, eat this and not that, the living or the nonliving, man or animal, but since *one must* eat in any case and since it is and tastes good to eat, and since there's no other definition of good . . ., *how* for goodness' sake should one *eat well* . . . ? (Derrida 1991: 115, emphasis orginal).

One cannot provide a ready answer to this question. One may only point at the necessity to keep the question alive. And what better text to keep it in the throes of an ethical conundrum than the *itihāsa* also called *Mahābhārata*?

Looking closely into a moment of expansive violence at the end of the Kurukṣetra war, one arrives at the violence constitutive of one's being, the moment of cannibalism that implicates the 'human' self. The carnage of the sleeping Pāṇḍava army and its allies escalates into the possibility of the destruction of the world at the moment of terror when Aśvatthāmā's *brahmaśira* confronts Arjuna's *brahmāstra*. The terrible moment fizzles out into the momentary death of Parikṣit. The moment is displaced forward into the destruction of the Yādavas as Kṛṣṇa watches ineffectually at the wholesale massacre of his clan. It is a total loss of the valiant maleness of the hero as Arjuna fails to 'protect' the Yādava women from the hands of the 'lowly' marauders. If one then goes back to the moment of terror in the *Sauptikaparvan*, what strikes first is that the incomprehensible terrible moment is produced through a clash of reasons, and not through unreason. Even the emotions of Aśvatthāmā had their own reasonable explanations and their own reasoned itineraries. The moment of terror as an outside to reason had been produced through the dynamics of reason. The resolutions had been marked by the reasons of certain structures of hegemony. The second point that becomes important at this juncture is that the terror produced by *ressentiment* repeats the structure of the rational terror of the dominant. It may even be more coercive and vengeful. Reason and emotion do not form a neat binary of opposed elements. Thirdly, in the given context of the *Mahābhārata*, the workings of reproductive heteronormativity take an interesting turn. The target of *brahmaśira* is deflected from the living Pāṇḍava brothers to the womb, the bearer of the male line of generation. This deflection of the target was also a neutralization. Thus, the threads of heterosexist generational textile had been pliant enough to absorb the shocks of imminent terror. Both the opposing sides in the moment of terror are human. The sublimity of human destruction — the sublime is not always aesthetic — is displaced onto the not-fully-human fetus. Yet, the fetus is also marked by the teleology of being human. The destruction is also displaced, one should not forget, in time and space to a later-day Dvārakā. And finally, the structures of violence, counter-violence and *ressentiments* acting in the production of terror do not absolve the responsibilities of the subject/s who produce or encounter terror. It remains necessary to address the intentions of the subjects who are produced as terrorizing or terror-hounded even when one is aware of the constructions of abstract power relations that operate to produce these subjects. Reading the *Sauptikaparvan* of the *Mahābhārata*, one may have glimpse of a certain training in the reorganization of desires and imaginations that might, and it may pretty well might not, render one's self a little responsive — if not responsible — to the mundane excesses of a terrorized world.

References

Bandyopadhyay, Sibaji. 2012a. 'A Return to Now', in *Sibaji Bandyopadhyay Reader*, 473–504. New Delhi: Worldview Publications.

———. 2012b. 'Defining *Terror*: A Freudian Exercise', in *Sibaji Bandyopadhyay Reader*, 359–472. New Delhi: Worldview Publications.

Bandyopadhyay, Sibaji. 2010. '*Mahābhārata*: Ekti Ashchorjo Muhurto', *Anustup* 45(1): 117–63.

———. 2008. *The Book of Night: A Moment from the Mahābhārata*, trans. Ipsita Chanda. Kolkata: Seagull Books.

———. 2002. *Uttampurush Ekbachan: Ekti Bhan*. Kolkata: Disha Sahitya.

Bhaduri, Nrisinha Prasad. 2009. *Mahabharater Pratinayak*. Kolkata: Ananda Publishers.

Bose, Buddhadeb. 2010[1974]. *Mahabharater Katha*. Kolkata: M. C. Sarkar and Sons Private Limited.

Chakrabarti, Arindam. 2008. 'Prasanga: Pratishodh', *Anustup*, 43(1): 15–41.

Chakravorty Spivak, Gayatri. 2004. 'Terror: A Speech After 9-11', *Boundary 2*, 31(2): 81–111.

———. 2005. 'The Moral Psychology of Revenge', *Journal of Human Values* 11(1): 31–36.

Das, Anirban. 2010. *Toward a Politics of the (Im)Possible: The Body in Third World Feminisms*. London, New York and New Delhi: Anthem Press.

Derrida, Jacques. 1991. '"Eating Well," or the Calculation of the Subject: An Interview with Jacques Derrida', in Eduardo Cadava, Peter Connor and Jean-Luc Nancy (eds), *Who Comes After the Subject*, 96–119. New York and London: Routledge.

———. 1989. *Memoires: For Paul de Man*, trans. Cecile Lindsay, Jonathan Culler, Eduardo Cadava, and Peggy Kamuf. Revised Edition. New York: Columbia University Press.

Deutscher, Penelope. 1998. 'Mourning the Other, Cultural Cannibalism, and the Politics of Friendship (Jacques Derrida and Luce Irigaray)', *Differences: A Journal of Feminist Cultural Studies*, 10(3): 159–84.

Hari Damodar Velankar (ed.). 1948. *The Mahābhārata for the First Time Critically Edited*, vol. 12: *Sauptikaparvan*. Pune: Bhandarkar Oriental Research Institute.

Dutt, M. N. (trans.). 2004. *Mahabharata: Translated into English from Original Sanskrit Text*, vol. 6. New Delhi: Parimal Publications.

P. Lal (trans.). 2008. *The Mahābhārata of Vyāsa*, vol. 10: *The Sauptika Parva*. Kolkata: Writers Workshop.

Hiṃsā–Ahiṃsā in the *Mahābhārata*

The Lonely Position of Yudhiṣṭhira

Gangeya Mukherji

I

The exercise of tracing the idea of non-violence in the *Mahābhārata* may appear as misdirected in view of the ostensible fact that the *Mahābhārata* is to all intents and purposes a text about violence and war. 'The daily happenings on the battle field are narrated in such greater detail that the *Mahābhārata* is known as the story mostly of a horrible war between them [cousins], with other stories here and there' (Chaturvedi 2007: 114). Coupled with this, the widespread impression is one of a general difficulty in compressing a massive and variegated literary work into one overarching theme. Indicating at the difficulties involved in any such endeavour, Vidya Nivas Mishra mentions some of the older commentaries on the *Mahābhārata*, written with an intention to outline one main theme as the central concern of the epic.[1] The *Mahābhārata* is explicitly not primarily a socio-political or philosophical text with cleanly demarcated premises, but essentially a work of literature containing the many dimensions of a human life. 'Though woven with myth and history and impregnated with Philosophy and Dharma, the *Mahābhārata* is primarily a poem. This fact has often been overlooked' (Mishra 1990: 19). But perhaps naturally, there are different and equally emphatic views on this problem regarding the *Mahābhārata*. Mukund Lath (1990: 113) calls the epic 'a very thoughtful work': 'It is not just an epic; in fact, one of the criticisms raised against it has been that it is too thoughtful. It cannot be an epic it contains too much thought'. Lath has traced *ānṛśaṃsya*,[2] along with *ahiṃsā*, as the central idea of the *Mahābhārata*. It will be relevant in this connection to point out that

[1] Mishra (1990: 19) mentions mainly the commentaries written by Madhavacharya, Sadananda Yati, Nilkantha Dikshita, and Anandavardhana.

[2] Lath states that in the *Mahābhārata* particularly, the term *ānṛśaṃsya* contains a 'supreme significance'. He defines *ānṛśaṃsya* as embodying the attitude of not being *nṛsaṃsa*. 'The word *nṛsaṃsa* is common enough in Sanskrit literature; it literally means one who injures man, from which other meanings follow such as mischievous, noxious, cruel, base, vile, malicious. *Ānṛśamsya* would then mean an attitude where such qualities are absent. But the word has more than a negative connotation; it signifies good-will, a fellow feeling, a deep sense of the other. A word which occurs often with *ānṛśaṃsya*, therefore, is *anukrośa*, to cry with another, to feel anothers pain' (1990: 115).

even though *hiṃsā* seems normally located in the epic, it is difficult to find sustained glorification of war per se, in the voice of the epic. A large body of scholars have agreed that the concern with non-violence as being a major agent in human relations is in fact central to a work that otherwise is taken to narrate mainly a destructive fratricidal war. Danielle Feller Jatavallabhula, one of the scholars who view the *Mahābhārata* war as a sacrifice, and in using the concept of sacrificial violence to negate its violent content, nevertheless draws the conclusion that the central theme of the *Mahābhārata* is the futility of war:

> On the whole, the pathos and the disgust with life reflected in the last *parvans* of the Mahābhārata are such, that one would feel tempted to say that the ultimate message of this text (and one which is certainly in keeping with the then-emerging idea of non-violence, but somewhat ironically, goes against the teachings on the social *dharma* of *kṣatriyas*) is that battles are not worth fighting and hence, sacrifices not worth performing (1999: 98).

But the *Mahābhārata* also foregrounds the inevitability of war in the affairs of state. This inevitability of war is conveyed through descriptions of situations and conflicts that are seemingly resolvable only through violent means. War also seemingly appears acceptable in the Brahminic tradition wherein the main aim of life is the preservation of *dharma* rather than the practice of *ahiṃsā*.

The justifications of war are twice conveyed in detail by Draupadī and the Pāṇḍava princes to Yudhiṣṭhira: for the first time when they attempted to convince Yudhiṣṭhira to go to war against the Kauravas; and for a second time when they attempted to dissuade a remorse-stricken Yudhiṣṭhira from his resolve to renounce the world, at the end of the war. Prominently, Kṛṣṇa asked both Yudhiṣṭhira and Arjuna to wage war for claiming the rights of the Pāṇḍavas, which he said was their duty: he said so to Yudhiṣṭhira towards the close of the *Udyogaparvan* and to Arjuna, mainly in the second chapter of the *Bhagavadgītā*. Similarly, in the *Udyogaparvan*, that self-respect and discharge of *Kṣatriya* duty intensely demanded the waging of war was conveyed first by Kuntī to Kṛṣṇa with the request that the same be, in turn, conveyed to her sons; and then by Karṇa to Kṛṣṇa, the former admitting to being convinced of the moral claims of Yudhiṣṭhira and also of the certainty of his victory, but even then praying to Kṛṣṇa against the averting of the fratricidal war, as it would be a great martial sacrificial rite worthy of the warrior class which should die heroically on the battlefield rather than in a nondescript manner from old age. Arguments contending that violence was a fact of life were also advanced in a different setting and context by the Dharmavyādha ('righteous' meat-seller) in the *Āraṇyakaparvan*. In the beginning of the *Śāntiparvan*, Bhīṣma counselled Yudhiṣṭhira to be always prepared for action and that the earth swallows up the king who is disinclined to battle.

The arguments in favour of the virtue of forbearance and against war were mainly advanced by Yudhiṣṭhira while replying to his brothers and Draupadī, as also, prominently, to Kṛṣṇa in the *Udyogaparvan*. The *Udyogaparvan* also contains a sincere and desperate appeal by Sañjaya to Yudhiṣṭhira, that his going to war would represent a falling from the path of virtue that he had ever so unswervingly followed. In addition to these dialogues, the idea of *ahiṃsā* is debated in the *Śāntiparvan*, which follows the conclusion of the war. These ideas of non-violence are organized mainly around four broad themes.[3] First, they are recorded as a general reaction against the sacrificial killing of animals, in a number of passages that describe kings, priests and ascetics expressing a horror of such sacrificial violence termed as *yajña hiṃsā*. This moral revulsion is said to have led, subsequently, to the substitution of living animals with vegetal/meditative oblations; according to Gandhi, the *Bhagavadgītā*, 'in deference to the moral spirit of the times, transformed and expanded the meanings of words, like "*yajña*", making *japa-yajña* (*yajña* in the form of the muttering of the sacred syllable) the "sovereign of sacrifices"' (Bedekar 1958: 121). The fact that the growing acceptance of the belief in *ahiṃsā* mainly caused vegetable offerings to gradually replace the traditional offerings of cooked flesh and *soma* at the sacrifices is also mentioned elsewhere.[4] The second theme emphasizes on *ahiṃsā* as the redemptive path in

[3] The discussion of *ahiṃsā* in the *Mahābhārata* in terms of these four broad categories draws initially on Bedekar (1958).

[4] Peter Hill, for instance, states: 'The great Vedic sacrifices, with their demand for animal offerings, are openly disparaged in various parts of the Epic. The growing concern with *ahiṃsā* or non-violence would seem to be the principal explanation' (2001: 249). In this connection, Hill mentions a well-known incident in the *Āśvamedhikaparvan*. A mongoose (or rather, anger previously transformed into a mongoose by a curse) came to tell Yudhiṣṭhira at the conclusion of the grand *Aśvamedha* sacrifice he had just performed that it was yet not 'equal to a *prastha* of powdered barley given by a liberal Brahman of Kurukshetra who was observing the *Unccha* vow' (Ganguli 2007, vol. XII, p. 155). The said Brahmin who was very poor had on one occasion offered entirely the meagre meal that his family was about to partake of, to a hungry guest who was actually the deity of Righteousness in disguise (ibid.: 155–62). Hill considers this episode 'as an interpolation reflecting society's growing concern with non-violence, a doctrine fervently promulgated by the Buddha and Mahavira, and preached by Asoka' (Hill 2001: 250). At the conclusion of this episode, Vaiśampāyana told Janmejaya that sacrifices were not to be given undue prominence, and that countless *ṛṣis* had attained paradise because of their penances. 'Abstention from injury as regards all creatures, contentment, conduct, sincerity, penances, self-restraint, truthfulness, and gifts are each equal in point of merit to sacrifice'(Ganguli 2007, vol. 12: 155). Vaiśampāyana further narrated to Janmejaya an incident where *ṛṣis*, who had been invited to a sacrifice performed by Indra, on seeing the misery of the animals about to be sacrificially slaughtered, protested to Indra against the principle of sacrificial killing that they called inauspicious and futile: 'The destruction of creatures can never be said to be an act of righteousness'. He was advised to offer, according to the *āgamas*, seeds of grain instead of living creatures (ibid.: 162 –64). It has been also opined that the story of anger appearing in the form of the aforementioned mongoose, is an interpolation by later priesthood which found the

a world which is overshadowed by the inevitability of death, with all vanity and ambition being ephemeral and ultimately ineffectual. This was emotively conveyed by Medhāvī to his father (Ganguli 2007, vol. 9: 286–89). Medhāvī understood the world as headed fast to destruction, in order to withstand which the quotidian religious activities of individuals were of no avail. He, instead, advocated the life of a renunciant that was lived without the taint of violence and passions, was aimed at realizing the ultimate truth of existence, and was the only way of transcending death. The ascetic Kapila and Syūmaraśmi, too, debated this very principle of the non-violent life which was possible to live only outside the secular world (ibid.: 255–66). On the other hand, the dialogue between the Brāhmaṇa ascetic Jajāli and the grocer Tulādhara was on the converse principle of non-violent life liveable in the material world itself and constitutes the third idea of *ahiṃsā*. This idea censures any form of livelihood or sacrifice that entailed cruelty to or death of living creatures. It considers this principle as having been enunciated in the Vedas. There is an implicit assumption that non-attachment, and even renunciation, is the enabling virtue for living a life that is non-violent to its core and that has been recommended in all the traditional tenets of wisdom and conduct. The practice of slavery that involves cruelty to human beings and such professions that routinely cause distress to animals as the ploughing of fields, the pulling of loads, as also the killing and selling the meat of animals and fish, are uniformly condemned. 'That mode of living which is founded upon a total harmlessness towards all creatures or (in case of actual necessity) upon a minimum of such harm, is the highest morality' (ibid.: 233). At this stage, Jajāli posed a question which reflects the constitutive principles of the position that violence is generatively located in the universe — a position also held by Arjuna in his arguments with Yudhiṣṭhira in the *Rājadharmānuśāsanaparvan* in the *Śāntiparvan* of the *Mahābhārata*.

> This course of duty that thou, O holder of scales, preachest, closes the door of heaven against all creatures and puts a stop to the very means of their subsistence. From agriculture comes food. That food offers subsistence even to thee. With the aid of animals and of crops and herbs, human beings, O trader, are enabled to support their existence. From animals and food sacrifices flow. Thy doctrines smack of atheism. This world will come to an end if the means by which life is supported have to be abandoned (ibid.: 238).

Responding to this possible reference to a predominant philosophy of the heterodox sects, the Tulādhara attempted to clarify and distance himself from any questioning of the Brahminical tradition, not so much by an adequate exposition

---

otherwise noble principle enunciated in the story, of an austere sacrifice performed under conditions of deprivation being superior to a grand sacrifice by a king, as too revolutionary, and, therefore, offered this elaborately constructed episode to detract from the power and immediacy of the censure of sacrifices (ibid.: 155n1).

of his basic principles as by a reiteration of the ideals of selfless action so prominently enshrined in the *Gītā*; he referred to the presence of these ideals even in the world of sacrifice which, he said, should ideally be performed in a simple manner and without any killing of animals: 'To the exclusion of all animals (which are certainly unclean as offering in sacrifices), the rice-ball is a worthy offering in sacrifices' (Ganguli 2007, vol. 9: 242).[5] The fourth category of discussion on *ahiṃ sā* is relatively more complex and figures in a remarkable, if difficult and perhaps essentially unresolved, dialogue between king Dyumatsena and his son Satyavat.[6] This dialogue indicates the ideas of human dignity, the ethics of deterrence, the making and the possibilities of the moral leadership of a king, and even the ethics of governance. Yudhiṣṭhira enquired of Bhīṣma about the ways in which a king could protect his subjects without having to take to violent means to do so. Bhīṣma narrated the instance of Satyavat advising his father against the practice of capital punishment; Satyavat argued that unrighteousness is intrinsically involved in taking life, even of the incorrigible criminal, since it violates what is sometimes described today as the bare body of a human being: 'Without destroying the body of the offender the king should do that unto him which is directed by the scriptures' (ibid.: 252). The body is not divested of human value even when it belongs to those who habitually associate with inauspicious practices such as those who pilfer 'the ornaments from cemeteries, and swearing apparel from men afflicted by spirits (and, therefore, deprived of senses)' (ibid.: 254). The killing of an offender results, in a way, in the killing of his dependents by depriving them of their only means of sustenance. Kings were enjoined to ensure the probity of their acts since people in lower stations of life generally emulated persons of eminence as regards the conduct of their lives. 'Good kings abundantly succeed in ruling their subjects properly with the aid of good conduct (instead of cruel or punitive inflictions)' (ibid.: 254). However, as in many instances in the epic, a medley of arguments converged in Satyavat's position: the salutary influence and public role of Brahmins; the morphing of royal conduct over the changing aeons; and the situations in which capital punishments are justifiable. However, it may be said that the basic theme of this dialogue underlines a major theme of the entire epic: the ethics of statecraft, and also the *dharma* that governs the conduct of the

[5] Tulādhara, however, makes a concession to a certain category of individuals: 'Creating sacrificial stakes (and other necessaries of Sacrifice) by simple fiats of the will, they perform many kinds of Sacrifice well-completed with abundant presents. One who is such a cleansed soul may slaughter a cow (as an offering in Sacrifice)' (Ganguli 2007, vol. 9: 241). Elsewhere, however, that a man could suffer the diminution of his accumulated merit by succumbing to the temptation of seemingly auspicious but actually inauspicious sacrificial killing is unequivocally conveyed through a psychological episode featuring Satya and Parṇ ada (ibid.: 275–78).

[6] For details of the Dyumatsena–Satyavat dialogue, see Ganguli (2007, vol. 9: 252–55).

enabled and the powerful, particularly because they are generally emulatory. In another episode narrated by Bhīṣma in the *Śāntiparvan*, the ascetic Vāmadeva told king Vasumanas: 'When the king, who is powerful, acts unrighteously towards the weak, they who take their birth in his race imitate the same conduct . . . The conduct of a king who is observant of his proper duties, is accepted by men in general as a model for imitation' (Ganguli 2007, vol. 8: 203). It is noteworthy that Vāmadeva further stated: 'The king should win victories without battles. Victories achieved by battles are not spoken of highly, O monarch, by the wise' (Ganguli 2007, vol. 9: 205).

This chapter particularly focuses on the dialogues regarding war as remedy and war as aggravation, conducted among the Pāṇḍavas because it was mainly among them that such debates were conducted and also because they were present in practically the major portion of the epic, and portrayed generally as victims of intrigue and injustice, and not governed in their intent and actions by the impulses of aggrandisement.

II

In the *Āraṇyakaparvan*, at an early stage of the 13-year period of exile for Pāṇḍavas, Draupadī blamed Yudhiṣṭhira for being indifferent to their degenerate condition and urged him to disregard his promise of living in exile for 13 years and to take immediate steps to avenge their insults by destroying the Kauravas. In this she referred to what she stated were the traditional precepts regarding the nature of Kṣatriyahood, revenge and forgiveness:

> It is said that there is no Kṣatriya in the world who is bereft of anger. I now behold in thee, however a refutation of the proverb! That Kṣatriya, O son of Prithā, who discovereth not his energy when the opportunity cometh, is ever disregarded by all creatures! Therefore, O, king, thou shouldst not extend thy forgiveness to the foe. Indeed, with thy energy, without doubt, thou mayst slay them all! So also, O king, that Kṣatriya who is not appeased when the time for forgiveness cometh, becometh unpopular with every creature and meeteth with death and destruction both in this and the other world! (Ganguli 2007, vol. 2: 57).

In support of her exhortations, she referred to a conversation between Prhlāda and Bali, regarding the relative merits of forgiveness and might. Prhlāda is reported to have stated that a person who is naturally forgiving falls into disrepute with his family and his attendants. He is disregarded and deceived by his servants; strangers and children speak slightingly toward him; and his wife is coveted by other men and acquires dubious habits herself. Thus, 'the learned applaud not a constant habit of forgiveness' (ibid.: 58). But this, in turn, does not also make might an unquestionable virtue. Pṛhlāda lists in detail the 'demerits of those that are never forgiving'. The man who gives way to unbridled rage soon becomes an object of scorn and hate, as a poisonous snake which harms the residents of the very house in which it takes shelter. Through his indiscriminate inflicting of punishment, the man of ill-advised might suffers the loss of wealth, of his friendships, and even his life. 'Therefore, should men never exhibit might in excess nor forgiveness on all occasions' (ibid.: 58–59). Draupadī then proceeded to narrate Pṛhlāda's listing of the categories which merited forgiveness and punishment respectively. This is a mix of the principled and the pragmatic. Offences by those who have done some service in the past, offences arising out of ignorance or out of some compulsion, and the first offence — all should be forgiven. Out of a fear of provoking an adverse public reaction, it became occasionally advisable to pardon the offences of certain persons against the state. Conversely, the second offence and offences done through deliberated intent, even if elaborate defences are created for these, should on no account go unpunished. Draupadī, arguing for a balance of forgiveness and persecution, stated that their unjust dispossession and exile, however, called for relentless persecution and destruction of the evil-minded Kurus: 'The humble and forgiving person is disregarded; while those that are fierce persecute others. He, indeed, is a king who hath recourse to both, each according to its time!' (ibid.: 59). We will return to Yudhiṣṭhira's response to this argument later in this chapter. For our present purpose, we will concentrate on Draupadī's contention that might/violence is not a dispensable means in human affairs, but is a necessary and potent resource in the life of a king, both as an individual and as a leader of his community. Her reference to violence as a means, rather than as a quality, draws on her contention that God is capricious rather than just. She reminded Yudhiṣṭhira that he had always regarded virtue as being more valuable to him than his own life: he could well give up his brothers and herself, but was incapable of swerving from the path of truth and justice. On the plane of rituals as well as conduct, he had always fulfilled all the obligations of worship, hospitality and charity. It was well known that his desire for kingship did not contradict the diktats of virtue. He was free from the taint of arrogance and pride even when he had become almost the lord of the earth for some time. Draupadī contended that she was familiar with the saying that he who protected virtue was protected in turn by virtue. But seeing the travails of her truth-seeking husband, she was inclined to disbelieve in that maxim. On the contrary, it seemed to her that the opposite of the saying was more correct: 'It seemeth that man can never attain prosperity in this world by virtue, gentleness, forgiveness, straight-forwardness and fear of censure!' (ibid.: 62). It was incomprehensible to her that the 'simple, gentle, liberal, modest, truthful' king could be inclined to the vice of gambling and, in a few reckless moments stake, lose his kingdom, his brothers and wife. For this reason, she was disposed to blaming not her husband, but the creator of the universe since it was well known that human beings were not independent agents of action but only subjects to the will of God: '[A]s a wooden doll is made to move its limbs by the wire-puller, so are creatures made to work by the Lord of all' (ibid.: 63). In saying so, significantly, she questioned the logic of a moral order sustaining the universe primarily because the creator himself appeared not as a dispassionate lawgiver, but as moved by the impulses that were perceptibly all too human — a creator who 'spreading illusion, slayeth his creatures by the instrumentality of his creatures'. The 'Supreme Lord, according to his pleasure, sporteth with His creatures, creating and destroying them, like a child with his toy (of soft earth)' (Ganguli 2007, vol. 2: 64). This question was perhaps natural coming from an epic heroine who is depicted as being at once fiery and thoughtful.[7] It is also strangely reminiscent of a similar statement from Shakespeare's famous tragedy, *King Lear*, regarding the 'vicious' nature of divine authority, uttered by Edgar at witnessing the suffering of his not entirely sinless father: 'As flies to wanton boys are we to the gods, / They kill us for their sport' (Shakespeare 1998, 4.1.38–39). Draupadī stated that her faith in the moral order was disturbed when Yudhiṣṭhira suffered and Duryodhana prospered: 'I do not speak highly of the Great Ordainer who suffereth such inequality' (Ganguli 2007, vol. 2: 64). She argued, paradoxically, that on the one hand, the fact of divine omnipotence simultaneously 'stained with the sin of every act' not the human doer but God himself; and that on the other hand, if the mortal actors were absolved of the sin of their deeds, then it followed that not God but individual might was the 'true cause of acts' (ibid.). Does this argument of Draupadī imply that there were, in effect, two situations prevailing in the philosophical universe, and in either of the situations — that of divine caprice, or that of a deistic universe — it was individual agency/might that was critical, and such moral questions as regarding non-violence and forgiveness were largely secondary. The nature of the universe either deprived individuals of any merit accruing from their virtuous acts, or it relegated virtue insofar as might, and not virtue, was the mover of worldly happenings. The individual thus became either supremely powerful, or supremely powerless in such a manner that the

---

[7] It would be appropriate to mention here that Vidya Nivas Mishra describes Ambā, Kuntī and Draupadī among the women; and Vyāsa, Vidura and Yudhiṣṭhira among the men, as the central protagonists of the epic. Mishra states that in a way, on one plane the *Mahābhārata* is essentially the story of the life and anguish of these six characters. Ambā, Kuntī and Draupadī are seen by him as perpetually tortured victims of an unjust social order. Draupadī, he says — she was born out of the flame of sacrificial fire that had been itself kindled as an act of retaliation; subsequently married, in an act of irony, Arjuna only to become a wife to five husbands; was virtually unprotected and publicly molested in the royal court in spite of having five protectors; and continuously agonized over her humiliation — is the most rebellious of these three women, in challenging a society of men, and is the only one who has a relationship of parity with the god Kṛṣṇa, who to the others is variously venerable, an adorable child, obscure, but to her a friend and thus with her in each of her crises: 'It is for this reason that Draupadī, unlike Amba and Kuntī, is not dependent on others, but that she stands on her own. It is because that Draupadī represents both a problem and its reconciliation that the author of *Mahābhārata* places Draupadī in the centre of the epic' (1998: 53; my translation).

question of the rightness of means was reduced in both cases to being a mere qualm. Since the divine is capricious and violent, the human beings deriving its impulses from the divine, will also inevitably have to be mighty and violent in order to claim their rights and occupy their rightful position. It needs to be noted that conversely this may imply that in the event of the universe being sustained and regulated by a moral order, violence would forever be a questionable attribute of the human self.

As mentioned earlier, we will examine Yudhiṣṭhira's significant reply to Draupadī at a later stage of our argument. Once again, Draupadī, however, refused to accept Yudhiṣṭhira's position conveyed in his reply. She clarified that although hers was apparently, as Yudhiṣṭhira said, the 'language of atheism', her attitude was not one of disrespect to the divine order, and that her statements on this subject should not be taken literally: 'Why should I disregard God, the lord of all creatures? Afflicted with woe, know me, O Bharata, to be only raving!' (Ganguli 2007, vol. 2: 67). She stated that it was really an illusion that human actions alone were capable of fetching desired results, whereas it was God who actually dispensed human fortunes according to the acts done in previous lives. Acts were, therefore, not so much as good or bad, but the 'result of God's arrangements'. But this, she said, referring to Manu, did not completely exclude human agency either: 'The man of action in this world generally meeteth with success' (ibid.: 69). For her, this human agency translated, in adverse situations such as that confronting Yudhiṣṭhira, into careful and vigilant action, guided chiefly by one's prowess:

> He should also wish evil unto his foe and his banishment. Without speaking of mortal man, if his foe were even the ocean or the hills, he should be guided by such motives. A person by his activity in searching for the holes of his enemies, dischargeth his debt to himself as also to his enemies (ibid.: 69).

The aforementioned argument of Draupadī, circular but unequivocal in its advocacy of a non-ethical and violent endeavour, was supported by Bhīma. Citing the authority of traditional sources on behaviour and statecraft, Bhīma criticized Yudhiṣṭhira's adherence to virtue and his submission to a life of exile in the forests as weakness and ignorance, unsuitable to any man of capability and spirit:

> This thy course of life is approved neither by Kṛṣṇa, nor Vibhatsu, nor by Abhimanyu, nor by Śriñjayas, nor by myself, nor by the sons of Mādrī. Afflicted with thy vows, thy cry is *Religion*! *Religion*! . . . It is because thou hast adopted a life of peace that thou feelest not this distress . . . Virtue is sometimes also the weakness of men . . . He that practiseth virtue for virtue's sake always suffereth. He can scarcely be called a wise man, for he knoweth not the purposes of virtue like a blind man incapable of perceiving the solar light (ibid.).

But Bhīma took care lest he appeared wholly to denounce virtue, arguing instead for what he said was the ideal balance of the ancients, between the pursuance of *dharma* (virtue), *artha* (wealth) and *kāma* (pleasure): 'One should not devote oneself to virtue alone, nor regard wealth as the highest object of one's wishes, nor pleasure, but should ever pursue all three' (Ganguli 2007, vol. 2: 72). Stating that nothing in the universe was higher than virtue, Bhīma then extended his argument with the logic of the various virtues advised for the different social orders; virtue thus became relative, not absolute. The repeated advocacy of violent means elsewhere in the epic, as here, is almost invariably based on a social and not a moral argument. He further argued that virtue was attainable by wealth, and might was the root of wealth: '[T]he person who throweth away like seeds a little of his virtue in order to gain a larger measure of virtue, is regarded as wise' (ibid.: 74). Moreover, as he stated, kingship was burdened with 'crookedness and unfairness' and with precepts that were opposed to 'tranquility and virtue'.

The latter half of the *Āraṇyakaparvan*, has a somewhat unique instance for the times, of a fowler/meat-seller giving a discourse on *dharma* to a virtuous ascetic called Kauśika. The *Mahābhārata* refers to the fowler (*vyādha*) as the Dharmavyādha or the righteous fowler, because of his conduct and wisdom. Enumerating the superior virtues, the fowler categorically stated: 'Truthfulness and abstention from doing injury to anyone, are virtues highly beneficial to all creatures. Of these, that latter is a cardinal virtue, and is based on truth' (Ganguli 2007, vol. 3: 429). At a later point, he explained that he followed his apparently cruel trade because of the sins committed by him in his past lives. This is the classic Dharmaśāstric assertion that station in life is determined by the accumulated consequences of the acts, virtuous or evil, of previous lives. Draupadī's argument, mentioned earlier, also adheres to this position, and her comment on the limitedness of human agency was likewise extended by the fowler to prove the indispensability of violence in life. The same argument was used later by Arjuna to justify the violence of the epic war. Although Dharmavyādha refrained from debating the moral issues related to the principles of war, his argument regarding the impossibility of a completely non-violent life appears to be an answer to the early Buddhist and Jaina canonical emphasis on *ahiṃsā*. We will later refer to the vexed contradictions within the Buddhist and Jaina doctrines on *ahiṃsā* as well. As if challenging the notion of the perpetual blemish on Kṣatriyahood regarding violence and war, Dharmavyādha asserted that contrary to popular perception, agriculture which was otherwise a commendable occupation actually involved good deal of violence to animal life: ploughing of the earth, for instance, resulted in the death of innumerable living creatures of the soil. As with the hunting of animals and eating their flesh, so even with the cutting of trees and herbs, loss of life of the many organisms present in trees and fruits, and even in water, was inevitable and inexorable: 'The whole creation, O Brāhmaṇa, is full of animals, sustaining itself with food derived from living organisms' (Ganguli 2007, vol. 2: 431–32). Fish preyed upon fish, certain species of animal preyed upon some other species, and some even preyed upon their own kind. Even enlightened men perforce destroyed unintentionally the organisms that fill the air while going about their quotidian routine. The fowler concluded: 'The commandment that people should not do harm to any creature, was ordained of old by men, who were ignorant of the true facts of the case. For, O Brāhmaṇa, there is not a man on the face of this earth, who is free from the sin of doing injury to animal life' (ibid.: 432).

In the *Udyogaparvan*, however, in a reversal of sorts, when Kṛṣṇa sought to elicit the Pāṇḍavas' opinion regarding the claiming of their inheritance, Bhīma, momentarily during the dialogues at this stage, and Arjuna and Nakula generally, expressed a desire for a non-violent and peaceful settlement with the Kauravas and entreated Kṛṣṇa to exert himself to this end. But at the same time, they were entirely prepared to go to war if necessary. Only Sahadeva and Sātyaki, recalling Draupadī's molestation at the royal court, appealed to Kṛṣṇa to provoke a war so that her humiliation could be avenged by slaying Duryodhana. Ironically, Sahadeva here alluded to the absoluteness of virtue rather than to its variability, in seeming to suggest that violence/war was actually opposed to virtue: 'If, O, Kṛṣṇa, Bhīma and Arjuna and king Yudhiṣṭhira the just are disposed to be virtuous, abandoning virtue I desire an encounter with Duryodhana in battle' (Ganguli 2007, vol. 4: 168). At this point, a weeping Draupadī emphatically asked for war against the Kauravas as enemies 'with whom peace cannot be established by either conciliation or presents, [and who] should be treated with severity by one desirous of saving his life' (ibid.: 169). She also drew attention to her humiliation and, in a dramatic manner, approached Kṛṣṇa, showing him her tresses that had been seized by Duḥśāsana at the Kuru court. She was, in fact, not at all inclined to the possibility of conciliating her enemies, saying that her father and her brothers, along with her sons and Abhimanyu, would take revenge on her behalf against the Kauravas should Bhīma and Arjuna become 'so low as to long for peace' (ibid.: 170). She was impelled by no other thought but that of revenge. Interestingly, at this time she also implicitly transposed morality against war, her statement indicating as if the epic were significantly conscious of the complexities involved in constructing intricately, i.e., through divergent and opposing voices, the logic of a just war, and also that to argue for even a just war against even reprehensible enemies was perhaps to argue ultimately against ethical principles: 'What peace can this heart of mine know unless I behold Duḥśāsana's dark arm severed from his trunk and pulverised to atoms? Thirteen long years have I passed in expectation of better times, hidding [*sic*] in my heart my wrath like a smouldering fire. And now pierced by Bhīma's wordy darts that heart of mine is about to break, for the mighty-armed Bhīma now casteth his eye on morality' (ibid.).

Later, in the *Udyogaparvan*, Kuntī — in a way anticipating some of the arguments presented by Kṛṣṇa to Arjuna, and by Arjuna to Yudhiṣṭhira — presented virtue not as an absolute but as a relative value pertaining differently to the different social orders with their differently ordained duties and responsibilities. These differences, according to her, ruled out any general ascription of immorality to violence and war. She told Kṛṣṇa that Yudhiṣṭhira, in his preference for non-violence, was actually causing his virtue to decrease. She desired that it be conveyed to Yudhiṣṭhira that: 'Thy understanding, affected by only the words of the Vedas, vieweth virtue alone. Cast thy eyes on the duties of thy own order, as ordained by the Self-create. For all ruthless deeds and for the protection of the people, from his (Brāhmaṇa's) arms was created the Kṣatriya, who is to depend upon the prowess of his own arms' (Ganguli 2007, vol. 4: 256). She cited the instance of sage Mucukunda adopting and discharging the duties of a powerful warrior king, on being gifted the sovereignty of earth by Vaiśravaṇa. Kuntī further cited from history the exhortations of Vidulā to her son Sañjaya who, on being vanquished, wanted to renounce the ways of the warrior class to which he belonged. Vidulā chastised her son for his pusillanimity, invoked the special duties of the warrior class and reminded him that it was better to die in battle than to live one's life in a 'low station': 'He is a man who cherisheth wrath and forgiveth not. He, on the other hand, who is forgiving and without wrath, is neither a man nor woman' (ibid.: 259). Seemingly, in complete accord with the views of Vidulā, Kuntī conveys the following message to Yudhiṣṭhira:

> Observe thou those kingly duties of thine that befit thy ancestry. That is not the conduct of the royal sage in which thou wishest to abide. Indeed, he that is stained by weakness of heart and adhereth to compassion, and is unsteady, never obtaineth the merit born of cherishing his subjects with love. That understanding according to which thou art mow acting was never wished (to thee) by Pāṇḍu, or myself, or thy grandsire while we uttered blessings on thee before; sacrifice, gift, merit, and bravery, subjects and children, greatness of soul, and might, and energy, these were always prayed by me for thee . . . Whether all this be righteous or unrighteous, you are to practise it, in consequence of your very birth . . . Mendicancy, therefore, is forbidden to thee. Nor is agriculture suited to thee. Thou art a Kṣatriya and therefore, the protector of all in distress. Thou art to live by the prowess of thy arms. O thou of mighty arms, recover thy paternal share of the kingdom which thou hast lost, by conciliation, or by working disunion among thy foes, or by gift of money and violence, or well directed policy (ibid.: 256–57).

This conversation between Kṛṣṇa and Kuntī was immediately followed by a slightly similar appeal by Karṇa to Kṛṣṇa to let the war occur, as it would be in the nature of a grand sacrifice, a *raṇayajña* to be recorded and forever related in

[8] Christopher Key Chapple, in one of his rather hasty interpretations of the main characters of the *Mahābhārata*, states quite the opposite of the actual on Karṇa's speech to Kṛṣṇa, in that Karṇa '*laments* the inevitability of war' (1995: 81; emphasis added). For this, Chapple cites as source Carrière (1987: 151). To cite a modern dramatic adaptation of the epic is not in itself academically objectionable, but to alternate seamlessly, as Chapple does, between the text of the epic and adaptations of it that describe scenes very differently from the main epic, may, however, pose genuine analytical problems. See Chapple (1995: 75–81, 135n1–136nn2–6).

the recitals of the *Brāhmaṇas*.[8] He invested the idea of war with the traditional values of honour and martyrdom, as also the customary *dharma* of the *Kṣatriyas*: 'The fame, O thou of Vṛṣṇi's race, the fame that they achieve in battles is the wealth that Kshtriyas own' (Ganguli 2007, vol. 4: 274). The characters in Karṇa's description of the imminent war were conceived in terms of sacrificial imagery, mainly in terms of ritualistic priesthood conducting a sacrificial rite.[9] He imagined Kṛṣṇa to be both the *Upadeṣṭṛ* and the *Adhvaryu*; Arjuna as the *Hotṛ*; his famed *Gāṇḍīva* (bow) as the sacrificial ladle, and his dreaded weapons as the *mantras*; Abhimanyu as the principal Vedic *mantra* to be chanted; Bhīma as the *Udgātṛ*; Nakula and Sahadeva as the slayers of sacrificial animals; and Yudhiṣṭhira 'of virtuous soul, ever engaged in *Japa* and *Homa*, ... [as the] *Brahmā* of that sacrifice' (ibid.: 273). From among the Kaurava, participants of the *raṇayajña*, Duryodhana would be the performer, with his army symbolizing his wife. Acknowledging his intense remorse for having insulted the Pāṇḍavas for the purposes of gratifying Duryodhana, Karṇa movingly said to Kṛṣṇa:

> When O Kṛṣṇa, thou wilt behold me slain by Arjuna, then will the *Punachiti* of this sacrifice commence. When [Bhīma] will drink the blood of the loudly roaring Duḥśāsana, then will the *Soma*-drinking of this sacrifice have taken place! . . . When mighty Bhīmasena will slay Duryodhana, then, O Madhava, will the sacrifice of Dhṛtarāṣṭra's be concluded . . . Oh, let this swelling host of Kṣatriyas perish by means of weapons on that most sacred of all spots in the three worlds, viz. Kurukṣetra, O Keśava . . . so that . . . the whole Kṣatriya order may attain to heaven. As long, O Janārdana, as the hills and the rivers will last so long will the fame of these achievements last . . . O Keśava, bring Kuntī's son (Arjuna) before me for battle, keeping forever this our discourse a secret, O chastiser of foes (ibid.: 274).

However, Kṛṣṇa, who was to favour war only as an inevitability and waging it as a duty towards the cause of justice to be discharged as dispassionately as possible, apparently refused to accept this emotive glorification of war. He prosaically indicated the terrible consequences of the war, rhetorically asking Karṇa whether winning the war was not altogether more appealing to him. Karṇa appeared to him fatally misguided; ignorance on matters of true virtue was a recipe for disaster, and he said as much to Karṇa: '[W]hen the destruction of all creatures approacheth, wrong assuming the semblance of right leaveth not the heart' (ibid.: 278).

Returning to the Pāṇḍava camp, Kṛṣṇa quite briefly narrated how Duryodhana spurned all efforts for a peaceful resolution of the conflict, including Kṛṣṇa's final suggestion that the Pāṇḍavas be given only five villages in which to live without any power, with the kingdom being retained by Duryodhana. He stated that war was now the only way to conflict-resolution. Even after this, when following his advice, the Pāṇḍavas prepared for the battle, Yudhiṣṭhira once again asked Kṛṣṇa

[9] See Jatavallabhula (1999) for details of other references to the *Mahābhārata* war as sacrifice.

about the true path of virtue to be followed in this situation. Kṛṣṇa very pithily indicated the evil nature of Duryodhana which could be subdued by force alone: 'As regards ourselves, we do not desire to make peace with the Kauravas by abandoning our property. War, therefore is that which should now take place' (Ganguli 2007, vol. 4: 297). Yudhiṣṭhira could not but express his misgivings. He had accepted war as a fait accompli, but nevertheless believed the impending slaughter to be evil. He felt that the cause of peace for which they had accepted the privations in the past was being defeated as if it were so ordained; and that all their strivings to avoid war had been fruitless and were progressively becoming hopeless as if by the contradictory logic in the avoidance of conflict with an adversary who was instinctively malevolent and unjust. This unsolicited, unwelcome and impending visitation of violent calamity was a cause for sorrow for him: 'What kind of victory shall we achieve by slaying our preceptors of venerable age' (ibid.). Arjuna sought to dispel the doubts of his sorrowing brother by reminding him of Vidura and Kuntī's injunctions for waging the war, none of whom would recommend an unrighteous course of action.

But on the battlefield, Yudhiṣṭhira's question came to haunt Arjuna. Very briefly thereon, Kṛṣṇa told Arjuna that war at that point was sinless. First, the fruit of an individual's actions was beyond his control, it lay with divine providence. Second, the soul was the essence of life and was indestructible, with only the body, at best an adjunct to living, being mortal. The individual was actually powerless to take life, and it was futile to grieve for something that one was not responsible for. Third, the individual could at the most discharge his duties without any attachment to the results thereof, and the foremost duty of the warrior was to fight a just and lawful war.[10]

The admonitions of the Pāṇḍava brothers and Draupadī to Yudhiṣṭhira to alleviate his resolve to renounce the world out of distress in the *Śāntiparvan*, basically repeated and, in the case of Arjuna, enlarged the arguments offered in this regard on various earlier occasions.[11] Arjuna, like as his brothers and Draupadī,

---

[10] It is relevant here to mention that the argument that one prominent aspect of virtue was its variability regarding the appropriate course of action commensurate with the respective callings of different social orders in different situations, had been outlined by Kṛṣṇa earlier in the epic, while replying to Sañjaya's exhortation to Yudhiṣṭhira to eschew war, in the *Udyogaparvan* (Ganguli 2007, vol. 4: 47–49). Asked for his opinion by Yudhiṣṭhira, Kṛṣṇa, hailed by Yudhiṣṭhira as 'the great judge of the propriety or otherwise of all acts', explained to Sañjaya: 'Supposing thou approvest of peace alone I should like to hear what thou mayst have to say to their question — which way doth the injunction of the religious lie, *viz.*, whether it is proper for the king to fight or not? — Thou must, O Sañjaya, take it into thy consideration the division of the four castes, and the scheme of duties allotted to each' (ibid.: 48).

[11] For the details of this argument of the Pāṇḍavas and Draupadī at this juncture of the narrative, and Yudhiṣṭhira's reply, see Ganguli (2007, vol. 6: 9–36).

took the traditional position on the duties of earthly life, of material necessities and their fulfillment, and on the instrumentality of *daṇḍa* or punishment in establishing a feasible and just state. Arjuna proceeded with a detailed outline of the kinds of *daṇḍa* to be used in different situations in what was an essentially Hobbesian world. 'If the rod of chastisement did not protect people, they would have sunk in the darkness of hell' (Ganguli 2007, vol. 8: 25). They tried to convince Yudhiṣṭhira that on the planes of duty, virtue, Vedic injunctions, and of law and justice, the just war was normative and proper. Bhīma reminded Yudhiṣṭhira of his equanimity in earlier situations of joy or sorrow: he had never allowed his mind to be tethered to incidents; he should not 'therefore, use [his] memory for becoming sad during times of bliss, or glad during times of woe' (Ganguli 2007, vol. 4: 29). Bhīma further argued that if his sense continued to be clouded by the recent events, he should also recollect the many injustices suffered by them in the past, to balance the immediacy of the *Mahābhārata* war. Violence begins in the minds of men, and its effects refuse to be erased from the minds of men. Perhaps indicating the possibility of this erasure, Bhīma pointed to a different war that must now engage Yudhiṣṭhira:

> Indeed that battle is now before thee in which there is no need of arrows, of friends, of relatives and kinsmen, but which will have to be fought with thy mind alone. If thou givest up thy life-breath before conquering in this battle, then, assuming another body, thou shalt have to fight these very foes again.[12] Therefore fight that battle this very day, O bull of Bharata's race, disregarding the concerns of thy body, and aided by thy own acts, conquer and identify with thy minds foe (ibid.: 29).[13]

The aforementioned statement by Bhīma can be seen as strikingly ironical. Throughout the epic, Yudhiṣṭhira determinedly fought this lonely battle, with results that were in the end subtly very different from those that visualized by Bhīma.

---

[12] It needs to be mentioned that, in the translator's note to this verse, Ganguli explains what Bhīma actually meant by this sentence: 'The meaning is that in consequence of prosperity and kingdom and, therefore, of the means of effecting thy salvation by sacrifice and gifts and other acts of piety, thou shalt have to be re-born and to renew this mental battle *with thy doubts*' (2007, vol. 8: 29n4, emphasis original).

[13] In a similar note, Ganguli comments: 'This is a difficult verse, and I am not sure that I have understood it correctly. *Gantavyam* is explained by Nilkantha as connected with *paramavyaktarūpasya*. According to Nilkantha, this means that thou shouldst go to, *i.e.* conquer, and identify thyself with, the *param* or foe of that which is of unmanifest form, the mind; of course, this would mean that Yudhiṣṭhira should identify himself with his own soul, for it is the soul which is his foe and with which he is battling. Such conquest and identification implies the cessation of the battle and, hence, the attainment of tranquillity' (2007, vol. 4: 29n5).

III

The arguments of Draupadī and Bhīma during the family discussion of the Pāṇḍavas in the *Āraṇyakaparvan*, have already been referred to in detail. The response of Yudhiṣṭhira is extremely significant not only to our present discussion but also to the development of the main themes of the epic. Yudhiṣṭhira, described in the epic as virtue incarnate, presented a cogent defence of the universality of certain ethical values. Calmly, he explained that anger was the undoing of the human possibility. How could he, therefore, adopt that emotion which Draupadī so passionately wished for him, even for the purpose of vanquishing the evil of Duryodhana? He did not wish to abandon the supreme virtue of forgiveness. He referred to the ascetic Kāśyapa's verses in praise of forgiveness that glorify forgiveness as a virtue, a sacrifice, the Vedas, the *śruti*: 'Forgiveness is *Brahma*; forgiveness is truth; forgiveness is stored ascetic merit; forgiveness protecteth the ascetic merit of the future; forgiveness is asceticism; forgiveness is holiness; and by forgiveness is it that the universe is held together' (Ganguli 2007, vol. 2: 61). He categorically rejected Draupadī's position that might and not virtue was the operative quality in the exercise of power and leadership. On the contrary, he asserted that forgiveness could be practised only by the truly resilient and for that reason was an essential attribute of kingship. Far from being an unrealistic position, this conveys the reality of a difficult world, raising, in turn, a major question: what is the ideal response to common forms of injustice and injury, and what are the behavioural connotations of this ideal response? Needless to say, this position also indicates the thinking of the *Mahābhārata* on this human predicament. Yudhiṣṭhira proceeded to further clarify his philosophic idea:

> Suyodhana deserveth not the kingdom. Therefore, hath he been unable to acquire forgiveness. I, however, deserve the sovereignty and therefore is it that forgiveness hath taken possession of me. Forgiveness and gentleness are the qualities of the self-possessed. They represent eternal virtue. I shall, therefore, truly adopt those qualities' (Ganguli 2007, vol. 24: 62).

Addressing Draupadī's anguish-ridden doubts regarding divine justice, he stated that he practised virtue not because he believed in their instrumental value, but because he believed in their intrinsic value:

> I give away, because it is my duty to give; I sacrifice because it is my duty to sacrifice . . . I accomplish to the best of my power whatever a person living in domesticity should do, regardless of the fact whether those acts have fruits or not . . . I act virtuously, not from the desire of reaping the fruits of virtue, but of not transgressing the ordinances of the Veda, and beholding also the conduct of the good and wise! My heart, O Kṛṣṇa, is naturally attracted towards virtue. The man who wisheth to reap the fruits of virtue is a trader in virtue (ibid.).

This last category of persons was for Yudhiṣṭhira not worthy of respect, as one should never calculate and nor even wish for the benefits accruing from one's meritorious actions. Although, he assured Draupadī that it is natural for the virtuous acts to have beneficent consequences and that she, on no account, should doubt the quality of divine justice. Apropos Bhīma's accusations and provocations, he reminded Bhīma that he should have protested against Yudhiṣṭhira staking his titles and his family during the game of dice itself, not now after he had given his pledge to honour the pact: 'But know, O Bhīma, my promise can never be untrue. I regard virtue as superior to life itself and a blessed state of celestial existence. Kingdom, sons, fame, and wealth — all these do not come up to even a sixteenth part of truth' (Ganguli 2007, vol. 24). V. S. Sukthankar has stated that this conversation, spread over a few chapters of the *Āraṇyakaparvan*, 'contain in the form of an animated controversy the substance of the entire ethical teaching of the epic' (1998: 74). Yudhiṣṭhira's stated position is highly significant for Sukthankar, as it naturally represents 'the "settled doctrine" (siddhānta) of the epic as opposed to the prima facie arguments (pūrvapakṣa) put forward by Draupadī and Bhīma' (ibid.).

But Yudhiṣṭhira presented a slightly more nuanced position, similar to that of Kṛṣṇa, while answering the entreaties of Sañjaya who had come to the Pāṇḍavas as the emissary of Dhṛtarāṣṭra in order to forestall an apparently imminent war with an appeal to the forbearance and righteousness of Yudhiṣṭhira. It should be mentioned in fairness to Sañjaya that more than being a mere emissary devoted to the interests of his king, he was essentially an honest and virtuous person who genuinely believed in *ahiṃsā* and the other virtues and sincerely wished for a solution that would protect the interests of the Pāṇḍavas. Aware of the fact that it was Yudhiṣṭhira alone who could transcend immediate concerns to espouse perpetual values, his appeal was informed and inspired by universal principles. Sañjaya began by stating that virtues earned in this transient human life should on no account be wasted on urgent material concerns, and that a life of mendicancy was superior to kingship wrested and wrought through the slaughter of human beings. Merit earned in this life, frequently and naturally through deprivation and suffering, was infinitely more valuable in the life after death. In stating so, Sañjaya sought to dismantle, through a traditional argument, the overriding legitimacy of war over the ages which has been constituted of the advocacy of the principle that, under an irregular and unjust dispensation, justice in this world can be established only by securing ones legitimate interests forcibly from illegitimate authority. He indicated that there were other more valuable planes of living which, however, had become impossible with the transgression of human values such as non-violence: 'O Ajātaśatru, if without war the Kurus will not yield thy share, I think, it is far better for thee to live upon alms in the kingdom of the Andhakas and Vṛṣṇis than obtain sovereignty by war' (Ganguli 2007, vol. 4: 44). He further argued that sovereignty obtained by the killing of preceptors and kinsmen would be a source of sorrow to Yudhiṣṭhira:

> Knowing all this, do *not* be engaged in war. If you are desirous of taking this course, because your counsellors desire the same, then give up (everything) to them, and run away. You should not fall away from this path which leads to the region of the gods! (Ganguli 2007, vol. 4: 45; emphasis in the original).

In response, Yudhiṣṭhira told Sañjaya that during uncommon situations, individuals were bound to the duties assigned to their respective social orders: '[V]irtue and vice, which are both eternal and absolute, exchange their aspects during seasons of distress. One should follow without deviation the duties prescribed for the order to which he belongs by birth' (ibid.: 46). Subsequently, however, Yudhiṣṭhira denounced the *kṣatriyadharma* as woeful and barren in a council wherein the Pāṇḍavas explored, with Kṛṣṇa, the rightful course of action open to them. As the rightful claimant to the Kuru throne, he was already burdened with the complaints of his brothers and Draupadī that he had been soft-hearted. By any standards, he had had enough provocation to wage a war. In this situation, therefore, his statement to Kṛṣṇa is classic: it initially listed almost all the conceivable reasons for going to war, as in the *pūrvapakṣa* of an argument and culminated in the complete demolition of the idea of war. Indeed, it may be speculated by some that going by the history of interpolations in the *Mahābhārata*, the latter part of Yudhiṣṭhira's statement reflects Jaina and Buddhist influences on the text. We are also not unaware of the possibility of a school of psychoanalysis putting forth the notion that in situations such as this, the real state of mind and its hidden but real desires and doubts are, in fact, expressed in the *pūrvapakṣa*, while the *uttarapakṣa* is a contrived set of arguments which betray the dominant social thought of the day, whereby the *pūrvapakṣa* is a genuine statement while the *uttarapakṣa* is hypocritical. However, we are inclined to consciously adopt the view that the *pūrvapakṣa* makes the arguments of the *uttarapakṣa* more comprehensive and therefore less contingent in nature, and we will proceed with that assumption in this discussion. The arguments that Yudhiṣṭhira put forward at this juncture conclusively rejected the very idea that a war could ever be just. It may be compulsively dictated by exigencies, its aim might be the establishment of a just order and it may even succeed in doing so, but almost immediately with its commencement, violations of the rules of war would inevitably occur. The spirit of his arguments was reflected in his overall stance and his utterances even after the war was over, till almost the end of the epic. In that sense he remained ironically the conscious dissenter in the great war, perpetually tormented by guilt and remorse. In this argument, he first cited the miserable condition of the Pāṇḍavas and their bounden duty to regain their due share of the kingdom. This he did with repeated references to the social codes of the day. Deprived of his lawful inheritance, a person is said to lose his sense of judgment and a profusion of socially disruptive consequences are said to occur from indigence and dishonour (ibid.: 154–55). Thus, their inheritance had to be claimed in order for them to practise their *dharma*. However, the possibility that it could only be accomplished by killing some of their kinsmen was abominable to Yudhiṣṭhira: 'What good, therefore, can there be in battle? Alas, such sinful practices are the duties of the Kṣatriya order! Ourselves have taken our births in that wretched order! Whether those practices be sinful or virtuous, any other than the profession of arms would be censurable for us' (ibid.: 155). His rebuttal of the first part of his own argument was based solely on moral/humanistic grounds. War howsoever glorified was cruel and unjust with little appeal as an equal competition between warriors. It also did not produce peace; the losers nursed their wounds, waiting to take their revenge:

> Sometimes one man killeth many, sometimes many and united together kill one. A coward may slay a hero, and one unknown to fame may slay a hero of celebrity . . . Under all circumstances, however, war is a sin. Who in striking another is not himself struck . . . Those that are quiet, modest, virtuous, and compassionate are generally stain in battle, while they that are wicked escape . . . Hostilities, waged over so long, cease not; for if there is even one alive in the enemy's family, narrators are never wanted to remind him of the past. Enmity, O Keśava, is never neutralised by enmity; on the other hand, it is fomented by enmity, like fire led by clarified butter. Therefore, there can be no peace without the annihilation of one party, for flaws may always be detected of which advantage may be taken by one side or the other . . . Indeed, when conciliation fails, frightful results follow. The learned have noticed all this in a canine contest . . . In such a contest, O Kṛṣṇa, the dog that is stronger, vanquishing his antagonist taketh the latter's meat. The same is exactly the case with men. There is no difference whatever . . . How may we, O Mādhava, preserve both our interest and virtue? (ibid.: 156–57).

Yudhiṣṭhira's ultimate reluctant consent to waging the war did not influence his value judgment on war. There are also Vedantic overtones in the position of Yudhiṣṭhira, informed by the concept of the indivisibility of self, of the striker of a blow not being himself immune from effects of the blow struck on another, as both are part of the one all pervading unity.

IV

Yudhiṣṭhira repeatedly took upon himself the responsibility for the manslaughter during the war. Even as he blamed the evil genius of Duryodhana for causing the war, he could not absolve himself of the primary responsibility for the bloodshed.[14]

---

14 Doubtless, Yudhiṣṭhira's personal sorrow was heightened by instances such as the collective remonstrance of the grieving women in the *Strīparvan* directed at him while he witnessed their lamentations on the banks of Gangā: 'Where, indeed, is that righteousness of the king, where is truth and compassion, since he has slain sires and brothers and preceptors and sons and friends? How, O mighty-armed one, hath thy heart become tranquil after causing Droṇa, and thy grandsire Bhīṣma, and Jayadratha, to be slaughtered? What need hast thou of sovereignty, after having seen thy sires and brothers, O Bharata, and the irrepressible Abhimanyu and the sons of Draupadī, thus slaughtered?' (Ganguli 2007, vol. 7: 17).

In the *Strīparvan*, presenting himself before a distraught Gāndhārī after the war, he said:

> Here is Yudhiṣṭhira, O goddess, that cruel slayer of thy sons! I deserve thy curses, for I am the cause of this universal destruction. Oh, curse me! I have no longer any need of life, for kingdom, for wealth! Having caused such friends to be slain, I have proved myself to be a great fool and a hater of friends' (Ganguli 2007, vol. 7: 22).[15]

In fact, in the early sections of the *Śāntiparvan*, he had arraigned *kṣatriyadharma* and aspired to renunciation (Ganguli 2007, vol. 8: 9–11). As mentioned earlier, Karṇa too had foreseen that Yudhiṣṭhira would be the *Brahmā* (chief priest) of the future *raṇayajña* at Kurukṣetra. Yudhiṣṭhira's insistence on bearing responsibility for the sins committed during the war was informed by the principle that the *Brahmā* of the *raṇayajña*, as in fact the *Brahmā* in any *yajña*, was ordained to supervise the performance of the war or any *yajña*, point out the faults that occurred, and rectify them by the conventional means of expiation; he also implicitly insisted on the first principle that as the bearer of the merits and demerits of the *raṇayajña* it was essential that he be cleansed of sin, and that real cleansing entailed the freedom from sin which was only possible through renunciation.[16] Perhaps, this war for claiming inheritance was so reprehensible to Yudhiṣṭhira in that it violated simultaneously two of the highest virtues, *anāsakti* (non-attachment) and *ānṛśaṃsya* (non-cruelty). Therefore, it is hardly a coincidence that in the epic, the constant votary of non-violence is also the most constant adherent to truth; it is actually indicative of the eternally stated interdependence of these two virtues.

Critics may speculate about the implications for the epic, of Yudhiṣṭhira's renouncing the throne rather than allowing himself to be crowned as the king. The response to this speculation may be seen to hinge on the nature as well as the expanse of the epic in question. Yudhiṣṭhira's denial of his own victory and a retirement from the kingdom would have imposed an abrupt moral ending on

---

[15] Yudhiṣṭhira is described as being terrified of Gāndhārī's righteous wrath at the fall of Duryodhana in the *Śalyaparvan*, and thereby entreating Kṛṣṇa to go to Hastināpura and pacify her anger, lest she destroyed the Pāṇḍavas 'by the fire of her mind' (see Ganguli 2007, vol. 7: 171–73). His humility and repentance before Gāndhārī may in this light be seen by critics, as contrived. But it may be pointed out that his characteristic humility and complete equanimity in dire situations, are in evidence throughout the epic and hardly merit such critical judgment.

[16] In this context,Yudhiṣṭhira told Arjuna: 'O Dhanañjaya, a perpetrated sin is expiated by auspicious acts, by publishing the act widely, by repentance, by alms-giving, by penances, by trips to *tirthas* after renunciation of everything, by constant meditation on the scriptures. Of all these, he that has practised renunciation is believed to be incapable of committing sins anew' (Ganguli 2007, vol. 8: 11). I have mentioned earlier that one such conventional expiatory act, the *Aśvamedha* sacrifice, was deemed to be of inferior merit.

the epic, reduced it to a narrative that was really about a family feud and deprived it of the dialogue between the universal and the contingent in the ethics of virtue, which unfolds through the searching, and gradually changing, questions posed by Yudhiṣṭhira to his preceptors.[17]

The loneliness of Yudhiṣṭhira derived as much from his positions as from the largeness of his character; whereas the vigorous play of activeness characterizes Arjuna, Yudhiṣṭhira has 'transcended the role of the mere human, he has attained a state beyond the constraints of the human limitation' (Mishra 1998: 67; my translation). Kṛṣṇa's fullsome praise for him evokes this transcendence.[18] There is often in literature a complex relationship between character and theme. Theme is a philosophical abstraction which needs to be experientially concretized through a character; the concrete is representative and hence not unique, and the character gains universality when it is treated as a theme. By investing a character with a special significance, it is as if the author enters into his own work, in attempting to make a statement of particular value. The *Mahābhārata* is distinctive from other similar narratives of dishonour and revenge, in the projection of its narrative on the ethical and metaphysical planes which is achieved in the interrelationship of the timelessness of the ethical questions that are grappled with, and through characters that express the 'tension between two ideal orders of beings, a moral type wherein

[17] The apparent ambiguity of the many closures in the *Mahābhārata* can be related to Nicholas Sutton's reading of the epic in another context: 'the tension between the ethics of morality and those of ritual action'. 'The epic here seems to explore the subtleties of *dharma*, using them to enhance the interest of the story it is telling, rather than accepting the role of a absolute arbiter of contentious doctrinal issues . . . *Dharma* is subtle, and the more it is discussed the more contentious it becomes; therefore to attempt to resolve it with simplistic statements of dogma is a folly that the epic renounces' (2000: 320). Sutton, in this connection, discusses the 'recurring tension in the narrative between Yudhiṣṭhira's moral sense and the dharmic duties imposed upon him' (ibid.: 305). For the details of the discussion see Sutton (2000: 317–20).

[18] Kṛṣṇa lauded Yudhiṣṭhira in the *Āraṇyakaparvan*: 'By you who have obeyed with truth and candour what your duty prescribed, have been won both this world and that to come! First you have studied, while performing religious duties; having acquired in a suitable way the whole science of arms, having won wealth by pursuing the methods prescribed for the military caste, you have celebrated all the time honoured sacrificial rites. You have taken no delight in sensual pleasures; you do not act, O lord of men, from motives of enjoyment, nor do you swerve from virtue from greed of riches; it is for this, you have been named the Virtuous King, O son of Prithā! Having won kingdoms and riches and means of enjoyment, your best delight has been charity and truth and practice of austerities, O king, and faith and mediation and forbearance and patience! When the population of Kuru-jangala beheld Kṛṣṇa outraged in the assembly hall, who but your self could brook that conduct, O Pandu's son, which was so repugnant both to virtue and usage?' (Ganguli 2007, vol. 3: 365–66).

the gods become incarnate as heroic individuals and an immoral — or rather an unmoral — type which it is the object of the former to destroy' (Sukthankar 1998: 63). Both of these qualities intermingle in the character of Yudhiṣṭhira. 'The Yudhiṣṭhira-ideal is thrown into sharp relief by the epic poets with the help of the contrasted character of his antagonist, Duryodhana' (ibid.: 77). This idea may be contestable for some scholars. For instance, Christopher Key Chapple equates — without substantiating his point — the position of Yudhiṣṭhira and Duryodhana: 'Duryodhana and Yudhiṣṭhira desire what the other has, without seeing the other as self' (1995: 81–82). I hope that my somewhat detailed exposition of Yudhiṣṭhira's position in the earlier section of this chapter serves as a substantive rebuttal of Chapple's comment. I am also unable to agree with Bimal Kṛisna Matilal's blurring of the ethical divide between Yudhiṣṭhira and Duryodhana. In one of his writings on the *Mahābhārata*, Matilal puzzlingly abstains from comprehensively analyzing the characters in question and instead confines himself to brief statements such as this obiter: 'Yudhiṣṭhira's *dharma* had a spiritual halo around it. Duryodhana's *dharma* was as material as the hard soil' (1995: 209).[19] Similarly, it is hardly possible to sustain the claim made by Gary A. Tubb in his critique of the *śāntarasa* in the *Mahābhārata*, that Yudhiṣṭhira aspired not for liberation from desire but for a kind of Valhalla, for which reason 'his actions could not be further from fulfilment of the most consistently mentioned aspect of freedom from attachment, indifference to friend or foe' (2007: 184). This passing remark carries no mention of the numerous passages in the epic, some of which have been cited earlier in this chapter and which almost completely negate Tubb's contention. Even a careful reading of the episode of Yudhiṣṭhira's ascent to heaven, which Tubb mentions without giving any detail, would dispel the notion that Yudhiṣṭhira at any stage at all coveted paradise.[20] Critics such as Sukthankar have seen the god Kṛṣṇa as the central figure of the epic. Arjuna is seen to personify the active quality of Kṛṣṇa. This thought can perhaps be extended to suggest, as indeed some have indirectly done, that Yudhiṣṭhira personifies the other attribute of godhead: permanent *vairāgya* (detachment), the essential quality of *mokṣa* (liberation). That is perhaps

[19] Matilal's other criticism of Yudhiṣṭhira lying to Droṇa (2002: 98) is much more difficult to answer; this episode has traditionally reflected the significant issue regarding truth and situational exceptionality.

[20] Tubb's reading of the *rasas* is also not very comprehensive. The *rasas* are states of mind, and not compartmentalized attitudes. The admittance into the mind of various *rasas* at different stages is natural; the individual is defined by the predominant *rasa* of his life, and not by the presence of a transient *rasa*. On another plane, even total embodiments of the *śāntarasa* like Mahāvīra have the suffix *vīra* attached to their name, which implies a degree of *vīrarasa* which in their case does not signify martial accomplishment but a victory achieved over one's own mind; traditionally, this category comprised the ultimate victor. I am grateful to Sibesh Bhattacharya for this interpretation.

why the authors of the epic have made Yudhiṣṭhira such a consistent opponent of violence and war. He is, along with Kṛṣṇa, one of the very few characters in the epic for whom can be said, only on a much grander scale and perhaps even on a different plane, what Bakhtin comments on the characteristic resilience of the archetypal heroes of the Greek novel: 'The hammer of events shatters nothing and forges nothing — it merely tries the durability of an already finished product. And the product passes the test' (2008: 107).

The *Mahābhārata* is similar to other epics insofar as the narrative hinges on the traditional bardic themes of dishonour and revenge.[21] But for our purposes it is distinguished by its equally important interrogation of seemingly established ideas of war and peace, and in its larger argument against violence. In its defining moments, the voice of the *Mahābhārata* shares anguish at the debasement of the human will by violence, divinely ordained or otherwise. Its approach to war is broadly similar to the Jaina and Buddhist views that on occasions violent means are necessary for establishing justice.[22] The injunction of the ban in biblical war texts proclaims that 'all human beings among the defeated are "devoted to destruction"' (Niditch 1993: 28). Although there is no evidence of there being anything in the *Mahābhārata* that is akin to a ban, it might be interesting to make a comparative study of the nuances of its idea of war against evil, and the psychology of the biblical 'ban-as-God's-justice ideology' that, as Niditch says, 'actually motivates and encourages war, implying that wars of extermination are desirable in order to purify the body politic of one's group, and to actualize divine judgment' (ibid.: 77). Tracing the broad outline of the *Mahābhārata*'s final shaping in the consciousness of a people, Buitenen writes:

> At a time when all the materials that were to go into the final redactorial version of the great epic (which transformed the *Bhārāta* into the *Mahābhārata*) were collected, materials that hailed from many milieus and many centuries, a change of sensitivity away from the war books had taken place, a change from the martial spirit toward a more reflective and in certain ways more quietistic mood. The war had ceased to be a glorious event for celebration and was to be regarded as a horrendous, blood-curdling finale to an aeon (1981: 3–4).

---

[21] Pradip Bhattacharya has tried to prove through references from the *Mahābhārata* that, contrary to popular perception, Draupadī had been dragged to the court by her hair but there had been no attempt to disrobe her: 'The internal and external evidence, therefore, indicate that the incident of attempted stripping that has ruled the popular imagination so powerfully and featured on stage, paintings, films and television as the fuse that set off the explosion destroying the Kṣatriya clans, was not part of the original text but was added later by one or more highly competent redactors' (2009: 98).

[22] See Schmithausen (1999) and Gethin (2007) for detailed discussions on Buddhist approach to violence; and Zydenbos (1999) and Dundas (2007) on Jaina approach.

The *Mahābhārata* may not contain a resolution of the issue of *hiṃsā–ahiṃsā*. Nevertheless, it demonstrates the virtue of Yudhiṣṭhira's lonely position, and in so doing, validates that position for our world of ideas.

References

Bakhtin, M. M. 2008. *The Dialogic Imagination: Four Essays*, trans. Caryl Emerson and Michael Holquist. Austin: University of Texas Press.

Bedekar, V. M. 1958. 'Ahiṃsā in the Mahābhārata — and Gandhi', in S. K. George (ed.), *Gandhi Marg*, 2(1): 119–25. Bombay: Gandhi Smarak Nidhi.

Bhattacharya, Pradip. 2009. 'Was Draupadī Ever Sought to be Disrobed?', in Kalyan Kumar Chakravarty (ed.), *Text and Variations of the Mahābhārata: Contextual, Regional and Performative Traditions*, pp. 89–99. New Delhi: Indira Gandhi National Centre for Arts (IGNCA).

Buitenen, J. A. B. van. 1981. *The Bhagavadgītā in the Mahābhārata*. Chicago: The University of Chicago Press.

Carrière, Jean-Claude. 1987. *The Mahābhārata: A Play Based upon the Indian Classic Epic*, trans. Peter Brook. New York: Harper & Row.

Chaturvedi, Badrinath. 2007. *The Mahābhārata: An Inquiry in the Human Condition*. New Delhi: Orient Longman.

Chapple, Christopher Key. 1998. *Nonviolence to Animals, Earth, and Self in Asian Traditions*. New Delhi: Sri Satguru Publications.

Dundas, Paul. 2007. 'The Non-violence of Violence: Jain Perspectives on Warfare, Asceticism and Worship', in John R. Hinnels and Richard King (eds), *Religion and Violence in South Asia: Theory and Practice*, pp. 41–61. London: Routledge.

Ganguli, Kisari Mohan (trans.). 2007[1893–96]. *The Mahābhārata of Kṛṣṇa-Dvaipāyana Vyāsa*, 12 vols. New Delhi: Munshiram Manoharlal.

Gethin, Rupert. 2007. 'Buddhist Monks, Buddhist Kings, Buddhist Violence: On the Early Buddhist Attitudes to Violence', in John R. Hinnels and Richard King (eds), *Religion and Violence in South Asia: Theory and Practice*, pp. 62–82. London: Routledge.

Hill, Peter. 2001. *Fate, Predestination and Human Action in the Mahābhārata: A Study in the History of Ideas*. New Delhi: Munshiram Manoharlal.

Jatavallabhula, Danielle Feller. 1999. 'Raṇayajña: The Mahābhārata War as a Sacrifice', in J. E. M. Houben and K. R. van Kooij (eds), *Violence Denied: Violence, Non-Violence, and the Rationalization of Violence in South Asian Cultural History*, pp. 69–103. Leiden, Boston and Koln: E. J. Brill.

Lath, Mukund. 1990. 'The Concept of *Ānṛśaṃsya* in the Mahābhārata', in R. N. Dandekar (ed.), *The Mahābhārata Revisited*, pp. 113–19. New Delhi: Sahitya Akademi.

Matilal, Bimal Krishna. 2002. 'Kṛṣṇa: In Defence of a Devious Divinity', in Jonardon Ganeri (ed.), *The Collected Essays of Bimal Krishna Matilal: Ethics and Epics*, pp. 91–108. New Delhi: Oxford University Press.

———. 1995. 'The Throne: Was Duryodhana Wrong', in G. R. Taneja and Vinod Sena (eds), *Literature East and West: Essays Presented to R. K. Dasgupta*, pp. 203–12. New Delhi: Allied Publishers.

Mishra, Vidya Nivas. 1998. *Mahābhārata kā Kavyārtha* (Hindi). New Delhi: National Publishing House.

———. 1990. 'Key-Note Address', in R. N. Dandekar (ed.), *The Mahābhārata Revisited*, pp. 19–36. New Delhi: Sahitya Akademi.

Niditch, Susan. 1993. *War in the Hebrew Bible: A Study in the Ethics of Violence*. New York: Oxford University Press.

Schmithausen, Lambert. 1999. 'Aspects of the Buddhist Attitude towards War', in J. E. M. Houben and K. R. van Kooij (eds), *Violence Denied: Violence, Non-Violence, and the Rationalization of Violence in South Asian Cultural History*, pp. 43–67. Leiden, Boston and Koln: E. J. Brill.

Shakespeare, William. 1998. *King Lear. The Arden Shakespeare*. London: Thomas Nelson and Sons Ltd.

Sukthankar, V. S. 1998[1957]. *On The Meaning of the Mahābhārata*. New Delhi: Motilal Banarsidass.

Sutton, Nicholas. 2000. *Religious Doctrines in the Mahābhārata*. New Delhi: Motilal Banarsidass.

Tubb, Gary A. 2007. 'Śāntarasa in the *Mahābhārata*', in Arvind Sharma (ed.), *Essays on the Mahābhārata*, pp. 171–203. New Delhi: Motilal Banarsidass.

Zydenbos, Robert J. 1999. 'Jainism as the Religion of Non-Violence', in J. E. M. Houben and K. R. van Kooij (eds), *Violence Denied: Violence, Non-Violence, and the Rationalization of Violence in South Asian Cultural History*, pp. 185–210. Leiden, Boston and Koln: E. J. Brill.

Just Words

An Ethics of Conversation in the Mahābhārata

Arindam Chakrabarti

Had speech (*vāk*) not been there, no one would be able to make known the distinction between just and unjust, true and false. Without the help of speech, neither good nor evil, neither the beautiful (dear to the heart) nor the repulsive would be articulately communicable. It is speech which makes all these known. Worship speech.

Chāndogya Upaniṣad VII.2.1.

Conversation, then, in which the Socratics are the best models, should have these qualities. It should be easy and not in the least dogmatic; it should have the spice of wit. And the one who engages in conversation should not debar others from participating in it, as if he were entering upon a private monopoly; but, as in other things, so in a general conversation he should think it not unfair for each to have his turn. He should observe, first and foremost, what the subject of conversation is. If it is grave, he should treat it with seriousness; if humorous, with wit. And above all, he should be on the watch that his conversation shall not betray some defect in his character. This is most likely to occur, when people in jest or in earnest take delight in making malicious and slanderous statements about the absent, on purpose to injure their reputations.

Cicero, *De Officiis* XXXVII (Cicero 1913: 134).

We call justice this face to face approach, in conversation.

Emmanuel Levinas, *Totality and Infinity* (Levinas 1969: 71).

From Ethics of Conversation to Ethics as Conversation

Conversation is central to the two-sided moral thinking of the *Mahābhārata*. Speaking is not just one among many kinds of human activity that are subject to moral appraisal and justification; it is the paradigmatic source of what we may call dialogic normativity. It is through the sieve of kind, accurate, reasoned, sincere, and candid conversation — discussing together (*sam* + *vada*) — that reflective human beings sift out good from bad, substance from chaff, correct from incorrect, virtuous from vicious conduct.[1]

> *na yaḥ samṛcche na punarhavītave, na saṁvādāya ramate /*
> *tasmānno adya samṛteruruṣyatam . . . //*
> (Save us, today, Mitra and Varuṇa,
> From those foes who *do not ask questions*,
> Do not offer sacrificial oblations, and
> *Do not rejoice at a conversation . . .*)

So prayed the Vedic seer (*Ṛgveda* VIII.101.4; translation and emphasis mine). Inquiry and conversation were as central to the culture of the Vedic people as were sacrificial rituals. Those who did not rejoice at a conversation were to be dreaded as enemies of culture. The same normative preoccupation with speech, communication and open debate[2] continued to be expressed in the *Mahābhārata* wherein it is both exemplified and self-critically theorized about.

Consider how the epic begins. Freshly back from the holy Naimiṣa forest, the bard named Ugraśravas ('Fierce to Hear') — son of Lomaharṣaṇa ('Hair-raising'),

---

[1] 'Here, as the wise ones filter out good from bad speech, as barley is sifted with a sieve, friends recognize the nature of real friendship and an auspicious sign is impressed upon their conversation' (*Ṛgveda* X.71.2).

[2] This culture of ritual debate in classical Indian philosophy has been preserved in the Tibetan Buddhist pedagogic tradition, which proves that it is compatible and continuous with the ethics of universal compassion, contrary to its appearance of combativeness. See *The Sound of Two Hands Clapping* by Georges Dreyfus. On the impact of this fondness for dialectic on Indian Philosophy, Johannes Bronkhorst remarks: 'I am speaking of the presence of a tradition of rational debate and inquiry. I use this expression to refer to a tradition that came to establish itself in India — or at least in the main philosophical schools — and that obliged thinkers to listen to the criticism of often unfriendly critics, even where it concerned their most sacred convictions, such as those supposedly based on revelation, tradition, or inspiration. Confrontations between thinkers so radically opposed to each other were no doubt facilitated by the debates organized from time to time by kings, about which we have some firsthand information from the pen of Chinese pilgrims visiting India in the middle centuries of the first millennium. Little is known about the reasons why, and the date when, this tradition of critical debate came to establish itself in India. Its effects, however, are visible in the efforts made by Indian thinkers to systematize their positions, to make them coherent and immune to criticism.

These reflections allow us to identify a particularly important factor in the development of Indian philosophy. Under pressure from competitors, the Indian thinkers of the early classical period were forced to do more than just preserve the teachings they had received; they had to improve and refine them — perhaps in order to avoid becoming the laughingstock of those they might have to confront at a royal court or on some other occasion' (Bronkhorst 2001).

the reputed *Sūta* (story-teller) — reported to the gathered sages the conversation that he had recently heard the conversation between Janamejaya and Vaiśampāyana. This conversation, in turn, was about the many conversations between Dhṛtarāṣṭra and Sañjaya, Bhīṣma and Ambā, Yudhiṣṭhira and the mysterious crane by the side of the lethal lake, Kauśika and Dharmavyādha ('righteous hunter'), Draupadī and Yudhiṣṭhira, Bhīṣma and Yudhiṣṭhira, Vasiṣṭha and Karāla Janaka, and many others. And of course, at the centre of this array of inter-discursive meta-narratives of conversations shines the most awesome conversation — *saṃvādam imam adbhutam* (*Gītā* XVIII.74) — between Kṛṣṇa and Arjuna, remembering, and again remembering which, Sañjaya told the blind king Dhṛtarāṣṭra , he could not stop shivering in awe and thrill.

Containing many such conversations with complex unanswered questions, this mammoth collection of *itihāsa* ('thus-it-was') stories is called *Jayākhyā Samhitā*. It is a continually redacted ancient compendium of conversations about even more ancient conversations, originally named *Jaya* which means victory. But whose victory is it? One cannot miss the irony of this title in the larger context of the epic because no one quite wins in this tale of a 'total war' whose longest chapter is called 'the book of peace' (*Śāntiparvan*). Eventually, we are told, justice and truth triumph, but one has to wait indefinitely for that victory to be visible, while, in the interim, all sorts of lies, deceptions and falsehoods seem to win and injustice thrives. In any finite timespan, one just sees everybody lose, every accumulation rushing towards decay, every rise ending in fall, every union culminating in separation, and every life terminating in death.[3] Just as messy as the human condition itself, it is a messy narrative of a war — a war of wits, weapons and sometimes just of words.

In this chapter, we analyze such a description of a war of words in the *Mahābhārata*. This dialogue is, in one sense, the most philosophical of all the conversations reported in the text because it is designed to be self-reflexive — *a conversation about how to converse well* and how not to converse in public. It can be called, borrowing from J. L. Austin (1975), a short treatise on how to do good and bad things with words. It is a battle of words between a philosopher king who claimed to be wiser and more liberated than outwardly world-renouncing monks and a stunningly beautiful and eloquent mendicant woman who talked lovelier than she looked, even as she eventually made the garrulous king speechless. The first speaker, Janaka — the legendary patriarch-patron of ancient Indian philosophy 'seminars' — started with a self-introduction but then hopped from topic to topic in a nervous desultory fashion, but the respondent, an itinerant nun ironically named Sulabhā ('Easy-to-Get' because she remained so hard to get for Janaka, in every sense of 'getting') structured her speech very cleverly, starting with

[3] *Sarve kṣayanta nicayaḥ patananta samucchruayaḥ / saṁyoga viprayoganta maraṇāntam ca jīvitam//* (*Śāntiparvan* 27.31, etc.).

a meta-discourse on discourse, and ending with a self-introduction. The bulk of the content of the dialogue, however, reflects the classic Indic tussle between two life-ideals: the Śramaṇic ideal of asceticism, monasticism and withdrawal from work supported by a broadly anti-essentialist metaphysics *versus* the Brahmanical ideal of flourishing householders' life, enjoyment and work, going with a world-affirming realism. At one level, therefore, it can be described as a dialogue between a *pravṛtta* (one leading an 'active' life) and a *nivṛtta* (one leading a contemplative life). To the extent that each party undermined and insulted and counter-insulted the other, both the talkers lost, though Sulabhā seemed to win because she had the last word. Of course, Truth alone wins, eventually, not falsehood — *satyam eva jayate na anṛtam* (*Muṇḍaka Upaniṣad* III.1.6), but we never quite know for sure the nature of this Truth. Ethical truth (*dharmasya tattvam*) remains hidden 'in the cave'.[4] There *is* a truth and it is possible to know it. The *Mahābhārata* is not anti-realist or skeptical about moral reality. But no one should claim exclusive privileged access to the truth about duty in all circumstances. The indecisiveness of the *Mahābhārata* as to who is the winner, Janaka or Sulabhā, narratively draws us nearer to the cognitive–discursive caution of never claiming dogmatically to have 'got it right'. Thus, the 'history' (in the sense of a narrative example) of this conversation can not only teach us thumb rules of 'just' speech and the ethico-political importance of difference-welcoming communication, but it also can help shatter our individualistic as well as collective prides and ego-centricity. The story seems to have been intended to train us to be fearless facers and speakers of truth about others and ourselves, and to beware of bullying swamping pontification or defensive self-aggrandizement.

Speaking to another human being is a free action which is governed by social rules of syntax and semantics and lexical conventions that we obey in order to give notice of both the speaker's and the listener/addressee's freedom.[5] This is

---

[4] In the first *Mahābhārata Today* workshop at Indian Institute of Advanced Study (IIAS), Shimla, in April 2010, I had suggested that 'cave' in this context means 'the depth of the heart', since there is a continuous use of the cave metaphor for the heart from the *Upaniṣads* to the *Mahābhārata*. In the Mokṣadharma conversation between the father and the son, for example, the homily ends with: 'Of what use is wealth for you, of friends, or wives, since, *Brāhmaṇa*, you are going to die. So, search for the self which is hidden in the cave. Where are your grandfathers and were would be your father?' (*Śāntiparvan* 175.38). The commentator glossed the word *guhā* here as 'intellect'. Whether it is the self or the true *dharma*, it is hard to find and must be searched for in the cave of one's own heart or intellect.

[5] The best contemporary theory of this ethical phenomenology of conversation is given by Ramchandra Gandhi (1984, 1974). Central to this theory is the idea of *sambodhana* or addressing the other, through which the speaker expresses an abandonment of causal power over the interlocutor invoking his/her freedom to respond of his/her own accord. *Sambodhana*, thus, becomes a revelation of the identity-in-face-to-face-ness between the speaker and the hearer and of the many-centeredness of the *ātman*.

why speaking is the human paradigm of voluntary rule-governed social action. We are socially obliged to do what we are 'told' to do. Perhaps, the bridging notion between speaking and ethical obligation would be the idea of 'giving one's word'. But I would like to deepen the connection between duty and interpersonal communication by trying to retrieve the idea of obligation from the moral psychology of dialogic deliberative exploration with another person and — in the latter half of the chapter — from the ancient Greek idea of 'fearless speaking of truth to power (*parrhesia*)'. Self-conscious rule-following consists in taking into account the interest — belief–desire–emotions — of others. Speaking is the arch-communicative freely rule-following action:

> Wishing to make a good statement, observing the subtle nature of morality, one should tell the truth in words which are non-hurtful, without engaging in calumny, free from deceptive deviousness, harshness, cruelty or malice. In this way, one should speak briefly with a non-distracted mind. The entire world is held together with (such) speech, if one talks properly, dispassionately and without vested interest (*Śāntiparvan* 215.12).

The world is bound up and held together (or kept awake) with words (*vāk-prabaddho hi saṃsāraḥ*, *Śāntiparvan* 215.11). From formal elocution or casual social chit-chat or gossip, to public dialogue or private tête-à-tête, friendly debate, collective deliberation, and caring conversation trying to search together for an obscure truth or determine one's duty especially at tough times of crisis, or simply asking 'how do you do?' — all kinds of speaking constitute the source of normativity. Words are deeds which, on most occasions, we claim credit for and ascribe culpability to. The social performance of such communicative acts is governed not only by lexical, syntactic and semantic rules, but also by ethical norms — norms that somehow spring from the very (context-sensitive) conditions and goals of the conversation one engages in. Much good, as well as much irremediable harm, can be done with informative, imaginative, persuasive, imperative, expressive, interrogative, entertaining, teaching, flattering, brainwashing, marketing, and other uses of words. In democracies run, and often ruined, by newspapers, advertisements, election campaigns, radio, television, the internet, facebook, and twitter, where face-to-face conversation is threatened, especially among the literate elite, by the omnipresence of remote-communication-technology — the virtues and vices of speech call for the most urgent attention.

Of course, the relationship between talking/theorizing about virtues and actual everyday *practice* of virtues remains controversial. Verbalization of and reflection on virtues of speech may or may not help speak virtuously. Does self-conscious articulation of a virtue help or hinder our practice of it? Does one censor and constrain the spontaneity and creative free flow of authentic speech by formulating an ethics of speech? If coercing others is violence and norms of good discourse tend to goad people to talk in a certain manner, then would not an ethics of discourse itself be an unethical enterprise? We will come back to these worries at the end of the chapter.

Three kinds of discourse (*kathā*) are distinguished by Gautama's *Nyāya Sūtra* (I.2.1–3): truth-seeking fair debate (*vāda*), wrangling to win (*jalpa*), and destructive disputation (*vitaṇḍā*, used by skeptics), the purpose of the last being mere refutation of the opponent. It is clear that the conversation we will examine in this chapter does not fall under any of these categories, although there is a touch of wrangling (*jalpa)* in Janaka's speech and a whiff of skeptical disputation (*vitaṇḍā*) in Sulabhā's. Some of the defects of speech that Sulabhā pointed out in Janaka's initial diatribe do, however, map on to the list of 'cases of defeat' given by *Nyāya Sūtra*, as will be mention later in the chapter.

Speech, Sacrifice and Violence in Vedic-Purāṇic Culture

In his magnum opus Vākyapadīya (*Of Sentences and Words*), *Bhartṛhari* provides us a clue to the deep connection between ethics and speech: 'All ought-to-be-done-s (*iti-kartavyatā*) of people are rooted in Word/Language (*śabda*)' (*Vākyapadīya* I.121). The standard interpretation of this is that here *śabda* means Vedic scripture. But even the idea that actions are known to be right when they are prescribed by the Vedas must not be rashly reduced to a 'divine command ethics', for Vedas were not taken as a personal God's commands by *Bhartṛhari* any more than by any *Mīmāṃsaka* or *Vedāntin.* But the new insight I derive from this very 'telling' verse, is that duties are what one is *told to do*, when the telling is done either by one's heart (*anukrośa* or outcry of the heart) or by no one in particular — a telling without a teller. In 'going up to someone'[6] in conversation, one performs one of the most moral actions one is humanly capable of. Responding to the calling, questioning, demanding, and reprimanding voice (or the face) of the other is rendered possible through the inner and public practice of speaking. It is this response to the other which constitutes the core of human moral life. In this sense, speaking is a sacrificial act, a ceremonial giving up of the solipsist reticent ego. Vedic ritual ethics — adapted to secular practice by the *Bhagavadgītā* — centred round the concept of sacrifice (*yajña*). Speech and war were both taken ritually as acts of sacrifice. Speech is fire, it burns and cooks. Trenchant words have been compared to sharp arrows, making archery a standard metaphor for public debate in the Vedic–Purāṇic literature. Recall Gārgī's challenging pair of questions compared to two killer arrows (in a symposium of philosophers, presided over by Janaka,

[6] 'Yes, meaning is like going upto someone'(Wittgenstein, *Philosophical Investigations*, Part 1, remark no. 458).

where Gārgī spoke up, even after being threatened by Yājñavalkya that she was crossing the limits of interrogation and her head would fall off if she asked any more questions):

> Just as an archer, son of some fierce king from Kāśī or Videha, lifts up and re-strings a bow which was once put down, aiming two sharp arrows at an enemy, I have risen again to ask you two questions, Yājñavalkya! If you can answer them, then I shall announce you to be the winner of this philosophical contest (*Bṛhadāraṅyaka Upaniṣad* III.6, 8).

The same metaphor of utterances as arrows reappears in the *Mahābhārata* verse: 'From the mouth spring out speech-arrows (*vāk-saayakaāḥ*) wounded by which, the victims suffer day and night, as they fall on other persons' hearts' (*Haṃsa Gītā* [*Sermon of the Swan*], in *Śāntiparvan* 299.9). Indeed, the gruesome scar (*bībhatsam kṣatam*) left by evil speech is said to be harder to heal than the damage done by an axe or piercing arrow (*Anuśāsanaparvan* 104.33).

As against this violent aspect of killer speech, which is to be abjured, there are at least three positive senses in which an act of talking to someone can be looked upon as a meritorious sacrifice. The concept of *yajña* (sacrifice) has an aspect of renunciation and an aspect of ritual violence to it, and the violence is sublimated and kept in control only through the practice of the ego-offering (*na-mama* ['not-mine'] = *namaḥ*) to the Other. The morally cleansing renunciation or relinquishment of ego works in three ways through speech.

First, participation in public language — since all language is public — requires relinquishing of privacy or exclusive ownership of one's ideas and sentiments. To speak one's mind sincerely is to give up exclusive proprietorship of one's ideas and let go of one's feelings. Telling is letting others know what one has come to know as beneficial truth. The truthful and reliable teller, i.e., *āpta*, thus, has been characterized in the *Nyāyabhāṣya*, as one who acts out of compassion towards others. When speech is used as a wounding weapon, to lie, to mislead, to plant seeds of mistrust between friends, to divide and rule, to sell for the sake of personal profit, to bribe, to blackmail, basically to take away rather than give, it thwarts and distorts this very purpose of *śabda*, just as the lethal crushing embrace of Bhīma by Dhṛtarāṣṭra at the end of the war perverted the purpose of a hug.

Second, from a very cryptic allusion in the ancient Ṛgvedic *Kauṣītaki Upaniṣad* 2.5, we come to know of the very ancient concept of *prāṇāgnihotra* ('internal fire-sacrifice') which construes any act of speaking as sacrificing one's breath to the fire-god of speech, while keeping quiet in order to breathe properly when one could have spoken is construed as offering one's speech to the fire of breath.[7]

[7] Abhinavagupta in his commentary on *Bhagavadgītā* IV.68 goes into fascinating esoteric details as to how teaching–learning can become a mutual knowledge-sacrifice performed by the teacher and the pupil.

Third, in a context of debate, in truth-seeking discourse (*vāda-kathā*), to speak and put forward one's position is to make oneself open to refutation and criticism. The *Caraka Saṃhitā* distinguishes between two kinds of discourse — disputative/aggressive (*vigṛhya*) and co-operative/friendly (*sandhāya*). But in both discourses, the speaker has to be ready to give up one's view if a fallacy is exposed in one's contention or argument. In a less structured conversation, assuming the role of a caring listener requires setting aside one's own egotistical interests and biases. Thus, speech-sacrifice deserves the title of a *satra*. This could be why actual sacrificial routines used to include a debate session, and sometimes the topic would be precisely whether the sacrifice had been successful or well-done or not. At the end of a *satra* or long sacrificial festival like the horse-sacrifice (*Aśvamedha*) that Yudhiṣṭhira performed after the war to cleanse himself of the sin of killing his kinsfolk, priests performing the roles of a reviler (*apagara*) and a praiser (*abhigara*) would come at the end, the former pointing out the failure and faults, and the latter the greatness and success of the sacrifice. At the end of his *Aśvamedha*, as Yudhiṣṭhira was about to enter back the royal citadel as the victorious king, and priests and guests were profusely praising his unparalleled generosity, we are told, a scary-looking black-eyed mongoose appeared and started berating the recently completed sacrifice. His body was half gold. He said that he used to live in a hole in the hut of a poor family who lived on scavenging grains from the fields after the crops had been harvested. When one day, in spite of being on the brink of starvation, all members of the family, one by one, gave away, their share of the last handful of cooked grains they had gathered, to a hungry guest, the family was welcomed to heaven as divine immortals. Witnessing all this, the mongoose came out of his hole and rolled on the left-over particles of this sacred food-offering. That turned one side of his body to gold. He came to Yudhiṣṭhira's sacrifice to try to make the other half golden too by rolling on the dust left over from the gift-giving ceremony. But there was nothing left. Hence, the sacrifice, for him was all in vain!

This interruptive story told by a fearlessly truth-speaking animal serves two purposes: to show that even the greatest ritual of gift-giving and sacrifice leaves someone utterly unfulfilled, and to show how completely selfless acts of hospitality can make mortals immortal. Sulabhā questioned Janaka's reputation of being truly liberated, while the mongoose questioned Yudhiṣṭhira's reputation of being consummately generous. In both cases, the speech of a stranger-guest disrupted the complacency of the powerful. With speech we give ourselves, but no giving is enough, since our debt and responsibility to the other is infinite.[8]

[8] Before we mine this unique *Mahābhārata* episode of a war of words, a linguistic battle between a philosopher king and a mendicant woman, in search for a virtue-ethics of speech, let us remind ourselves of the modern European/Jewish ethical philosophy of speech articulated by Emmanuel Levinas: 'Speech first founds community by *giving*, by presenting the phenomenon as given; and it gives by thematizing. The given is the work of a sentence' (1969: 98).

We hear of a set of verses beginning with 'Do not be a heart-breaker, do not speak cruelly, . . . a wise man does not hurl such verbal attacks on others' (*Sabhāparvan* 66.6), in the voice of Vidura, the lone pro-Pāṇḍava voice of virtue in Dhṛtarāṣṭra's corrupt court, just when Draupadī had been staked as a bet and lost in the rigged game of dice, and Karṇa and Duryodhana were staging the public stripping of their cousins' wife using heart-breaking abusive language. The same set of warnings against verbal abuse is repeated in the *Haṃsa Gītā* (*Śāntiparvan* 299.8–10) and again in the conversation between Umā and Maheśvara (*Anuśāsanaparvan* 104.33–34). Verbal abuse must have been as commonly committed an offence then as it is now.

The Encounter and Its Narrational Context

Towards the end of the sprawling *Śāntiparvan* (Chapter 56) , Yudhiṣṭhira, himself ageing and watching his gallant grandfather Bhīṣma wait for death on his bed of arrows with stoic resignation, expressed his worry about how to win over the twin scourges of human existence, ageing and death. Could they be overcome by immense wealth, very long life, ascetic austerities, memorable work or erudition, or by some alchemical rejuvenation? In response, Bhīṣma repeated a short conversation between king Janaka and his illustrious *Sāṃkhya* teacher Pañcaśikha. After an extremely poetic meditation on how time is devouring every being who is born and carrying us constantly closer to death, Pañcaśikha summarized, as it were, the second chapter of *Bhagavadgītā* to the effect that there is a deathless self in each of us, identifying with which one ought to neither celebrate birth nor lament death, and live through charity and worship, without violating traditional ethical codes. Yudhiṣṭhira came back with the central question of the *Mahābhārata*, obviously alluding to Janaka's fame as a saintly regent who attained the same spiritual emancipation that ascetics sought, without renouncing worldly activities: 'Could one ever attain liberation — that ultimate aim of life — without giving up one's involvement with the social life of a householder?' (*Śāntiparvan* 320.1). That Bhīṣma told this Janaka–Sulabhā story when he was asked this question makes us wonder exactly how Bhīṣma wanted to answer the question. The story clearly shows that Janaka pompously claimed for himself the status of a liberated soul, but his spiritual and soteriological pride was shattered by the sharp and eloquent mendicant woman who fearlessly told him the truth and exposed him to be 'not quite there yet'. So, what should Yudhiṣṭhira learn from this story? Surely, he was not being told to emulate Sulabhā, nor could he be expected to model himself on the pathetic character of Janaka. Was he supposed to learn that a king, while enjoying his wealth, reputation and power, could be really as free and morally as elevated as a mendicant woman who remained genuinely unperturbed by the worst public humiliation? It seems that the text is a resounding 'no' to this question. Rather, Bhīṣma seems to be warning Yudhiṣṭhira that even the most well-trained philosopher-king could turn out to be a self-deluded 'liberation'-talker (*mokṣa-vārttika*, as Sulabhā called him) while trying angrily to prove that the monastic guest was an imposter! In the larger context, such a message by a dying royal grandfather who was showing Yudhiṣṭhira how to remain tranquil and free while discharging one's royal duties is at best quizzical and at worst cynical. But that is how *Mahābhārata* deals with ethical issues, telling inspiring stories, but then adding narrative caveats of indeterminacy and alternative views to a decisively preferred solution to a moral problem. Can one attain *mokṣa* without becoming a *sannyāsin* (renouncer)? The narrative answer through the Sulabhā story seems to be a profoundly wry: 'Yes, of course, but . . .'.

Even if it is taken as a 'narrative caveat', we do not know if we should take it as a dialogue which happened between two people in the 'age of virtues' (*dharma yuge*) or as a metaphor of a struggle that happened in Janaka's own mind. Just as the *Gītā* happens in the 'space of morality' (*dharma kṣetre*), this dialogue is said to have taken place in the 'time of morality' (*dharma yuge*). Could it be a time of reckoning that comes in everyone's life when inside their their soul and body two sides argue against each other, and the debate, if fair and even, keeps them walking the middle path, if the debate is fair and even? This doubt arises because of a very puzzling preparatory statement made by Bhīṣma, the didactic story-teller:[9]

> Listen to this conversation between a man who was liberated in the midst of the pomp of royal insignias and umbrellas and a woman who was equally liberated with the formal monastic signs of carrying a triple staff and a water-pot — *a conversation that happened in one single locus* (*Śāntiparvan* 320.19).

Commentator Nīlakaṇṭha interprets this 'locus' somewhat oddly to mean that two souls can occupy one single gross body because the body is nothing but a house of the self. He comments: 'The significance of this story is that each of them left their identification with the gross external body' and got together in a single body. Well, that would be interesting. Whose body, Janaka's or Sulabhā's, we need to get clear but we cannot. Does Bhīṣma want us to imagine that Sulabhā literally entered the body of Janaka? Or is it simply the royal assembly hall in Mithilā that is being spoken of as 'one location'? That would be a disappointing and implausible interpretation. Nīlakaṇṭha gets carried away and remarks: 'By means of this story, the point is being made that just as the house is not the self of the house-owner, in a single subtle body, two individual souls (*jīva*s) can exist for some time, hence neither the gross nor the subtle body is the self of the person'. But, did not the dialogue happen publicly because Janaka was chastised by Sulabhā for bringing up unseemly suspicions in the middle of an assembly, and Janaka complained that Sulabhā was trying to overpower his entire cabinet of ministers and eyeing even his courtiers? So, perhaps, the suggestion is that even public dialogues happen

---

[9] *Ekasmin adhiṣṭhāne saṃvādaḥ śrūyatām ayam.*

simultaneously inside each interlocutor's body, or perhaps, within the body of the single Vedic–Purāṇic cultural ethos, the tussle between masculine power/knowledge and feminine frank speech and renunciation was constantly happening? Is this a dialogue happening inside the listener's body, be it Yudhiṣṭhira's or ours? Or, is it a conversation of cultures, between the *Rajarṣi/Kṣatriya/* urban culture and the Śramaṇic/monastic/wilderness counterculture? Is this a dramatization of the perpetual inner 'unhomeliness' of the Indic mind?

Even the stereotypes are reversed here. In the dialogue between the victorious but disenchanted king Yudhiṣṭhira and the bitterly ambitious queen Draupadī, at the end of the total war, the virtuous husband wished to quit the world of power, and the enraged wife called him insane and urged him to enjoy the kingdom, power and prosperity. In the Janaka–Sulabhā story, on the contrary, the female voice representing unworldliness derided the life of a king, whereas the insecure and aggressive male voice defended the socially engaged royal life as an authentic practice of detachment in the midst of opulence!

We break up both the speeches of Janaka and Sulabhā into several segments and try to analyze them from different angles. Fortunately, we do not have to solve the historical riddle as to whether the Janaka of *Bṛhadāraṇyaka Upaniṣad*, the Janaka of *Rāmāyaṇa* who adopted Sītā as his daughter, and the Janaka spoken of in the *Śāntiparvan* (320.4–6) are the same or namesakes. Here, we are given another tell-tale sobriquet of Janaka, *Dharmadhvaja* (flag-waver of *dharma*). In this name the seed of pretentiousness is already present because in *Mahābhārata*'s Sanskrit the word *dharmadhvajin* refers in a derogatory manner to a man who shows off how righteous and pious he is. This flag-waving pious king is introduced as someone who attained the fruit of complete renunciation (*sannyāsa phalika*) without leaving his kingship. He performed his scripturally enjoined duty as a king perfectly, controlling his senses while ruling the earth. His fame as one learned in the Vedas, an efficient ruler and a spiritually emancipated philosopher made other kings yearn to be like him.

The identity of Sulabhā, our second protagonist, is shrouded in mystery though one could conjecture some vague link with a lost part of the Vedic corpus called *Saulabhya Brāhmaṇa*. We are told that in the same age of *dharma*, an alms-begging female called Sulabhā, belonging to the mendicant order, practised the regimen of *Yoga* and wandered over the whole earth. In course of her wanderings, Sulabhā heard from many staff-carrying ascetics of different places that the ruler of Mithilā was a living-liberated person of perfect wisdom. Hearing so about king Janaka and curious whether it was true or not, Sulabhā sought a personal interview with Janaka. One adjective of the mendicant woman that is very significant is that she 'moved as fast as a light speedy missile' (*laghv-astra-gati-gāminī*, *Śāntiparvan* 320.11). Clearly, it is an epithet of her super-quick wit transferred to her physical motion, but the narrator also wished to remind us that her mind was working like an *astra* — a weapon — in this conversation. No wonder Janaka was on the defensive from the very get go.

At the start, of course, Janaka showed ritual hospitality to Sulabhā, his unexpected guest. For a householder, Bhīṣma told Yudhiṣṭhira: 'there is no other God except the guest'.[10] Janaka offered Sulabhā a special couch, got her feet washed and welcomed her with fine food. But when Sulabhā made eye-contact with Janaka, apparently arresting the king in a psychic lock (*yoga-bandha*), Janaka felt uncomfortable. In that assembly of master commentators on religious and philosophical texts, as Janaka sat surrounded by his ministers, this *yoga*-adept *bhikṣuki* (female mendicant) entered his intellect with her intellect.[11]

The Perturbed Philosopher-King's Pompous Peroration

Ravished, confused and threatened by the young nun's irresistible physical charm and extraordinary yogic powers, the philosopher king started rambling in the royal assembly. First, he threw a volley of questions at her. Then, he embarked on a long self-flattering elocution about his own intellectual pedigree and his philosophical position. Thereafter, he brought a slew of charges against Sulabhā — allegations of hiding her real caste and origins, having illicit designs, and disturbing the social order in several ways by proposing to create several kinds of unhealthy hybridity.

Before we get into the actual dialogue between them, we must first take a look at the psycho-social power structure of the communicative platform: Sulabhā was supposed to ask the questions and catch a glimpse of Janaka's soul to check if it was really liberated or not. In order to do that she captured the king's attention with some *yoga-bandhas* (*bandha* is in plural because at many levels she held Janaka as a 'captive audience'). As if casting a hypnotic spell on him, she made him talk

---

[10] *Tasmād gṛhasthāśramasthasya nānyad daivatamasti vai/ ṛte'tithim . . .//* (*Anuśāsanaparvan* 2.90).

[11] Nīlakaṇṭha raises here some fascinating philosophical questions. Given that one's own intellect is internal to the individual and another person's intellect is entirely inaccessible to oneself, how could this 'intellectual entering' happen? His answer invokes the Vedāntic as well as *Sāṃkhya* doctrine that *buddhi-sattva* is, after all, a material substance, and through the visual sense-organ — itself physical — it can come out and take the shape of the object, which in this case would be the intellect of another person. This is the peculiar *Advaita Vedānta* doctrine of perception where the *antaḥkaraṇa* is like a liquid which can actually spill out through a sensory channel and assume the form of an external object and return to give rise to an apparent modification of consciousness which is felt like a piece of perceptual awareness. Basically, with special concentration techniques, a direct perception of other's mental states and thoughts is held to be possible. Nīlakaṇṭha also keeps up the battle-metaphor for this encounter, calling both the intellects of Janaka and Sulabhā weapons (*buddhi astra*) which are equal to one another in power.

first, rather rave randomly. The text uses a rare adverb *utsmayan* (*Śāntiparvan* 320.18) to describe Janaka's attitude. What does *utsmayan* mean? Literally, it can be broken into *ut* ('up') and *smayan* ('derisively smiling'), so it must mean 'with a supercilious derisive attitude'. Nīlakaṇṭha conjectures that it means 'showing pride in his own invincibility'. Taking up her testing spirit as a challenge, combatively Janaka started the war of words with a slew of questions: 'Where are you from, where are you off to, who do you belong to? In your education, age, and caste, I suspect something not quite right'. Trying to show that he was not overpowered by her,[12] Janaka said, 'Your ladyship! Where have you practised this ascetic life *(kva carya iyam kṛta)*? Who do you belong to? From where have you come? Where are you headed?' (*Śāntiparvan* 320.20).

Without waiting for an answer, arrogantly and insecurely, Janaka volunteered to speak about himself , his state of liberation and about two traditional ways of attaining it: the way of knowledge and the way of action. Then, he claimed that his teacher had trained him in a third middle way which enabled him to possess the highest knowledge of ultimate reality and the self, without giving up social, domestic and ritual actions. He further said that he might look like an ordinary monarch attached to his royal privileges and powers, but actually he was a liberated sage (in fact, several times in the *Mahābhārata*, Janaka's tagline has been quoted as his sign of consummate wisdom and detachment: 'Either even this body is not mine, or the entire world is mine, and what is it to me if Mithilā is burnt down?') and was uniquely qualified to give her some philosophical lessons! Introducing himself as the most favourite disciple of the venerable Pañcaśikha, belonging to the mendicant order, of Parāśara's ancestry, Janaka claimed that he was not only fully conversant with *Sāṃkhya* and *Yoga* but he also had personally attained liberation and perfect equanimity and tranquility of mind. Indeed, his equality of attitude towards friends and foes had reached such a perfection that he felt the same towards one who smeared sandalwood paste on his right hand and one who tried to chop off his left hand. But, giving expression to, as it were, a renunciation-envy, he kept harping on a jealous comparison with the shaven-headed, triple-staff-bearing nun:

> Look at me, how am I any less liberated than you are. If emancipatory knowledge can come from bearing those three sticks, why cannot such knowledge come from bearing the scepter of a king? All actions are motivated by the desire to relieve some pain, including the action of leaving home and adopting the life of an alms-begging spiritual practitioner. If a king relieves his pain by having a golden parasol held above his head and a monk relieves his pain by wearing ochre robes and triple-staff, why should one be loftier than the other with respect to spiritual enlightenment? (*Śāntiparvan* 320.42–50).

---

[12] *Svasya anabhibhūtatvam darśayan,* according to Nīlakaṇṭha.

Anticipating the charge that a king could not ever be spiritually liberated because he had to reward and punish his subjects and thus get involved with their good and bad deeds, Janaka remarked that even monks reprimanded some people and placated others, so they were just as involved as a king whereas the king could be just as uninvolved if he practised being a disinterested witness inside while being outwardly engaged in political activities:

> The wearing of ochre robes, shaving of the head, bearing of the triple stick, and the water-pot — these are the outward signs of one's monastic mode of life. These have no value in aiding one to the attainment of liberation. There is no special metaphysical freedom in being penniless and no necessary bondage associated with owning property. The fetters constituted by kingdom and affluence, my tie to attachments, I have cut off with the sword of renunciation sharpened on the whetting stone of the scriptures dealing with spiritual release (*Śāntiparvan* 320.47–52).

Minus the tirade against external monasticism, the words of wisdom that Janaka said are very much consonant with the ones we find, for instance, in third, fourth, ninth and 18th chapters of the *Bhagavadgītā*. He applied to himself the description 'treating a clod of earth, a piece of stone, and a lump of gold as the same' (*Śāntiparvan* 320.37) which we also find in the *Gītā* VI.8. But notice the high rhetoric of self-flattery which soon degenerates into a repetitious defensive drone. 'That is who I am, freed from all attachments and no less disinterested in worldly things than you are'. Such overt conceit, which almost begins to sound like the self-refutation 'No one is as non-egotistical as I am', is then betrayed by further self-refuting statements, such as 'I have developed a certain trusting affection towards you, so I think that your monastic appearance is a false front'(*Śāntiparvan* 320.53). Janaka got entangled in his own mood-swing between attraction and alarm, trying to at once impress her and instruct and rebuke her, as he started telling Sulabhā that her demeanor did not befit the mode of life to which she professed allegiance. 'You have a shapely body bursting (*agryam*) with beauty and youth, yet you are apparently under a vow of asceticism. That is the ground of my suspicion'. At this point, the text of Janaka's speech became a bit obscure and controversial. *Śāntiparvan* 320.55 starts by stating that Sulabhā's carrying the triple-staff is a mark of desirelessness, and her being 'obviously' full of desire (Janaka imagined all through that Sulabhā was basically seducing him!). Is is not fair or justified to argue that she was not maintaining whatever vow she had taken. According to one reading, the verse ends with 'A liberated person does not have anything to hide' (*na muktasya asti gopanā*); according to another version, 'A completely liberated person should protect herself' (*vimuktasya asti gopanā*). Nīlakaṇṭha plays with both readings. In any case, Janaka got more and more upset protesting against Sulabhā's entry not only into his city and palace, but into his heart without her having any right to do so. What seems to be happening has a perennial gender-economic pattern to it. It is the familiar kind of masculine narcissism which turns into anger when snubbed and blames its own weak incontinence on the woman's 'unruly and deviant' (because the patriarch could not figure it out) sexuality, completely ignoring the intellectual content of the woman's engagement.[13]

Janaka's Four Allegations against Sulabhā

> Firstly, you are mixing *varṇas*, you belong to the foremost of all the orders, being a *Brāhmaṇa* woman. I am a *Kṣatriya*. There is no union for the two of us. Do not cause an intermixture of *varṇas* (colours/castes). You have committed yourself to *mokṣa*-oriented life-stage of a mendicant recluse, whereas I live in the domestic stage of life, This, your entering into my palace and my body and mind, therefore, is another evil you have done, for it produces an unnatural confusion of two incompatible stages of life. I do not know whether you belong to my own *gotra* (kinship-lineage) or not. And you do not know what *gotra* I belong to. If by chance we are of the same kinship line, our union would be a third kind of illicit intermixture [indirectly, endogamy]. If, again, your husband is alive, somewhere far away, then by adulterously getting together with me you are committing the fourth sin of violation of conjugal *dharma* (*Śāntiparvan* 320.59–62).

The fourth he called *dharmasaṃkara* in a rather strained sense because it was not a case of mixing of two *dharmas*. The concept shifts from hybridity (in case of the first two intermixtures she was charged with) to hypocrisy and possibly adultery. What it amounted to was the charge of cheating on Sulabhā's hypothetical spouse. Not only did Janaka project his own lust on to Sulabhā — a perennial patriarchal trait of blaming the victim — his language became ruder and ruder until he used the abusive word 'wicked woman' (*duṣṭā*) and complained that she had exposed herself to be a whore-like character. The speech that began by noting that Sulabhā deserved to be honoured (*mānārhā*) ended with the strange allegation that by casting seductive glances at the king and his respectable courtiers, the fraudulent nun was attempting to win an occult sexual victory over the entire court of Janaka! The most frightened and confused words of reproach from Janaka are the following:

> Moreover, this occult connection that you have brought about between you and me, by entering my body and mind, with God knows what design, is like the mixture of

[13] There have been some studies of the gender dynamics behind the Sulabhā-Janaka exchange, notably by Ruth Vanita (2003). But more detailed study needs to be done on the *Mahābhārata*'s deliberately ambiguous stance regarding the respectful, method-conscious, systematic dismantling of male dominance done by Sulabhā in her public debate with Janaka, literally the Patriarch. In this essay, I have focused mostly on the ethics of speech and fearless speaking of truth to power, but the gender politics of conversation, for example between Draupadī and Yudhiṣṭhira, between Sulabhā and Janaka, between Gāndhārī and Kṛṣṇa, and between Gārgī and Janaka, remains an equally important area of research not explored by this essay.

> poison and ambrosia [ensuring both death and immortality?]. The union of a willing pair of a man and a woman is eternally enjoyable like ambrosia. But this unavailability of any loving man for you [and your trying to mate with me, an unwilling partner] is as abominable as poison (*Śāntiparvan* 320.69).

Showing touchiness unbecoming for a metaphysical monarch, Janaka blurted out: 'Do not touch [me], do not give up [your sacred vow of abstinence].[14] Be assured that I am an honest righteous man. Now go and follow the dictates of your own scriptures' (*Śāntiparvan* 320.70). Let us pause here a little to consider how the threatened sage-king was trying to *control or deny his own inappropriate desire* for possessing this female ascetic by playing an offensive game as the best defense.

Fake *Yogi*s and Pretentious Sage-Kings: Interlude on Desire and Hypocrisy

Both parties of the dialogue ended up calling the other a hypocrite of some sort. Next to cruelty, the *Mahābhārata* decries hypocrisy as a common vice. The virtue that ensues from eliminating hypocrisy is straightness, sincerity and authenticity (*ārjava*), a kind of honesty that amounts to the practice of truthfulness. The *Mahābhārata* bristles with harsh warnings against hypocrisy, especially ostentatious performance of piety and austerity for the sake of attaining social prestige. For instance, Kṛṣṇa warns in the *Gītā* (III.6): 'Repressing the motor-organs externally, one who internally keeps thinking about the objects of sensual enjoyment, he is called an "imposter" and he is self-deluded'. Elsewhere, the religious hypocrite is spoken of more unforgivingly: 'Cruel inside but sweet in speech, like wells concealed in grass, these mean creatures go around waving the flag of righteousness, using religion as a bird-catching trap-cage (*dharma-vaitaṃsika*)' (*Śāntiparvan* 158.18). This seems to be a description of modern-day god-men. Some of the words used by Janaka against Sulabhā and mendicant (Śramaṇic) wandering monks in general were used against Janaka himself by his wife Kauśalyā when, once in chapter 18 of the *Śāntiparvan*, he had shaved his head and was getting ready to leave his family and retire to an ascetic life of a monk. Monks were called by her (Janaka's wife) simple parasites whose vow of poverty and living on a handful of grains could be sustained only by householders who made enough money and looked after the welfare of society. Janaka, surely, was not one of those hypocrites posturing as a 'holy man'. Rather, he suspected Sulabhā to be such a 'fake saint'. In his dialogue with Sulabhā, he himself came pretty close to being a self-deceiving insecure character, simply because of his grandiose claims about his own liberated status and his unconcealed vulnerability to the attractions of this powerful

---

[14] The text here is uncertain: it could be *mā spārkṣīḥ* ('do not touch'), or *mā tyākṣīḥ* ('do not give up').

parrhesiastes (we will explore what that meant in Greco-Roman literature, following Michel Foucault's analysis) who wanted to inhabit him for only one day just to check him out. Desire had surely overtaken him but he showed how unshaken he was. He was miffed but he tried to maintain, though not with much success, a calm appearance.

At least in this episode, Janaka's intellectual and spiritual pride made him utterly self-blind. He refused to recognize that it was he who had been smitten by Sulabhā and not the other way around. He claimed to have conquered his own passions, and tried to show up the officially ascetic passion-renouncer to be overcome by lust for him! In the process, he only made himself a laughing stalk for Desire who speaks in his own voice in the *Âśvamedhikaparvan* of the *Mahābhārata*:

> No living being can defeat me without an appropriate method, though some try hard to kill me with a weapon they know to be powerful. For them, I re-emerge anew in that very weapon.
>
> When for example, some people try to destroy me by means of sacrificial rituals, ceremoniously giving away various kinds of precious gifts, I, Desire, appear in their minds again, in the form of a craving for heaven or reputation, like a pious soul reborn as a living moving sentient creature.
>
> When some people try to destroy me by constant contemplation of Veda and Vedānta, I reappear in their philosophical egos, imperceptibly as the elemental soul is present in a subtle form even in immobile plants.
>
> . . . The learned one exerts himself to get rid of me by striving to attain liberation (*mokṣa*). I dance and laugh at him, because he sits right in the middle of his burning Desire for freedom!
>
> Thus, am I one perennial force, never to be killed by any embodied being, unless they adopt appropriate technique (*Kāma Gītā* [*Sermon of Desire*] in *Āśvamedhikaparvan* 13.12–18).

When Janaka was rebuked by his wife (*Śāntiparvan* 18) for his inauthentic resignation, his lack of commitment to family duties and his escapist inclination towards renouncing domestic life in search of emancipatory wisdom and transcendence, he learnt to embrace the life of a dutiful husband and king, with an inner resignation and equipoise. He would now be rebuked again, from the diametrically opposite point of view, for his unacknowledged over-attachment to his royal position, by a nun who found him not resigned enough. Yudhiṣṭhira was told this story because he was also similarly upbraided — and indeed diagnosed as clinically insane — by Draupadī for expressing a desire to become a mendicant alms-begging monk. Persuaded to opt for the other extreme, he might have overestimated the worth of his *Kṣatriya* paradigm of a Janaka-like, free-in-the world engaged king. How is the *karmayoga* (*Yoga*) versus *jñānayoga* (*Sāṃkhya*) tussle panning out here?

At the end of the war when Yudhiṣṭhira could not stop feeling guilty and disillusioned, and wanted to leave the kingdom and become a mendicant ascetic, the sharp-tongued Draupadī once again took her eldest husband to task and bracketed him with 'those anti-social anti-Vedic heretics' when he refused to rejoice at the five brothers' final triumph over the Kaurava regime of evil. Calling herself the unluckiest of all women with bitter sarcasm, Draupadī mockingly suggested:

> If your brothers have not gone equally insane along with you, they should now lock you up along with the heretics (*nāstikas*, possibly Ājīvikas) and themselves enjoy and rule the earth. Someone like you going astray from the path of duty deserves to be treated as a mentally deranged person with medicinal herbs, incense, snuff and eye-ointments (*Śāntiparvan* 14.33–35).

Yudhiṣṭhira — whom I see more in the image of the conscientious reader of the *Mahābhārata*, rather than the hero — remained in a double-bind till the end as to whether to lead the life of aggressive action and consumption of the world, or to retire to the forest and get immersed in contemplative inaction and detachment? He put his dilemma most succinctly in response to Arjuna: 'Both are injunctions of the Vedas "Do the work" and "Renounce all work"' (*ubhayam veda-vacanam kuru karma, tyaja iti ca*) (*Śāntiparvan* 19.1).

To come back to the story that Bhīṣma continued to narrate:

> Though rebuffed by the king's unpleasant, unreasonable, and inappropriate desultory sentences, the dignified Sulabhā did not show any signs of being shaken or upset. After the king was done speaking these words, Sulabhā started speaking with calmness and grit. She was charming to look at but her words were even more charming (*Śāntiparvan* 320.76–77).

The text thus teases us to make sure we focus on her logic rather than on her looks, which is something that Janaka, the typical male philosopher, apparently had a hard time doing.

Sulabhā's Discourse on the Norms of Civil Discourse[15]

Apparently ignoring all the abusive aspersions levelled at her, Sulabhā quietly started with her rules of decent discourse: 'Speech must be free from the nine blemishes of expression and nine blemishes of intent that taint the understanding. Discourse should also, while putting forward the purported meaning with perspicuity, possess eighteen well-known qualities' (*Śāntiparvan* 320.78). In

---

[15] The statements cited from Janaka–Sulabhā dialogue in this section can be found in *Śāntiparvan* 320.20–75 (Janaka's speech) and 320.78–190 (Sulabhā's speech).

dramatic contrast to the flustered, personal and angry manner of Janaka's speech, Sulabhā's response was patient, methodical, and impersonal, with a formal meta-discourse on the ethics of discourse. As if ignoring all these personal questions, she spoke in abstract generality about how, ideally, meaningful words should be combined into sentences in order to perform obligatory communicative acts. Her refusal to retaliate verbally reminds us of the formulation of what is the noblest human virtue in the *Haṃsa Gītā* (*Śāntiparvan* 299.20): 'When I am cursed I do not curse back, self-control is the door to immortality, and I am telling you this sacred secret: "There is nothing higher than being human"'.

The 18 virtues of talk that Sulabhā listed consist of avoidance of 18 verbal vices, divided into nine faults of performance and nine faults of intent. The nine flaws of performance are as follows: (*a*) verboseness; (*b*) offensive/vulgar words (described beautifully as 'that from which only turning away is pleasurable' [*parānmukhasukham*], which, in turn, reflexively captures what she was doing with Janaka's vulgar speech: enjoying it by ignoring it!); (*c*) untruth; (*d*) utterances flouting all three 'human ends', viz., justice/righteousness, prosperity and pleasure; (*e*) uncultured or ungrammatical speech; (*f*) incomplete, too laconic and scanty speech; (*g*) strained, tortured phrases (The Sanskrit word for this particular infelicity of speech is *kaṣṭa-śabdam*, of which an interesting example supplied by Nīlakaṇṭha's gloss is the use of the word *vijitātmabhavadveṣi* to refer to Karṇa because he was the rival [*dveṣi*] of Arjuna, the son [*ātmabhava*] of Indra, who, in turn, was won (*jita*) by Garuḍa (*vi*); (*h*) arrogant (out-of-turn) talk; and (*i*) unreasonable, irrelevant speech.

While listing the nine flaws of judgment (*buddhi*) or intention, Sulabhā adopted a first-person voice saying: 'I shall never speak with these sorts of intent' (*Śāntiparvan* 320.90), but it is clear that she was obliquely shaming Janaka by doing a psychological analysis of how *he* spoke.

So, the cognitive–affective improprieties of speech listed by Sulabhā, along with their illustrative examples, are as follows.

(*a*) Speaking out of lust: Janaka's repeated mention of Sulabhā's young shapely body and its beauty, and his assumption that she was sexually interested in Janaka show that this was how he was speaking.
(*b*) Speaking out of rage: This is exemplified by the subtext of Janaka's statement, 'Why have you come to my kingdom, by closeness to which influential person have you gained access to my palace? How dare you create four kinds of illicit mingling? You are a lose woman! Don't touch me!'.
(*c*) Speaking out of fear: This is reflected in Janaka's paranoia that Sulabhā wanted to win over his entire entourage and all the men in his assembly.
(*d*) Speaking out of greed: This would apply to most contemporary marketing talk that one is taught in management schools and much contemporary profit-making journalism. But the *Mahābhārata* is supremely sensitive about greedy teachers of science and philosophy who sell their intellectual

capital. In a fine passage (of the crucial Chapter 142 of *Śāntiparvan* from which I glean the clearest recommendation of 'two-sided moral thinking'), Bhīṣma castigated such greedy falsely wise people (*mithyā-vijñāninaḥ*): 'By berating others' knowledge-disciplines, those who advertise their own knowledge-disciplines, using their discourse as weapons or arrows, know them to be demonic knowledge-merchants (*Śāntiparvan* 142.15–16) Was Sulabhā insinuating that Janaka was one of these greedy self-promoting 'academics' since he was selling his own learning and glorifying his own philosophical lineage and berating the monastic tradition represented by her?

(*e*) Speaking out of smallness/diffidence: 'Am I less dispassionate than you just because I am sitting on a throne under a golden canopy?'

(*f*) Speaking out of undignified egotism: 'There is no one else who can speak of *mokṣa* other than me!'

(*g*) Speaking out of shame: Being 'caught' as clearly enamoured by a young nun in the presence of all his courtiers, flatterers and ministers was really embarrassing for Janaka, provoking his allegations against her!

(*h*) Speaking out of pity for the interlocutor: I feel sorry for you that you never found a husband equal to your caliber, and that you wanted to unite with me but I cannot oblige you!

(*i*) Speaking out of conceit: The entire speech of Janaka is an illustration of this fault.

Thereafter, Sulabhā also gave a list of positive verbal virtues. Good sentences should be:

(*a*) complete (*upetārtham*), i.e., they should not leave out any signified meaning unsaid;

(*b*) non-equivocal and coherent (*abhinnārtham*);

(*c*) judicious and logically well-constructed (*nyāyavṛttam*);

(*d*) concise, not too long-winded (*na ca adhikam*);

(*e*) full of grace, richness of nuance, evenness of flow, etc. (not rough, harsh, or coarse, the adjective used is *ślakṣṇam*, a word deserving a lot of research); and

(*f*) not leaving room for doubt or vagueness (*na ca sandigdham*).

In a public setting, one's speech ought to show: (*a*) acuteness or subtlety;[16] (*b*) proper division and enumeration of pro-s and con-s; (*c*) well-planned sequence

---

[16] It is most fascinating to observe how Kisari Mohan Ganguli, the 19th-century translator of the *Mahābhārata*, has illustrated and interpreted these obscure terms for virtues and vices of discourse by applying them to the most heated debates on social reform which had

of what is to be discussed after what; (*d*) an unasserted initial statement of the thesis to be proved and a concluding one with a QED; and (*e*) an articulate open statement of the discourse-driving purpose (desire or aversion).

Compare all of these requisites of 'proper' speech with the 22 'occasions of defeat' (*nigraha-sthānas*), i.e., checkmate situations in open debate, as per the ancient *Nyāya* school of philosophy (*Nyāya Sūtra* V.2.1–24): loss of thesis; change of thesis; contradicting one's own contention; giving up one's own thesis; shifting the ground/reason; irrelevant speech, i.e, dodging digression; gibberish or

---

been going on at that time in Calcutta and India at large. It is, therefore, pertinent to note certain footnotes from Ganguli's translation, which try to apply Sulabhā's hermeneutic criteria to the textual interpretative debate raging about widow-remarriage in late-19th-century Bengal:

> *Sauksmyam*, is literally minuteness. It means ambiguity here. I have rendered verse 81 very closely to give the reader an idea of the extreme terseness of these verses. For bringing out the meaning of the verse, the following illustration may serve. A sentence is composed containing some words each of which is employed in diverse senses, *as the well-known verse of Parasara which has been interpreted to sanction the remarriage of Hindu widows*. Here, the object indicated by the words used are varied. Definite knowledge of the meaning of each word is arrived at by means of distinctions, *i.e.*, by distinguishing each meaning from every other. In such cases, the understanding before arriving at the definite meaning, rests in succession upon diverse points, now upon one, now upon another. Indeed, the true meaning is to be arrived at in such cases by a process of elimination. When such processes become necessary and or seizing the sense of any sentence, the fault is said to be the fault of minuteness or ambiguity (Ganguli 1883–96, *Śāntiparvan*, Section CCXXI: 63, n. 1, emphasis added).
>
> To take the same example; first take the well-known words of Parasara as really sanctioning the remarriage of widows. Several words in the verse would point to this meaning, several others would not. Weighing probabilities and reasons, let the meaning be tentatively adopted that second husbands are sanctioned by the Rishi for the Hindu widow. This is Sankhya' (ibid.: 63, n. 2).
>
> Having tentatively adopted the meaning the second husbands are sanctioned by the verse referred to, the conclusion should be either its acceptance or rejection. By seeing the incompatibility of the tentative meaning with other settled conclusions in respect of other texts or other writers, the tentative meaning is capable of being rejected, and the final conclusion arrived at, to the effect, that the second husband is to be taken only according to the *Niyoga-vidhi* and not by marriage (ibid.: 63, n. 3).
>
> By occurrence of these five characteristics together is meant that when these are properly attended to by a speaker or writer, only then can his sentence be said to be complete and intelligible. In Nyaya philosophy, the five requisites are *Pratijna*, *Hetu*, *Udaharana*, *Upanaya*, and *Nigamana*. In the Mimansa philosophy, the five requisites have been named differently. *Vishaya*, *Samsaya*, *Purvapaksha*, *Uttara*, and *Nirnaya* (ibid.: 64, n. 2).

incomprehensible speech; reversal of pre-fixed order; omission of one or more steps; adding unnecessary steps; repetition; silence, i.e., failure of respond, after repeated query; lack of intelligence; evasion; suffering from the same fault as the opponent; failing to censure a patent fault in an opponent; censuring the faultless; conceding a theory that one regards as mistaken; and citing a pseudo-reason/committing an inferential fallacy. We can see a lot of overlap and similar methodological concern in the two lists.

Finally, Sulabhā formulated, in a couple of terse verses, her central general norm for good communication, 'just talk' as we have called it, her normative philosophy of language: When the speaker, the listener, and the sentence take equal shares, without losing any part, into what is intended to be said, only then, O King, does such meaning come to light (*vaktā śrotā ca vākyam ca yadā tvavikalam nṛpa/ samam eti vivakṣāyām tadāso'rthaḥ prākaśate//*) (*Śāntiparvan* 320.91).

In *Alice in Wonderland*, after using words whimsically with complete semantic anarchy, Humpty Dumpty asked imperiously: Between the established conventions of a language and the occasion-specific intention of the speaker who is to be the master? Sulabhā came to the heart of this three-cornered tussle between the speaker's meaning, the hearer's meaning and the sentence-meaning, by enunciating a principle of equal priority.

Neither the bully, nor the self-effacing guesser of the hearer's individual interests, nor even the impersonal lexicon should have control over successful communication of meaning. In the political economy of conversation, giving unequal power to what the speaker unilaterally wants to say leads to one kind of semantic oppression. Especially when, like Janaka, the speaker tries to pass off his own interest as the interest of the interlocutor and belittles the listener by second-guessing what she wants to say before she has even spoken, the tyranny of the speaker's meaning can lead to a total failure of communication. Sulabhā put this succinctly by way of telling Janaka that all this talk of 'desire for intercourse' had nothing to do with the listener's interest, and that Janaka was projecting his own desire as the desire of the other: *svārtham āha parārtham ca*. If, on the contrary, the speaker completely throws away his own objectives and tries to speak from the point of view of the hearer, 'doubts and suspicions' (*viśāṃkā*) tend to arise out of such a situation because one suspects that the speaker is not being sincere. 'Only he is a speaker proper who speaks without going against his own intentions or the

---

These characteristics, the commentator points out, though numbering 16, include the four and 20 mentioned by Bhojadeva in his Rhetoric called *Saraswati-kanthabharana* (ibid.: 64, n. 3).

Ganguly also comments critically on other contemporary translators. For instance, he states: '*Pararthame* means, as the commentator explains, of excellent sense. It does not mean *Paraprayojanam* as wrongly rendered by the Burdwan translator. The latter's version of the text is thoroughly unmeaning' (ibid.: 64, n. 4).

intentions of the hearer'. This attention to equality in meaning-determination, I argue, has a deeper connection with the *Mahābhārata*'s unusual definition of cruelty as flaunted inequality. In *Śāntiparvan* 164.6, Bhīṣma described a cruel person as one who was mean, controlling, harsh, over-anxious, pompous, user of foul words, proud advertiser of his own acts of gift, praiser of his own clan or kind, and — most importantly — not ready to share and distribute power and wealth equally (*a-saṃvibhāgī*). It is amazing how many of these features we find in Janaka's behaviour in this episode. In a final definition, Bhīṣma equated cruelty with shameless over-consumption of edible, drinkable and lickable delicacies, while the 'eyes of the poor'[17] are watching (*Śāntiparvan* 164.11). There is, thus, a connection between linguistic, conversational semantic justice and economic justice that Vyāsa, Bhīṣma and Sulabhā are drawing our attention to.[18]

Sulabhā's Theory of Birth and a Proto-Buddhist Metaphysics of Personal Identity[19]

'You have asked me who I am, where I am coming from, etc. Listen to my reply, O king, with undivided attention' — with this preface, Sulabhā played a verbal trick. Instead of answering the king's questions with her biographical details first, she turned the query 'where have you come from' into a general metaphysical question of the origin of an embodied individual, a question of personal identity. Sulabhā's theory of birth is also relevant here because Janaka could well be prying into her personal history in order to explore the possibility of persuading her to give up monastic life and perhaps become one his consorts.

'As lac and wood, as grains of dust and drops of water, exist commingled when brought together — this is how a clay-puppet on a wooden frame is made — even so are the beings of all creatures. Sound, touch, taste, form, and scent, these and the senses, though diverse in respect of their essences, exist yet in a state of amalgam' (*Śāntiparvan* 320.94–98). The description of the human person in terms of aggregation of physical elements and sensory capacities reminds us of the Buddhist theory that reduces the so called self into five psychophysical aggregates. Subsequently (*Śāntiparvan* 320.57), Sulabhā would call the state or polity a seven-part amalgam (*saṃghāta*), with a clear hint at the comparison between a state and a person. The word *saṃghāta* used here by Sulabhā should remind us of the *Sāṃkhya* text *Sāṃkhyakārikā* which argues for the existence of Consciousness/Self on the basis

[17] I allude here to the subtle and sarcastic story 'Eyes of the Poor' by Baudelaire (1970).

[18] An imaginative way to re-interpret this connection between semantic justice and equality could be found in the works of Jacques Ranciere, *Disagreement: Politics and Philosophy* (1998) and *The Politics of Aesthetics: The Distribution of the Sensible*, which talk about equal distribution in the context of aesthetic justice, precisely the kind of 'distribution of sharing' (*saṁvibhāga*) that the cruel bully of a speaker refuses to do.

of the first premise that every unconscious amalgam exists telelogically for the sake of something other than the physical amalgam (*saṃghāta parārthatvat*). It is also reminiscent of one of the names of the body in the *Caraka Saṃhitā*, *saṃhanana*. These cognate words both mean an amalgam. Sulabhā anticipated (or echoed) the Buddha's theory of the human person by factorizing it into the sense-organs, the constantly changing cells and particles, and came very close to a five-*skandha* kind of No-Self view. You cannot ask a *skandha*, a sense organ 'Who are you?' because the eye does not see itself, nor does the ear hear itself. Sulabhā's political ontology of the human person might very well represent a now extinct school of early *Sāṃkhya* which came close to a Buddhist reductionism about the self.

As a proto-Buddhist metaphysican, Sulabhā explicitly referred to the *Vaiśeṣika* rivals and rejected their dualistic distinction between unchanging soul and changing body. She told the king:

> Myself, yourself and all other embodied beings are evolutes of that Unmanifest *Prakṛti*. Insemination and other [embryonic] conditions are due to the mixture of semen and blood. In consequence of insemination, there first appears [what] is called by the name of *kalala*. From *kalala* arises what is called *budbuda* [bubble]. From the stage called *budbuda* springs what is called *peśī*. From the condition called *peśī* that stage arises in which the various limbs become manifested. From this last condition appear nails and hair. At the end of the ninth month, O king of Mithilā, the creature takes its birth so that, its sex being known, it comes to be called a boy or girl. When the creature issues out of the womb, the form it presents is such that its nails and fingers seem to be of like burnished copper. From infancy to youth and from youth to old age, as the creature advances from one stage into another, the form presented in the previous stage disappears. The constituent elements of the body, which serve diverse functions in the general economy, undergo change every moment in every creature. Those changes, however, are so minute that they cannot be noticed. The birth of the minute cells, and their death, in each successive condition, cannot be marked, O king, even as one cannot mark the changes in the flame of a burning lamp (*Śāntiparvan* 320.115–20).[20]

---

[19] The statements cited in this section are from *Śāntiparvan* 320.95–124.

[20] Ganguli, in the spirit of Hindu revivalism, comments:

> The fact then of continual change of particles in the body was well-known to the Hindu sages. This discovery is not new of modern physiology. Elsewhere it has been shown that Harvey's great discovery about the circulation of the blood was not unknown to the Rishis (1883–96, *Śāntiparvan*, Section CCXXI: 67, n. 1).
>
> The instance mentioned for illustrating the change of corporal particles is certainly a very happy one. The flame of a burning lamp, though perfectly steady (as in a breezeless spot), is really the result of the successive combustion of particles of oil and the successive extinguishment of such combustion Both this and the previous verse have been rendered inaccurately by K. P. Singha' (ibid.: 67, n. 2).

In the narrative, this segment of Sulabhā's speech helped her deflect Janaka's personal questions, but in our historical analysis, this segment clearly identifies the mendicant woman as coming from a proto-Buddhist non-Brahmanical tradition of anti-essentialist metaphysics of personal identity.

Questioning the Gender-Biased Questions Asked by the Liberated Patriarch

When such is the state of the bodies of all creatures — i.e., when that which is called the body is changing incessantly even like the speedy galloping pace of a steed of good mettle — who then has come whence or not whence, or whose is it or whose is it not, or whence does it not arise? What connection does there exist between creatures and their own bodies? As from the contact of flint with iron, or from two sticks of wood when rubbed against each other, fire is generated, even so are creatures generated from the combination of the 30 principles that Sulabhā went through one by one in a systematic exposition which sounds similar to an Adrāra Kālama type of ontology. Showing the king that she was better acquainted with *Sāṃkhya* and other theories of embodiment, Sulabhā then mocked at the king's alleged equanimity and liberal attitude of non-discrimination between friends and enemies, self and other, etc. If he did not see any differences, why did the difference between man and woman, young and old, beautiful and ugly, householder and renouncer matter so much to him? If he saw the same all pervasive consciousness everywhere, why did not he see himself in her, and if he did why he was so threatened by the possibility that she might unite with him?

> What indications of liberation can be said to occur in that king who acts as others act towards enemies and allies and neutrals and in victory and truce and war? What indications of Emancipation occur in him who does not know the true nature of the aggregate of three as manifested in seven ways in all acts and who, on that account, is attached to that aggregate of three? What indications of liberation exist in him who fails to cast an equal eye on the agreeable, on the weak, and the strong? (*Śāntiparvan* 320.148–64).

Of Human and Royal Bondage: Deconstructing Kingship

> Unworthy as you are of it, your posturing as an liberation person should be exposed by your well-wishers! This endeavour to attain to liberation (when you have so many faults) is like the use of medicine by a patient who indulges in all kinds of forbidden food and practices. O chastiser of foes, reflecting upon spouses and other sources of attachment, one should behold these in one's own soul. What else can be looked upon as the indication of liberation? Listen now to me as I speak in detail of these and certain other minute sources of attachment appertaining to the four

well-known acts (of lying down for slumber, enjoyment, eating, and dressing) to which you are still bound though you profess to have taken to the path of liberation. That man who has to rule the whole world must, indeed, be a single sovereign without a second. He is obliged to live in only a single palace. In that palace he has again only one sleeping chamber. In that chamber he has, again, only one bed on which at night he is to lie down. Half that bed again he is obliged to give to his Queen-consort. This may serve as an example of how little the king's share is of all he is said to own. This is the case with his objects of enjoyment, with the food he eats, and with the robes he wears. He is thus attached to a very limited share of all things. He is, again, attached to the duties of rewarding and punishing. The king is always dependent on others. He enjoys a very small share of all he is supposed to own, and to that small share he is forced to be attached (as well as others are attached to their respective possessions). In the matter also of peace and war, the king cannot be said to be independent. In the matter of women, of sports and other kinds of enjoyment, the king's inclinations are exceedingly circumscribed. In the matter of taking counsel and in the assembly of his ministers and council-members what independence can the king be said to have? When, indeed, he sets his orders on other men, he is said to be thoroughly independent. But then the moment after, in the several matters of his orders, his independence is barred by the very men whom he has ordered. If the king desires to sleep, he cannot gratify his desire, resisted by those who have business to transact with him. He must sleep when permitted, and while sleeping he is obliged to wake up for attending to those that have urgent business with him — bathe, touch, drink, eat, pour libations in the fire, perform sacrifices, speak, hear — these are the words which kings have to hear from others and hearing them have to slave to those that utter them. Men come in batches to the king and solicit him for gifts. Being, however, the protector of the general treasury, he cannot make gifts unto even the most deserving. If he makes gifts, the treasury becomes exhausted. If he does not, disappointed solicitors look upon him with hostile eyes. He becomes vexed and as the result of this, misanthropic feelings soon invade his mind. If many wise and heroic and wealthy men reside together, the king's mind begins to be filled with distrust in consequence. Even when there is no cause of fear, the king entertains fear of those that always wait upon and worship him. Those I have mentioned, O king, also find fault with him. Behold, in what way the king's fears may arise from even them! Then, again, all men are kings in their own houses. All men, again, in their own houses are householders. Like kings, O Janaka, all men in their own houses chastise and reward. Like kings, others also have sons and spouses and their own selves and treasuries and friends and stores. In these respects the king is not different from other men. Alas, the land is ruined, the city is gutted by fire, the foremost of elephants is dead! When such things happen, his majesty the king succumbs to grief like any other mortal, little regarding that these impressions are all due to ignorance and error. The king is seldom freed from mental griefs caused by desire and aversion and fear. He is generally afflicted also by headaches and diverse diseases of the kind. The king is afflicted (like others) by all couples of opposites (as pleasure and pain, etc). He is alarmed at everything. Indeed, full of foes and impediments as kingdom is, the king, while he enjoys it, passes nights of sleeplessness. Sovereignty, therefore, is blessed with an exceedingly small share of happiness. The misery with which it is endowed is very great. It is as unsubstantial as burning flames fed by straw or the bubbles of froth seen on the surface of water. Who is there that would like to obtain sovereignty, or, having acquired sovereignty, can hope to win tranquility? You regard this kingdom and this palace to be yours. You think also this army, this treasury, and these counsellers to belong to you. Whose, however, in reality are they, and whose are they not? Allies, ministers, capital, provinces, punishment, treasury, and the king, these seven which constitute the limbs of a kingdom exist, depending upon one another, like three sticks standing with one another's support. The merits of each are set off by the merits of the others. Which of them can be said to be superior to the rest? At those times those particular ones are regarded as distinguished above the rest when some important end is served through their agency. Superiority, for the time being, is said to attach to that one whose efficacy is thus seen. The seven limbs already mentioned, O best of kings, and the three others, forming an aggregate of ten, supporting one another, are said to enjoy the kingdom like the king himself. That king who is endowed with great energy and who is firmly attached to Kṣatriya practices, should be satisfied with only a tenth part of the produce of the subject's field. Other kings are seen to be satisfied with less than a tenth part of such produce. There is no one who owns the kingly office without someone else owning it in the world, and there is no kingdom without a king. If there be no kingdom, there can be no righteousness, and if there be no righteousness, whence can liberation arise? If it be true that you have been emancipated from all bonds, what harm have I done you by entering your person with only my Intellect? With Yatis, among all orders of men, the custom is to dwell in uninhabited or deserted abodes. What harm then have I done to whom by entering your understanding which is truly of real knowledge? I have not touched you, O king, with my hands, of arms, or feet, or thighs, O sinless one, or with any other part of the body. You art born in a high race. You have modesty. You have foresight. Whether the act has been good or bad, my entrance into your body has been a private one, concerning us two only. Was it not improper for you to publish that private act before all your court? These Brāhmanas are all worthy of respect. They are foremost of preceptors. You also are entitled to their respect, being their king. Doing them reverence, you art entitled to receive reverence from them. Reflecting on all this, it was not proper for you to proclaim before these foremost of men the fact of this congress between two persons of opposite sexes, if, indeed, you are really acquainted with the rules of propriety in respect of speech.

O king of Mithilā, I am staying in you without touching you at all even like a drop of water on a lotus leaf that stays on it without drenching it in the least. If on the other hand, you are aware of my touch as I am allegedly touching you, your liberating wisdom has been quite fruitless, since you are still so perturbed. Thus, you seem to have fallen off from the home-attached familial mode of life, but you have not yet attained the freedom (sought by those who leave their homes in search of liberation) that is so difficult to arrive at. You are living in a limbo between the two, like a mokṣa-talker, someone who merely gossips and lectures about liberation (but is not actually anywhere near his own liberation). The contact of one that is emancipated with another that has been so, or Puruṣa with Prakṛti, cannot lead to an intermingling of the kind you dread. Only those that regard the soul to be identical with the body, and that think the several orders and modes of life to be really different from one another, are open to the error of supposing an intermingling to be possible. My body is different from yours. But my soul is not different from your soul. When I am able to realise this, I have not the slightest doubt that my understanding is really not staying in yours though I have entered into you by Yoga.

Apropos of the charge of intermixture and inappropriate touch or intimacy, Sulabhā spoke like a Buddhist logician who questioned the very nature of relation or mixture of two distinct things. She was the last person to attempt any mixing or mingling or touching, as she suggested, by bringing in suddenly an image of a series of things which appeared to be together but stayed quite distinct from one another:

A pot is borne in the hand. In the pot is milk. On the milk is a fly. Though the hand and the pot, the pot and the milk, and the milk and the fly exist together, yet are they all distinct from each other. The pot does not share the nature of the milk. Nor does the milk get mixed up with the fly. The condition of each is contained in itself, and can never be altered by the condition of that other with which it may temporarily exist. In this manner, caste, gender, and practices, though they may exist together with and in a person that is liberated, do not really attach to him or her. How then can an intermingling of orders be possible in consequence of this union of myself with you, even if it were imagined? (*Śāntiparvan* 320.77–79).[21]

Sulabhā's Exemplary Self-introduction: Candour without Boasting

In Bhīṣma's narrative of the Janaka–Sulabhā dialogue, finally, with a calm self-assurance, Sulabhā met the spurious allegations levelled by Janaka by telling him who she was and what lineage she belonged to:

Then, again, I am actually not of a higher social order (*varṇa*) than you are Nor do I belong to the *Vaiśya* or *Śūdra* castes. I am, O king, of the same order with you, borne of a pure *Kṣatriya* race. There was a royal sage of the name of Pradhāna. You must have heard of him. I am born in his race, and my name is Sulabhā. In the sacrifices performed by my ancestors, the foremost of the gods, viz., Indra, used to come, accompanied by Droṇa and Śataśṛṅga, and Cakradvāra [and other presiding

[21] This argument from discreetness of the relata in a relational situation reminds us of Dharmakīrti's dictum in his *Sambandha Parikṣā* (*Examination of Relation*): 'Entities are by themselves unrelated, it is our imagination which connects them' (*amiśrāḥ svayam bhāvāḥ tān yojayati kalpanā*).

> deities of the great mountains]. Born in such a race, it was found that no suitable groom was available for me. Instructed then in the religion of Emancipation, I wander over the Earth alone, observant of the practices of asceticism. I practice no hypocrisy in the matter of the life of Renunciation. I am not a thief that appropriates what belongs to others. I am not an illicit intermixer of the practices belonging to the different orders. I am firm in the practices that belong to that mode of life to which I properly belong. I am firm and steady in my vows. I never utter any word without reflecting on its propriety. I did not come to see you, without having thinking about it properly, O monarch! Having heard that your understanding has been purified by the religious practice of the path of liberation, I came here from desire of some benefit. Indeed, it was for enquiring of you about Emancipation that I had come. I am not saying this taking sides and favoring my own kind or class (*na vargastha*) [recall, description of the cruel person in *Śāntiparvan* 164: 5–6 as one who 'does not practice even distribution or sharing of goods, and who keeps praising his own class or kind'].
>
> I do not say it for glorifying myself and humiliating my opponents. But I say it, impelled by sincerity only. What I say is, he that is emancipated never indulges in that intellectual dialectical disputation for the sake of victory. He, on the other hand, is really emancipated who devotes himself to Brahma, that sole seat of tranquility. As a person of the mendicant order resides for only one night in an empty house [and leaves it the next morning], even after the same manner I shall reside for this one night in thy person [which, as I have already said, is like an empty chamber, being destitute of knowledge].
>
> You have honored me with conversational hospitality [this, in the contest, is high sarcasm]. Now, having slept this one night in your empty person, which I have made my temporary home, O ruler of Mithilā, tomorrow I shall depart.

Thereafter, Bhīṣma continued, 'Hearing these useful and significant sentences supported with reason, king Janaka did not say anything more after this'.

The *Nyāya*[22] classification of this losing outcome in a debate would 'cannot think of what to say' (*apratibhā*), and this state is typically represented by the gesture of hanging one's head in shame and trying to write on the ground with one's finger.[23]

Foucault on *Parrhesia*

In stark contrast to the flustered and angry tone of Janaka's increasingly indecent speech, we have seen how Sulabhā's response started patiently, methodically and didactically, with a formal meta-discourse on the ethics of discourse. As if ignoring all these personal questions and nasty aspersions, she spoke in abstract generality about how, ideally, one should speak in public, not out of fear or lust, shame or pride.

Was Sulabhā Practising Parrhesia?

In his very last series of public lectures at the College de France, Michel Foucault excavated and examined the concept of *parrhesia* — an essentially normative character trait of citizens of a democracy who should enjoy *isogoria* or equal rights of speaking. Used or exemplified widely in the Greco-Roman world, between 5th century BCE to 5th century CE by authors, such as Euripides, Plato, Aristotle (minimally), the cynics, Plutarch, Epictetus, Seneca, and others, the word is apparently derived from *pan* which means 'all', and *rhema* which means 'telling together', i.e., telling all.

One who tells all the truth, unflatteringly and fearlessly, against power, was called a *parrhesisates*. While claiming that this idea is exclusively Greek, Foucault considers, together with typical Euro-centric misgivings and 'sanctioned ignorance',[24] the possibility that the relentlessly argumentative Indian Âjīvika philosophers (culturally continuous with Buddhists and Jains), whom the Greeks called *gymnosophists*, might have influenced the cynic self-examination and meditative practices, which was conceptualized as telling the whole truth about oneself to oneself. In Foucault's own words: '*Parrhesia* is a kind of verbal activity where the speaker has a specific relation to truth, through frankness, to his own life, through danger, to other people and himself, through criticism, and a specific relation to moral law, through freedom and duty' (2001: 19; Nielson 1995).

Is *parrhesia* itself a figure of speech, a rhetorical device? If it is, then how do we deal with Levinas' strong objection that all rhetoric is violence to the interlocutor, that in genuine conversation the speaker's candour should take the form of offering up one's thoughts without fear or tact, a ' saying is a denuding of denuding' (Levinas 1998: 49)?

Foucault would have a nice response in terms of what is called *svabhāvokti alaṃkāra* (the figure of zero-rhetoric) in Sanskrit rhetoric. The classic example of this is the dialogue between Alexander, the Macedonian ruler, and Diogenes, the street-dwelling cynic philosopher. The Gārgī–Yājñavalkya episode or the Sulabhā–Janaka episode would also serve as a good example.

When comparing Gārgī Vācaknavī with Sulabhā, we see certain crucial differences between them. Gārgī was obviously a self-appointed 'examiner' or judge in the public contest for (another?) Janaka's cows with gilded horns. She was snubbed once, but she came back with two sharp questions. She compared her

---

[22] Commentary *Nyāyabhāṣya* on *Nyāyasūtra* V.2.18.

[23] See Thakur and Raghavan 1964 for Jayanta Bhaṭṭa's *Āgama Ḍambara* that describes a Buddhist teacher Dharmottara, when vanquished and silenced by Sankarṣana, the *mīmāṃsaka*, as writing on the ground speechless (*bhūmim alikhati*).

[24] I owe this phrase to Gayatri Chakravorty Spivak, personal communication.

own queries with killer arrows flung by warriors from Kāśī or Videha. The exact words inaugurating this second round of Gārgī's daring of Yajnavalkya are of great interest.

Kierkegaard calls Socrates the ideal teacher because he is as 'un-bribable' as the dead. In India, where the centuries old tradition of sycophancy shows no sign of dying in the public sphere, notwithstanding our recent alertness about corruption in business and state bureaucracy, a richer notion of truth-telling and *parrhesia* is badly needed as a corrective. One thing Sulabhā teaches us is how *not* to flatter a politically and academically reputed and powerful king and how to subject spiritual fame to rational public scrutiny.

Comparing Alexander and Diogenes, Raikva and Janaśruti, and Janaka and Sulabhā

What constitutes truth-telling as a virtue is one of the most troubled questions of the *Mahābhārata*. In the *Śāntiparvan* (109.4–16), Bhīṣma problematizes truth and truth telling. As in the *Yogasūtra* which takes non-violence to be stronger virtue and calls truth-resulting in harm and violence to be untruth, Bhīṣma also subjects truth to three more basic tests. If a factual truth fails these tests in a certain situation, then Bhīṣma warns that sometimes truth should not be told, and in its place even telling a falsehood may be ethically preferable. This is not meant as a general rule that unpleasant truths should not be spoken or falsehoods which benefit people count as truths. Which particular situations call for overriding the universal dictate of truth-telling is, admittedly, hard to determine. A richer notion of truth emerges with three overarching principles of justice that Bhīṣma formulates: justice has been commanded for the sake of overall flourishing of people, and whatever is connected to flourishing is just. Justice is called *dharma* because it holds society together, and whatever promotes holding together is just. Justice has been commanded for the sake of avoidance of injury, and whatever is connected to the virtue of non-injury is just. Especially at the time of crisis, we cannot act on any simple set of principles, but need more complex and nuanced deliberations before and after we act. In another context, therefore, Bhīṣma speaks of 13 aspects of the full-blooded virtue of truthfulness. These 13 'structures' of Truth are: (*a*) equity, (*b*) self-control, (*c*) non-rivalry/non-competitiveness, (*d*) forgiveness, (*e*) shame, (*f*) forbearance, (*g*) lack of envy, (*h*) renunciation, (*i*) contemplativeness, (*j*) dignity, (*k*) tenacity/patience, (*l*) empathy/crying out of the heart at other's suffering, and (*m*) non-injury. (Alternatively, the list starts with Truth itself and then collapses non-rivalry/non-competitiveness and lack of envy into a single virtue of non-jealousy).

Speech is uttered for the purpose of transferring one's knowledge to another. It can only be said to have been employed for the good of others and not for their injury if it is not deceptive, confusing or barren in knowledge. If, however, it proves to be injurious to living beings even though uttered as such, it is not truth; it is only a sin. By this outward appearance, this is a facsimile of virtue, and one gets into painful darkness. Therefore, let everyone examine well and then utter truth for the benefit of all living beings (*Yogasūtra* II.30).

Here Vyāsa agrees with the *Mahābhārata* account in seeing *satya* as opposed not to *asatya* but to sin (*pāpa*). Even if what one says is accurate, Vācaspati Miśra clarifies, if it is not spoken for the sake of benefitting others, it is only the semblance of truth, not truth.In *Yogasūtra* II.33, Vācaspati explains that deception, confusion and futility are three conditions that preclude an utterance's qualifying as true. A deceptive (*vañcita*) utterance, he says, is one that does not communicate the idea that is in the mind of the utterer to the mind of the audience. This would apply to strategic uses of equivocation and to mental reservation, as well as to straightforward misinformation. A confused (*bhrānta*) utterance is one wherein the utterer is sincere but does not actually know the truth. An utterance can be futile, or 'barren of knowledge' (*pratipattivandhya*), for two reasons. First, the audience may not understand it, perhaps because of language barrier or because the utterer and audience are not in close proximity (I cannot claim to have told you something if I whispered it under my breath while you were at the other end of the room — or across the country). Second, the utterance may be nonsensical, as is the case of Lewis Carroll's famous poem 'Jabberwocky', or it may make sense but have no object, as would be the case of discussing whether the queen of the United States parts her hair on the left or right.

Some Objections to the Very Idea of Ethics of Conversation

In ancient Indian medical methodology, the norms of debate were not only laid down but also often theorized and critically examined. There were debates about what should be the rules of debate and the exact role of a neutral judge or jury. But can one ethically consistently formulate norms of correct conversation or debate? Would not a *compelling* discourse on the norms of non-coercive conversation be operationally self-refuting? This would sound like a good objection to the very idea of the rules of Free Speech. If all persuasive rhetoric is violence to the other, is not Sulabhā's moralistic persuasion to avoid 18 types of bad language or bad motives for speaking itself a form of verbal coercion? It managed to silence Janaka, after all, and scored a kind of verbal victory for the female ascetic.

The point of friendly speech is not to coerce, dominate or enslave, but to enter into a freedom-celebrating acknowledgement of mutual epistemic dependence between the speaker and the one spoken to. Hence, any speech which pushes around and curtails the freedom and spontaneity of others is unethical. Any imperative of the form 'you must talk to others this way rather than that way' curtails the freedom and spontaneity of natural human speech. Therefore, any formulation of the ethics of speech would be itself unethical as a speech-act.

To this conundrum my response would got as follows:

We must distinguish between the causal, hegemonic, 'power-buttressed', or even benefit-promising, heteronomous 'must' on the one hand, and the moral 'must' which is autonomous, on the other. The moral obligation to speak the truth non-aggressively and non-injurously but fearlessly, consists precisely in feeling spontaneously self-constrained to relinquish power.

In his last work, *Truth and Truthfulness*, Bernard Williams recommends, somewhat in the anti-Kantian spirit of the *Mahābhārata* (which, unlike Kant, endorses life-saving lies), that there is no 'moral LAW' or universalizable rules of right speech. There are moral virtues of speech which have to be imbibed and exemplified according to the speaker's particular relationship with the hearer. The 13 forms of Truth enumerated by Bhīṣma may help us develop such a virtue ethics of truth-telling in the face of power. The *Mīmāṃsā* theory of the imperative verb-ending as immediately goading or generating an urge (*ārthabhāvanā*) to act according to the rule has to be given up or tinkered with, before we can interpret imperatives, such as 'do not bull-shit your students or your teachers', or 'do not lie to your citizens, just to win votes or wage wars', in a way that does not generate the aforementioned paradox. As Jayanta Bhaṭṭa stated in his unique 8th-century philosophical play *Āgama-Ḍambara* ('The Tumult of Traditions'), Act One:

> If what is legitimate is uttered, briefly, in a statement containing one's final conclusion in a nutshell, if pompous discourse abounding in verbal tricks, sophistical refutations, and cases of defeat is shunned, with no malice in the heart, no rudeness in speech and no frown in the eyebrows, then everywhere we would be members of assemblies of debates among disciplined people.

Indeed, the word used in this verse for 'members of assembly' in Sanskrit literally means 'civilized' or 'civil' (*sabhya*, i.e, *sabhāyāḥ yogyāḥ*). Although Jayanta must have written the logical play partly to illustrate the debate-related topics of *Nyāya Sūtras*, such as play on words, sophistical rejoinders and cases of defeat and fallacies of argumentation, the context of 'Tumult of Traditions' is a crisis of governance very much alive for the contemporary world rife with conflicts centred on religious identity.

We should compare, first, the powers against which Diogenes and Sulabhā showed the courage to speak the truth. Janaka and Alexander were both monarchs surrounded by ministers, courtiers and bodyguards. Alexander was carrying a lance of his own, while Janaka sat in the comfort of his throne and royal regalia under a golden umbrella. Alexander, being a student of Aristotle, was famed for his knowledge; Janaka, too, proudly proclaimed himself to be the pupil of Pañcaśikha, a *bhikṣu*, and yet ranted against the home-abjuring holy beggars.

Now, let us compare Diogenes with Raikvā Sayugva in the *Chāndogya Upaniṣad*. Both were street-dwelling philosopher-sages. When Janaśruti came to check Raikvā

Sayugva out and found him scratching his scabs sitting under a parked cart, Sayugvā Raikva started by addressing the regent as a *Śūdra*: 'You are a king of the *kṣatriya* caste, but you are no better than a wage-labourer servant because you expect to buy knowledge in exchange of a wage or remuneration'. Was Raikva acting as a *parrhesiast* here? Itinerant journalists and public intellectuals (like P. Sainath, the Indian journalist of the farmer suicides reportage fame) are contemporary counterparts of Sulabhā going around critically examining reputed political leaders, public figures and heads of states, practising *parrhesia*, and not just exposing their pretenses but also making them more self-critical and vigilant in the process, with no personal gain. *Chāndogya Upaniṣad* tells us of another street-dwelling lout of a philosopher who shattered the intellectual pride of a wise king

To bring the discussion back to modern times, one should recall Gandhi's 'Fearless Speech' delivered with wit but without arrogance, at the great Ahmedabad trial of March 1922:

> I have no desire whatsoever to conceal from this court the fact that to preach disaffection towards the existing system of Government has become almost a passion with me, and the Advocate-General is entirely in the right when he says that my preaching of disaffection did not commence with my connection with Young India but that it commenced much earlier, and in the statement that I am about to read, it will be my painful duty to admit before this court that it commenced much earlier than the period stated by the Advocate-General. It is a painful duty with me but I have to discharge that duty knowing the responsibility that rests upon my shoulders, and I wish to endorse all the blame that the learned Advocate-General has thrown on my shoulders in connection with the Bombay occurrences, Madras occurrences and the Chauri Chaura occurrences. He is quite right when he says, that as a man of responsibility, a man having received a fair share of education, having had a fair share of experience of this world, I should have known the consequences of every one of my acts. I know them. I knew that I was playing with fire. I ran the risk and if I was set free I would still do the same . . .
>
> I am endeavoring to show to my countrymen that violent non-co-operation only multiples evil, and that as evil can only be sustained by violence, withdrawal of support from evil requires complete abstention from violence. Non-violence implies voluntary submission to the penalty for non-co-operation with evil. I am here, therefore, to invite and submit cheerfully to the highest penalty that can be inflicted upon me for what in law is deliberate crime, and what appears to me to be the highest duty of a citizen. The only course open to you, the Judge and the assessors, is either to resign your posts and thus dissociate yourselves from evil, if you feel that the law you are called upon to administer is an evil, and that in reality I am innocent, or to inflict on me the severest penalty, if you believe that the system and the law you are assisting to administer are good for the people of this country, and that my activity is, therefore, injurious to the common weal.

The only rhetoric here is the fully transparent cut-and-dried logic of it which goes somewhat like this:

> The current law dictates that if I have spread anti-colonial sentiments, I should be severely punished. It is my duty to spread anti-colonial sentiments, and I have done so, and if released I shall do so again. A law that regards an obligatory duty as a punishable offence is evil law. Hence the current law is evil law. To non-violently non-cooperate with such evil law is to keep breaking it and take the consequences. That is what I am doing.'

Conclusion: Yama as Double-sided *Dharma*

The Vedic–Purāṇic tradition was not, by any standard, non-violent. It was at least as addicted to war and conflict as the cultures of Greek and Roman antiquity. Yet, not only the Śramaṇic counter-culture but also the mainstream Vedic Brāhmaṇical tradition itself took 'non-violence to all living beings' as an overriding 'universal great vow' (*sārvabhauma mahāvratam*, in Aranya 2000: 212). The *Mahābhārata*, too, is never tired of extolling non-cruelty as the paramount virtue. Was its upholding of non-violence as a regulative ideal, then, sheer hypocrisy or double-think? Perhaps, a civilization idealizes non-cruelty and non-injury as virtues only to the extent that it finds cruelty and collective deliberate injury rampant in its own actual history. Judged by this thumb-rule and given the obsessive idealization of non-violence, the ancient Indic societies must have been pretty violent on an average. But one of their common central civilizational features remained their obsessive attention to the power of spoken words that led, at least, the Ājīvika, Vedic, Jaina, and Buddhist intellectual elite to an ethics of inquiry and dialogue, *saṃpṛccha and saṃvāda* (togetherness-in-discourse and inquiry) as a method of dissipating violence, negotiating conflict and managing anger.

The *Mahābhārata* itself, with which one is supposed to interpret and elaborate the Vedas, remains acutely aware of the obverse role of speech as an instigator rather than a dissipator of violence. Sometimes, verbal negotiations and persuasion fail. When words fail, then weapons, more or less lethal, have to be brandished if not used and thereafter destruction happens if they are used. Yet, it was a civilizational project of the Vedic Buddhist and Jaina intellectual elite to sublimate collective rage in the form of rule-abiding debate both as a sport, a public spectacle and a method for reaching a common middle ground in case of a conflict of policies and philosophies.

Grudgingly or proudly, Indian society has been pluralistic for as long as its past is knowable. Here, the *un*availability of a singular dominant philosophy, *non*-universality of every moral ideal and *un*resolved tension among conflicting cults and ideologies have always promoted a chaotic survival-in-disunity. Such a society cannot afford to lose its philosophical heritage of friendly discourse or verbal contests in the name of any monolithic cultural integration or nationalistic development. Even if it periodically succumbs to a total war with a resigned apocalyptic prevision of inevitable collective doom, the embattled armies must at least wait for 18 unhurried chapters of ethico-metaphysical dialogue to be conducted first. This, admittedly, is a myth. But it is a myth that the Indian people have always lived by. Multiculturalism always gathers its own discontents and egoistic aggression of Other-welcoming openness.[25] The actual future of Indian aggression is as unpredictable as its past remains irretrievable. But we cannot permit either the jingoistic symbol of 'our great golden Hindu heritage' or the homogenizing materialism of global capitalism or communism stamp out the culture of *brahmodya* or public philosophical debate.

As I finish writing this chapter, the gruesome second bomb attack on Mumbai is rocking India. The counter-violence, however, remains verbal.

All conversations — unless they are lost in sophistry and rhetoric — tend to be a negotiation between the self and the other, between verbal hospitality and verbal contest, between the agonistic and altruistic elements.

I am trying to re-orient our cultural self-construction towards the power-dismantling power of public dialogical speech. Speech, I am fully aware, can become hate speech, brain-washing addiction-inducing advertisement, befuddling rhetoric of a demagogue or that mass-mesmerizing technique of lying which is called election-campaign in a democracy. Too often has the Word — even the sacred Indian Word — been used to fuel ferocity and spread divisiveness rather than seek the truth or form discursive communities. Yet, the plurality-nurturing nature of speech that cares for truth, as against the difference, opens up a conceptual space for *hope* for the future by effacing the hubris of ballistic masculinity. With the deafening noise of cell-phones and political campaigns, all this talk about reasoned debate in the public sphere may sound like a whimpering hope for a utopia. But if words have the power to inflame collective revenge, they also have the power to initiate reconciliation. With some epistemic humility and self-sacrifice, we can even *construct* a dialogic foundation for a more humane society led by honest, caring, hesitant conversations.

---

[25] Amartya Sen (2005) has laudably drawn attention to the ancient and continuous Indian culture of debate and dissidence, but has simplistically attributed it only to the skeptical and heterdox traditions. Although Buddhist logic and materialist *Cārvāka* dialectic made great advances in skeptical epistemology and debate-theory, the spirit of questioning one's most sacred dogmas and the practice of engaging in public debates as seriously as taking part in sacrificial rituals is inherent to the both the Vedic and the Śramaṇic cultures. Yet both have an equally strong mystical undercurrent which regards speech and discourse as distracting noise to be silenced by some transcendence. Sen's analysis, not unexpectedly, lacks sensitivity to these complexities. Sen seems completely unaware of the presence of what I am calling two-sided moral thinking in the *Mahābhārata*.

How should we talk to one another? Is speech a way to control, dissipate or vent violence? How can we make sure that our words heal, build and create rather than hurt, destroy and kill? According to the Ṛgvedic hymn to knowledge (*jñāna sūkta,* X.71), speech was born out of love spilling out as addressing of the second self; thus, we violate its basic nature if we use it to hate and humiliate others. If speech — who only reveals her inner body to the humble lover — is used aggressively to win debates and vanquish opponents without compassion for less gifted speakers in the community, then such selfish speech goes in vain, without nourishing the society. As the *Mahābhārata* states: 'For the sake of flourishing growth of living beings ethical conduct is prescribed, so one should ascertain that to be *Dharma* which is connected to flourishing' (*Śāntiparvan* 109.10).

With the requisite philosophical reflexivity, if we pay attention to the words the *Mahābhārata* uses to describe the words exchanged during this mysterious encounter between the knowledge-proud king and the quietly daring, sharp young nun, we are likely to derive some major hermeneutic insights into the 'presuppositions of human communication'.

In the opening sentence of this chapter, I have used a provocative characterization of the *Mahābhārata* ethics as 'two-sided'. Let me end by providing a supporting text for this not-entirely-happy adjective of the messy morality that emerges out of the numerous conflicting illustrative narratives of the *Mahābhārata*. After hearing an outrageous story of ravenous Viśvāmitra who had claimed to be 'doing the right thing' by deciding to eat the stale rump of a dead dog stolen forcibly from an untouchable hunter, during a severe famine, Yudhiṣṭhira confessed that he was so confused about what was right and what was wrong that he lost all zest for living a righteous life and his sense of justice was slackening. In response to his moral epistemic pessimism, Bhīṣma characterized the applied ethics of a king to be 'never one-sided'. Bhishma said to Yudhiṣṭhira:

> I have not been instructing you about justice and duty on the basis of what I have heard from the Vedas alone. What I have told you is the result of my own intuition and practice (*prajñā-samavahāra*). This is the honey — the essence — that the wise thinkers have collected from life. A king cannot go through his course in the world relying on a one-branched morality . . . Attend to these words of mine. Only kings that are possessed of superior intelligence can rule, expecting victory. A king should provide for the observance of morality by the aid of his own understanding, being guided by knowledge gleaned from various sources . . . Righteousness sometimes takes the shape of unrighteousness and vice versa. He who does not know this, becomes confounded when confronted by an actual instance of this double aspect of situations. Before the occasion comes, one should, O Bharata, be ready with two opposite kinds of understandings of a situation (*Śāntiparvan* 142.4–8).

In Bhīṣma's incisive articulation, the king — and as Sulabhā reminds us, each of us is a king in our own house, in this house called the body (*sarve sve sve gṛhe rājā, Śāntiparvan* 320.47) — has to traverse a forking path of choices. Unless he equips himself ahead of time with two-sided thinking, in his journey he could be paralyzed with doubts. In order to be morally knowledgeable, he has to be *dvaidha-jña*, i.e., 'one who knows two-ways of looking at the situation', not one who is vacillating.

From our trans-traditional anachronistic analysis of the Janaka–Sulabhā exchange, so far, we have learned at least the following lessons which together can help us reconstruct such a dialogic ethics of two-sidedness.

First, though speech can be both aggressive and caring, face-to-face verbal communication — as long as it abides by the ethics of speech — brings two human beings closer together by pruning the prickly egos of both sides and compelling us to respect the self (speaker), the other (hearer) and the impersonal norms of the language (speech itself) equally. Through such hospitable, heart-sharing and knowledge-sharing use of words, the meaning of different kinds of friendship is known by friends — *atrā sakhāyaḥ sakhyāni jānate* (*Ṛgveda* X.7.2; cf. Levinas 1998: 5).

Second, the truth-finding deliberative aspect of conversation and logically organized debate, when internalized, helps us know both sides of a moral issue, by subjecting our own biases to welcome criticism. Free critical conversation is expected to deepen into a kind of 'moral care of the self' by curbing our *philautia* (egoistic self-love), making us review our own actions and desires as an external *parrhesiastes* would do. As Foucault comments:

> And the main effect of this parrhesiastic struggle with power is not to bring the interlocutor to a new truth, or to a new level of self-awareness; it is to lead the interlocutor to internalize this parrehesiastic struggle — to fight within himself against his own faults (2001: 133).

Third, the ethical and political potential of power-disruptive fearless speech that is exemplified in Sulabhā's speech to Janaka or Diogenes' speech to Alexander the Great has immense relevance for our word-dominated life of digital mass-media and tele-communication.

Finally, conversation has to be the central means of attaining moral knowledge when the morality is two-sided. Even the Ṛgvedic prayer for protecting the culture of debate and inquiry is significantly addressed to two gods coupled in a *dvandva* compound: Mitra–Varuna, roughly the sun and the ocean, two complementary aspects of cosmic order and law!

By following a one-branched *dharma* no one, not just political leaders and monarchs, can conduct a self-critical other-responsive ethical life. That is why the narrative ethics of the *Mahābhārata* remains dialogical, and begins and ends with open debates where each is supposed to take both sides. All these ethical binaries are transcended, of course, in *mokṣa*, at the end, but then the transcendence is also transcended, just as Janaka, the self-proclaimd liberated person, had to be liberated from his liberation. One has to be unattached even to the detachment, renounce the renunciation of right and wrong,[26] and then enjoy living a natural light-footed spontaneously moral life. But that is another story.

References

Aranya, Swami Hariharananda (ed.). 2000. *Yoga Philosophy of Patanjali with Bhasvati*. 4th enlarged ed. Kolkata: University of Calcutta.

Austin, J. L. 1975[1962]. *How to Do Things with Words*, William James Lectures, ed. J. O. Urmson. Oxford: Oxford University Press.

Baudelaire, Charles. 1970. *Paris Spleen*. New York: New Directions Publishers.

Bronkhorst, Johannes. 2001. 'The Peacock's Egg: Bhartròhari on Language and Reality', *Philosophy East & West*, 51(4): 474–91.

Caraka Saṁhitā. 1981. New Delhi: Munshiram Manoharlal.

Cicero, Marcus Tulliua. 1913. *De Officius*, trans. Walter Miller. Cambridge, MA: Harvard University Press.

Dreyfus, Georges. 2003. *The Sound of Two Hands Clapping*, The Education of a Tibetan Buddhist Monk. Berkeley: University of California Press.

Foucault, Michel. 2001. *Fearless Speech*, ed. Joseph Pearson. Los Angeles: Semiotext(e).

Gandhi, Ramchandra. 1984. *I am Thou: Meditations on the Truth of India*. Pune: Philosophical Quarterly Publications, University of Poona.

———. 1974. *Presupppositions of Human Communication*. New Delhi: Oxford University Press.

Ganguli, Kisari Mohan (trans.). 1883–96. *The Mahabharata of Krishna-Dwaipayana Vyasa*, 4 vols. http://www.sacred-texts.com/hin/maha/ (accessed 9 October 2013).

Kinjavadekar, Pandit Ramachandra Shastri (ed.). 1979. *Mahābhārata*, vol. 5: *Śāntiparvan*, with Nīlakaṇṭha's Commentary. New Delhi: Oriental Books Reprint Services and Munshiram Manoharlal.

Levinas, Emmanuel. 1998. *Otherwise Than Being: Or Beyond Essence*, trans. Alphonso Lingis. Pittsburg: Duquesne University Press.

———. 1969. *Totality and Infinity: An Essay on Exteriority*, trans. Alphonso Lingis. Pittsburg: Duquesne University Press.

Mishra, Shrinarayan (ed.). 1992. *Pātañjalayogadarśanam: Vācaspatimiśraviracita-Tatvavaiśaradī-Vijñānabhikṣukrta-Yogavārtikavibhūṣita-Vyāsabhāṣyasametam*. New Delhi: Bharatiya Vidya Prakashan.

Neilsen, Greg. 1995. 'Bakhtin and Habermas: Towards a Transcultural Ethics', *Theory and Society*, 24(6): 803–35.

[26] The actual verse is in *Shanti parvan*, Mbh XII, Ch 316, verses 40–43, of Critical Edition.

Nicholson, Hugh. 2010. 'The Shift from Agonistic to Non-Agonistic Debate in Early Nyāya', *Journal of Indian Philosophy*, 38: 75–95.

Ranciere, Jacques. 1999. *Disagreement: Politics and Philosophy*, Minneapolis: University of Minnesota Press.

———. 2004. *The Politics of Aesthetics: The Distribution of the Sensible*. London: Continuum.

Ṛgveda-Saṃhitā with Sāyaṇa's Commentary. 1972. Pune: Vaidik Samshodhan Mandal.

Sambandhaparīkṣā-The philosophy of relations: containting the Sanskrit text and English translation of Dherma Kirtti's Sambandhaparikṣā with Prabhācanḍra's commentary by V. N. Jha. 1990. Delhi: Sri Satguru Publications.

Sāṁkhyakārika by Iśvarakṛṣṇa, with the Commentary of Gauḍapāda. 1964. Pune: Oriental Book Agency.

Sen, Amartya. 2005. *The Argumentative Indian: Writings on Indian History, Culture and Identity*. London: Penguin.

Śrīmadbhagavadgītā, Madhusūdansarasvatī Viracita, 'Guḍhārthadīpika' Vyākhyāsahita. 1975. Varanasi: Chowkhamba.

Ten Principal Upaniṣads with Śaṅkara Bhaṣya. 1978[1968]. New Delhi: Motilal Banarasidass.

Thakur, Anantalal and V. Raghavan (ed.). 1964. *Ṣaṇmatanāṭakāparābhidham Āgamaḍambaraṃ Nāmarūpakam*. Darbhanga: Mithila Vidyapitha.

The Nyāya-sūtras of Gautama: with the Bhāsya of Vātsyāyana and the Vārtika of Uḍḍyoṭakara, trans. Gaṅgānāṭha Jhā. 1984. Delhi: Motilal Banarasidass.

Vanita, Ruth. 2003. 'The Self is not Gendered: Sulabhā's Debate with King Janaka', *NWSA Journal*, 15(2): 76–93.

Vākyapadiyam. Ambākartrisamākhyayā vyākhyayā sahitam. Ko. A. Subrahmanya-Ayyara-Sampurnananda. 1963. Samskrita Vishwavidyalaya.

Williams, Bernard. 2002. *Truth and Truthfulness: An Essay in Genealogy*. Princeton University Press.

Wittgenstein, Ludwig. 1998. *Philosophical Investigations*, Part 1, Oxford: Basil Blackwell.

About the Editors

Arindam Chakrabarti is Professor, Department of Philosophy, University of Hawaii, Manoa, USA. He has taught at University of Calcutta, Kolkata; University College London; University of Washington, Seattle; and University of Delhi, New Delhi. He holds BA and MA degrees in philosophy from Presidency College, Kolkata; and D Phil. degree from University of Oxford. He has authored and edited several books in English, Sanskrit and Bengali, that include: *Denying Existence: The Logic, Epistemology and Pragmatics of Negative Existentials and Fictional Discourse* (1997), *Universals, Concepts and Qualities: New Essays on the Meaning of Predicates* (co-edited with Peter Strawson, 2006), and *Deho, Geho, Bondhutva* (2008). He has also published more than 80 articles and reviews. His recent essays are centred on the theme of 'body' each of which is a product of a tensed but spontaneous co-mingling of Western and Indian streams of thought.

Sibaji Bandyopadhyay is Professor of Cultural Studies at the Centre for Studies in Social Sciences, Calcutta (CSSSC). Formerly, he was Professor of Comparative Literature at Jadavpur University, Kolkata. He has written profusely in both Bengali and English on subjects ranging from children's literature to politics of translation, particularly with reference to the Gītā. His publications include: *The Colonial Chronotope* (1994), *Prasanga: Jibanananda* (2011: new edition), *Sibaji Bandyopadhyay Reader* (2012), *Galileo, Through a Trapdoor: A Performative Response to Chittrovanu Mazumdar* (2013), *Gopal-Rakhal Dvandasamas* (2013: new edition). Besides essays, some of his other works include: *Uttampurush Ekbachan* (play: 2002)[English translation: *The Book of the Night* (2008)], *Guhalipi* (poetry: 2002), *Madhyarekha* (an anthology of poems, stories, plays and essays: 2009), *Ekti Barir Galpo* (film-script: 2013). He is also the recipient of the Vidyasagar Memorial Award and the Sisir Kumar Das Memorial Award.

Notes on Contributors

Nrisinha Prasad Bhaduri was Associate Professor of Sanskrit at Gurudas College, University of Calcutta, Kolkata. He has worked extensively on classical Sanskrit texts, especially the *Mahābhārata*, and has published books in Bengali, including *Vālmīkir Rāma O Rāmāyaṇa*, *Kaliyuga*, *Mahābhārater Choy Prabīṇ*, *Bhāratayuddha Ebong Kṛṣṇa*, *Mahābhārater Laghu-guru*, *Kṛṣṇa, Kuntī Ebong Kounteya*, and *Caitanyadeva*. He is currently engaged in a project, funded by the Department of Higher Education, Government of West Bengal, on the preparation of an encyclopedic dictionary of the *Mahābhārata*, the *Rāmāyaṇa* and the *Puraṇa*s.

Saroja Bhate was Professor of Sanskrit and Head of the Department of Sanskrit and Prakrit Languages at University of Pune; and Secretary of Bhandarkar Oriental Research Institute, Pune. She has published 10 books and about 70 research papers on Sanskrit grammar, *Subhāṣita*s and other subjects. She was a visiting professor and fellow in many universities and institutes abroad, including those in Cambridge, Oxford, Berlin, Paris, Lousanne, and Peking. She has also received many national honours, such as the Ideal Teacher award, the Veda-Vyāsa Puraskar from University Grants Commission (UGC) and the Rashtrapati Puraskar from Government of India. She is presently Maharashtra government's nominee on the Regulating Council of Bhandarkar Oriental Research Institute; a member of the Board of Management of Rashtriya Sanskrit Sansthan, New Delhi; and President of Prajna Pathashala Mandal, Wai, Maharashtra.

Sibesh Bhattacharya was Professor of Ancient History Culture and Archaeology, University of Allahabad; National Fellow at Indian Institute of Advanced Study (IIAS), Shimla (2001–04); and President of Indian Social Science Congress (1999). He has authored three books, edited two volumes and contributed some 50 odd articles to national and international journals and chapters to edited volumes.

Uma Chakravarti taught history in various capacities in Miranda House, University of Delhi from 1966 to 2006. She writes on early Indian history, the 19th century and on contemporary India with a special focus on the margins in Indian society. She has been associated with the movements for democratic rights and women's rights since the 1970s and has also made two filims on women in history, *A Quite Little Entry* (2010) and *Fragments of a Past* (2012).

Vrinda Dalmiya is Professor of Philosophy at University of Hawaii, Manoa; and currently a fellow at IIAS. She has also taught in the Department of History and Philosophy, Montana State University, Montana, USA; and Indian Institute of Technology (IIT), Delhi. Her interests are in feminist epistemology, care ethics, disability studies, and environmental ethics. She has published several journal articles in these areas. She is currently researching on articulating a feminist virtue epistemology using the methodology of comparative philosophy.

Anirban Das is Faculty in Cultural Studies at the Centre for Studies in Social Sciences (CSSS), Kolkata. He also teaches feminist theory, as visiting faculty, in the Women's Studies Programs at Jadavpur University and University of Calcutta. He has published essays on feminist theory, postcolonial theory, deconstruction and the history of medical epistemology. He has edited the first comprehensive volume on deconstruction in Bengali titled *Banglay Binirman/Abinirman* (2007); and authored a book titled *Toward a Politics of the (Im)Possible: The Body in Third World Feminisms* (2010). His current cross-disciplinary research interests lie in political and ethical consequences of Marxian and poststructuralist thought; feminist epistemology and ethics; and feminist imperatives in the translation of 'science' in the postcolonial setting.

Enakshi Mitra is Assistant Professor in the Department of Philosophy, University of Delhi. Her areas of teaching and research interest includes logic, philosophy of language, philosophy of mind, and philosophy of action. She has also published several articles in journals and chapters in edited volumes.

Gangeya Mukherji teaches English at Mahamati Prannath Mahavidyalaya, Mau, Chitrakoot, Madhya Pradesh, India. He was a consultant for the preparation of the Nomination Dossier for Santiniketan as a UNESCO World Heritage Site, and a fellow at IIAS. His research interest lies in capacious concepts and intellectual history of India, especially in the nineteenth century. He has recently authored *An Alternative Idea of India: Tagore and Vivekanada* (2011) and edited *Learning Non-violence* (forthcoming). He is currently writing a monograph on the political thought of M. K. Gandhi and Rabindranath Tagore.

Prabal Kumar Sen was Professor of Philosophy at University of Calcutta. His main area of interest comprises different branches of Indian philosophy. He has edited from manuscripts, a number of philosophical texts in Sanskrit, and also translated portions of some such texts in Bengali. He has also contributed a number of articles to various journals and anthologies.

Radhavallabh Tripathi is Vice-Chancellor of Rashtriya Sanskrit Sansthan, New Delhi. He has taught at the universities in Udaipur, Rajasthan; and Sagar, Madhya Pradesh, both in India. Well-known for his studies on *Nāmyaśāstra* and *Sāhityaśāstra*, Professor Tripathi has published 157 books and 202 research papers, and has received more than 25 national and international awards and honours for his literary contributions. He has accomplished academic assignments in many countries, including Holland, Austria, Germany, Thailand, UK, Nepal, Bhutan, and USA.

Index